THE PRACTICAL TUTOR

The
Practical Tutor

EMILY MEYER

LOUISE Z. SMITH

New York   Oxford
OXFORD UNIVERSITY PRESS
1987

Oxford University Press

Oxford   New York   Toronto
Delhi   Bombay   Calcutta   Madras   Karachi
Petaling Jaya   Singapore   Hong Kong   Tokyo
Nairobi   Dar es Salaam   Cape Town
Melbourne   Auckland

and associated companies in
Beirut   Berlin   Ibadan   Nicosia

Library of Congress Cataloging-in-Publication Data
Meyer, Emily.
The practical tutor.
Includes bibliographies and index.
1. English language—Rhetoric—Study and teaching.
2. Tutors and tutoring.   I. Smith, Louise Z.   II. Title.
PE1404.M48   1986   808'.042'07   86-5335
ISBN 0-19-504109-7
ISBN 0-19-503865-7 (pbk)

9 8 7
Printed in the United States of America
on acid-free paper

ACKNOWLEDGMENTS

This book, like tutoring, is a collaborative effort, so we want to begin it by thanking those who have, in some way, written it with us. First, we must thank our mentors, Ann E. Berthoff and Eunice Helmkamp McGuire, who guided our thinking and teaching. We are grateful as well to Stephanie Hanks, Susan Irvings, George W. Smith, and Vivian Zamel for advising us on individual chapters and to Neal H. Bruss for being the clear-minded, resourceful reader of every chapter. A Faculty Development Grant from the College of Arts and Sciences of the University of Massachusetts at Boston supported Ruth Hart Shilakowsky's cheerful, computer-fearless preparation of the manuscript. The calm optimism of our editor, William P. Sisler, sustained us, and the professionalism of associate editor Wendy Warren Keebler and copy editor Judy Jamison eased the book's production.

Boston   E.M.
April 1987   L.Z.S.

CONTENTS

INTRODUCTION AND SUGGESTIONS
FOR USING THIS BOOK

This text is a practical guide to tutoring composition. It is intended for anyone assisting adult writers at various levels in formal and informal educational settings: literacy programs, colleges, and workplaces. We hope that undergraduate tutors, graduate teaching assistants—anyone planning a teaching career in any discipline who recognizes the importance and difficulty of helping writers learn to write well—will find our chapters valuable. We hope, as well, that supervisors of writing centers or programs in community agencies, educational institutions, and firms will encourage their staff to use this book as a resource.

The Practical Tutor attempts to alert its readers to issues that frequently arise in writing tutorials. Because tutors are usually themselves strong writers, their writing is often considerably more advanced than that of the writers with whom they work, and they may take for granted the very skills most difficult for inexperienced writers to attain. Accordingly, the chapters describe the problems of various kinds of writers, some with little experience in writing and others who are more practiced but still need assistance. In exploring these problems and their causes, the book also summarizes recent research and thinking in the field of composition in order to familiarize tutors with the composing process as it is now understood. Much has been learned about this process over the past ten years, primarily that generating, forming, reconsidering, editing, and revising are continuous rather than sequential processes. (We represent this continuity on the cover of this book with the Möbius strip—a figure made by turning one end of a rectangular ribbon 180 degrees and then fastening it to the other end, so that it has only one unending side.) We think it important that tutors be aware of the research and its pedagogical implications. Many tutors, for instance, have taken traditional composition courses that presume that writing is a linear rather than a recursive activity. Even if tutors have not, as writers, actually employed the conventional procedures that follow from such thinking, they might feel obliged to transmit what they believe to be the party line. Most importantly, the chapters offer practical applications of current theory. By using examples of writers' compositions and including sample dialogues between tutors and writers, the book suggests how to talk with writers, how to help them learn to think, read, and write more critically. Inexperienced tutors tend to talk descriptively or prescriptively about writers' essays without realizing that doing so may confuse writers and hinder the growth of their independence. *The Practical Tutor* helps tutors learn how to formulate questions rather than to make corrections or additions for writers.

We begin the book with chapters on getting acquainted with writers and on the special nature of tutorial dialogue. Next, we discuss tutorial strategies appropriate to important aspects of composing: helping writers generate ideas fluently, helping them form concepts, helping them shape papers, and then helping writers with surface issues such as punctuation and spelling. We have chosen this sequence because we believe that this is the order in which problems ought, ordinarily, to be addressed. Young children speak when they have something to say, and they do not worry about correctness; the more they speak, the more correct their speaking becomes. Similarly, writers need to have something they want to say before they have either occasion or incentive to perfect it.

While reading the chapters sequentially may be advantageous, it is not essential, especially since each chapter refers readers to other portions of the book that treat related issues. Our chapter sequence suggests how tutors can progressively help writers to overcome difficulties, but since some writers are more advanced than others and may not experience all the problems we describe, we have designed the book in such a way that it can be used in any order that is suitable to tutors' practical needs. Tutors who are not working with writers on fluency problems, for instance, may begin with later chapters and refer to the earlier ones as necessary.

We assume that many of our readers will use this book in formal training programs or courses, so we have divided the materials into fourteen chapters to correspond with the number of weeks in a semester. A course might devote one week to each chapter, but such a division is not necessary. If, for example, computer-assisted instruction were not integral to a program, Chapter 14 might be omitted and more time devoted to one of the longer chapters, such as "Reading and Writing across the Disciplines" (Chapter 11) or "Tutoring Spelling and Vocabulary" (Chapter 13).

While *The Practical Tutor* need not be used in a formal course, we have found a seminar desirable because it helps tutors see their work not as a series of disconnected encounters but as a continuous, practical learning process. In addition, offering formal training helps to affirm a principle only now gaining acceptance: that composition is an established field of intellectual inquiry. In order to assist the development of formal training programs, we have created questions and assignments for the reader, which are integrated into each chapter and marked by arrows. We have also included at the end of each chapter suggestions for classroom activities and writing exercises that provide practice in forming tutorial strategies and questions. In addition, we offer chapter bibliographies to invite deeper exploration of issues than class time permits. In our own seminar, we require tutors to prepare either two short papers or one long project on a topic related to their tutoring experience. By affording the opportunity for further reading, we encourage tutors to become researchers. Finally, we include suggestions for journal entries in hopes that tutors will record comments about the chapters, jot down thoughts about their own composing processes, and reflect upon their tutoring experiences. It is often useful to record thoughts about a particular tutoring session: to speculate about sources of the writer's difficulties and try to recall what was said, what went well, what did not, and to consider what could be done next time. When used in a course, these journals can help teachers or supervisors guide tutors. We assume that mentors will not evaluate the journals but will comment on them to stimulate further thinking about composition, offer suggestions for working with particular writers, and recommend further reading. The more detailed the tutors' recollections of tutoring sessions, the more helpful their supervisors can be. The basic premise of this book is that writing is a way to form ideas, to make meaning, to discover one's thoughts, so we want our readers to write about composing, their own and others', as a way to encourage reflection on the subject.

PART ONE

Getting Acquainted:
Writers and Compositions

1

Meeting the Writer

Writing tutorials take place in a variety of contexts. In some colleges, they are linked to a student's course work and are supervised or conducted by an instructor. In other institutions and workplaces, tutorials are furnished by auxiliary services such as writing labs and writing centers. Sometimes, tutors unaffiliated with a school are privately engaged. Variations of these tutorial formats can also be found, each calling for certain distinct procedures.

No matter what setting provides for a tutorial, however, its basic purpose is unvarying: it is to help writers gain the confidence and skill necessary for them to write well independently. The process through which tutors help writers learn to do so differs in complexity and duration depending on each writer's ability, level of achievement, previous experience, attitudes, values, and availability. Initially, tutors need to gather information about these factors in order to establish a plan for the sessions. Writers using tutorials need information too. If they are to respond frankly and constructively to questions, they must know something about their tutors and the settings in which they work.

➤ As a way to get yourself thinking specifically about what you and the person you tutor need to know, imagine that you are going to meet a candidate for tutoring for the first time. Make a list of questions that you would want to ask. Then imagine that you are the writer, that you have never previously been tutored and know very little about the program. How might you feel about attending a session, and what would you want to know about the tutor and the program? Make a second list of questions. Add to it anything else that you think a writer ought to know but might not think to ask (or might hesitate to ask) about your tutorial program. Now compare your lists with the samples (page 6). These lists can be adapted to or abbreviated for the particular setting in which you tutor. Perhaps your program provides questionnaires and descriptive handouts; many programs do. These are particularly useful when it is likely that a tutor will meet a writer only once or twice, as is often the case in drop-in centers. If handouts are distributed and questionnaires filled out prior to the first session, less time needs to be devoted to information gathering. In other programs writers are more apt to see their tutors regularly, so more of the first meeting can be spent getting acquainted. If this is true in your case, you may want to bring and refer to a list of questions, but do not be surprised if the conversation does not follow the sequence you predicted. Writers may ask unanticipated questions or may volunteer information without prompting. This need not be disturbing. If the conversation flows naturally, if the tutor does not keep rigidly to a preconceived format, the writer will be more likely to relax, talk easily, and listen well. Almost any order will do as long as the primary aims of getting acquainted, making preliminary assessments, and establishing ground rules are accomplished.

To suggest what an initial session between a tutor and a writer might be like, we have included the recollection of one of our tutors (Chuck Anastas, a graduate of the University of Massachusetts, Boston) of his first meeting with a student. He recorded the session in his journal, a practice that we hope you will follow. This tutor had been assigned to help students in the freshman English class in which the writer was enrolled. The arrangement was intended to foster long-term tutorials where necessary, so a lengthy first interview was appropriate, particularly since, as it turned out, the writer was experiencing many problems. Keep the following questions in mind as you read the dialogue, and when you finish reading, answer them in writing:

- What kind of information does Chuck try to gather? What reasons might he have for asking questions that do not directly concern the student's writing?
- What do James's comments reveal about him as a person, as a student, and as a writer? What kinds of problems do you think he is experiencing?
- What strengths do you observe in Chuck's approach? What might he have done differently? Why?

JIM: You the tutor?

CHUCK: Ya, hi, I'm Chuck.

JIM: Hi.

CHUCK: You're Jim, right?

5 JIM: James.

CHUCK: OK, let's go sit down. . . . James, you're in Nancy's class, right?

JAMES: Ya.

CHUCK: The 5:30 class, right?

JAMES: Ya.

10 CHUCK: How do you like it?

JAMES: It's OK.

CHUCK: Do you like Nancy's teaching?

JAMES: She's all right.

CHUCK: How are you doing in the class?

15 JAMES: Well, I'm havin' my troubles.

CHUCK: Ya?

JAMES: Ya, I guess I can't write too good. *[pause]* I guess I need some help on grammar.

CHUCK: What do you mean?

20 JAMES: Well, for one thing, I don't know where commas go.

CHUCK: Ya.

JAMES: And Nancy says I need ta know how ta organize things, ya know, like paragraphs. *[pause]*

CHUCK: Nancy says that—what do you say?

25 JAMES: Well, I guess she's right, I mean, I know what I want ta say most of the time, I just don't know how ta put it on paper.

CHUCK: Ya, it's not easy to do.

JAMES: I hear that.

CHUCK: Anything else?

30 JAMES: Not really.

CHUCK: How do you like the classes?

JAMES: They're good, they're alright. I know what's goin' on.

CHUCK: How about the readings?

JAMES: They're OK.

35 CHUCK: Like them?

JAMES: Sometimes. *[pause]*

CHUCK: Do you take any other classes besides Nancy's?

JAMES: Ya, ah, history.

CHUCK: How do you like it?

40 JAMES: Not so much.

CHUCK: Why?

JAMES: The guy's boring. He just talks.

CHUCK: No discussion . . . ?

JAMES: Sometimes.

45 CHUCK: What are you reading for the class?

JAMES: We got ah textbook.

CHUCK: Got much writing?

JAMES: We gotta do three papers, and we got two tests.

CHUCK: That's a lot.

50 JAMES: Too much.

CHUCK: Got enough time for both courses?

JAMES: I don't know.

CHUCK: What do you do during the day?

JAMES: I'm ah meat cutter. (secretary, insurance clerk, janitor, bartender, waitper-
55 son, bankteller, etc.)

QUESTIONS IN EARLY SESSIONS

Tutor might ask writer:

1. What's your schedule like this semester? How many courses are you taking and when are you free?
2. Are you taking a writing course now? Or courses that require much reading and writing?
3. Besides school, what other responsibilities do you have?
4. What kind of experience with writing have you had? In school? On the job?
5. How do you feel about writing?
6. What sort of procedures do you follow when you write a paper? What do you do first? Last? (and with this paper?)
7. About how much time do you spend preparing an essay (did you spend preparing this essay)?
8. What problems as a writer do you think you have?
9. What brought you to the tutoring program?
10. What do you hope to gain from these tutoring sessions?
11. What questions do you have about the tutorial and about my role as a tutor?

Writer might ask or think:

1. Who are you? What's your connection with my teacher? Will the teacher know I'm coming?
2. Have you taken this course?
3. Will you help me with all my writing assignments or just with English?
4. Will I have to do extra assignments?
5. Will you proofread my papers?
6. How often will we meet?
7. What happens if I miss a session?
8. Do I have to pay for this service?
9. How much time should I spend writing my papers?
10. Will my grades improve?
11. What kinds of people get tutored?
12. How come writing is easy for you and hard for me? (A common misperception among novice writers is that teachers and tutors find writing easy.)

CHUCK: Got a heavy schedule.

JAMES: *[sighs]* Ya.

CHUCK: It's hard making time for class work.

JAMES: Makin' the classes ain't bad, it's the homework that's tough. I'd just as
60   soon lay back when I get home, know what I mean?

CHUCK: Ya, I've done it, working and classes. It's tough.

JAMES: Ya, right.

CHUCK: What do you do when you're not working, or going to class, or studying?

JAMES: Sleepin', man!

65 CHUCK: Not a bad idea. *[pause]* Well, you said you needed work on commas,
        and organizing your paragraphs, right?

JAMES: Ya.

CHUCK: Anything else?

JAMES: Well, I don't always know how to make ah sentence, I mean, where to
70   put the period, ya know?

CHUCK: Ya. *[pause]* OK, sentences, periods, commas, and organizing para-
        graphs, right?

JAMES: Ya, right.

CHUCK: Got any papers that you've written?

75 JAMES: Ya, got one from Nancy's class. She said ta bring it.

CHUCK: Good, now how about reading it for me.

JAMES: No.

CHUCK: Don't feel like it?

JAMES: Na, I mean, I don't like reading much.

80 CHUCK: OK, can I read it?

JAMES: Ya, sure.

CHUCK: Give me about ten minutes, OK?

JAMES: Ya, OK, I'm gonna get coffee while ya read it.

CHUCK: Good, ah, how about getting me one while you're there.

. . .

85 CHUCK: Thanks for the coffee. While you were gone I looked over your assign-
        ment and the paper Nancy gave back to you. She wants you to add a couple
        of paragraphs. How about writing them and getting together tomorrow?

JAMES: Ya. Maybe I can drop in around ten, but I might have to take my grand-
        mother to the dentist, so it might not be 'til around noon, OK?

90 CHUCK: Well, actually, I've got a lot of reading of my own to do. I want to meet
        you, but let's figure out a sure time, OK?

JAMES: Well . . . aren't ya always here? I mean, I thought ya worked here.

CHUCK: Ya, well, I do work here, but only a few hours. So if you do have to help
        your grandmother, then I can't meet ya and can't get paid.

95 JAMES: I hear that.

CHUCK: Look, here's my phone number. Why don't you call me tonight?

JAMES: OK.

CHUCK: Can I have your number, just in case you miss me? I really want to be sure we get back together on those new paragraphs.

100 JAMES: Sure. Well, ah, . . . see ya sometime tomorrow.

Getting Acquainted, Establishing Trust, Providing Gauges

Chuck proceeds in a friendly, informal manner that tries to put James at ease. When James indicates that he prefers to be called by his given name, he may imply that he does not yet feel comfortable or finds the nickname condescending. Perhaps James feels that seeing a tutor is degrading, is an admission of stupidity. If so, using his formal name may be a way for him to preserve his dignity in a conversation with someone who has greater competence and authority. On the other hand, he may just like his given name. Chuck may not know exactly why James does not want to be called "Jim," but he defers to James's preference and, in so doing, may begin to gain James's trust.

Chuck may also have made James feel more comfortable by expressing sympathy for James's heavy schedule (57) and by revealing that he himself has found it difficult to combine school and work (61–64). If James has been thinking that he lacks capability, Chuck has reassured him that feeling burdened by the double responsibility is understandable. By sharing his experience as a student, Chuck may have relieved James.

A tutor's own practices as a writer and, more generally, as a student can provide gauges that help writers like James see themselves more positively and operate more realistically. For example, tutors might let writers know how much time they allocate for the completion of assignments. Inexperienced writers frequently assume that "good writers" polish off in minutes assignments that, in reality, require hours. A tutor could say, "It usually takes me about . . . (approximation) to complete this kind of work," or "Most people allow . . . (approximation) for this sort of assignment." The second variation is probably more helpful, since writers often idealize their tutors and would be likely to think, "If it takes my tutor an hour, it'll take me three or four."

Most people learn more easily when they feel secure and confident than when they feel threatened and hesitant. Chuck's questions about James's schedule, his feelings about his classes and about his job suggest Chuck's interest and concern. He has begun to create the supportive atmosphere that is vital for good collaboration. At the same time, these questions serve another important purpose: they help Chuck begin to assess both the causes and the nature of James's difficulties.

Identifying the Causes and Nature of Writers' Problems

Identifying the causes of a specific problem is crucial, because they determine what measures should be taken. If tutors do not gather enough information, they may adopt inappropriate strategies. For instance, suppose Chuck had not asked background questions but had plunged into a session on punctuation once James had named it as a trouble spot (20). Chuck might not have discovered, for one thing, that an external force, James' heavy schedule, may be contributing to his problem (38–57). If writers are not composing well because they are too tired or pressed to spend the requisite time on an assignment, it might be wise to discuss the advisability of reducing the number of their classes or work hours. That discussion might be one alternative for Chuck to consider, but he does not foreclose the discussion once a possible cause has presented itself. Instead, Chuck wisely asks a number of general questions and receives responses that suggest more than one source of difficulty.

A clue to another potential cause appears toward the end of the session, when James says he doesn't like reading much (79). He may be indicating that he finds seeking help humiliating, but he may also not like to read aloud because he cannot read well. At some future time, Chuck would probably explore this issue further in order to determine whether, in fact, James has a reading problem and, if so, how it bears on his writing problems. If he does not comprehend well what he reads, his inability to supply the paragraphs that his teacher requires comes as no surprise. James's failure to develop his essays, then, may be caused by a reading problem or by his fatigue. On the other hand, his exhaustion may be a symptom rather than a cause. James's lethargic comments, his lack of enthusiasm about his classes and his assignments, may indicate that he feels discouraged rather than disinterested, in which case, Chuck may need to plan "fail-safe" exercises that will demonstrate to James that he *can* succeed. In order to form hypotheses such as these, tutors must listen carefully to distinguish underlying meanings in writers' comments. If you are not certain which of several possible causes is responsible for a problem, you can, without confronting a writer with your interpretations, form what Robert Langs calls a "silent hypothesis" (308–311, 640–641). You can experiment to see if your first hunch is the actual cause. If it is not, you can try your next best guess. You may not be able to form a conclusion in one session, but you can at least begin to explore probable sources of difficulty.

Listening to and Waiting for Responses

Chuck might never uncover all of these potential reasons for James's poor performance if he did not ask as many questions as he does, and it is greatly to his credit that he questions neither intrusively nor threateningly. Notice, for instance, the way he allows James to define his problems. James initially describes them very generally: "I can't write too good" (17). At this point, Chuck could have intervened with a follow-up question, but, instead, he waits to see if James will identify the problems more specifically. He does not risk intimidating James with a barrage of questions but instead gives James the opportunity to expand his idea. Such pauses in the conversation (17, 23, 36, 44) may make Chuck feel awkward, as if he ought to fill in the silence with some comment. But because he waits, he obtains more information than he would have with rapid-fire questioning or lengthy remarks. Chuck does, however, ask for clarification when James says that he needs "help with grammar." This is a catchall phrase that students use to describe a number of problems, some of which are not grammatical. James, for instance, names punctuation as his difficulty with "grammar."

When the student reports what his teacher says he should work on, Chuck's encouraging "Ya" helps him determine whether James himself thinks that he has problems with organization or whether he is merely dutifully reporting without perceiving the difficulty. Listening to the way in which a writer describes his problems can, then, be instructive. It can tell you how accurate the writer's self-assessment is and whether he minimizes or maximizes the seriousness of his difficulties. Chuck's effort to determine how James views his problems is important because his approach will vary depending on whether or not James sees the organizational failures.

Chuck could, however, have phrased his question, "Nancy says that—what do you say?" (24) more felicitously; for instance, he might have said, "Could you talk a bit more about organization? I'm not sure what you mean by this." "What do you say?" could be construed as Chuck's attempt to align himself with the student against the instructor. Such an alliance would be dangerous in that it could encourage the student to blame the instructor and to avoid dealing with the problem. At the same time, this sort of compact could undermine the tutor's working relationship with the instructor (assuming there is one). If, as sometimes happens, a student tries to engage your sympathies against a teacher, you are better off to maintain a neutral position than to take sides in a dispute about which you have only partial information. You can productively refocus the session on academic issues rather than on personal ones with such comments as, "I really can't judge whether the professor has a grudge against you, but his comments on your paper indicate that he thinks you need to work on phrasing more clearly, so let's work on that." If the student's complaints seem justified, you can confirm without criticizing the instructor. Let's say, for instance, a student claims that her professor's assignments are unmanageably vague or difficult. If you agree about the specific assignment at hand, you might say, "Well, I certainly find this one hard, but let's see if we can break it into parts we can handle."

Maintaining Neutrality

At the same time you avoid getting embroiled in a conflict between student and professor, you can maintain the student's trust and promote his candor by assuring him that his comments will be kept confidential. Some students do not want anyone to know that they are receiving assistance and would be more apt to see a tutor if reassured as to the confidentiality of the sessions. If the structure of your program makes conferences with the student's professor advisable (such contacts can be invaluable in clarifying the instructor's expectations and assignments), you would be wise to obtain the student's permission to consult with the instructor and to state that your purpose is either to report only on what topics you have covered or to seek information about work to be done. You may, at times, prefer a three-way conference in order to avoid miscommunication or distrust.

To return to the dialogue, we have seen that Chuck has slowly and patiently questioned James in order to find out what skills James thinks he needs to improve. Then, Chuck turns to another source of information, James's essay (74). A writer may not always describe his problems fully or accurately, and you can judge this once you have seen the writing. James briefly suggests that he has trouble developing papers, and Nancy's directive that several paragraphs be added confirms this assessment.

Setting Priorities and Clarifying Procedures

Even if what a writer describes as his largest problem may, in your view, be only a minor one, you might be wise to start with it simply because the writer's concern may motivate him to work on it more than on some issue you have identified. A writer who feels helpless will feel more in control if she names the problem and sets the agenda. If the writer's priority is not the same as the professor's (or yours), you could point this out and let the writer decide the topic to be covered in the session. Clearly, you and the writer need to reach an agreement about what you are going to work on, how often you should meet, for what length of time, and so on.

Another method of establishing priorities when a writer's essay contains many problems is to identify patterns of error and then to concentrate on the one that most seriously obstructs a reader's understanding. Instead of going over the paper line by line and jumping from one type of problem to another (a strategy that can devastate writers and diffuse their mental energy), you can ask yourself, "What is most confusing to me?" or "Why am I not understanding?" before choosing a problem on which to focus. If you use this method, you are well advised to ask questions about the writer's ideas before considering mechanical problems such as spelling and punctuation (Chapter 3 discusses this issue at greater length).

In order to understand the context in which he is working, a writer needs to know what your expectations are just as you need to understand his. For instance, you should explain that tutoring will help him learn how to improve his own writing, that it is not a tutor's function to rewrite or edit his papers for him. It is also essential to agree on how either you or the writer can cancel or reschedule an appointment. (It is a good idea to purchase an appointment book and bring it to tutoring sessions.) In the dialogue, Chuck has to correct James's misimpression that tutors are available at all times. When Chuck suggests that they set a definite meeting time, James's hesitation may imply that he is not sure that he wants to be tutored. Chuck gives him an "out" by suggesting the exchange of phone numbers. This gives James some time to reflect. When Chuck says he will call if James does not phone, he expresses active interest in helping, but he is not pressing for an immediate commitment. If James does not call, Chuck could phone (on the assumption that James just needs a bit of encouragement), and he would then have to judge from James's responses whether to abandon efforts to meet him. There is little point in trying to force people to get tutoring assistance if they do not want it, but diffident or discouraged students might overcome their misgivings if they had evidence that someone was eager to help them.

Accomplishing a Task and Assigning a Task

In addition to agreeing on an agenda and clarifying procedures, it is a good idea to try, at the end of the first meeting, to get some small writing task accomplished so that the writer can see some concrete and immediate benefits of tutoring. Chuck evidently feels that he does not have time to tackle any problem in the first session, but perhaps James would have agreed to a subsequent one if they had spent a few minutes working on a problem he or Nancy, the instructor, had identified. For example, halfway through the dialogue, James says he knows what he wants to say but doesn't know how to put it on paper. Chuck then learns that Nancy has asked James to add some paragraphs. Perhaps Chuck could have asked James to list some concepts or form some questions from which he could later generate those paragraphs at home. (Chapters 3 and 4 will discuss ways of generating ideas.) Chuck wisely does give James a specific task for the next meeting, but in the session he could have helped James figure out a way to complete the task. If writers accomplish some writing in the session and are given tasks for the next one, the likelihood of their return increases and your time is used efficiently.

In the dialogue, Chuck asks James to complete an assignment that must be turned in to the instructor, not for supplementary work. Since James already feels overburdened, additional assignments might overwhelm him. However, if a writer has time or inclination, or if the instructor specifically requests that such work be done, a tutor could readily assign it. The tutor's latitude increases when writers request tutorial assistance, not in conjunction with course work, but for general self-improvement.

Making Referrals

As you become acquainted with a writer and his problems, you may discover that you are not qualified to handle them or that they are inappropriate for a writing tutorial. Such is the situation in the following dialogue between a tutor and a student enrolled in the second semester of a freshman composition course. After you read the dialogue, write a critique of the session. What has the tutor done well? What would you have done differently?

SALLY: Hi. I'm Sally. I'm the tutor here. How can I help you?

RALPH: I came here because Mr. Larson says I have to, but I don't see why I should be here.

SALLY: Oh. Well, what does Mr. Larson think the problem is?

5   RALPH: Oh, I don't know. He's such a jerk. He really hates me. I mean, no matter what I do it's wrong. Nothing I do is right.

SALLY: That's hard, I know, but we better concentrate on your writing problem. Are you having any difficulties in your other classes?

RALPH: I told you. Don't you listen? My only problem is Larson. He's a real

10   bastard, so you're wasting your time.

SALLY: Maybe if we try to figure out what he is specifically criticizing in your papers, we can convince him that you're trying to improve.

RALPH: Oh, nothing's going to please him. I mean, I write terrific papers, I mean, publishable, you know.

15 SALLY: Did you bring any papers with you?

RALPH: Here's one I wrote for him last week. It's freshman comp crap. You know the kind of thing. Sometimes, I'd like to tell him what an ass he is.

SALLY: He says here that you're not answering the question but that instead you're judging the author. You are criticizing Orwell when you were asked to il-
20 lustrate the dangers of at least two of the misuses of language he describes.

RALPH: Orwell doesn't know what he's talking about. Obviously, we all use language differently. He's just a put-down artist.

SALLY: But whether or not that's so is beside the point. You are being asked to show what's dangerous about bandwagon slogans, and so on.

25 RALPH: You and Larson are just alike. You don't get it.

SALLY: You know, you really sound angry. You don't like what Larson says or what Orwell says or what I say. Look, [getting exasperated] I'm trying to help you but you sure aren't making it easy. Maybe you should talk to a counselor.

30 RALPH: That does it! [he leaves]

.   .   .

Sally begins the session very well by being supportive and by trying to get Ralph to focus on his writing problem. He, however, is too angry to do so. Sally is undoubtedly correct that he ought to seek counseling, but, unfortunately, she gets caught up in his anger and struggles with him. Probably frustrated by her inability to help him, she interprets his behavior aloud and makes the referral in a hostile way. If she had been able to remain calm and nonconfrontive, she might have gotten farther. Consider this alternative to the end of the dialogue:

SALLY: It must be painful to be in a class where you feel that the teacher doesn't understand your ideas. Is there anyone else that you feel this way about?

RALPH: It's just the same thing with my father. He doesn't get it either.

SALLY: That must be very frustrating. Have you ever thought of seeing a counselor
5 about this?

RALPH: Oh great. Now you think I'm crazy.

SALLY: No, I'm not saying that at all. What I'm suggesting is that you might want to see a counselor to help you figure out why nobody "gets" what you're saying. That would help you learn how to express ideas in a way that people
10 WILL understand. You have some sophisticated ideas in your essays but you say that people don't "get" what you're saying.

RALPH: So how is a counselor going to help with that?

SALLY: I'm not a counselor, but I've seen people in similar situations who went for counseling and felt they got a lot out of it. It might be worth seeing somebody over at the counseling center once or twice just to give it a try.

In this version, Sally attempts to be empathic: she tries to imagine what someone like Ralph would be feeling and to describe the sensation. Yet she does not label his feelings, nor does she characterize his problem. In the first dialogue, by contrast, her summary of Ralph's various angers (26–28) is apt but sounds accusatory. Here she adopts Ralph's idiom in order to make him feel understood (she picks up his "nobody gets it") and makes the referral by suggesting that his experience is not uncommon and that others have found counseling useful, thereby implying that he is neither deranged nor unique. Her suggestion that he go on a trial basis sounds less urgent and frightening than if she had said, "You really ought to go. I think you need help." Someone like Ralph may resist counseling no matter how patient and artful the tutor is, but at least, when Sally makes a referral, she has acted responsibly by giving the advice she deems appropriate and indicating the limits of her role.

This is not to say that you should avoid all discussion of personal problems, only that you have to decide on the extent to which you should become involved in them. Sometimes writers whose behavior is less extreme than Ralph's simply need to air their dilemmas; until they do so, they cannot concentrate on their writing. It is as if their anxiety or anger creates static that impairs their ability to hear what the tutor is trying to say about their writing. Once given the opportunity to unburden themselves, they may be better able to listen and to discuss their writing. If, however, a writer consciously or unconsciously uses personal issues to procrastinate, you can redirect the discussion or make a referral, whichever the situation calls for. Since the link between academic and emotional difficulties is so strong, tutors often serve informally as counselors. Helping a student to develop self-discipline, self-esteem, and confidence can be legitimate forms of assistance. But whenever you feel that the issues raised by a writer are too complex or disturbing for you, that you are out of your depth, then it is time to make a referral as gently as possible.

While some writing problems are, at base, psychological, others are physiological. If a student squints when reading and complains of headaches, you could ask when he last had his eyes examined. He may simply need glasses. If a writer frequently reverses letters when forming written words, he may be showing signs of a language disorder. If you see such signs, suggest that the writer seek a diagnosis from a learning disabilities specialist or from a hospital language disorders unit. Whatever the problem, if you are in doubt about its nature or its solution, consult a supervisor if you have one, and if not, someone in your institution with the appropriate expertise.

Helping with Anxiety, Frustration, and Anger

While learning disabilities and severe psychological disorders should be treated by people with specialized training, tutors can help writers overcome some emotional conflicts as well as some external circumstances that obstruct academic progress. It is certainly appropriate for a tutor to teach a student how to assess his situation realistically and how to deal with it constructively. A writer's behavioral and circumstantial problems may not surface immediately, but to give you some idea of the kinds that you are likely to observe at some point and that are within a tutor's province, we have listed some student comments that reflect typical difficulties.

1. I want you to help me raise my grade in English. I'm not doing real well, and I'm flunking French, too. My advisor thinks I should drop it so I can concentrate on my other courses, but I can't do that. It would mean that I'd graduate later, and I can't. I can't stay a student forever. I can't afford it. Look, I'm already in debt, and I'm working forty hours a week. I have two jobs that don't pay much. I want to graduate and get a decent job, and dropping a course will only put off graduation. So if I can just pass English, everything will be OK.

2. I'm swamped. I'll never get all of this work done. I have two papers and a midterm due next week, and I haven't had time to do much work on anything. Maybe I should withdraw from school. It's too much work for me.

3. I want you to help me write a paper for my Sociology of the Family course. It's supposed to be a five- to seven-page comparison of the parent–child relationships in three studies we read. I haven't started it yet. When is it due? Tomorrow.

4. I have to write about my reactions to Miss Havisham in *Great Expectations*. I don't know what to say. You told me that you read it. Can you help me get started? I mean, what did you think of her?

5. I'm an "A" student, but I have this terrible problem writing. It takes me forever to get anything done. I agonize over every word. Now I have to do a paper for my Shakespeare seminar, and I'm paralyzed. Nothing comes out. I have a topic, but I can't get anything written. I write something and I scratch it out. I'm really blocked.

6. You're really not helping me. You said we were going to work on the paper I wrote on *Heart of Darkness,* but all you do is ask me a million questions about the guy who tells the story—er, Marlowe. This is not doing me any good.

➤ Before reading further, decide how you would respond to each of these comments. Write an imaginary dialogue between each speaker and yourself, or ask a fellow tutor to join you in some role-playing: one of you can be the tutor, the other the writer, and you can alternate roles.

Making the situation concrete

1. I want you to help me raise my grade in English. I'm not doing real well, and I'm flunking French, too. My advisor thinks I should drop it so I can concentrate on my other courses, but I can't do that. It would mean that I'd graduate later, and I can't. I can't stay a student forever. I can't afford it. Look, I'm already in debt, and I'm working forty hours a week. I have two jobs that don't pay much. I want to graduate and get a decent job, and dropping a course will only put off graduation. So if I can just pass English, everything will be OK.

While some (but not many) people might successfully combine full-time study with full-time work, this student evidently cannot. His overambitious schedule must at least contribute to if not account for his troubles in French and English, but he has been either unable or unwilling to see the merit of his advisor's suggestion that he drop one course in order to pass the others. Like an unfortunate number of students, he cannot acknowledge that his aspirations are unrealistic, that he cannot achieve all of his objectives simultaneously, that he must defer some so he can achieve others.

A tutor could help him accept real limitations and decide which goals are paramount by encouraging the student to "concretize" his situation (to coin the psychological term), and then to evaluate it. You could ask such a writer to list all the assignments he has due for the next week or two and to approximate the time required for the completion of each one. Then you could help him make an hourly schedule and fill in all the time already allocated for classes, work, meals, transportation, religious observance, child care, and so on (Figure 1). Finally, the student could fit his assignments into the remaining spaces. If, as in the example, the student has overcommitted himself, that will become apparent: he will not be able to find in the schedule the amount of time he has budgeted for his homework. Having confronted this reality, he is more likely to concede that he must give up something than when his advisor first suggested it. In general, when one reasons out a problem oneself, the solution is clearer than if one simply hears it from someone else, and it is less humiliating to admit an error of judgment on the basis of one's own rather than someone else's reasoning. Instead of lecturing, a tutor can suggest a means by which a student can discover for himself what his situation is and what his choices are.

If this young man were to make out a schedule, it is doubtful that he would choose to reduce his work hours, since he is in financial straits. That leaves course reduction as an alternative, but the student does not want to delay his graduation. If, however, he were to make no adjustment in his schedule, it is likely that he would fail French and perhaps English as well. A tutor might ask what effect failing French and/or English might have on the student's grade-point average and on his chances for graduating on time. This would be another way to ensure that the student look objectively at his circumstances.

Interpreting and responding—withholding judgment

2. I'm swamped. I'll never get all of this work done. I have two papers and a midterm due next week and I haven't had time to do much work on anything. Maybe I should withdraw from school. It's too much work for me.

Like the student in the first example, this woman needs to evaluate her situation more realistically and to plan more carefully. However, while the young man in the first example may have overestimated his ability to complete several projects simultaneously, this person may be underestimating hers. Probably she feels overwhelmed by the rush of assignments, a rush that often occurs at midterm or semester's end, and her anxiety has paralyzed and demoralized her. Many students are unprepared for the amount of work expected in college. They arrive without having developed the necessary study habits. If the tutor were to suggest that she adopt an hourly schedule prior to exams or other times of pressure, she would probably see, after blocking out her time (presuming she is not carrying an unreasonable load), that she had a sufficient number of hours to complete her papers

SAMPLE STUDY SCHEDULE

	MON.	TUES.	WED.	THURS.	FRI.	SAT.	SUN.
9	read art history	West. Civ. 113		West. Civ. 113		← job at bookstore →	
10	start english paper due thursday	English 101	meet with English tutor	English 101 [PAPER]			
11	aerobics	Soc 101	aerobics	Soc 101	aerobics	do the laundry and errands	
12	lunch	lunch	lunch	lunch	lunch		
1	Art Hist. 100	study bio. →	Art Hist. 100	← job at bookstore →	Art. Hist. 100		
2	Biology 102		Biology 102		Biology 102		
3	meet Andy for coffee	take a break →	Bio. Lab.			dinner	
4	work more on English paper		→				
5	↓	read soc →	take a break				basketball game with Andy
6	dinner	dinner	dinner	dinner			
7	read biology	start Art History paper due next week	finish English paper →	dinner			
8	review for West. Civ. quiz		read soc.	work on first draft of Art History paper			
9	→			→			↓
10		→					

Figure 1

and prepare for exams. This would, in all likelihood, reduce her anxiety although it would probably not eliminate it altogether. Once again, if people learn to look dispassionately at their situations, they are better able to resolve their dilemmas and to adjust their behavior. Offering students opportunities and methods for assessing their circumstances is more helpful than cheering them on with general encouragements such as, "You can do it. I know you can. Just try a little harder." This woman might be further discouraged by such well-intended words because she might feel that she could not live up to the tutor's expectation. Supportive remarks work best when combined with practical strategies that foster realism or activism, or as positive reinforcement for actual achievement.

Once she found that her tasks were more manageable than she had thought, the student in this example would probably abandon the idea of withdrawing from her classes. Her comments imply that she feels frightened, out of control, and in this context, the wish to leave school sounds more like a signal for help than an actual desire. The order created by the study schedule would probably calm her, help her to regulate herself, and, consequently, the idea of withdrawing would likely be forgotten. However, in other cases, when students express the wish to withdraw, their subtexts may be different from this woman's.

Some students consciously or unconsciously create situations like hers; that is, they procrastinate. While some do so out of fear, others do so because they fundamentally do not want to be in school at the time. Some are not interested in classes and would prefer a job in the "real" world. Others encounter external circumstances that make staying in school unwise: perhaps a parent has fallen ill and needs care; perhaps some combination of events—eviction and debt, for example—makes withdrawal advisable. Yet it is hard for tutors to accept and confirm this conclusion. After all, they are aligned with academic enterprise. They may, furthermore, mistakenly believe that their tutoring can be considered successful only if the student performs well in school: they have an investment in the student's achievement. They may therefore try to dissuade the student from withdrawing when the student has a valid reason for doing so. Making decisions for a student is not the tutor's function. When someone is considering alternate directions, a tutor can offer realistic observations without making value judgments and can ask questions that help a student reach an independent conclusion. Consider the following dialogue between a student, Kathy, and her tutor, Janice:

KATHY: I don't know. I really think I should quit school and help out at our family's restaurant. Since my uncle died, there's no one to work with the wholesalers, you know, order the food and all, and I think I could do that, but my Dad keeps after me to stay in school. *[pause]*

5   JANICE: Uh-huh. Your dad thinks you should try to finish?

KATHY: Yeh. But you know, it's really dumb. I'm only here because he wants me to be here. I'm not so crazy about classes. He's going to pass the business on to me and my little brother anyway. Studying philosophy doesn't teach me how to run a restaurant, but being there does.

10   JANICE: That's true. On the other hand, what you learn in college might have a different kind of value. I don't mean practical or vocational. I mean it can change or expand the way you think about almost everything.

KATHY: Hmm, well, maybe. But right now, what I want to do is help out at the restaurant.

15 JANICE: Has your dad considered hiring someone to do your uncle's job?

KATHY: No. He wouldn't. It's a family business, and he wants me to help him out and go to school, but I can't hack both.

JANICE: Why do you think he wants you to stay in school?

KATHY: No one else in the family has gone to college. I'd be the first. He's real
20 proud, and I think he wants to be able to tell his friends that his kid graduated from college.

JANICE: How do you feel about staying in school?

KATHY: Well, right now, I really want to learn the business. I mean, maybe I could go back to college later, part time, at night, like. Maybe I'd be more
25 into it later than I am now.

JANICE: Sounds as if you know what you want but that you have to convince your father.

KATHY: Yeh, and that won't be easy.

JANICE: Maybe we could work that out together. I can help you figure out how to
30 talk to him, I think. Suppose I act as if I'm him, your dad I mean, and you practice what you want to say.

Without advocating any position, Janice raises issues that Kathy may not have considered (the nonvocational value of education, the possibility of hiring an outsider). Having tried to help Kathy think the matter through fully, Janice recognizes that Kathy has made up her mind, accepts the decision, and offers to assist in its actualization. Janice might have reached a different decision herself, but she does not try to impose her own perspective on Kathy. Rather, she presents ideas for Kathy's consideration.

Meeting the immediate crisis

3. I want you to help me write a paper for my Sociology of the Family course. It's supposed to be a five- to seven-page comparison of the parent–child relationships in three studies we read. I haven't started it yet. When is it due? Tomorrow.

This writer has made an unrealistic request, and a tutor, upon hearing it, might reasonably wonder why she waited so long to start the paper, what she expects him to do (after all, the paper cannot be completed in a single meeting), and whether the session can be put to good use. If Sidney, a tutor, were to voice these concerns to Mary, a writer, the conversation might go something like this:

SIDNEY: How come you waited so long to come here?

MARY: Well, I had a lot of other work to do.

SIDNEY: Well, it's too bad you didn't come sooner. I'd like to help you, but what did you think we could do in an hour? I mean, we can't get the paper done.

MARY: Uh, no. But I brought the essays with me.

SIDNEY: Well, that's not going to do me much good; I don't see how I can help you with this one. There just isn't time. If you get another assignment, come see me at least a week in advance.

➤ Before reading further, write a critique of Sidney's approach.

· · ·

While Sidney's frustration is understandable, he could have used the session to greater advantage. He has certainly made clear that tutors have no alchemical formulae for producing instant essays and that Mary must allocate more time for her assignments. However, there are more tactful and constructive ways of making the same points. Furthermore, Sidney need not have lost the opportunity of helping Mary meet her immediate crisis. Instead of focusing his questions on why Mary has used poor judgment, he could have proceeded as follows:

SIDNEY: Gee, it's too bad you didn't come sooner. You don't have much time left to do this paper. What would happen if you asked your professor for an extension?

MARY: I didn't think of that. Do you think it's OK?

SIDNEY: Sure, but if it isn't, you could turn the paper in late. That way we could have more time to work on it. It'd probably be better to turn in a good paper late than something you dashed off in an hour. But you'll have to decide, because some professors take off points for lateness.

MARY: Uh, I didn't know that. But the professor hasn't said that.

SIDNEY: How about checking that out after this session? Maybe you can start on the paper by listing characteristics of each of the relationships and seeing where the similarities and differences are.

In this version, Sidney helps Mary move forward. He helps her realize that this writing project will consume considerable time, and he immediately suggests two plans of action. He could, toward the end of the meeting, briefly mention the advisability of a study schedule and might suggest another meeting to set one up, but he has wisely concentrated on Mary's chief concern, which is how to get the paper written.

Helping the writer do the work

4. I have to write about my reactions to Miss Havisham in *Great Expectations*. I don't know what to say. You told me that you read it. Can you help me get started? I mean, what did you think of her?

This writer is asking, in effect, that the tutor write the paper for him. This request could be a deliberate attempt to manipulate the tutor, but more likely it is an unconscious effort motivated by the student's diffidence and inexperience. He may simply not know how to get started; he may not be aware of any methods for generating ideas, so he turns to the tutor for answers. In such a situation, a tutor might be tempted to offer her own ideas: she might want to share her enthusiasm about the literature; she might think that she could stimulate the student's thinking by talking about the character herself. The problem with this approach is that the tutor would provide the ideas for the paper instead of teaching the writer how to form independent reactions. In the dialogue below, Sharon, a tutor, asks questions that help the writer, Bob, discover what he does think of Miss Havisham:

SHARON: I think she's really interesting and very complicated. If I had to write this paper, I think I'd start jotting down words that occurred to me as I tried to picture her or remember what she did, just to get myself rolling. How about trying that?

5   BOB: OK, but I don't remember much. *[pause]*

SHARON: Well, how about starting with specific things she did or what she said? You could list that and then to the right of the page you could write how you feel about each item or what you would call it.

BOB: You mean like the way she talked about how she brought up Estella?

Instead of refusing outright to characterize Miss Havisham, Sharon responds noncommittally with "interesting" and "complicated," general words suggesting that the subject is rich in possibility. She then quickly introduces a procedure that will help Bob form his own response, and she resists his implicit invitation to offer her own views (6).

Making the writing task manageable: overcoming blocks

5. I'm an "A" student, but I have this terrible problem writing. It takes me forever to get anything done. I agonize over every word. Now I have to do a paper for my Shakespeare seminar and I'm paralyzed. Nothing comes out. I have a topic, but I can't get anything written. I write something and I scratch it out. I'm really blocked.

One might not suspect that a person who gets high marks would find composing so difficult, but the situation is all too common: perfectionists, who set unrealistically high standards of achievement, and self-doubters, who think nothing they do can approach competence, all suffer this distress. Since the woman in this example, unlike the writer in the second example (page 16), writes "A" papers, a tutor might be even more apt to assume that all that was required was a pep talk, something like "Well, you're getting 'A's' so you must be doing something right. Just try to relax a bit and go ahead and write. It'll be fine." As in the earlier case, however, such a comment could make the writer feel worse rather than better. "This tutor is expecting so much from me," she might think, "that I'll never be able to do the job he thinks I can do." If a tutor offered praise in hopes of encouraging her, the tutor would have ignored or at least discounted the writer's extreme discomfort.

One way a tutor could alleviate some of this writer's anxiety is to try to make the project seem manageable, that is, to divide it into a series of small operations so that it becomes less overwhelming. If the tutor were to suggest several meetings and to propose that a specific task be accomplished in time for each meeting, the assignment might not seem as daunting to the writer. Alternatively, a tutor could find out what sort of procedures the writer habitually follows when composing. Such a person may harbor some misconceptions about the composing process (a process that will be described in subsequent chapters) and consequently may not be proceeding as efficiently as is possible.

Deflecting anger, acknowledging error, changing tack

6. You're really not helping me. You said we were going to work on the paper I wrote on *Heart of Darkness,* but all you do is ask me a million questions about the guy who tells the story— er, Marlowe. This is not doing me any good.

In this example, the writer has become angry at the tutor, and the question is, how should a tutor respond to such attacks? Below is David's response to Bernie's anger. Before reading our analysis, write a critique of David's approach: what might he have done differently, how and why?

DAVID: What do you mean, I'm not helping you? What do you think I'm trying to do? What do you think those questions were for, anyway?

BERNIE: Well, you don't have to get so worked up!

DAVID: I was just trying to get you to say stuff you could've said in the paper.

5 BERNIE: You don't have to yell at me, for Chrissakes.

DAVID: I'm trying to help you and you fight me every step of the way.

BERNIE: Well you could start helping me and stop yelling at me.

DAVID: I'm not yelling, I'm just . . .

BERNIE: Yes you are . . .

. . .

Because David takes Bernie's criticism personally, he becomes defensive and inadvertently turns the session into a shouting match. David probably tries to justify his actions and lashes out because he feels that his competence as a tutor has been questioned. Bernie does not see or will not acknowledge that David is trying to help, and that frustrates David. He reacts angrily to the criticism and escalates the tension. Had he considered why Bernie might be upset and had he deflected Bernie's anger, he might have led a more productive session. Perhaps Bernie did not know why David was asking all those questions. Maybe David did not explain their purpose clearly. In such an event, some of Bernie's anger might be justified, and once this were conceded, David might resume discussion of the essay. On the other hand, perhaps Bernie became annoyed because he did not know what answers to give and felt that his ignorance was being exposed. Perhaps he felt badgered by the queries, or perhaps he felt guilty about not having suc- ceeded with his first try on the essay. For any of these reasons, Bernie might be turning anger that is really directed at himself against his tutor instead. With these possibilities in mind, David could have proceeded as follows:

10 DAVID: I'm sorry. Maybe I should have explained more clearly why I was asking these questions. I think the essay needs to be filled out; it needs to say more about your topic, the narrator in *Heart of Darkness*.

BERNIE: Yeh, well, it felt as if you were jumping all over me.

DAVID: It did? I'm really sorry. I didn't mean to do that. But what you just said 15 to me about the narrator could be useful. Before you forget it, write it down. You can use it in your paper.

BERNIE: OK. I said the narrator is sort of in the story and out of it at the same time.

DAVID: That's really an important idea that you could talk some more about, I 20 don't want to throw you by asking a lot of questions again. Maybe we could figure out together what you could ask yourself about what ''being in'' and ''being out'' of the story means, so your reader will see what you mean and why you think so.

In this version, David defuses Bernie's anger by acknowledging the possibility that he has erred. He is able to distinguish between the intention and the effect of the questions he asked, so he apologizes for any distress he may inadvertently have caused Bernie. This sort of recognition and conciliation on the tutor's part can turn an impasse into a productive session. Then, too, David alters his tutoring strategy when he resumes discussion of the essay. Since his questioning intimidated Bernie, David tries to make the tutoring process seem to Bernie less adversarial, more collaborative. Together they will devise a method by means of which Bernie will generate the missing details. David has, figuratively, asked Bernie to sit next to him rather than across from him.

Summary

Initially, you will need to establish rapport, obtain information about the nature and sources of a writer's problems, and clarify and agree upon objectives and procedures. Tactful, well-paced questions, careful listening, empathic comments, and information about your own experience as a writer help to elicit useful information and build trust. Maintaining confidentiality also promotes good relationships with a writer's instructors. Getting to know a writer, assessing her difficulties, and testing your hypotheses require time and patience, so you may need more than one session to complete the process.

Because academic and personal problems are often connected, tutoring does entail some informal counseling. However, since offering writing assistance is a tutor's main responsibility, you are well advised to refer someone suffering severe emotional distress to a counselor. Less severe behavioral problems can be addressed by such methods as "concretizing" a situation, responding without judging, addressing an immediate crisis, activating a writer, breaking a project into manageable tasks, offering practical strategies—not just vague encouragement—deflecting anger, and changing one's tack. Academic problems such as learning disabilities require greater expertise than most tutors possess. Consulting a supervisor or making a referral is wise when you suspect that a writer has a disability.

If a writer sees immediate benefits from tutoring, he will be more likely to attend further sessions, so accomplishing some writing task in the first session is advisable when you anticipate an extended tutorial. Establishing an agenda for future sessions and giving an assignment also increase the likelihood of the writer's return. Such planning makes efficient use of the writer's and your time.

SUGGESTIONS FOR JOURNAL ENTRIES

1. As soon as possible after you have met with a writer for the first time, record the session in your journal. Write your observations of the writer's general appearance, attitude, gestures, and so on. Analyze the session. What went well, what did not? What would you like to have done differently? What hypotheses can you make about the student, the sources of difficulty, and the prospect for change? What course of action is in order?

2. Write about the kinds of adjustments you had to make when you enrolled in college. How do they compare to those that the writers described in this chapter (or any that you encounter as a tutor) experienced? How did you react to the new situation, and how did you adjust? Are your experiences transferable? That is, could you use what you yourself learned to assist a writer? How?

3. Jot down reactions to the ideas presented in this chapter.

4. Record any instances of behavioral problems that you observed in the writers with whom you work. What was your reaction? What was your hypothesis, and how did you proceed?

SUGGESTIONS FOR FURTHER WRITING

1. A female student in a college "developmental" writing course arrives for a tutoring session with the paper below written in response to the following topic: "Write a description of your neighborhood. Make it detailed enough to distinguish it from any other neighborhood."

   a. List the strengths and problems you identify. Then list all the possible causes for the problems.

   b. Write down some questions that you might ask this writer in an initial meeting. Or, write an imaginary dialogue between you and this writer.

   My Neighborhood, by Lucille H.

   I live in Dorchester. I grew up there so it farmiliar. The people nice, everbody get along. Living in a three-decker apartment the neighbors are known to me. Mostly middle income families. I like kids playing on the street on my way to work. Its a happy place. In summer people sit out on there porches. George Roche buy all the kids ice cream. The landlord live somewhere else so things break down like heat in winter, but mostly we do fine.

2. Below is an *excerpt* from a paper a second-semester freshman composition student presented to his tutor. The excerpt is taken from his response to this topic: "In his letter to his father, Kafka says that he does not blame his parent for the suffering the son experienced as a boy. Yet information in the letter suggests that Kafka does resent his father's behavior. What is it about his father that Kafka seems to resent? What is your evidence?"

   a. What problems do you observe? List them and their potential causes.

   b. What kinds of questions would you address to the writer? What recommendations might you make? List these or write an imaginary dialogue between you and the writer.

   What Kafka resents, by Stephen P.

   Kafka implies that his father was overbaering and hypocritical. The discription of his father's behavoir in the swimming incident is enough to make anyone despise the man. The father is always belittling the boy, making him feel worthless and inferior.

   Then, too, Kafka shows that his father is a do-as-I-say, not-as-I-do type. He criticizes the boy's table manners and then voilates the very rules he imposes on the boy. While Kafka dosen't explicitly say his father is bad tempered or inconsistent, the man's actions speak for themselves.

3. Below are some comments that reflect more examples of typical behavioral problems experienced by student writers. Analyze each comment and indicate how you would respond to it, or write an imaginary dialogue.

a. Could you do this exercise for me, just to show me how to do it, because I really don't understand.

b. I didn't do my assignment for our session. My boyfriend and I broke up two days ago and I can't concentrate, I'm so sick about it.

c. I just know I'm going to get a bad grade on this paper. Read it, you'll see. It's really terrible.

d. My professor told me to come and talk to you about the paper I wrote for her on *Billy Budd*. Where is the paper? I didn't bring it.

e. I came here to work on my writing and you're asking me all these personal questions that are none of your business. If you don't start helping me, I'm leaving.

SUGGESTIONS FOR CLASS ACTIVITIES

1. Break into groups of three for some role-playing. Use dialogues and situations provided in this chapter or situations that you have experienced. One person can observe while the remaining two play tutor and writer. Stop after just a few minutes. Then let the observer comment and the actors explain what they felt was occurring, what went well, and so on.

2. Break into small groups and share experiences regarding initial meetings with writers. Give each other ideas about how to handle difficult situations.

3. Discuss your answers to the exercises in "Suggestions for Further Writing."

SUGGESTIONS FOR FURTHER READING

Beck, Paula, Thomas A. Hawkins, and Marcia Silner. "Training and Using Peer Tutors." *College English* 40 (1978): 432–449.

Bridges, Charles W., Ed. *Training the New Teacher of College Composition.* Urbana, IL: NCTE, 1986.

Bruffee, Kenneth A. "Collaborative Learning: Some Practical Models." *College English* 34 (1973): 634–643.

———. *A Short Course in Writing: Practical Rhetoric for Composition Courses, Writing Workshops, and Tutor Training Programs.* 2nd ed. Cambridge, MA: Winthrop, 1980.

Bruner, Jerome S. "The Nature and Uses of Immaturity." *American Psychologist* 63 (1972): 687–705.

Clark, Beverly Lyon, *Talking about Writing: A Guide for Tutor and Teacher Conferences.* Ann Arbor: University of Michigan Press, 1985.

Fanelli, Gerard. "Locus of Control." In *Motivation in Education.* Ed. Samuel Ball. Psychology Series. Ed. Allen J. Edwards. New York: Academic Press, 1977. 45–66.

Freire, Paulo. *Education for a Critical Consciousness.* New York: Seabury Press, 1973.

Friedman, Paul G. *Interpersonal Communication: Innovation in Instruction.* Aspects of Learning Series. Washington, DC: National Education Association, 1978.

Goldstein, Arnold P., and Frederick H. Kanfer, Eds. *Helping People Change: A Textbook of Methods.* New York: Pergamon Press, 1975.

Harris, Muriel. "Individual Diagnosis: Searching for Causes Not Symptoms of Writing Deficiencies." *College English* 40 (1978): 318–323.

———. *Teaching One-to-One: The Writing Conference.* Urbana, IL: NCTE, 1986.

Hawkins, Thomas A. *Group Inquiry Techniques for Teaching Writing.* Urbana, IL: ERIC/NCTE, 1976.

———. "Training Peer Tutors in the Art of Teaching." *College English* 37 (1976): 440–449.

Hill, W. Fawett. *Learning through Discussion: Guide for Leaders and Members of Discussion Groups.* Beverly Hills, CA: Sage Publications, 1969.

Langs, Robert. *The Listening Process.* New York and London: Jason Aronson, 1978.

Lefcourt, Herbert. "Locus of Control and Coping with Life's Events." *Personality: Basic Aspects and Current Research.* Ed. Ervin Staub. Englewood Cliffs, NJ: Prentice-Hall, 1980, 200–235.

Luft, Joseph. *Group Process: An Introduction to Group Dynamics.* 2nd ed. Palo Alto: Mayfield Publication Co., 1970.

Maslow, A. H. *Motivation and Personality.* 2nd ed. New York: Harper and Row. 1970.

Neugarten, Bernice. "Adult Personality: A Developmental View." *Human Development* 9 (1966): 61–73.

Ohlson, E. La Monte. *Identification of Specific Learning Disabilities.* Champaign, IL: Research Press Co. 1978.

Troyka, Lynn Quitman. "Perspectives on Legacies and Literacy in the 1980's." *College Composition and Communications* 32 (1982): 252–262.

Wood, David, J. S. Bruner, and Gail Ross. "The Role of Tutoring in Problem Solving." *Journal of Child Psychology and Psychiatry* 17 (1976): 89–100.

2

Engaging in Dialogue

Most people will tell you that soap operas are junk, but they have educational value. They tell you about reality and the problems people have. You learn about how to solve problems from watching even if they aren't your own problems. You get all involved with the people and this is what makes you want to keep watching. What will happen next? In my dormitory, everybody rushes in to watch *General Hospital*. You could hear a pin drop. If Luke and Laura get married, we will have a party. So, you see, soap operas are a way of life.

This essay, written by a college student, leaves its readers unsatisfied. It raises but leaves unanswered many questions: In what sense are soap operas "educational"? What does the writer mean by "reality" and "problems"? What kinds of problems? How does watching soap operas help one learn how to solve problems? Who are Luke and Laura? What does the asserted "educational value" of these problems have to do with their being a "a way of life"? A more experienced writer might have considered these questions in the process of composing and consequently have made the essay more explicit, but inexperienced writers tend not to reflect on their ideas. They do not question their thoughts, and, as a result, their compositions are not fully elaborated.

Experienced writers have developed an inner monitor, another "self," that comments and questions as the writing self sets down ideas, and it is this voice that helps the writer specify and connect his ideas. "The self proposes, the other self considers. The self makes, the other self evaluates. The two selves collaborate: a problem is spotted, discussed, defined; solutions are proposed, rejected, suggested, attempted, tested, discarded, accepted" (Murray, 140). This process resembles conversation, and indeed some theorists have argued that we learn to question our writing selves, or, more fundamentally, that we develop as thinkers by internalizing the linguistic structures of conversation. Although the relationships among thinking, speaking, and writing have not yet been fully and precisely established, what we "experience as reflective thought" seems "related causally to social conversation" (Bruffee, 639).

Why then, since most writers can communicate orally, do inexperienced writers fail to elaborate their ideas? Why, in other words, do they not operate dialogically in composing? John Schafer (27), among others, has suggested that

> conversation dialogues are different from dialogues found in essays. When we converse, or at least when we converse with friends, we need not be explicit because we share a great deal of knowledge with our hearers . . . The monologues students write often have a dialogic quality, but to understand the question and answer or statement and elaboration exchanges set up, we must be able to read the mind of the writer.

Schafer's theory offers only a partial explanation of the soap opera paper's omissions. It may explain why the writer did not identify Luke and Laura: she might have assumed that all of her readers were familiar with the characters in *General Hospital,* or she might have been addressing herself, not an imagined audience. Inexperienced writers often compose associatively, as if writing down their thoughts as they occur. They do not communicate to a reader and are not conscious that their audience may not share the contexts or assumptions underlying the sentences. These writers leave out crucial information, producing prose that is elliptical or "writer-based," as opposed to prose that is directed to a reader, or "reader based" (Flower).

Schafer's explanation is consistent with Flower's characterization of inexperienced writers, but it does not fully account for the writer's failure to explain general concepts such as "educational value" or "problems." His view assumes that the writer has already formulated questions and answers that elaborate the meaning of these terms, but that she has not expressed them all in writing; if one could read her mind, one would find the missing information there, already formed. However, it may be that the author of the soap opera paper does not know precisely what she means by "educational value" or "problems." She may have used these terms uncritically, without perceiving the need to define them for herself. She may have asked herself a preliminary question, such as, "What do I gain from watching these soap operas?" but she probably did not ask the necessary follow-up questions once she decided that the programs have "educational value." In other words, it is likely that, like many inexperienced writers, she has not *sufficiently* developed a dialogic habit of mind.

Some have ascribed this kind of failure to developmental factors; other attribute it to deficient oral skill, and still others to cultural background. (For an overview of these perspectives, see Kroll and Schafer.) Whatever the cause, the inexperienced writer's "other self" exists, if at all, in a nascent state, and its growth must be stimulated if the writer is to mature. The tutorial conference is an ideal format for such stimulation because it is truly dialogical, consisting of two speakers, unlike a class, where the writer is not the sole respondent. By commenting and asking questions, a tutor can temporarily stand in as an inexperienced writer's questioning self. The writer hears and responds to the kinds of questions he should be asking himself. The conversation provides practice that will help him internalize dialogic linguistic structures and thereby develop his critical faculties. Conversation, then, is a preparation for independent thinking and writing. It is the "major means of developing language and thought" (Moffett, 73).

While such dialogue can indirectly make writers aware of the necessity to reflect on their ideas, tutors can make this point more explicitly by calling attention to the kinds of questions they have raised in a session. Tutors can also suggest that writers keep double-entry notebooks (Berthoff) in which they first write freely on one side and then comment on their ideas on the other. Such an exercise shifts the dialogic activity from speaking to writing. Just as a tutor's questions foster critical thinking, they make writers audience-aware and can help them transform "writer-based" prose into "reader-based" prose, writing that is purposefully directed to an audience. By asking for further definition or information, tutors can help writers begin to gauge what their readers need to know.

What sorts of observations and queries will, then, promote genuine dialogue between tutor and writer? What can a tutor say to help a writer qualify, alter, or expand an idea? If a tutor stands in for a writer's "other self," it might seem to follow that she should make the same kinds of comments that she would make about her own writing. Such remarks, however, tend to be too abstract and too technical for a basic writer, who lacks academic vocabulary, critical skills and an understanding of composing tasks. Tutors, after all, are usually strong writers, and if they comment as if advising themselves, they may take for granted the very skills and concepts most difficult for basic writers to master.

Consider the following example: Genevieve, a college student in a basic writing course, is asked to write a description of a person she knows well. Before handing her paper in, she shows it to her tutor, Gail, who reads what is reproduced below:

> My friend Stella would do anything for you, she is always there when you need her and listens to you. We have been good friends for years. She got married when we finished high school and now she has a darling baby boy that looks just like her. She says she wants to come to college once the baby is a little older. I hope she comes soon so we can take classes together like we did when we were little.

GAIL: This seems like a good beginning, but it needs to be more developed.

GENEVIEVE: Uh-huh. So what do you mean? Should I start over?

GAIL: No, I didn't say that. I just meant you need to say more, you know, give more details.

GENEVIEVE: You mean, hmm, like what?

GAIL: Like develop the idea that she would do anything for you.

GENEVIEVE: Well, she would. I mean, she's that way. What do you want me to say?

➤ Before reading further, write a critique of Gail's approach: What is she doing well? What should she have done differently? What else might she have done to help Genevieve expand her essay?

The Dangers of Descriptive Responses

Genevieve's paper does suffer from a lack of "development," but because she is an inexperienced writer, she does not know what that term means or what she ought to do to "develop" her paper. Gail fails to see that Genevieve is unaccustomed to talking about writing, anybody's writing, and that she is unfamiliar with vocabulary used to name or describe elements of composition. Specifically, Genevieve does not realize that in this context, "develop" means that she should add examples or specific details that illustrate her general assertions, but when Gail tells her this she still does not know how to generate them. She would be less confused and would offer more if Gail asked the kinds of questions that would produce the desired "text." Consider this alternate conversation:

GAIL: I think you have a good beginning here, but I'd really like to know more about your friend. You said that she'd do anything for you. What sort of thing did you have in mind? What special things has she done to make you think so?

5   GENEVIEVE: Well, um, like, maybe it sounds silly, but once my car died and it was winter and it was cold and I called her from the garage. She came right over and picked me up. It was late and she was probably in the middle of dinner and she had to come a long way. But she never thought about it. She just came.

10   GAIL: Great. That helps me understand what you meant. How about writing that down and using it as an example in the paper? It makes your general idea that she would do anything for her friends a lot clearer.

Instead of abstractly describing the writer's problem as lack of "development," Gail, in this version, asks a direct question that elicits the missing information. Only when Genevieve has supplied it, has said what her friend did, does the tutor use terms that describe what has been accomplished ("example" of "general idea"). To inexperienced writers, such terms mean most when applied, as in this case, to an actual text. Genevieve is now apt to grasp and to use these terms herself because she can see to what they refer. Gail, having called what the writer has supplied an "example," could then ask her to find other places in the essay that could be similarly expanded. With some practice, Genevieve should be able to check her own work to see if she needs to illustrate at any point.

There are really two adjustments in tutoring strategy here: one is that the tutor has turned statements into questions, and the other, that she has phrased them in ordinary, accessible language. For inexperienced writers like Genevieve, the specialized, "academic" language that describes elements of composition is too vague and too intimidating to be useful, but tutors can phrase the same concepts in everyday vocabulary. For example,

ACADEMIC TERMINOLOGY	EVERYDAY LANGUAGE
How can you illustrate your topic sentence?	Why do you think this? What makes you think so? Where have you seen this?
What transitional device could link these two ideas?	What's the connection between this and that? Why did you say this before that?
What is your thesis?	What's the main idea you want me to come away with? What is it that you want me to think or do on the basis of what you said?

The Dangers of Evaluation and General Prescription

Just as descriptive commentary can baffle novice writers, general evaluations can mystify and often upset them. Here is another tutor's response to Genevieve's paper. After you read it, write down some specific suggestions for the tutor. In what ways might he have been more helpful?

SEAN: I'm sure your friend is a nice person, but this paper isn't good, first of all, because it's so general, and then your topics keep jumping around. You need to organize this and make it cohere, stick together.

GENEVIEVE: Oh.

5 SEAN: To start with, you're going to have to give more details. She could be anybody. You didn't make her special, different from anybody else.

GENEVIEVE: I really worked hard on this. I guess I just don't know how to write.

SEAN: Well, don't be so general. Give details.

GENEVIEVE: I don't know. Maybe I should choose someone else to write about.

10 SEAN: I think you can write about Stella, but just be more specific, for openers.

Sean begins with a summary of the paper's shortcomings. Unfortunately, this demoralizes Genevieve, who is made to feel that her efforts were worthless and that her essay does not merit revision. Sean may have felt that Genevieve should be told what is wrong in order that she improve, but he overwhelms her with criticisms and confuses her with vague prescriptions. The more constructive approach in this situation is not, however, to ignore the writer's problems in order to spare her feelings. Rather, it is to focus more clearly and ask neutral questions instead of offering negative assessments and general advice.

Sean does not seem to realize that several of the problems about which he has commented (shifting from subtopic to subtopic rapidly, using unsupported generalizations) emanate from the same source. If he had assessed her essay more carefully, he might have focused the discussion on that issue, and, instead of criticizing, he might have asked commonsense, specific questions, the kinds of questions she should be asking herself in order to generate the missing material.

A tutor must almost necessarily evaluate a writer's work (as we pointed out in Chapter 1) in order to decide how to proceed. However, these judgments should not be voiced; rather, they should be converted into questions that educe from the writers whatever material is required. When you speak as a respondent rather than as a critic, novice writers gain a better sense of what needs to be done. They also feel less negative about themselves and their writing than if they feel judged. More practiced writers and writers with high self-esteem may benefit from the kind of evaluation or prescription that a tutor might make about his own writing, but such comments are usually counterproductive when addressed to basic writers.

Pace and Tone of Questions

If a tutor's questions are to be effective, they must be carefully timed and delivered. How would Genevieve react if a tutor trying to help her add details said,

"When you said that Stella would do anything for you, what'd you mean by anything? I mean really anything, or what? And would she do this for everybody or just a close friend like you? And does that have anything to do with the sentence that says you've been best friends for years?"

Genevieve would probably feel beset by this volley of questions. Which is she to answer first? How is she to remember them all? A writer who feels cross-examined is likely to freeze or to become flustered. To avoid this, you can pace questions slowly and can add encouraging "um hums" and nods that cue the writer to continue. You can also consciously modulate your tone of voice so that your questions do not sound inquisitorial or hostile. A question such as "What do you mean by that?" can be encouraging or intimidating depending on the way it is voiced and what gestures accompany it. Such subtleties of delivery can greatly affect a writer's response, so you might want to use a tape recorder in practice sessions in order to adjust the pitch, volume, and intonation of your questions.

Using Open-Ended Questions, Repetition, and Summary

Our assertion that questions draw better responses from inexperienced writers than decriptions and evaluations is not without qualification. As we have already indicated, the questions must be well paced and worded in language comprehensible to the writer. Other aspects of phrasing must be considered, as well, if tutorial dialogues are to help writers expand and qualify their ideas. Consider the following example: Al, a student in a developmental writing course, has to write about a "personal experience you've had with pollution." He tells his tutor, Stan, that he does not know what to write. Stan, in the dialogue below, tries to help Al generate some ideas.

STAN: Well, there are many kinds of pollution. There's air and water, for instance. How about air pollution?

AL: Yeah. I read in the paper that there's a lot of it, but I don't know much about it.

5   STAN: Well, think about your experience. How about telling about what you're aware of in school. I notice that it's real stuffy in here. Very little air circulates. What else do you notice?

AL: The smoke?

STAN: Sure, And how about all the stuff from the chem labs? What does that
10   smell like? It bothers my eyes. How about you?

Stan is certainly wise to steer Al toward writing about his own "experience," instead of summarizing newspaper accounts. However, Stan's comments and questions are so directive that they control Al's responses. It is the tutor here and not the writer who decides the subject (which kind of pollution) and even what details are to be included (poor ventilation and smells from the chem lab). Presumably, Stan assumes that his questions will prompt Al to begin thinking, that they will give Al some ideas to start with, but this strategy may make Al feel even less capable of generating material because Stan does it so well. Such a diffident writer could become dependent on the tutor for ideas instead of creating his own. (A person who sees writing as an unpleasant or useless requirement might even take advantage of a tutor like Stan by deliberately letting him do all the work.) Had Al been given the opportunity, he might have chosen a different kind of pollution and might have recalled different sensory details from those Stan suggests. A more open-ended approach, as indicated below, would allow the writer to choose his own topic, explore it more freely, and create original responses:

STAN: When you hear of the word "pollution," what do you think of?

AL: Well, I read an article on air pollution in the newspaper.

STAN: Do you have any direct experience with air pollution, anything you can remember?

5   AL: I don't think so. Let me see. Well, I come to school on the subway. It gets pretty foul in the trains and in the stations.

STAN: OK. I'm not sure what you mean by foul. Can you tell me by talking about what you see and smell?

AL: There's an awful lot of garbage everywhere. Paper on the trains and in the
10   stations, candy wrappers, cigarettes, and God, those graffiti, I mean, they're really gross. Maybe I can't call them pollution, but they really are, sort of.

STAN: Go on.

AL: Well, pollution is a dirtying-up, isn't it? and those graffiti do that in a number of ways—real dirt and dirty words.

15   STAN: Yes, that's a neat idea.

AL: And then there's all that garbage.

STAN: That garbage?

AL: You've seen it. Like I said, the candy wrappers, the discarded newspapers, butts, I even slipped on somebody's spit once.

20   STAN: OK, great. You've mentioned a lot of stuff here, the graffitti, the paper, the saliva, and you said that polluting means dirtying. It's good that you are starting to define it.

AL: It's . . . [pause] what I'm describing isn't really what experts mean when they talk about stuff, like, you know, industrial waste in the water or in the
25   air, but it's what I'm most aware of.

STAN: That'd be a good thing to say in your paper.

        · · ·

The questions in the second version are quite differently phrased. They invite the writer to describe his own experience, not one that is selected for him, and to provide his own details rather than to amplify those suggested by the tutor. In this dialogue, the tutor occasionally elicits detail by repeating some of the writer's phrases as questions that ask for specification ("That garbage?" line 17, for example). Questions like, "When you hear the word 'pollution,' what do you think of?" also call for specification without controlling the content of the response. Because the tutor volunteers less, the writer offers more. As a result, the essay he writes will more truly be the product of his thinking, not his tutor's.

Furthermore, the tutor's comments allow Al's thoughts to move freely, so much so that he changes his topic. He begins talking about air pollution, but his recollections do not, as he realizes, fit that category. Instead of forcing him back to his original topic, Stan wisely lets him talk his way through to a different one and calls attention to this shift by summarizing what Al has said. This makes Al think some more about how to name or define the kind of pollution he has experienced.

A paraphrase or summary is distinguishable from and preferable to the kind of remark that reinterprets or adds to the writer's material. For instance, Stan might have said to Al, "You seem to be saying that there are figurative forms of pollution." But this does the writer's thinking for him. Even if a more sophisticated writer's "other self" might offer such a comment, it is best to let the writer add it himself. Stan could have *asked* Al to find a name for the pollution of words. The tutor, then, is a stand-in for the writer's other self only insofar as he questions or summarizes what the writer has generated. The tutor is not the answering self, in other words.

A tutor's paraphrase or summary offers a writer an opportunity to reflect on what he has said so far. This reflection is similar to what writers do as they revise drafts, and the discussion between tutor and writer is a precursor of that activity, particularly if the tutor jots down what the writer says or instructs the writer to take notes as she talks.

The·kinds of questions and responses that encourage a writer to remark on her preliminary ideas (be they oral or written) include the following:

GENERAL AMPLIFICATION:	Tell me more about
CLARIFICATION:	I'm not sure what you mean by————; would you explain that a bit?
SPECIFICATION:	Which one did you have in mind? Where did that happen? For example? Like what? Would you give an instance, please?
QUALIFICATION:	What exceptions can you think of? When was this not true?
PARAPHRASE OR SUMMARY:	Let me see if I can sum up what you just said: In this paragraph, you said that You told me that

Some of these forms can be combined: "Earlier you said that Macbeth's problem is his ambition. Here you say that Lady Macbeth wants her husband to succeed. What is the connection between these ideas?" Here, summary is combined with a call for specification.

Open-ended questions, then, spur a writer to think independently. They also invite him to talk and write more extensively. A tutor's careless phrasing can restrict not only what the writer discusses but also how much he says. Consider the example below, in which Ann, the tutor, tries to help Ron generate some ideas for the "describe your experience with pollution" assignment.

ANN: You said you wanted to talk about water pollution in your area?

RON: Yes. I live four blocks from the bay, and there's a marina there that messes up everything.

ANN: Do you mean that the boats dump their waste in the water?

5   RON: Yes.

ANN: Do the people also throw their garbage overboard?

RON: Yes.

ANN: Has the marine life been affected?

10 RON: Yes it has. You can't fish anymore. It's not safe.

In an attempt to get Ron to specify what "messing up" the bay means, Ann asks a series of questions that call for a yes-or-no answer. These are problematic in two ways: first, they do not require elaboration, and second, the questions supply the details for the writer instead of eliciting them. When Ann asks, "Do you mean that the boats dump their waste?" she seems to be calling for specification or qualification but actually restricts the discussion to what *she* imagines "messing up" means. Unfortunately, in this dialogue, it is Ann, not Ron, who is
➤ doing most of the work because of the way she has phrased her questions. Before reading further, write an improved version of the dialogue between Ann and Ron, one in which Ann invites the writer to speak with greater freedom and at greater length.

.   .   .

If Ann had asked, "What do you mean when you say the harbor is messed up?" she would have given Ron the opportunity to speak more spontaneously and volubly. Even if Ron were to respond vaguely, for instance, if he said, "Oh, you know, people mess it up," Ann could ask a specifying question that capitalizes on his addition of "people" as the malefactors. Basing her question on his response, she might say, "Which people do you mean?" She would than be taking her lead from him, not vice versa.

A tutor's questions, then, should derive from the context created by the writer, so a tutor must necessarily listen carefully and make judicious use of the writer's vocabulary. Considerable time and practice may be required before a tutor acquires skill in questioning, but the cultivation of this art is essential for good tutoring, tutoring that enables a writer to formulate new ideas.

Dealing with Errors of Fact or Logic

So far, we have mentioned ways in which tutors can assist writers to amplify their ideas. Their "errors" are errors of omission, not errors of fact or logic. But when a writer does make false or poorly reasoned statements, the same kind of questioning that we have already recommended is appropriate. Evaluative remarks are even more destructive in this context. Comments from a tutor such as "That's ridiculous!" or "Where in the world did you get that idea?" or "Oh, come now, you can do better than that,'' only humiliate and offend. Instead of berating the student or the essay, a tutor can ask questions or make comments that help a writer test his assumptions or conclusions. ''What evidence can you provide to support that idea?'' or ''Tell me why you think so?'' are more promising openings for discussions in which the tutor can help the writer correct her own errors.

It is important, however, that you make certain that these questions are not covert evaluations, that instead they ask the writer for arguments or evidence so that you can help the writer detect logical fallacies or misstatements. Let us say a writer has brought to a tutoring session an interpretation of Matthew Arnold's celebrated poem, ''Dover Beach.'' The writer asserts that the speaker of the poem is in France, standing at a seaview window and addressing his loved one in England. The speaker, however, is actually in Dover, as the title implies, but the tutor wants neither to hurt the writer's feelings nor to give away the answer that the writer should discover for himself.

TUTOR: You say the speaker is in France. Are you sure?

WRITER: *[blushing]* No, I guess not. *[pause]*

TUTOR: Well, where is he?

WRITER: I don't know. I thought he was sort of composing out loud.

The question, ''Are you sure?'' is rhetorical, just another way of saying, ''You're wrong.'' The writer senses this and changes his position only because he has picked up the cue, not because he has thought the matter through. He says what he thinks the tutor wants him to say and does not question his original response. Instead, the tutor could have said, ''I can see why you think the speaker is at the window, but can you tell me why you think he's in France?'' This would have made the writer retrace his thinking, and in the process he might have found that his evidence did not hold up or simply was not there. The tutor could ask more questions that help the writer offer a new interpretation. Questions like ''Are you sure?'' ''Is it really?'' and ''Don't you think that . . . ?'' are irritating because the phrasing is disingenuous, and the tutor sounds condescending if not sarcastic. If a writer has made an obvious mistake, it might be kinder and more productive to point out the error, gently, than to humiliate her with these nonquestions. A tutor could let the writer know that she must rethink an issue and then reopen the questioning, for example, ''I think you're going to have trouble substantiating that one. Perhaps if you told me what made you think so, we could go back and check the text.'' This approach would probably be a less embarrassing way of alerting a writer that she has erred than the rhetorical question or a confrontive remark like, ''Well, then why is the poem called 'Dover Beach'?'' which would probably make the writer feel quite stupid. Asking for substantiation in a nonthreatening way (''Could you explain why you think the speaker is in France?'' or ''What details in the text made you think the speaker was in France?'') requires the writer to test her own hypotheses, to argue with herself, in effect, and thus to engage in that crucial dialogue that is basic to good thinking and good writing. If the tutor points out the right answer, if the tutor makes the correction for the writer, what has the writer learned? The right answer, but not how to determine it.

There are situations, however, in which a writer has no way of finding an answer during a conference. In such cases, a tutor can identify an issue requiring clarification and can suggest that the writer do some research before turning the paper in.

While the process of asking questions and waiting for a writer to offer a ''correct'' response can be tedious and difficult, it accomplishes a good deal more than telling a writer what to think or criticizing him for being wrong. We recommend questioning over evaluating, because questioning encourages writers to think dialogically and, ultimately, independently. While this chapter has introduced general strategies for engaging students in dialogue, the following two chapters discuss more formal ways in which tutors can help writers learn how to generate and shape ideas.

Summary

Inexperienced writers tend not to reflect on their ideas. They do not question their thoughts, and, as a result, their compositions are not fully elaborated. Experienced writers, by contrast, have developed another ''self'' that questions and comments as the writing self sets down ideas. When tutors engage in dialogue with writers, they temporarily stand in for the writer's ''other self'' and help writers develop the dialogical habit of mind that is necessary to good writing.

You can help a writer elaborate and refine ideas by asking thoughtful, specific questions. This practice is preferable to supplying answers, offering evaluations, or giving general advice, because it encourages the writer to do the thinking. Questions should be slowly paced and modulated in tone to prevent a writer from feeling interrogated. Questions that call for amplification, specification, or qualification help a writer expand preliminary ideas. Questions that encourage a writer to test her hypotheses and examine her evidence help her correct erroneous or illogical statements. Your questions will be more helpful to an inexperienced writer if they are phrased in everyday language rather than in technical, academic terminology. They will help a writer think freely, independently, and critically if they are open-ended and carefully phrased to avoid embarrassing a writer, controlling her responses, or elaborating for her. You can also summarize a writer's ideas to provide the opportunity for her to reflect and comment on them.

SUGGESTIONS FOR JOURNAL ENTRIES

1. Observe yourself as a writer. Do you tend to "talk to yourself" as you write, or do you have a different equivalent of the writer's "other self" described by Murray? What sort of process do you generally follow as you write? What works well? What does not? What procedures that you use might be helpful to the writers with whom you work?

2. If you are meeting with writers similar to those described in this chapter, describe your conferences. How have you helped the writers elaborate on their ideas? What worked? What did not? What would you do differently next time? If you are working with more advanced writers, comment on the extent to which the strategies suggested in this chapter are helpful to them.

3. Try writing a "double-entry" journal of the sort described on page 29. In the left-hand column, write freely your reactions to the ideas presented in the chapter. Then, on the right-hand side, comment on your comments. This is another way to set up a dialogue with yourself as a writer and a useful exercise for the writer with whom you work.

SUGGESTIONS FOR FURTHER WRITING

1. Transform comments:

Turn the following evaluations into questions that will elicit a useful revision:

    a. This is too wordy.

    b. This doesn't have enough reasons.

    c. This isn't clear.

    d. This doesn't tell me what the outcome was.

    e. This fails to establish any relationship between point A and point B.

    f. This language is too general (too specific).

Rephrase the following questions by substituting everyday language for technical or abstract vocabulary:

    a. What substantiation can you provide for this point?

    b. How can you restructure this argument?

    c. What devices of cohesion could connect the ideas in this paragraph?

    d. What qualification can be made about this point?

2. Below you will find three student papers that require elaboration. Describe how you would draw further information from the writers or write an imaginary dialogue between you and each writer.

A. ASSIGNMENT: *Description of an experience that is "educational" or that has changed the way you think*

My greatest enjoyment is sitting and reading a newspaper. It is one pleasure I have and when people at social gatherings utter these words, "Don't believe what you read in the newspaper" I quietly think of all the knowledge I have acquired from this very hobby.

A crossword offers a challenge that could not be compared to any other hobby. It demands full concentration yet provides entertainment at the same time.

The real estate section, cars and things offered for sale section, are really interesting when I scan over them and sometimes I try to imagine the people that are offering these items for sale.

A home and garden section in any newspaper provides a world of information for those that are interested in that sort of thing.

Sports sections in most papers are very informative. This section can be addictive to those who are sport buffs.

If one ever sat and read the news they could certainly say they are getting a bargain in these inflationary times.

B. ASSIGNMENT: *Description of a place*

1. The Town Pier, the center of harbor activity, is overlooked by both the clipper Ship Hotel and Front Street, the business district of town. One of the main events that goes on daily at the Pier is the unloading of fish from the various fishing vessels. Another purpose the Pier suits is as an office for the Harbor Master who regulates everything from boat moorings to clamming licenses. A third

example of the usefulness of the Town Pier is that it serves as a docking place for visiting seamen and also for the Town's boat owners' dinghies.

C. ASSIGNMENT: *Two things mistakenly believed to be unlike (500 words)*

The Armed Services and the Universities

I believe that the Armed Services and the colleges are alike in many aspects in certain areas. Taken my discussion from my friend who joined the Navy the same time I started school. We write back to each other. He explains how Navy life is to me, I in turn explain college life to him. What I found to my surprise that both of our lives are similar in many points.

5   I found that we both found a new life better than what we were doing before. We both found something that we want to do for the time being. I like what I'm doing now, and he also like what he's doing.

We both gained a lot of self-confidence in ourselves. To do what I must do for self-preservation. We both understand to make our own decision in life. Too stand-up on our two feet. We both learn

10   what life is all about, we grew up alot. We both can talk intelligable on certain subject. We can understand ourselves and other better. I feel know that I help someone instead of somebody helping me.

We both learn discipline, conformity, being on time and being responsible young adults. We learn it but wanting to change and bettering ourselfs. It's better being this way in having alwas having

15   something to do and keeping ourselves occupied.

It awaken both of us, instead of given up in life, we found what was wrong with both of us and conquered the problem.

My friend is presently attending school in the Navy. He is studying for a electrian Mate. When he get out he wants to become a electrician. I doing the same thing with my future, and seeking to

20   gain my career in life.

We both have alot of time to party and do the things just to give us pleasure and enjoyment. I'll be traveling soon to a new school. Living in a new environment. Learning new things, seeing new things and trying to my life a little easier by learning. Also my friend will be doing the same thing only he will be doing on a ship.

SUGGESTIONS FOR CLASS ACTIVITIES

1. Using the sample papers provided in "Suggestions for Further Writing," do some role-playing. Ask your partner to comment on the usefulness of the questions you ask, their pacing, phrasing, and delivery.

2. Using situations you have encountered in tutoring, do some role-playing. If you try to imitate the behavior of someone you had difficulty working with, you may get ideas from your fellow tutors.

3. Bring in assignments that writers have shown you. Use them in role-playing exercises in which the "writer" needs to get started.

4. Bring in copies of initial drafts written by writers with whom you have worked. Describe how you help each writer; if you have access to the final versions, duplicate and bring them in. Or, use the first drafts for role-playing exercises in which you assume the writer's role and let your classmates practice tutoring.

SUGGESTIONS FOR FURTHER READING

Barnes, Douglas, James Britton, and Harold Rosen. *Language, the Learner and the School.* Baltimore: Penguin, 1971.

Berthoff, Ann E. *Forming, Thinking, Writing.* Part II. Rochelle Park, NJ: Hayden, 1978.

Britton, James. *Language and Learning*. Hammondsworth: Penguin, 1978.

Bruffee, Kenneth. "Collaborative Learning and the 'Conversation of Mankind.' " *College English* 46 (1978): 635–652.

Emig, Janet. "Writing as a Mode of Learning." *College Composition and Communication* 28 (1977): 122–127.

Flower, Linda. "Writer-based Prose: A Cognitive Basis for Writing Problems." *College English* 41 (1979): 19–37.

Halpern, Jeanne W. "Differences between Speaking and Writing and Their Implications for Teaching." *College Composition and Communication* 35 (1984): 345–357.

Jacobs, Suzanne, and Adela Karliner. "Helping Writers to Think: The Effect of Speech Roles in Individual Conferences on the Quality of Thought." *College English* 38 (1977): 489–505.

Kroll, Barry M. "Developmental Relationships between Speaking and Writing." In *Exploring Speaking–Writing Relationships: Connections and Contrasts*. Eds. Barry M. Kroll and Roberta J. Vann. Urbana, Ill: NCTE, 1981. 32–54.

Lawrence, Mary. *Writing as a Thinking Process*. Ann Arbor: University of Michigan Press, 1974.

Liggett, Sarah. "The Relationship between Speaking and Writing: An Annotated Bibliography." *College Composition and Communication* 35 (1984): 334–344.

Lunsford, Andrea. "Cognitive Development and the Basic Writer." *College English* 41 (1979): 38–46.

———. "Aristotelian vs. Rogerian Argument: A Reassessment." *College Composition and Communication* 30 (1979): 146–151.

Moffett, James. *Teaching the Universe of Discourse*. Boston: Houghton, Mifflin, 1983.

Murray, Donald. "Teaching the Other Self: The Writer's First Reader." *College Composition and Communication* 33 (1982): 140–147.

———. *A Writer Teaches Writing*. 2nd ed. Boston: Houghton, Mifflin, 1985. Chapter 8.

Schafer, John. "The Linguistic Analysis of Spoken and Written Texts." Reprinted in Kroll, 1–31.

Shaughnessy, Mina P. *Errors and Expectations*. New York: Oxford University Press, 1977. Introduction, Chapter 7.

Vygotsky, L. S. *Thought and Language*. Trans. E. Hanfman and G. Vahar. Cambridge, MA: MIT Press, 1962.

Wilson, John. *Thinking with Concepts*. Cambridge: Cambridge University Press, 1971.

Wood, David, J. S. Bruner, and Gail Ross. "The Role of Tutoring in Problem-Solving." *Journal of Child Psychology and Psychiatry* 17(2) (1976): 89–100.

PART TWO

Composing Processes: Generating Ideas

3

Promoting Fluency I: Getting Started

Chapter 2 considered ways in which tutorial dialogue can help writers to *elaborate* their ideas, to make the transition from writer-based to reader-based prose. Writers who do not elaborate their ideas lack *fluency*. The term "fluency" is more commonly applied to speaking, particularly to speaking a foreign language, than to writing. "She has fluency in Russian" usually means, "she handles Russian *pronunciation, syntax,* and *inflections* comfortably, and her *vocabulary* is large and diverse enough to enable her to express ideas on a variety of subjects and in a variety of social and rhetorical contexts." When "fluency" is applied to writing, however, it has less to do with correct and appropriate language per se and more to do with meaning, with having something to say, and with getting it down on paper with some sense of ease rather than of strain. In *Writing for the Inexperienced Writer: Fluency, Shape, and Correctness,* Marlene Griffith defines "fluency" as distinct from "shape" and "correctness" in writing:

> By fluency, I mean the ability to write down one's observations or thoughts or feelings, *to think out loud on paper.* By shape, I mean structure, form, organization, whether this be of the piece as a whole, of a paragraph, or of a sentence; it includes sentence patterns and paragraph development. By correctness, I mean such things as spelling and punctuation, the use of the "s" and the apostrophe. I am not suggesting absolute separation of these categories; . . . . (67; emphasis added)

While indeed there is no "absolute separation" of fluency, shape, and correctness (because writing processes are nonlinear), fluency must be developed first. After all, until a writer has generated some raw material, has recalled and/or gathered "something to say," there is nothing to shape, nothing to correct. A major difference between nonfluent and fluent writers is, however, the amount of time they allow for invention throughout the writing process. Nonfluent writers may short-circuit invention and write very little, as if they really have "nothing to say." In contrast, fluent writers give themselves plenty of time and space to generate raw *material* for paragraphs and essays early in the writing process, and they remain open to further invention, to the bright ideas that may occur to them as they shape and correct. Because the papers of nonfluent writers are often full of errors, tutors may feel tempted to tinker with these smaller, more immediate "fixable" problems instead of tackling the larger questions of meaning. Both writers and tutors may assume—wrongly, we believe—that correctness is more important than meaning. But a writer must generate plenty of material to compose effectively. Emphasizing correctness too early in the writing process may intimidate and silence a writer, just as correcting a young child's grammar may intimidate and silence her, whereas encouraging her to form whole constructions, however incorrect, helps her to communicate her meanings. That is why, unless for some reason a teacher explicitly says otherwise or a writer expresses a strong preference to the contrary, fluency should take priority in tutorial dialogue with writers who are not yet elaborating their ideas. Accordingly, later chapters will consider techniques for shaping ideas and for correcting sentence problems and punctuation. This chapter presents informal and formal techniques by which tutors sitting beside writers, as partners on "their side" of the paper rather than as judges on the "other side," can help them develop fluency.

Writers Who Lack Fluency

We discern two kinds of nonfluent writers: reticent writers, who generate very little material, and self-censoring writers, who judge their initial ideas so severely that they have a lot of trouble getting started (but are fluent once they get going). Before we present techniques for tutoring, we want to take a closer look at each group.

Reticent writers

Most reticent writers have not received helpful writing instruction in school. In addition, some writers get little practice because our culture often does not promote writing. Circumstances that impede a writer's progress are familiar: TV watching, school disruption, students moving from school to school. These reticent, inexperienced writers are seldom inexperienced people, however. Their lives as students, workers, parents, and citizens are often rich in experiences about which they definitely do have something to say.

However, academic assignments may seldom call upon them to write on those topics about which they are well-informed and articulate *speakers*. Their ideas may seem to dry up as soon as they start to write. That is because speaking to some extent calls upon skills different from writing. (We have touched on this subject in Chapter 2 and will say more about the differences in Chapter 8.) While speaking, they can easily keep their thoughts in mind, can use tone and gesture to indicate the relationships among ideas, and can use audience response to gauge when they have gotten their ideas across or when they need to give further explanation. But as Sondra Perl has observed, when they write, they worry about the look as well as the sound of their ideas, about such things as spelling, punctuation, paragraph indentation, and penmanship. They begin to edit for correctness, consulting the dictionary and grammar handbook before they have even gotten many of their ideas down on paper. Thus, they run out of time and produce only a few sentences. Moreover, these frequent distractions make them lose track of what they want to say, and they eventually stop in frustration.

Reticent writers may also lack fluency as a result of their socialization. Our conversations with students over the years have revealed several factors. Writers may have been taught that deference and diffidence are signs of politeness and that children, especially girls, "should be seen and not heard." Girls may have been taught that boys prefer girlfriends who ask them questions about themselves and are good listeners. While some cultures prize lively family debates as opportunities for friendly exchanges of wit and erudition, others regard differences of opinion as uncomfortable quarrels that must be avoided or quickly smoothed over. People who grow up with these kinds of attitudes usually have little oral fluency and little confidence in their ability to communicate. They may believe that they have little to say that anyone else would want to hear, much less read. So they write very short, undeveloped papers.

Self-censoring writers

Peter Elbow has described two attitudes that are involved in the composing process: "the accepting mentality needed for abundant invention and the rejecting mentality needed for tough-minded criticism" ("Embracing Contraries in the Teaching Process," 339). If associative writers (who will be discussed in Chapter 6) are too accepting and invent too abundantly and superficially, perfectionistic, self-censoring writers are too rejecting, so tough on themselves that before they can even get started, their inner voices are already muttering, "That's a dumb/boring/too obvious/too obscure idea," or "I don't know enough about that," or "That idea will never pan out," or "Professor Scribbly would hate that subject," or even "Professor Scrawley hates me!" Self-censoring writers have often received formal writing instruction strongly emphasizing correctness; they have been taught rules that supposedly produce and protect "good writing," rules like "First think of what you want to say, and then write your outline" or "Never use a semicolon with a coordinating conjunction." They have read enough to appreciate all-too-keenly the gap between their amateur attempts and the work of professional writers.

Self-censoring writers typically sit for hours in front of blank paper, wracking their brains for ideas that will be interesting and significant enough to please both themselves and the highly critical readers they imagine; they (like the "blocked" writers we will describe in Chapter 4) perform mental gyrations in order to think ideas all the way through before beginning to write, and once they do begin putting words on paper, they insist on perfecting each sentence—choosing just the right words and refining the sentence structure—before framing the next. Sondra Perl's "basic writers" are not the only slaves of premature editing; some graduate students laboriously perfect sentences and even chapters, only to discard them later. Premature editing is insidiously destructive to both reticent and self-censoring writers, because it allows them to believe that they have been substantively revising their papers when, in fact, they have merely been tinkering. All but the most seriously self-censoring writers eventually do get their papers written, but at immense costs in time, anxiety, and intellectual energy.

The processes of composing are actually quite different from what these two groups of writers suppose. James Britton explains in *The Development of Writing Abilities (11–18)* that students begin thinking and writing in "expressive language," which includes informal talk, notes, journal writing, and early drafts; later on, they use "transactional writing" to elaborate and explain their personal ideas in order to inform and perhaps to persuade an impersonal audience that might need to have certain kinds of information and lines of reasoning more explicitly spelled out. Britton and other composition researchers note the tendency of writers to skip over the middle speculative stage, a stage that is essential to the process of moving from expressive ("writer-based") to transactional ("reader-based") prose (as Chapter 2 explains). Without it, papers are often empty, artificial, and merely correct. Promoting fluency, opening up access to thought, necessitates prolonging the incubation period in which writers can engage themselves with the subject, can turn it this way and that and explain it to themselves before becoming concerned with explaining it to others. Tutorial dialogue enables writers to talk to real people, their tutors, rather than to some very demanding or hostile imaginary audience, and it prolongs speculative thinking.

Reticent and self-censoring writers also share a misperception about how "good writers" write. While they may picture "the great American novelist" amidst crumpled pages and overflowing ashtrays, really *good* academic writers, they imagine, sit down at their typewriters, insert pristine sheets of bond paper, and pour forth logical, polished prose on the very first try. Whoever can't do that, can't write. Ironically, the seemingly inevitable *rightness* of professional writing does not reveal the untidy processes by which the professionals *got* it right. The messiness of invention—as seen in Donald Murray's rambling daybooks (see *A Writer Teaches Writing*), or in the "Poems in Process" section of the *Norton Anthology of English Literature* (4th ed., II, 2513–2533), or even in the cutting and pasting by which more experienced student writers produce their papers— remains undisclosed to these writers.

Thinking out loud on paper may intimidate reticent writers and frustrate self-censoring writers. They (and sometimes their tutors) may wish they could avoid the stresses of invention and get on with easier tasks such as organizing or editing. But as Marlene Griffith explains, thinking aloud on paper brings writers back to their own language and experience, making "inner experience known by translating it into words and thus putting it outside one's self." And it also connects writers' inner experiences with the outer experiences they glean from books and lectures, "filtering [outer experience] through the mind's eye and I, thus letting it *be* known." As Griffith concludes, "Genuine fluency generates and opens up access to thought" (29–30). By sharing your ways of "thinking out loud on paper," revealing your own untidy composing processes, and insisting that fluency receive priority, you can help reticent and self-censoring writers.

Fluency Promotes Correctness

The experiences of Marlene Griffith in the Bay Area Writing Project, of Sondra Perl and Peter Elbow, and of many other researchers in composition show that as writers gain fluency, many of their problems with correctness mysteriously vanish. This may seem dubious. While we know that correctness does not *entirely* take care of itself—and several chapters of this book are devoted to techniques tutors can use to promote it—we have seen that, indeed, as writers become more fluent, many of their problems with sentence structure, grammar, spelling, punctuation, and mechanics DO begin to clear up. We do not yet know why this happens, but composition researchers are investigating several hypotheses. Their investigations will undoubtedly lead to refinement of tutoring techniques. Meanwhile, our best advice to tutors is "Don't count on it, but when you see it happening, congratulate the writer, and enjoy!"

Promoting Fluency: Listing and Mapping

Chapter 2 suggested the kinds of questions you can ask in order to get writers to talk about their subjects. In addition to using these general strategies, you can use the informal techniques of listing and mapping by means of which writers can proceed from talking to jotting their ideas on paper. These techniques promote fluency by helping writers think dialogically and analytically.

Listing is a primary means of promoting fluency. As tutorial dialogue proceeds, the writer thinks out loud and gradually associates one thing with another. The tutor listens for associations that seem especially interesting to the writer and asks further questions about them. These associations can be the basis of a preliminary list. Once the associational list is fairly full, the tutor helps a writer sort it, placing similar items in clusters and naming each cluster according to the quality its members share. The names of categories can be used to generate further information. (Their use for shaping will be discussed in Chapters 5 and 6.) Although at the beginning of the dialogue you might transcribe a writer's comments to allow him to concentrate fully on generating thoughts, he should assume this task as soon as possible (unless his very laborious handwriting impedes the progress of the dialogue). Listing shows reticent and self-censoring writers that in fact they have more to say about a subject than they might have thought in the beginning; it assuages their fear of the blank page; and it prompts them to recall further information and ideas.

Mapping is a nonlinear, graphic representation of tutorial dialogue using only the writer's *key words;* it seems to integrate the functions of both hemispheres of the brain by combining visual with verbal learning styles (Boyle). For a paper about "irrigation," a writer might put down anywhere on a piece of scratch paper an assortment of terms, perhaps first "more crops," then "waste-water pollution," then "selenium and arsenic," then "kills ducks," and so forth, gradually generating a map like that in Figure 2. As words appear here and there on the

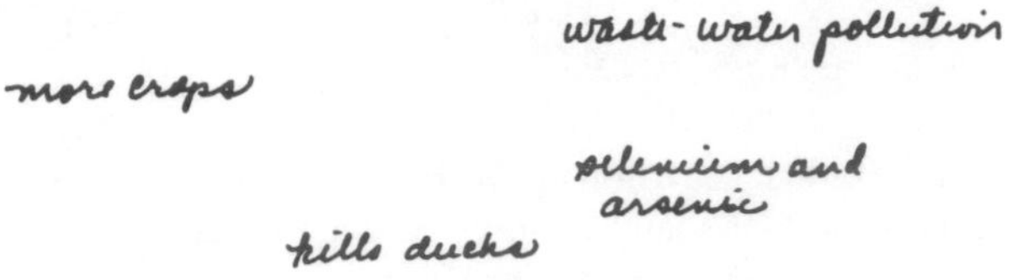

waste-water pollution

more crops

selenium and arsenic

kills ducks

Figure 2

page, some writers, especially so-called visual learners, may draw in connections they might not have noticed in purely verbal dialogue. Seeing these might also prompt them to add more words and to draw more connections (Figure 3). Mapping is more than just a nonvertical list, because as each word appears on the map, it may in turn prompt the writer to come up with a variety of associated words. After plenty of material is set forth, you can help the writer look for similar items and gather them into clusters. The writer can then redraw the map, clustering these items and naming each cluster according to the quality its members share. Some words may appear in more than one group, indicating potential connections. Some words may not fit into any group and may be set aside. One group of words may engage a writer's interest to the extent that a whole new list or map may be developed about it. While a list records ideas simply in a vertical line, a map records them helter-skelter on a page, thus leaving room for unforeseen associations. In the spirit of helpfulness, you might be tempted to write the words in patterns of your own design, but (as with offering contributions to a verbal list) doing so would prevent writers from making their own connections and thus would usurp the writers' "thinking out loud on paper." Mapping, like listing, is most useful when it prolongs free association and prevents both premature closure and premature editing. In later chapters, we will say more about

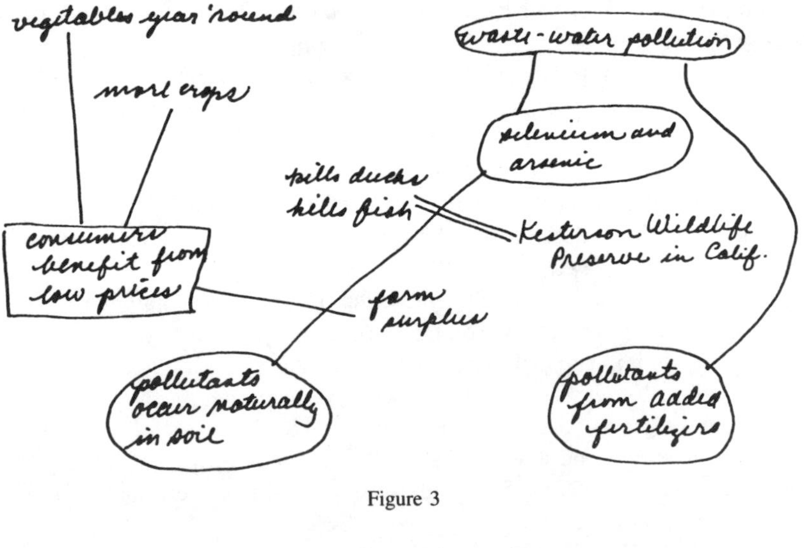

vegetables year 'round

more crops

waste-water pollution

selenium and arsenic

kills ducks
kills fish

consumers benefit from low prices

Kesterson Wildlife Preserve in Calif.

farm surplus

pollutants occur naturally in soil

pollutants from added fertilizers

Figure 3

techniques of grouping, renaming, and connecting groups of ideas, all of which are more relevant to "shape" than to "fluency."

Listing and mapping could help Carol, the writer of the paper reproduced as Figure 4, to overcome her extreme lack of fluency. She is an adult enrolled in a precollege writing course in an open-admissions program. Although Carol is much less experienced in writing than the novice writers we discussed in Chapter 2, she is not at all atypical of students in many open-door junior colleges today. She does not write elaborated prose, but her life experiences, including work as a nurse's aide and a waitress, *do* provide her with "something to say." Read her paper, try to imagine what kind of person she is, and take a few minutes to write a dialogue (using the techniques presented in Chapters 1 and 2) through which

My job

1   I reely like my job. My job is a waitress. At
2   Howard johnsons one the hiway by the statium.
3   I use to be waitress at Holidan in. But
4   Hojos better to me I think 30 34 every body get along
5   good ther I think 46

6   Wonday Bob Richards come into Hojos Holiday
7   in. He report sports on TV. He is good. He is
8   funny I think. 68

9   My friend Shirley work at Hojos. in the
10 morning. Tips good at night. I think. 81 83

11   Hojos serve good food. Friday Wednesday fish
12 Try all you can eat. Tips are good on Winesday I
13 think. 102

14   People come after the football games. It is
15 fun after the games. 114 to me I think. 118

16   I reely like my job. 123

Figure 4

Carol and Joe, her tutor, get acquainted and establish something of Carol's prior experience with writing.

> Carol wrote the draft (Figure 4) in response to the assignment, "Write a 500-word paper describing a job you liked or disliked." Keeping in mind our profile of reticent writers, please read her draft and take a few moments to write out your responses to these questions:

- What kinds of problems do you observe in the draft?
- What *does* the writer know about composition?
- What do her statements imply about how she feels about what she is saying?
- Where do you see opportunities to help her elaborate?

. . .

You probably noticed not only lack of fluency, but also many problems with correctness (misspellings, confusion of homonyms, missing words, incorrect verb forms, incomplete sentences) and shaping (statements unrelated to the topic, the job itself; confusing shifts from one workplace to the other) that characterize the papers of nonfluent writers. The paper shows *some* grasp of paragraphing (each paragraph is about a different idea), but it is hard to tell whether or not the paragraphing is deliberate. Carol is worried about length; as the superscripts show, she is counting words and tacking on "I think" or "to me I think" to two completed sentences (lines 10 and 15). Elsewhere (lines 5 and 8), "I think" may indicate both a feeling of "having nothing to say" that anyone would want to read about and a diffidence about the validity of her reactions. The very short paragraphs leave the reader asking questions: Does she like waitressing in general? Or only at Howard Johnson's? Does she like it because of the customers? The co-workers? The tips? What do "good" (lines 5, 7, 10, 12) and "fun" (line 15) mean? To help her "think out loud on paper," tutorial dialogue might proceed as follows:

CAROL: *[after Joe has read the draft]* Pretty bad, huh?

JOE: Well, I don't see anything we can't work on. What do you think is "pretty bad"?

CAROL: Everything. Grammar. I worked for two hours, and I still need 377 more
5   words.

JOE: Well, before we work on sentences, I'd like to know more about your work at Hojo's.

CAROL: Shirley was nice. She showed me a lot.

JOE: Like what?

10 CAROL: You know. *[pauses]* Where things were kept. *[pauses]* How to carry a lot of things at once, how to set down the plates nice and quiet. . . .

JOE: You said it was fun sometimes. . . .

CAROL: Yes, she kidded. With the customers. You know—regulars at the Fish Fry. Her fans.

15 JOE: She had fans. . . .

CAROL: Yes. You know Bob Richards? From TV? *[Joe nods.]* He would come in for coffee after taping over at the stadium. *[pauses]* She'd bring him his coffee right away, without him even ordering. She knew what he liked.

JOE: Bob liked that. . . .

20 CAROL: Yeah. She made the customers feel like they were company.

By reading the assignment and draft attentively and by asking Carol to identify her concerns, Joe treats her as a serious and responsible writer. He keeps in mind that she wants to work on her incomplete sentences but postpones this issue of correctness until she has elaborated her ideas. (Chapter 8 will discuss ways of dealing with sentence problems.)

Now that Joe's questions have helped Carol elaborate her original statement that working as a waitress was sometimes fun, he might begin jotting a preliminary list (Figure 5):

JOE: Like company. That's neat. Let's try to get some of these ideas down on paper. What did you say . . . ? *[As Carol dictates, Joe lists a few terms and then passes the list to her so she can add to it.]*

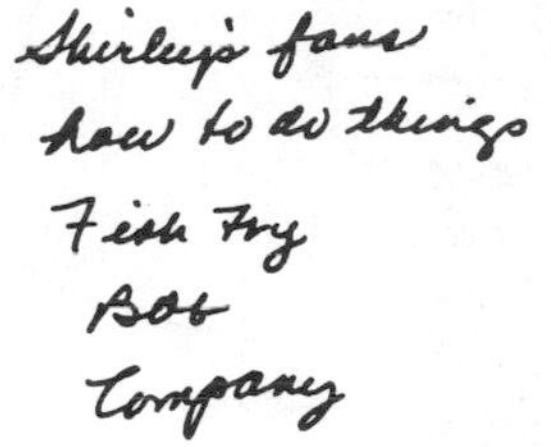

Shirley's fans
how to do things
Fish Fry
Bob
Company

Figure 5

Good. Tell me some more about your job.

25 CAROL: Well, the manager was a real pain. Wanting to take us out, you know! *[writes "manager" on the list]*

JOE: What else?

CAROL: The cook! What a nice guy!

JOE: Now you're rolling! Just say some words as fast as you can think of them
30   and add them to the list, OK?

CAROL: OK. Tired . . . smile . . . good food . . . turkey dinner . . . 28 flavors . . . stadium . . . *[she writes these]*

JOE: How about the things she showed you. You know. The things you mentioned earlier.

35 CAROL: Oh, yeah. *[adds these]*

JOE: Which of these could go together?

CAROL: I don't know. They all go together, don't they?

JOE: How do you mean?

CAROL: They are all about my job?

40   JOE: Yes, they are. But supposing you wanted to sort them out into groups. Which ones *could* go together?

    CAROL: Hmmmm . . . Bob was Shirley's fan. *[draws a line between "Bob" and "Shirley's fans"]* *[pauses]* So was the company. And the cook. *[draws connecting lines]*

45   JOE: That's good. What do they all have in common?

    CAROL: They're all Shirley's fans.

    JOE: Yes. Could you write "fans" beside that cluster? *[Carol writes.]* OK. What else goes together?

    CAROL: The things Shirley showed me how to do. *[draws connecting lines]* OK.
50   Those are all skills. *[labels the items "skills"]* Hmmm . . . smiling when you're tired is a skill too. *[draws in the connection]*

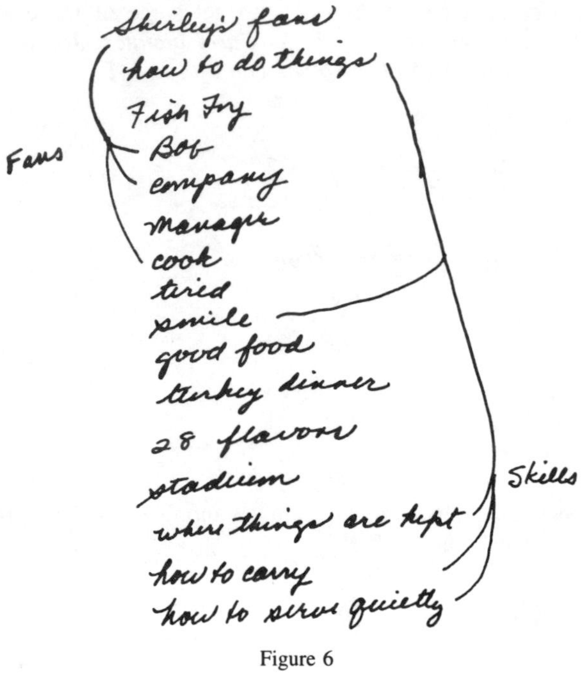

Figure 6

As Carol identifies the similar items, clusters them, and names the common quality of each cluster (Figure 6), she finds new connections (for instance, the connection between smiling and the other skills Shirley taught her). Joe could continue questioning her in this way until most, if not all, of the items listed were part of a cluster. The leftover items could be set aside for later use or discarded. Joe could now help Carol elaborate the two groups, "fans" and "skills." By listing, grouping, and naming, Carol has realized that she has more to say about her experience than she thought at first. She has gained fluency.

Sometimes, however, a vertical list constrains writers. They may feel unable to change its apparent sequence (even though that sequence is entirely associational). Supposing that the list generated above affected Carol that way, making it hard for her to see that "Shirley's fans" and "Bob" went together. Because its random visual appearance defies sequence, mapping might be a good alternative strategy for helping her see the possible connection. Let's go back to the point at which Joe asks Carol to begin sorting:

JOE: Which of these could go together?

CAROL: I don't know. They all go together, don't they?

55 JOE: Yes, in a way. They're all about your job. Let's try making a map. I'll read the items on your list, and you write them down helter-skelter on a piece of scratch paper. Don't try to arrange them, just write them any old way, OK? *[Carol writes the items.]*

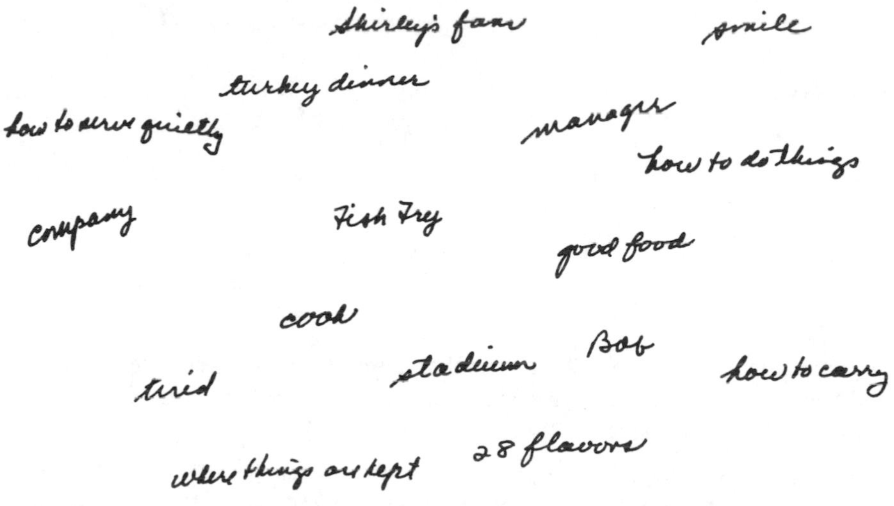

Shirley's fans   smile

turkey dinner

how to serve quietly   manager

                                  how to do things

company   fish fry

                              good food

            cool

tired   stadium   Bob   how to carry

        where things are kept   28 flavors

Figure 7

By listing her associations rapidly from conversation (Figure 7), Carol generates more topics. After she has generated quite a few, Joe might direct his questions toward those that seemed to interest her, thus helping her expand her ideas further (Figure 8):

JOE: It sounds like you've got a lot to say about the manager.

CAROL: For sure! He would take it out on you. You know. If you wouldn't date
60 him.

JOE: How do you mean?

CAROL: He'd give you a table where nobody would want to sit. Or tell the busboys to clear someone else's table. Let you wait. That way your tips would be low.

65   JOE: Could you add those to the map too?

     CAROL: Sure. *[writes]*

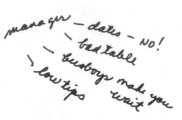

Figure 8

By asking more questions about the other items Carol showed interest in, Joe could similarly help her develop each. Then he could help her cluster similar items and name the clusters (Figure 9):

     JOE: You've got a lot of material now. Let's see what items you could cluster together on the map. It's probably easier to redraw it than get too many lines tangled up. Here's some more paper.

70   CAROL: OK. Well, Shirley and the cook were nice. So was Bob. They go together. *[lists them together]*

     JOE: Good.

     CAROL: 28 flavors goes with turkey dinner *[writes]* . . . tired and smile *[writes]* . . . the manager . . . well, I'm going to put him with "tired" and "smile"
75   because I had to smile at him when I was tired to death of him!

     JOE: I can see what you mean! What would you call that cluster of items?

     CAROL: Pains! *[labels the cluster]*

     Joe: What about the other clusters you've got so far?

     CAROL: Well . . . 28 flavors and turkey are "benefits." And "friends" fits Shir-
80   ley, Bob, and the cook. *[writes]* Hmmm . . . "friends" and "benefits" go together: good parts of working at Hojo's. And "pains" are bad parts.

JOE: How about connecting them?

CAROL: *[She crosses out "pains" and relabels both clusters.]*

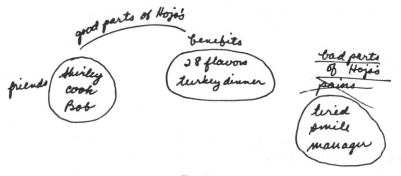

Figure 9

As with listing, there would probably be some items on the map that Carol found uninteresting; if so, she could set them aside, either to be used later (if she needed more material) or to be discarded. At this point in the dialogue, mapping, clustering, and naming enable Carol to begin noticing relationships; in other words, she has increased her fluency and is beginning to shape her draft.

Promoting Fluency: Heuristics

In addition to the informal processes of questioning, listing, and mapping that we have just considered, there are also more formal ways of inventing material: heuristics. An *heuristic* is a tool for systematically discovering information about a subject or a problem and asking fruitful questions about it. Listing and mapping are means of gathering information, but since they employ relatively free association, they are rather more open than systematic. Heuristics are not algorithmic, either. The algorithms for long division or for calculating monthly principal and interest payments on a thirty-year mortgage at 12 percent always follow the same steps in a fixed order and arrive at the same results for the same data. Rule-governed procedures always are (or can be discovered to be) conscious and logical. Heuristics, on the other hand, are not rule-governed procedures that specify a certain, unvarying series of particular steps to be carried out mechanically. They always involve some trial and error as well as some intuition. Those presented in this chapter can be used for promoting fluency and for helping writers to shape or organize their papers, but for purposes of discussion, Chapter 3 emphasizes their use for promoting fluency. We describe a number of tools so that if a writer does not feel comfortable with one, you can introduce another. You may also choose to combine a few of the simpler ones.

HDWDWW

This acronym stands for Berthoff's sentence: **How does who do what and why?** It helps writers generate ideas by naming agent, action, manner, purpose. She uses, as an example, HDWDWW to generate information about snowshoes: *How do they work? How* are they manufactured? Out of what materials? *Who* manufactures them? *Who* sells them? *Who* buys them? *Who* uses them? *Why* are they used? She could add further questions, such as When? For whom? And to whom? Supposing that Phil needs to write an essay for his politics course explaining how various interest groups view the issue of waste-water pollution from irrigation projects in the San Joaquin Valley. Although he read the assigned essays twice, he feels overwhelmed by the complexity of the issue. By using the heuristic to construct a chart, his tutor, Manuel, might help Phil to overcome his self-censorship and to recall information:

MANUEL: Who has an interest in resolving this issue?

PHIL: Well, obviously the farmers themselves. And consumers. Manufacturers of fertilizers? Contractors? Oh, and of course the environmentalists! That's all, I guess.

5   MANUEL: OK, let's list those on this piece of scratch paper. If you think of others, we can add them as we go along. *[begins a chart]*

WHO

farmers

consumers

10   manufacturers

contractors

environmentalists

OK. What do these people do about waste-water?

PHIL: Well, the environmentalists are trying to shut down the projects. But the
15   farmers want to keep them going, so they can produce more fruit and vegetables. Most consumers, I guess, want low produce prices all year, so they would want to keep the projects going. *[pauses]*

MANUEL: OK, let's just add what you said to the list we started. Could you make a new column for "does what"?

20   PHIL: *[adds the new column and fills in the chart]*

WHO	DOES WHAT	WHY
farmers	want to keep projects going	more produce
consumers	want to keep projects going	low prices
manufacturers		
contractors		
environmentalists	want to close projects	pollution

MANUEL: Good. How about the other people?

PHIL: Well, the manufacturers depend on selling fertilizer and tractors to those farmers, and the more land is irrigated, the more farms there are, so I guess
30   they would support projects. And the contractors make money building the

irrigation systems—and they build the factories that build the tractors, too. So they'd support the projects. *[fills in the chart]*

Hey, you know, that reminds me that the manufacturers and contractors hired lobbyists to fight against the environmentalists who were trying to stop the pollution of the wildlife preserve by waste-water runoff from irrigation projects. *[adds "lobbyists" to the "who" column and continues to fill in the chart.]*

Well, of course, some consumers are environmentalists, so they would sacrifice low food prices in order to protect the birds and fish. *[adds a new line to the "consumers" category on the chart]*

WHO	DOES WHAT	WHY
farmers	want to keep projects going	more produce
consumers	want to keep projects going	low prices
	sacrifice low food prices	support environmentalists
manufacturers	support projects	need customers
contractors	support projects	need contracts
environmentalists	want to close projects	pollution
lobbyists	work for manufacturers and contractors	keep projects
	work for environmentalists	protect birds and fish

Because the heuristic is so systematic, it can help Phil generate a lot of material without becoming confused and discouraged by the complexity of the relationships he sees; when he recalls that interest groups may have mixed motives, as the consumers do, the chart can help him keep track of them. When one category expands, so do others. The "why" of this heuristic can powerfully generate material. For example, a HDWDWW sentence beginning "Contractors support irrigation projects" could be completed in a number of ways: "because they think the danger of pollution is exaggerated" or "because they are developing ways of removing the pollutants that wash out of the soil" or "because they can get additional contracts to build warehouses for storing the surplus food grown by means of irrigation projects." Before you read on, take a few minutes to write out sentences in which you apply this heuristic to a topic of your choice.

Double-entry listing

In Chapter 2, we explained the importance of dialogical thinking as a means of generating and structuring ideas. Drawing a line down the middle of the page and listing oppositions (by which we mean not merely differences, but relationships of many kinds) on either side can help writers elaborate their ideas. Like HDWDWW, the double-entry list uses a *form* to generate material for composing. As Berthoff says, "Like every other aspect of the composing process, opposing goes on all the time. Seeing something with respect to, in terms of, in relation to something else involves oppositions, the forms of relatedness" (77). Joe and Carol could have begun with a double-entry list (instead of mapping or HDWDWW), labeling the two columns *"who* comes to the Fish Fry?" and *"why?"* or *"working with* Shirley" and "working *without* Shirley." Supposing that Nell, a self-

censoring writer, feels she has "nothing to say" in a paper about "urban violence." Her tutor, Ros, could ask her to think of oppositions to it:

ROS: Let's draw a line down the middle of the page and write the subject on one
    side. Then we can put other ideas on the opposite side. Just start writing
    down anything you think of about "urban violence."

NELL: OK. Well, I guess if there's "urban violence," there must be "rural vio-
5   lence." *[begins the list]*

ROS: What does the phrase "urban violence" bring to mind?

NELL: My mother was in L.A. during the Watts riot. And how about the riots in
    Detroit? I don't recall when . . . *[pauses]*

ROS: Well, we can look up the dates later. What else?

10 NELL: Mugging! I've *seen* that! And what you don't see but you often hear about
    nowadays, child abuse. And other kinds of domestic violence. *[adds these to
    the "other" column]*

SUBJECT	"OTHER" ELEMENT
urban violence	rural violence
urban violence	the Watts riots of 1964
	the Detroit riots
urban violence	mugging
	child abuse
	domestic violence

The double-entry list helps Nell recall material by relating her subject, "urban
violence," to some "other" elements. Now Ros might help her explore the nature
of the relationship:

20 ROS: What kind of relationship do you see between "urban violence" and mug-
    ging, child abuse, and domestic violence?

NELL: They're *kinds* of urban violence?

ROS: Yes. Let's try to think of other kinds.

NELL: Auto theft. Arson. Vandalism. Armed robbery. *[adds these to the list]*

25 ROS: Could you ask about *kinds* of other things on the list?

NELL: Why not kinds of rural violence? Moonshining can get pretty risky, I un-
    derstand. Did you hear about the cattle rustlers over in Keswick County
    stealing the prize bulls—they're worth hundreds of thousands, for breeding
    you know. Probably child abuse and domestic violence go on in the country
30   as well as in the city. *[adds to her list]*

SUBJECT	"OTHER" ELEMENT
urban violence	rural violence
child abuse	child abuse
domestic violence	domestic violence
	moonshining
auto theft	rustling cattle

By seeking oppositions, Nell identifies a kind of relationship (between a class and
an example) and applies the question "What kinds are there?" to the earlier opposition between "urban" and "rural." Ros could proceed by asking her further
questions that would help identify other kinds of relationships between the subject
and "other" elements:

KIND OF RELATIONSHIP	SUBJECT	"OTHER" ELEMENT
class/class	urban violence	rural violence
class/member	urban violence	the Watts riots
general/particular	urban violence	mugging, arson, etc.
particular/general	urban violence	crime

40

Of course, there are many other possible relationships (Chapter 4 will say more about them). Before you continue reading, take a few minutes to construct a series of questions you could use to help a writer generate material using one or more of the other oppositions listed above.

Diagrams

Besides the charts derived from HDWDWW and double-entry listing, other simple diagrams can help reticent and self-censoring writers to recall information. One is a circle diagram, with the subject in the middle and questions surrounding it like spokes. The spokes can consist of two or three questions, or some of the standard journalistic array (Who? What? Where? When? Why? How?), or as many questions (even the "twenty questions" given in some writing texts) as tutor and writer consider relevant to the topic. Manuel could begin helping Phil with a circle diagram instead of HDWDWW (see Figure 10). Instead of tackling the assigned topic immediately, Manuel might ask Phil for some more general information in order to break through the barrier of self-censorship:

MANUEL: I'm not really familiar with this question. Could you just explain what it's all about? What pollutants are we talking about?

PHIL: The pollutants are arsenic and selenium.

MANUEL: How do they get into the water?

5 PHIL: Well, you might think they come from artificial sources, like insecticides and fertilizers. But actually, they occur naturally in the soil in very small amounts.

MANUEL: One way for us to keep track of what you've said and get some further information is to use this circle diagram. We'll write your subject, "San Joaquin waste-water pollution" in the center. Then we'll make spokes for various questions. So far, you've got spokes for "What pollutants?" and "How do they get in the soil?" *[begins a circle diagram and then passes it to Phil]*

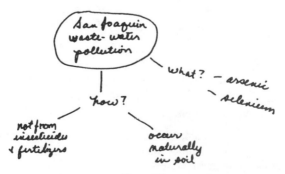

Figure 10

I'm confused. If arsenic and selenium occur naturally, how does the pollu-
15   tion occur?

PHIL: I said "small amounts." The problem comes when relatively large amounts
wash from the soil when the irrigation water runs off into a pond or lake,
like the Kesterson Wildlife Refuge. *[adds to diagram]* Hmm. I guess I could
ask, "To whom?"

20 MANUEL: Good.

PHIL: *[adds a new "to whom" spoke]* The fish and ducks die. And scientists have
found deformed bird embryos, so there's a genetic problem in addition to
the effect on individual animals.

Now that Phil has gotten started, Manuel can begin to focus the dialogue more
directly on the assignment (see Figure 11):

MANUEL: You've got a lot of information now. Let's take another look at the
25   assignment and see if we're on target. *[They reread the assignment together.]*

PHIL: I'm supposed to be talking about interest groups. OK. I'll add another spoke
for "Who is interested?" Well, obviously the farmers themselves. And consumers. Manufacturers of fertilizers? Contractors? Oh, and of course the
30   environmentalists! *[adds these]* That's all, I guess.

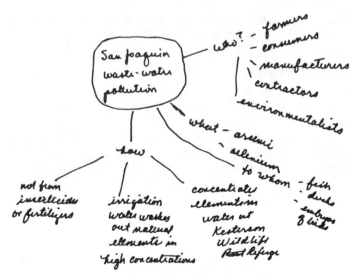

Figure 11

The questions on one spoke can generate further information by becoming the
subjects for new circles (see Figure 12):

MANUEL: Let's make some smaller diagrams for each interest group and ask the
same kinds of questions about them. *[draws circles for each interest group]*
How about the farmers? *[passes the diagram to Phil]*

PHIL: Who? Well, let's see. It's not the smaller farmers, but those who belong to
35   co-ops. And the huge farms owned by corporations. You know, agribusi-
ness. *[adds "who" spoke]* Why? Because they want to bring more land
under cultivation, and they want to raise several crops a year without depending on a rainy season.

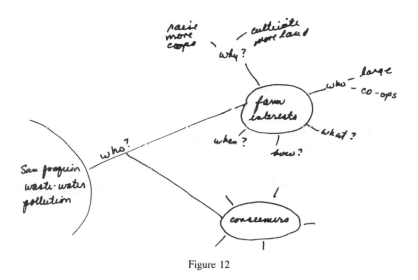

Figure 12

As Phil begins to ask himself similar questions about each of the interest groups,
he overcomes his self-censorship and finds out that he has plenty to say about this
complex political issue. He becomes more fluent and more independent.

Tree diagrams

Similarly, tree diagrams can help generate ideas for assignments that entail clas-
sifications (What are the kinds of this? What are the alternative ways to do that?)
or conditions (the familiar "if yes, X . . . if no, Y" and "if . . . then . . .
else" of computer flowcharts). For example, Manuel could help Phil elaborate his
recognition that one interest group might have mixed reactions to the problem (see
Figure 13):

MANUEL: You said that some consumers might support the projects but others
would not. Let's talk some more about that.

PHIL: Sure. On one side, everybody wants to pay low prices for their food, and
since plentiful supply reduces prices, they would support irrigation projects.

5   MANUEL: Why would the other consumers?

PHIL: They don't like high food prices, but they are willing to get along without
the irrigation in order to protect the environment.

MANUEL: Let's draw a diagram of these two responses. *[begins a tree diagram
with "for" and "against" and then passes it to Phil]*

10   PHIL: *[adds a branch to "for" and "against"]* Also, consumers have to pay taxes
to store food surpluses, so extra production can cost them more than they
save at the grocery store. *[adds a second branch to "against"]* But they
also save taxes when the larger farms create more jobs, so more people are
employed and pay income tax and don't collect welfare. *[adds a second
15   branch to "for"]*

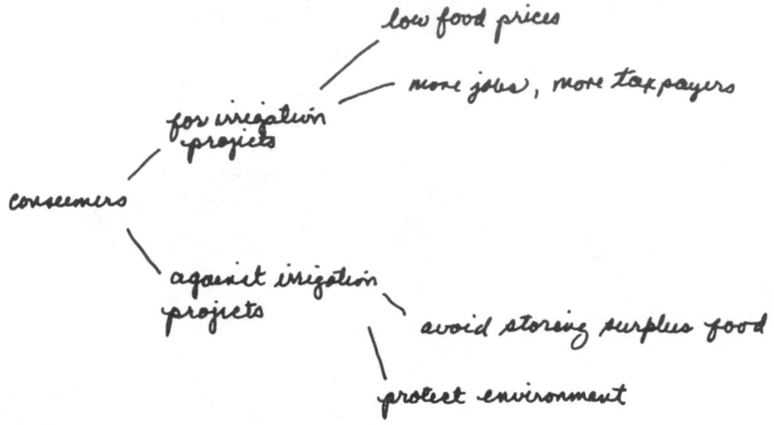

Figure 13

For both circle diagrams and tree diagrams, the tutor and writer decide how many
and which questions are appropriate to ask, given the amount of time, as well as
the length and scope of the assignment. The process of questioning (as in listing
and mapping) nudges writers toward recalling ideas and finding they have more
to say about a subject than they supposed at first.

Matrices

A matrix is a two-dimensional array of information (although mathematical matrices may have more than two dimensions), in which one axis lists questions or
criteria to be applied to the items listed on the other axis. Like the double-entry
or oppositional list, it helps writers elaborate their ideas by seeing them as relationships. Phil and Manuel created a matrix by using the horizontal axis to ask
the same three questions ("Who? Does what? Why?") about each of the interest
groups listed on the vertical axis. The matrix grew out of their conversation,
instead of being constructed at the outset as a chart full of empty spaces to be
filled in. Questions need not be limited by HDWDWW, but can be suggested by
the key terms listed in an assignment. (Chapter 4 will say more about analyzing
the language of assignments.) Matrices are more complex, more powerfully analytical heuristics than the simple diagrams we have just presented, and they require special care when used in tutorial conferences. Even simple assignments,
such as "Compare and contrast the benefits and disadvantages of two products
you use regularly," could produce a matrix complex enough to intimidate many

writers, especially diffident ones like Carol, by simultaneously presenting too many empty spaces to fill up:

	PRODUCT A	PRODUCT B
SIMILARITIES		
BENEFITS		
DISADVANTAGES		
DIFFERENCES		
BENEFITS		
DISADVANTAGES		

If you are helping diffident writers generate ideas, you would be well advised to use this chapter's conversational techniques and simple diagrams that "picture" the ideas produced during the conversation. If you are working with more experienced writers who have plenty of information in mind (or who perhaps feel overwhelmed by having too much information and too many questions in mind), you can use matrices more productively. Still, it is wise to avoid presenting writers with fully constructed matrices; it is better to help them construct the matrices by asking them to analyze assignments and to think of the questions they want to ask about the subject.

For instance, suppose that Tammy has been trying unsuccessfully to think of ideas for the assignment, "Write an essay explaining what constitutes a 'star' performance in popular music." Although she is seldom seen without her Walkman, she nevertheless feels that she "has nothing to say." Allison, her tutor, could ask her to name several singers whom she considers "stars," and then begin to name their qualities:

TAMMY: I've started over and over on this paper, and I just can't do it! I mean, how should I know what "star" means?

ALLISON: Well, who are your favorite singers right now?

5   TAMMY: Cyndi Lauper, for sure! And Tina Turner just won a Grammy Award for "What's Love Got to Do with It," which is a great song. Before Cyndi, I guess I liked Donna Summer best. Even my mother was singing "She Works Hard for Her Money, So You Better Treat Her Right!"

ALLISON: Did you like it too?

TAMMY: Not as much as the others. Oh—I *loved* "The Rose."

10   ALLISON: OK, let's put their names down. *[lists names across the top of a piece of scratch paper]* So what would you say makes them "stars"?

TAMMY: The hit songs, I guess. Did you see Cyndi singing "Time after Time" on the Grammy Award show last week?

ALLISON: Yes. I thought she was terrific too. Let's put down the songs as one

15   thing that makes them "stars." *[begins a vertical list with "hit songs" and then hands the chart to Tammy]*

	"STAR" VOCALISTS		
"STAR"	Cyndi Lauper	Tina Turner	Bette Midler
HIT SONG	"Time after Time"	"What's Love Got to Do with It?	"The Rose"

20

ALLISON: Could you tell me some more about these?

TAMMY: Well, they're all really dramatic performers. I mean, they don't just stand there and sing. They make it seem like there's a story behind the song. And of course, they all dance too.

25 ALLISON: How about listing "dramatize" and "dance" right below "hit song"? *[Tammy writes.]* Could you say some more about what you mean by "dramatize"?

TAMMY: Well . . . I guess I don't mean that Cyndi is acting out things that really happened to her in real life. She's creating a character, but you have the
30 *feeling* that the character is based on her own real experience. That's *why* she can act it so well. Cyndi just seems like a person who could pick up the pieces of a love affair "time after time." And the song repeats that idea, "If you fall, I will catch you, I'll be waiting, time after time." Kind of like a refrain.

35 ALLISON: *Dramatic* character seems to coincide with her real personality? That's clearer than just "dramatize"—why don't you change it on your list?

TAMMY: Right. And the character's role is kind of captured by that refrain. I better add "refrain" too. *[writes]*

ALLISON: Good, I'm glad you added "refrain." . . .

40 TAMMY: Hmmmm . . . what other songs have refrains too? . . . These refrains express the character's dramatic conflict. Like Tina Turner says she's been hurt too often, and now she's "taking on a new direction," one that doesn't depend on a "second-hand emotion" like love. But "The Rose" says you have to be willing to take risks in love. *[adds these to the list]*

45

		"STAR" VOCALISTS	
STAR	Cyndi Lauper	Tina Turner	Bette Midler
hit song	"Time after Time"	"What's Love Got to Do with It"	"The Rose"
dance			
character dramatizes	pick up pieces	take on a new direction	take risks
real life			
refrain	"If you fall, etc."	"What's love but a second-hand emotion?"	————

50

ALLISON: That's good. You're cruising! What else?

55 TAMMY: Oh, oh. I haven't said anything about dance yet! Let's see . . . it really is part of the dramatic performance of the song.

Allison could proceed by asking Tammy to elaborate this statement about dance and to add whatever other categories seemed appropriate. Once Tammy has elaborated some ideas about what constitutes a "star" performance, Allison might use HDWDWW to help her relate a few ideas at a time:

ALLISON: So let's pick up some of the qualities you've described. Which seem most important to you now?

TAMMY: I guess the dramatic character.

60   ALLISON: What does the dramatic character *do* for a "star" performance?

    TAMMY: *The dramatic character seems to match the singer's real personality.* You know, things we know about her from her publicity. That's why Cyndi's "Time after Time," or even "Girls Just Want to Have Fun," are star performances. And the character's dramatic conflict is expressed in the refrain.

65   ALLISON: It sounds like you better add "publicity" to your list of categories. *[Tammy writes.]*

Since Tammy seems to be very interested in the songs themselves, the tutorial dialogue could focus on intensively elaborating information about the lyrics, the connections between the "real-life" image created by publicity and the dramatic characters featured in performances, and so on. Tammy might also want to elaborate extensively, by adding new names to the horizontal axis and new categories (say, costumes) to the vertical axis. Either way, by using the matrix, she will ask the same questions about each performer, and her systematic inquiry will help her test her developing criteria for recognizing a "star" performance.

Such a matrix can help writers ask the same questions about each member of a class of things being compared. It can help them avoid the confusion of switching question categories; for instance, in comparing two performers, the matrix could help them avoid accidentally asking about the publicity of one and the costumes of the other. It can also help writers realize that they have so much to say about one of the subjects, that they can set aside the rest of the matrix and concentrate on making a new submatrix for just one category.

A much more elaborate, nine-part matrix is the "tagmemic" grid, devised by Richard Young, Alton Becker, and Kenneth Pike in *Rhetoric: Discovery and Change.* "Tagmemic" comes from a Greek root "tassein," to put in order, and Kenneth Pike's "tagmemics" is an effort to put in order a unified grammar of verbal and nonverbal human behavior. In our experience, a matrix this complex can overwhelm writers and make them feel as if they must "fill in the blanks," rather than follow the direction of their own ideas. However, some tutors might find tagmemics helpful to fairly advanced writers.

Summary

Inexperienced writers often lack fluency. They have trouble thinking of what to say or trusting what they do think of saying on paper. With these writers, work on fluency should ordinarily precede attention to shaping and correcting ideas because writers need to have expressed some thoughts before they can organize and then style them. Nonfluent writers may be reticent or self-censoring. The former may not have been encouraged to communicate in speaking or in writing and often have not received useful composition instruction. The latter may have a little more training, but they recognize the gap between their amateur attempts and the work of professionals, and they fear harsh criticism. Both types of writers concern themselves prematurely with correctness. They try to refine each sentence before forming a new one, so they spend a great deal of time producing very little text. They assume that really good writers compose orderly, grammatical prose without having to add, move, or change ideas, or to correct phrasing. This misperception intimidates and constrains nonfluent writers.

You can help these writers begin to "think aloud on paper" by introducing informal and formal methods of generating ideas. Asking writers to list single words or phrases encourages the reticent and self-censoring to throw down ideas without worrying about sentence sense, paragraphing, or punctuation. When they produce lists, writers see that they do have something to say, and seeing the words often makes them think of connections and additions. Mapping resembles listing except that writers place words randomly on a sheet of paper instead of in a vertical line. This procedure can encourage spontaneity and free association. Like listing, mapping prevents premature closure and premature editing.

You can also introduce formal heuristics that writers can use to generate and elaborate ideas. Heuristics like "How does who do what and why?" and double-entry lists stimulate dialogical thinking. When writers create charts by using these methods, circle or tree diagrams, or matrices, they can keep track of ideas they have generated and can then begin to identify relationships among their preliminary ideas. You can introduce one or a combination of these strategies, or you can offer an alternative if a writer does not take to the one you initially select.

SUGGESTIONS FOR JOURNAL ENTRIES

1. In your journal, write a description of how your own composing processes have changed as you have become a more experienced writer.

2. Which of the ways of promoting fluency seems least familiar to you? Try it out on the topic of your choice, in order to see how it works for you. After your experiment, write your response to it: Will you use it again or not? Why?

3. Describe a conference in which you have recognized that your tutee to some extent resembles the reticent or self-censoring writers described in this chapter.

SUGGESTIONS FOR FURTHER WRITING

1. Write a dialogue in which you use listing and mapping to help a reticent writer elaborate ideas for a paper on "Describe a recreational activity that you especially enjoy."

2. Write a dialogue in which you use HDWDWW to help the same reticent writer with the same assignment.

3. Write a dialogue in which you use HDWDWW to help a self-censoring writer elaborate ideas for the same assignment. Ask for other tutors' responses, and compare yours with theirs.

4. Write a pair of dialogues using one of the diagrams, first with a reticent writer and then with a self-censoring writer. How do your two dialogues differ?

SUGGESTIONS FOR CLASS ACTIVITIES

1. With two classmates, one a "writer" and the other an observer, read aloud the dialogue you wrote using listing and mapping. Ask the observer to evaluate its plausibility and effectiveness and to suggest alternatives. Then, extemporaneously role-play at least one of these alternatives and ask the observer to compare the two versions.

2. With two classmates, one a "reticent writer" and the other an observer, read aloud the dialogue you wrote for using HDWDWW above. Ask the observer to evaluate its plausibility and effectiveness and to suggest alternatives. Then, extemporaneously role-play at least one of these alternatives and ask the observer to compare the two versions.

3. Follow the directions for exercise 2 above with a "self-censoring writer."

4. Compare your observations on the uses of diagrams with reticent and self-censoring writers (exercise 4 under "Suggestions for Further Writing") with those of other tutors.

SUGGESTIONS FOR FURTHER READING

Berthoff, Ann E. *Forming, Thinking, Writing.* Rochelle Park, NJ: Hayden, 1978.

Boyle, Owen. "Mapping and Composing." In *Teaching Writing: Essays from the Bay Area Writing Project.* Ed. Gerald Camp. Montclair, NJ: Boynton/Cook, 1982. 191–220.

Britton, James, et al. *The Development of Writing Abilities (11–18).* London: Macmillan Education Ltd., 1975.

Buckley, Marilyn Hanf. "Mapping and Thinking." In *Teaching Writing: Essays from the Bay Area Writing Project.* Ed. Gerald Camp. Montclair, NJ: Boynton/Cook, 1982. 184–191.

Cambourne, Brian. "Oral and Written Relationships: A Reading Perspective." In *Speaking–Writing Relationships: Connections and Contrasts.* Eds. Barry M. Kroll and Roberta J. Vann. Urbana, IL: NCTE, 1981. 82–98.

Collins, James L. "Speaking, Writing, and Teaching for Meaning." In *Speaking–Writing Relationships: Connections and Contrasts.* Eds. Barry M. Kroll and Roberta J. Vann. Urbana, IL: NCTE, 1981. 196–214.

Cooper, Marilyn M. "The Ecology of Writing." *College English* 48 (1986): 364–375.

Elbow, Peter. *Writing Without Teachers.* New York: Oxford University Press, 1973.

―――. "Embracing Contraries in the Teaching Process." *College English* 45 (1983): 327–339

Emig, Janet. *The Composing Processes of Twelfth Graders.* Urbana, IL: NCTE, 1971.

Flower, Linda. *Problem-Solving Strategies for Writing.* New York: Harcourt Brace Jovanovich, 1981.

Griffith, Marlene. "Writing for the Inexperienced Writer: Fluency, Shape and Correctness." In *Teaching Writing: Essays from the Bay Area Writing Project.* Ed. Gerald Camp. Montclair, NJ: Boynton/Cook, 1982. 67–96.

Heath, Shirley Brice. *Ways with Words.* Cambridge University Press, 1983.

MacDonald, Susan Peck. "Specificity in Context: Some Difficulties for the Inexperienced Writer." *College Composition and Communication* 37 (1986): 195–203.

Moffett, James. "Liberating Inner Speech." *College Composition and Communication* 36 (1985): 304–308.

Moffett, James. *Teaching the Universe of Discourse.* Boston: Houghton Mifflin, 1968.

Murray, Donald M. *A Writer Teaches Writing.* 2nd ed. Boston: Houghton Mifflin, 1985.

Perl, Sondra. "A Look at Basic Writers in the Process of Composing." In *Basic Writing: Essays for Teachers, Researchers, Administrators.* Eds. Lawrence N. Kasden and Daniel R. Hoeber. Urbana, IL: NCTE, 1980, 13–32.

Schor, Sandra. "Composition Strategy as Translation." *College English* 48 (1986): 187–194.

Young, Richard E., Alton L. Becker, and Kenneth L. Pike. *Rhetoric: Discovery and Change.* New York: Harcourt, 1970.

4
Promoting Fluency II: Deepening Critical Analysis

Besides feeling that they have "nothing to say," some writers may lack fluency because they have been taught an artificially linear view of composing, a view that interferes with the recursive composing process native to writers at all levels of skill and experience. Tutors can reassure writers that it is all right, actually desirable, to do what comes naturally—to follow their recursive "instincts"—instead of forcing themselves to follow the linear patterns their earlier writing instruction may have provided.

Two Notions of the Writing Process: Linear and Recursive

The linear notion of composition, propounded by texts such as Warriner's *English Grammar and Composition,* holds that composing is a step-by-step process: choosing and limiting the subject; assembling materials; outlining; writing the first draft; revising; writing the final draft. In this model, writers first *think* of their ideas, then *transcribe* them, marching straight ahead, idea by idea, right through from the first word to the last, and finally *proofread* the "finished" product. In *Problem-Solving Strategies for Writing* (50), Linda Flower diagrams the linear model:

```
PLAN       o o o o o o o o
GENERATE                  o o o o o o o o
DESIGN                                  o o o o o o o o
EDIT                                                  o o o o o o o  DONE
           - - - - - - - - - - - - - -  TIME  - - - - - - - - - - - - - - - - →
```

Flower calls this model "simple-minded," because it ignores reality: her (and other researchers') observations of writers in the act of composing show that they do not really behave in this way.

Instead (according to various findings by Flower and Hayes, Perl, Emig, and others), real writers normally compose by going back and forth among the activities of planning, generating, organizing, and editing. Flower diagrams the actual composing process (50):

PLAN	o o o o o	o o o	o o
GENERATE	o o o o o	o o o	o o
DESIGN	o o o o o o	o o o o	
EDIT	o	o	

- - - - - - - - - - - TEN MINUTES - - - - - - - - - - - - - →

A writer (who is not trying to follow a linear process she has been taught is "correct") might read the assignment, begin to write a sentence, rearrange some words in the sentence, pause to consult the dictionary, rearrange more words, pause to look back at the assignment again, locate a key word and resume writing, perhaps rephrasing the initial sentence and checking punctuation. Pausing again, she might review the assignment, reread her first sentences, and generate several more sentences that dichotomize or classify the key word into smaller, more manageable parts or that express a string of associations with it. Perl (24) calls these movements "shuttling":

> Careful study revealed that the students wrote by shuttling back and forth from the sense of what they wanted to say forward to the words on the page and back from the words on the page to their intended meaning. This back-and-forth movement appears to be a recurrent feature that may be characteristic of composing even among skilled writers. At one moment students are writing, moving their ideas and their discourse forward; at the next they are backtracking, rereading, and digesting what has been written.

"Shuttling," or dialogical thinking, naturally goes on throughout the composing process, and writers who allow it to happen usually have little difficulty with fluency. For Perl and Flower, "planning" does not mean "first think of your ideas," as the linear model holds; instead, it means sensing what the whole composition should say and beginning to work toward that tentative sense of the whole. Whereas "designing" in the linear model means making a quite static outline, in the recursive model it means a flexibly "retrospective structuring." Both aspects, "the reaching back and the sensing of forward movements have a clarifying effect," and they promote development of meaning by fostering construction and discovery:

> Writers construct their discourse inasmuch as they begin with a sense of what they want to write. . . . Rereading or backwards movements become a way of assessing whether or not the words on the page adequately capture the original sense intended. Constructing simultaneously affords discovery. Writers know more fully what they mean only after having written it. In this way the explicit written form serves as a window on the implicit sense with which one began.

(26)

While pausing to hunt prematurely for surface errors usually interferes with elaboration of ideas (as we said in Chapter 3), Perl suggests that such editing may also function positively, as a delaying action that allows a writer to reconsider the language of the assignment in relation to what has been written thus far, to construct and discover meaning that is "right with the self" and thus conducive to fluency. Such critical "shuttling" from key rhetorical and conceptual terms of an assignment, from the overall problem to various of its parts, can be a very productive composing strategy because it makes writers think dialogically (see Chapter 2). However, linear notions of the writing process, whether assumed or learned, may seriously interfere with such thinking, and, consequently, with fluency and critical analysis. Then, writers get stuck.

Some linear writers try to figure out whole essays before writing a single word. A few people can actually do this for fairly short essays on simple topics. But for most writers, performing such intellectual gyrations is like trying to do long division mentally. Whereas the perfectionistic self-censoring writers in Chapter 3 reject their ideas as boring or dumb, these writers become overwhelmed by the sheer complexity of planning a whole paper before starting to write. Frustrated and confused, they may *stop* in despair, hoping that inspiration may strike eventually. When it does not (because inspiration strikes most often when one is in the midst of writing, rather than waiting to begin), they become even more anxious. Their writing process might look this way:

PLAN   o o o o o o o o o o o o o o o o o o   STOP

GENERATE

DESIGN

EDIT

— — — — — — — — — — — — TIME   — — — — — — — — — — — — — — →

Planning becomes so elaborate and confusing that these writers never engage in the other three activities. Unlike reticent and self-censoring writers, who produce very little, these writers never begin generating; instead of getting "done," they stop.

Other linear writers, having been taught to compose by constructing outlines, are somewhat better off. But not much. They often use merely formal labels—introduction, body, conclusion—instead of adjusting their outlines to the specifications of particular writing assignments; they name the parts without telling how the paper will develop them. Take, for example, the following outline for a paper about the uses of laboratory animals:

     I. INTRODUCTION

     II. BODY
        A. Drug experiments
        B. Nutrition experiments
        C. Cosmetics experiments

     III. CONCLUSION

The formal labels do not help the writer to state propositions (such as, "For basically frivolous reasons, cosmetics experiments inflict suffering on animals.") and do not logically articulate the connections between parts (Are drug and nutrition experiments *alike* in some way? Are they *different* from cosmetics experiments? Were drug experiments historically antecedent to the others?). If the outline *did* articulate the propositions, the writers would have less trouble finding ideas they really wanted to express. They would have something they wanted to say. Although they *could* try to generate material, these writers do not. Their writing process might be diagrammed thus:

```
PLAN       o o o o o o o o o o o o o o o o o o o o o o o o o o
GENERATE                                            o o o o   DONE
DESIGN
EDIT
           - - - - - - - - - - - - - TIME  - - - - - - - - - - - - - - - ->
```

After constructing a formal outline, these writers "march" straight through it, fleshing out each item with a few sentences; then they consider the paper done. Even though their loosely constructed outlines express only the most common-place responses to writing assignments, they feel very reluctant to "shuttle," to rearrange or augment them conceptually during the composing process. Instead, they cling to the original, static plan and crank out empty, boring, and extremely brief papers often expressed in cramped and stilted language that does not engage their audiences.

You can use the strategies in this chapter to help writers unlearn the linear strategies that interfere with their ability to generate "something to say" and ana-lyze it critically. The writers described in Chapter 3 and in this chapter have much in common, and the heuristics we have previously described are also appropriate for helping linear writers; however, Chapter 4's techniques are especially useful in helping writers to minimize the interference of linear composing processes they have been taught and to engage in nonlinear, dialogical strategies for prolonging the constructive and exploratory processes of critical analysis.

Distinguishing Editing from Dialogical Thinking

Although (as Perl observes) there is no absolute line between the deceptive recur-siveness of premature editing (see Chapter 3) and the more genuine recursiveness of critical "shuttling" (since changing a word may be just tinkering or may be redefining a concept), you can promote fluency by helping writers to distinguish between the two activities. Then they can postpone the distractions of editing until fairly late in the composing process, after they have "shuttled" among other as-pects of writing. An example of how premature editing interferes with generating ideas is the following draft written by Tim, a college freshman, who came to class empty-handed on the day his paper on Loren Eiseley's "The Brown Wasps" (see box) was due. Tim told his tutor, Walt, that he had "gotten stuck" and showed him a crumpled paragraph (one of several that had missed the overflowing wastebasket; see Figure 14) and the assignment sheet:

> Assignment: Loren Eiseley opens "The Brown Wasps" with a lengthy paragraph comparing wasps and people. Explain in as much detail as you can the comparison he makes. Then explain how it relates to the main point of his essay.

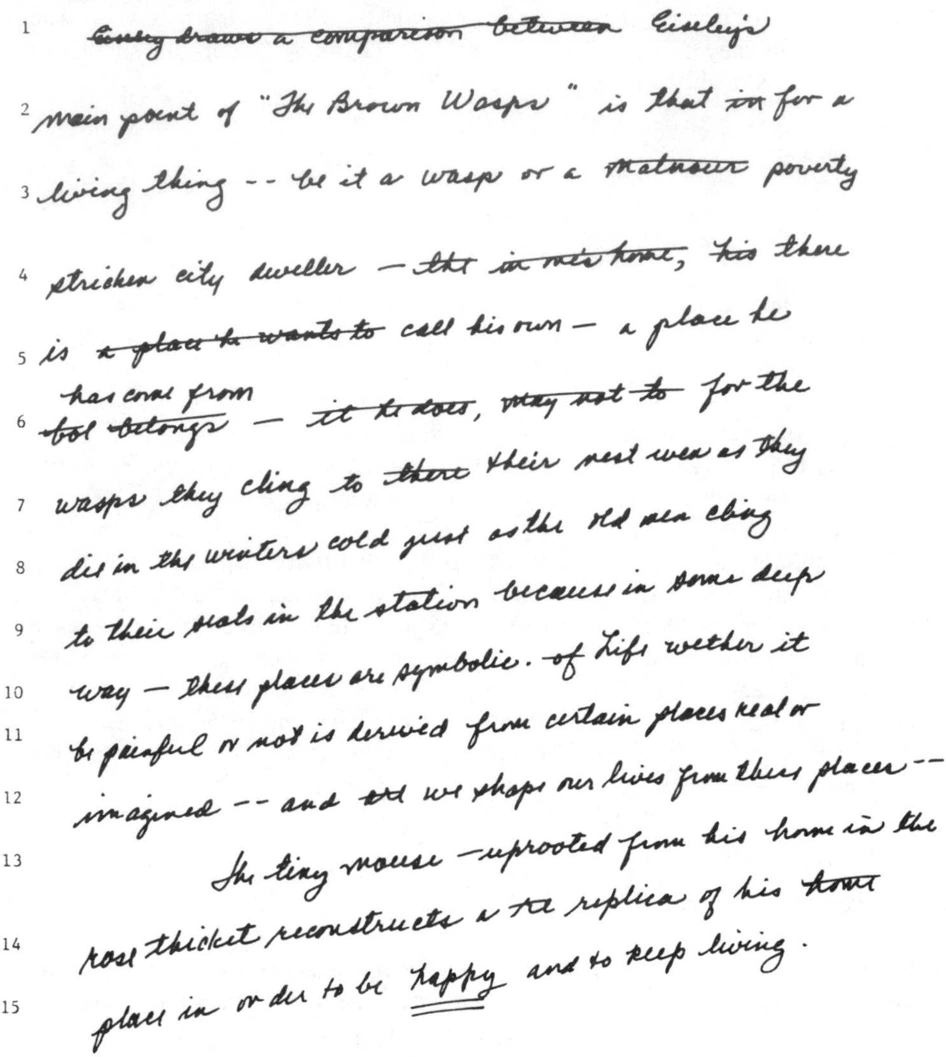

1 ~~Easley drew a comparison between~~ Eiseley's

2 main point of "The Brown Wasps" is that ~~in~~ for a

3 living thing -- be it a wasp or a ~~malnour~~ poverty

4 stricken city dweller — ~~tht in nts hont;~~ his there

5 is ~~a place he wants~~ to call his own — a place he

has come from

6 ~~bel belongs~~ — it ~~it does,~~ ~~may not to~~ for the

7 wasps they cling to ~~there~~ their nest ~~wen~~ as they

8 die in the winters cold just as the old men cling

9 to their seals in the station because in some deep

10 way — these places are symbolic. of Life wether it

11 be painful or not is derived from certain places real or

12 imagined -- and ~~we~~ we shape our lives from these places --

13 The tiny mouse —uprooted from his home in the

14 rose thicket reconstructs ~~a~~ the replica of his ~~home~~

15 place in order to be <u>happy</u> and to keep living.

Figure 14

Instead of starting immediately to work on the paper, Walt could ask Tim to describe the process by which he composed the paragraph:

WALT: Before we get started on what you wrote, would you mind telling me how you went about writing?

TIM: I rewrote my opening lines so often, I felt like I was practicing my penman-ship!

5 WALT: Judging by the looks of the paper, it seems as if some parts were easier to write than others.

TIM: Yeah. Right here. [points to lines 7–12] When I got to this part about the wasps and old men, I really took off.

Loren Eiseley, "The Brown Wasps," paragraph 1

There is a corner in the waiting room of one of the great Eastern stations where women never sit. It is always in the shadow and overhung by rows of lockers. It is, however, always frequented—not so much by genuine travelers as by the dying. It is here that a certain element of the abandoned poor seeks a refuge out of the weather, clinging for a few hours longer to the city that has fathered them. In a precisely similar manner I have seen, on a sunny day in midwinter, a few old brown wasps creep slowly over an abandoned wasp nest in a thicket. Numbed and forgetful and frost-blackened, the hum of the spring hive still resounded faintly in their sodden tissues. Then the temperature would fall and they would drop away into the white oblivion of the snow. Here in the station it is in no way different save that the city is busy in its snows. But the old ones cling to their seats as though these were symbolic and could not be given up. Now and then they sleep, their gray old heads resting with painful awkwardness on the backs of the benches.

WALT: I see what you mean. What were you trying to do in the first seven lines
10   that gave you so much trouble?

TIM: Well . . . they were my introduction.

WALT: How would you describe the kinds of changes you were making in those
       opening lines?

TIM: I was looking for the right words. Like right here my writing looks like trial
15   and error. I'm discarding "in" in favor of "for" (2) and then I'm searching
       for the right phrase, changing my mind three times (4). Wow!

WALT: Yes, you were editing for connective words. And afterwards?

TIM: Well, in the next few lines, I guess I decided that "poverty-stricken" was
       more accurate than just "malnourished" (3). *[pauses]* Hmmm . . . then I
20   was trying to pin down the meaning of "home," not just a place the man
       wants to call home or *belongs to,* but a place he has *come from* (5–6).

WALT: So what's the difference between those kinds of changes and the ones you
       were making earlier?

TIM: When I was editing for connective words, I didn't know yet what I was
25   trying to connect with what? But the later changes were zeroing in on my
       exact meaning?

WALT: I think that makes sense.

TIM: Afterwards, I knew what I wanted to say. Just tell about Eiseley's compari-
       son between the wasps and men.

30 WALT: And the words just came naturally?

TIM: Well, compared to the beginning they did. I felt Eiseley's idea could apply
       to all of us, including me, so I wrote, "we shape our lives from these
       places" (12).

WALT: OK, so what do the observations you just made suggest about your writing
35   process?

TIM: I guess maybe I was trying to make a perfect introduction before I actually knew what I was trying to introduce?

WALT: OK. So what could you do differently next time?

TIM: I guess I should just try to get something on paper and worry about the exact
40   wording later.

By observing his own draft, Tim now recognizes that "getting something on paper" first and perfecting it later is better than planning everything in his head and trying in vain to say it exactly right the first time. Flower calls this strategy of putting down some word or other, or even leaving a blank line, rather than getting stuck, "satisficing" (39). Walt could continue the dialogue by helping Tim distinguish between premature editing and critical "shuttling" among concepts in his paragraph.

Keeping Tim's dialogical thinking within the scope of the assignment might be Walt's concluding objective for this tutorial session. Tim might say that even though the mouse (13–15) was not in Eiseley's opening paragraph, mentioning it might at least prove he had read the homework. Walt could then show Tim some ways of keeping the words flowing—making lists, trying HDWDWW and other heuristics we described in Chapter 3—and of checking to see how the emerging draft fits the assignment.

Promoting Critical Analysis: The Language of Assignments

Even though all writers need to analyze the language of assignments, many writers pay little attention to it. In so doing, they miss opportunities to identify key concepts and relationships and to think critically about them. Many of Chapter 3's heuristics employ the language of assignments to figure out the alternatives for tree diagrams and to designate the headings for double entry lists or for matrices. Analyzing the language of assignments includes circling key concepts, interpreting imperatives, identifying signal words, and exploring assignments phrased as practical questions of fact, process, or relationship. Such analysis is one way in which tutors can stimulate linear writers to engage in dialogical thinking.

Circling key concepts

This simple technique can help linear writers to subdivide the problem posed by the assignment and to play speculatively with possible relationships among parts, instead of carrying the whole assignment in their heads. Take, for instance, the following assignment: "Compare and contrast the objectives and achievements of the Nazi occupation of Europe and the Soviet occupation of Eastern Europe." A writer might extract two pairs of concepts: "objectives/achievements" and "Nazi occupation/Soviet occupation." Combining the pairs in various ways, a tutor could ask questions such as, "What were the objectives of the Nazi occupation? What were the objectives of the Soviet occupation?" and so on, gradually shifting the question-asking responsibility to the writer. By identifying and variously combining key concepts, writers can get beyond merely presenting "information" and begin to articulate propositions about how the key concepts are related to one another.

Interpreting imperatives

The imperatives used in some assignments are the marching orders that tell writers what to do: "compare and contrast," "explain the causes," "define," "describe the process of," and so on. You can help writers take note of imperatives and perhaps use them in conjunction with double-entry or oppositional lists, circle or tree diagrams, and matrices (as Chapter 3 explains). For instance, you can help writers to see that questions like "Consider the impact of . . ." or "What are the possible results of . . ." are cause/effect questions that can be analyzed by means of tree diagrams. In the assignment about Nazis and Soviets, a tutor could use the imperatives "compare" or "contrast" to help a writer make a simple matrix:

	OBJECTIVES	ACHIEVEMENTS
SIMILARITIES	Item 1 Item 2 Item 3	
DIFFERENCES Nazis Soviets	Item 1 Item 2 Item 1 Item 2	

Besides helping writers to identify the *kinds* of information required for the assignment, imperatives in assignments provide options for *organizing* that information in order to articulate and develop concepts. A tutor and a writer could experiment with the three organizational "invitations" embedded in the assignment above:

MODEL I	MODEL II	MODEL III

I. Nazi occupation
  A. Objectives
  B. Achievements
II. Soviet occupation
  A. Objectives
  B. Achievements
III. Similarities and differences
	I. Objectives
	  A. Similarities
	    1. Item—Nazi/Soviet
	    2. Item—Nazi/Soviet
	    3. Item—Nazi/Soviet
	  B. Differences
	    1. Item—Nazi/Soviet
	    2. Item—Nazi/Soviet
	II. Achievements
	  A. Similarities
	    1. Item—Nazi/Soviet
	    2. Item—Nazi/Soviet
	  B. Differences
	    1. Item—Nazi/Soviet
	    2. Item—Nazi/Soviet
		I. Similarities
		  A. Objectives
		    1. Item—Nazi/Soviet
		    2. Item—Nazi/Soviet
		  B. Achievements
		    1. Item—Nazi/Soviet
		    2. Item—Nazi/Soviet
		II. Differences
		  A. Objectives
		    1. Item—Nazi/Soviet
		    2. Item—Nazi/Soviet
		  B. Achievements
		    1. Item—Nazi/Soviet
		    2. Item—Nazi/Soviet

If a tutor were to ask, "What relative emphasis do the imperative terms 'compare/contrast' get in each of these three models?" a writer might recognize that by relegating "similarities and differences" to the last third of the essay, Model I *de*emphasizes the imperatives in this assignment. Models II and III, both of which make "similarities and differences" major organizing features, respond more exactly to these imperatives. The writer could choose between them, depending upon her inclination after gleaning the source materials.

Identifying signal words

You can also help writers consider what kinds of language can be used to accomplish the task named by an assignment's directions. For example, if an assignment calls for comparison/contrast, you can ask what kinds of words establish similarities and differences. A writer could be asked to jot down these words for later use both in analyzing what he reads (about which Chapter 11 will say more) and in writing his own essay. (In this case, words listed might include "differ from," "contrast with," "but," "on the other hand," "similarly," "both," "parallel," "like," and so forth.) Below is a list of the kinds of signal words that you might ask writers to look for in their reading and use to generate ideas for their own essays:

SIGNAL WORDS

PART/WHOLE: includes, overlaps, example of, same kind of _____ as, part of, made up of, complementary to

LIST: one, another, besides, also, furthermore, too, more, and, in addition, three things, several, many, a few

TIME: begins, next, then, from here, soon, shortly, after, meanwhile, later, at last, finally, first, second

COMPARISON/ CONTRAST: similar, like, in the same way, all comparative forms of adjectives and adverbs (e.g., better, worse, faster, more slowly); but, however, nevertheless, yet, on the other hand, other, those, former, latter, different

CAUSE/EFFECT: because, consequently, for this reason, therefore, on that account, hence, as a result of, so that, since, resulting in

CLIMAX: finally, thus, in conclusion, in summary, looking back, all superlative forms of the adjective and adverb (e.g., most, best, worst, least, most important, least important, most quickly)

By helping writers analyze the key concepts and the signal words in the language of assignments, you can help linear writers to move back and forth among key terms in order to establish relationships among them and to identify many options for generating ideas. The same procedure can prevent other writers from reading assignments too superficially and composing too associatively.

Exploring assignments phrased as questions

Whereas some assignments use imperatives, many use interrogatives: instead of explicitly telling the writer "your paper should do this," such assignments ask the writer questions like "why?" "how?" "to what extent?" or "which is more probable?'' A history assignment on the Normandy Invasion might ask writers to draw upon readings in journalism and military history in order to answer a wide array of practical interrogatives. Together, a tutor and a writer could figure out that the following questions of fact implicitly require the writer to *list:*

Who reported the Normandy Invasion for the American press?

What events of the Invasion did the reporters then consider ''historic''?

When did the secret British preparations for the Invasion become public knowledge?

Where were the reporters when they observed the Invasion?

To analyze such questions, the tutor could ask the writer to list any number of items—names of radio and newspaper reporters, various definitions of ''historic,'' kinds of secret preparations, locations, and means of observation—depending on the evidence available. Tutor and writer might have more difficulty in figuring out how to address the following questions calling for descriptions of *process:*

How were RAF aircraft secretly constructed and then concealed on the airfields near London? (descriptive)

How can civilian logistical support for such an operation be rallied without sacrificing security? (prescriptive)

The writer might simply answer ''how?'' by listing ''in what ways?'' Additionally, both of these questions are probably directing the writer to examine *causes and effects,* describing steps in a process (''What was done early, and what was done later?'') or prescribing *conditions* for a process to work (''If this result is desired, then what must be done first? What next? What last?''). Thus, these questions give the writer less flexibility, because she must describe or prescribe the parts (or steps) in a whole process. To help the writer explore the ''how?'' of these questions, the tutor could ask her to recall her readings in order to describe the normal security precautions, to list what extra precautions were taken and what steps were needed to avoid calling attention to them, and so on. The tutor could also help the writer see that each of these process questions indicates that the paper should address two sets of key concepts (construction/concealment; support/security).

In the following assignment, the query ''why?'' implicitly directs the writer to ''explain the causes and effects of . . .'':

Why did General Eisenhower decide to delay the Invasion? In retrospect, to what extent did the events that ensued justify his decision?

A tutor might begin by asking a writer to make two lists, one naming what Eisenhower expected the delay to achieve, the other naming the events that ensued. Next, the tutor might help her sort the second list into three groups of events: those that did realize Eisenhower's expectations, those that failed to realize them, and those that he had not anticipated at all. Finally, by asking, ''In what ways and how much did the outcomes fulfill Eisenhower's expectations?'' the tutor could help her to decide the extent to which the decision was justified.

Assignments may ask writers to address a variety of other relationships. They may ask questions about *definition* and *degree,* which invite writers to use signal words expressing part/whole and comparison/contrast:

> *To what extent* can Hitler's, Churchill's, and Roosevelt's radio broadcasts all be considered "propaganda"?
>
> *Which gave better* reporting of the Invasion, Edward R. Murrow on radio or Ernie Pyle in "Stars and Stripes?"

Implicit in each of these interrogatives is the directive *define.* In the first topic, the writer must define "propaganda" before he can judge the extent to which the broadcasts fit the criteria. A tutor could ask the writer questions about what the dictionary and the course readings say "propaganda" means. Next, the tutor could ask, "With which parts of the whole definition of 'propaganda' do each leader's broadcasts correspond?"). "To what extent" may also mean "how much" or "to what degree," as in "to what extent did the reporters agree about allied preparedness?"

The topic concerning Murrow and Pyle is a little more demanding, since one cannot simply look up a definition of "good reporting"; this topic asks for evaluation by degree. The tutor could help a writer formulate a working definition of "good reporting" by means of which to judge each reporter. A tutor could ask a writer to build the definition by relating personal experience ("What constitutes "good reporting" in 1987?") to historical knowledge ("What do your readings say or imply constituted 'good reporting' in 1944?"). The tutor could then help the writer decide *the extent to which* Murrow's and Pyle's reporting matched these criteria and whether one was *better* than the other or whether they were simply *different.* Besides using the techniques for making matrices (described in Chapter 3), the tutor could invite the writer to employ the signal words for comparison/contrast in beginning to formulate responses to these assignments.

Some assignments require writers to perform several kinds of analysis. For example, directives to list, to define, and to compare/contrast are implied in the following history assignment about logical consistency:

> *On what grounds* can one *deplore* the bombing of Coventry *yet approve* the bombing of Dresden?

"Grounds" are philosophical reasons, causes, and/or motives for actions, decisions, and/or beliefs (Toulmin). Initially, a tutor could ask a writer to *list* whatever justifications his history texts agree upon *for* bombing a city; through this procedure, the possible "grounds" would be defined (A–E in the grid below). Second, a tutor could ask him to make two more lists: reasons given for bombing Coventry (A, C, M, N); reasons given for bombing Dresden (A, C, D, X, Y). Third, they could *compare/contrast* the list for each city with the list of grounds; if a reason for bombing one city does not match any of the "grounds," then it cannot justify bombing that city (M, N, X, and Y). Some grounds might apply to neither (B and E). However, if a reason for bombing a particular city does match one of the "grounds," then that reason "justifies" bombing that city (A, C, and D below). Finally, the tutor could help him compare the matching reasons-and-grounds, seeing which grounds apply to both cities, and which apply only to one of them. If he finds a "ground" that applies to Dresden (D) but not to Coventry, then that would be a "ground" to *"deplore* the bombing of Coventry and *approve* the bombing of Dresden." (If, however, they found that all the grounds applied to both cities, they would inevitably conclude, "There are no grounds upon which one could approve the bombing of Dresden yet deplore the bombing of Coventry.") As they undertook each step, they could draw a chart:

	STEP 2, LISTING Reasons for bombing Dresden: A, C, D, X, Y	Reasons for bombing Coventry: A, C, M, N
STEP 1, DEFINING Course proposes these as grounds for bombing cities:		
		STEP 3, COMPARING/CONTRASTING
A	A	A
B	—	—
C	C	C
D	D	□
		STEP 4, CONTRASTING
E	—	
	—	
but does not mention these as grounds:	X Y	M N

Similarly, the following assignment about policy implicitly directs the writer to perform several analytical steps:

> *Should* modern leaders like Chancellor Helmut Kohl and President Ronald Reagan use public ceremonies to promote reconciliation?

➤ This time, rather than provide a list of questions you could ask, we would like you to pause and formulate a list of possible questions yourself. Our purpose is to help you internalize the process of analysis, just as you must help writers to do in order to become independent. Although you may usefully *model* analytical processes for writers, to continue to do so indefinitely would risk doing the writers' thinking for them; gradually, try to encourage writers to ask their own questions (we have mentioned this in Chapter 1, but it bears repeating here).

Of course, you would probably not ask all of these questions in any one tutorial conference. To do so would risk overwhelming linear writers by making them think the question were more complex than they might have foreseen. By identifying key concepts, noting imperatives, employing signal words, and analyzing the imperatives implied in practical interrogatives, you can help writers identify the important parts of writing assignments and can help writers think critically.

Promoting Critical Analysis: Problem-Solving Strategies

Seeing writing as real communication

Sometimes writing assignments can *seem* like merely academic exercises, asking writers to present the information given in a course; as such, they can seem quite unrelated to the writers' "real" world. Writers may feel called upon simply to repeat what their readings and lectures have said, without seeing the purpose, the practical significance, of their writing. Paolo Freire, describing in *Education for a Critical Consciousness* and *The Politics of Education* his adult literacy programs in Brazil, speaks of the vital importance of a writer's seeing a piece of writing not in terms of what it *is about*, but in terms of what it will *do*, how it will enable the writer to take a "stance of intervention" by using reading and writing to effect changes. For example, in response to the first assignment about the Normandy invasion ("Who reported the Normandy invasion for the American press?"), a writer could present information *about* the reporters' biographies, public images, means of taking notes and writing reports, partnerships with photographers, contractual relations with their newspapers, and so on. To make such information meaningful to the writer, a tutor could ask practical questions about what it suggests readers should *do* or think. For instance, a tutor could ask, "Why is it important in 1987 to know about how a reporter–photographer team covered an event in World War II?" The writer might respond by suggesting that some readers might take action (for example, reporters who aspired to become New Journalists like Tom Wolfe and Jimmy Breslin, intent upon presenting their personal experiences of public events, might begin to hire photographers as essential partners) or that they might change their attitudes (for example, TV audiences might find in the work of reporter–photographer teams an antidote for skewed and partial presentation of history as docudrama). Such questions help writers see their papers as occasions for practical communication, for promoting readers' assent and, perhaps, action.

Rephrasing assignments to analyze their academic, rhetorical, and practical purposes

Besides analyzing the language of assignments, you can employ Freire's insight to help writers rephrase assignments as problems concerning the purpose of the assignment and the audience for whom it is intended. Since most academic papers are assigned in courses and read by teachers, you could focus first on the academic purposes of the assignment, such as "Why was this topic assigned in this course? How does it fit in with the other readings, lectures, and other paper assignments?" or, if the choice were left up to the writer, "Why did you choose this topic for this course or occasion?"

Since every real communication is meant to be *received by someone*—not necessarily someone in an academic setting—*for some reason*, you could help writers think about intended readers whom their papers might persuade to do or think something. Questions like the following might help writers imagine relationships with their readers in order to determine how to approach them:

> What does my intended reader already know about this problem?
>
> Why does my intended reader need to know about this problem?
>
> What interest(s) does my intended reader share with me regarding this issue?
>
> On what aspects of this problem might my reader disagree with me? Why? How can I overcome or defuse opposition?

What kind of person do I want to project myself as being? What's my style? Why?

You can also help writers identify practical purposes for assignments, since all problems are *problems for someone*. An academic assignment like "Write a 1000 word review of Leni Riefenstahl's propaganda documentary film *Triumph of the Will* (1935)" entails practical problems for filmmakers, editors, and politicians, who need to understand technical and conceptual relationships between "propaganda" and "documentary" and to assess how films affect the public's understanding of their policies. To identify the practical problems implicit in this assignment, a tutor could ask a writer questions like the following:

For whom is the film a problem?

What groups have interests in solving these problems? Why?

What groups have interests in not solving them? Why?

Who should be responsible for solving them? Who actually is? Why?

Who else should know about them? Who, if anyone, should not know?

What is the major conflict each of the interest groups faces?

How does the "good" of one group affect the "goods" of the other interest groups? Of the larger community?

Since, like problems, all solutions are *solutions for someone*, the tutor could help the writer explore alternatives by asking questions such as these:

What could be done, or could have been done, to solve this problem?

What side effects might, or did, a particular solution have? For whom?

Who might oppose a particular solution? Why?

Just as in a single tutorial session you would not ask all of the groups of questions analyzing the language of the assignment, so you would want to select carefully the kinds and numbers of problem-solving questions, depending on the responses of the writer. By adjusting the questions, heuristics, and pacing of the tutorial dialogue to writers' needs, you can use problem-solving questions to help writers see papers as sets of small, do-able tasks. As they internalize these problem-solving questions, writers can learn to move among them as they gradually build up their compositions. Instead of trying to compose linearly, writers can learn to alternate among brief periods of generating ideas about one of the practical or rhetorical subproblems, reviewing and rephrasing the topic, generating some more, briefly editing (perhaps by renaming a concept), rereading what has been written and checking to see how it fits the assignment, generating some more, and so forth. This kind of critical "shuttling" among problems promotes the in-depth conceptual analysis underlying genuine fluency.

Promoting Fluency and Critical Analysis through Incubation

Acquiring fluency and analytical skill through the techniques presented in Chapters 3 and 4 takes time. Beyond the conference, once the writer leaves you and starts to work independently, he needs time for incubation, time to try listing and

HDWDWW, and then maybe one or more of the diagrams or problem-solving strategies. After that, he needs more time to do other things—to walk out to the coffee shop, to feed the cat, to fold the laundry—while the paper assignment sits quietly at the back of the mind, until an idea hatches—Eureka! Then he needs time to see how the discovery may lead him astray and must be saved for another day, or how it may alter and enrich his incubating idea. Since inexperienced writers often do not realize that lengthy reflection makes part of the composing process, you can share your own experiences as a writer to reassure them and to help them listen to their ruminations more attentively (see Chapter 1).

Combining the Strategies: A Sample Session with a Linear Writer

In any given tutorial conference, a tutor would need to select just a few of the strategies for analyzing the language of assignments and for using problem-solving techniques. In the following dialogue, the tutor selects strategies by picking up cues from the writer. Dinah, a writer in an introductory sociology course, finds herself unable to write on the assignment, "Describe how your neighborhood has changed in the last twenty years." She tells Reed, her tutor, that the harder she thinks about the assignment, the more overwhelmed she feels by the complexity of the changes her neighborhood has undergone. She has tried to decide what to say before writing and now does not know where to begin. Reed might begin their session by helping her to analyze the language of the assignment:

REED: What is the assignment asking you to do?

DINAH: I'm supposed to say how my neighborhood has changed between 1965 and 1985. It ought to be easy, since I've lived there all my life. But I'm so confused! I don't know if I'm supposed to say in what ways the neighbor-
5   hood was different in 1965 from today. Or if I'm supposed to say what brought the changes about.

REED: So, according to what you just said, the word "how" in the assignment gives you two alternatives. You can *name the ways* in which it changed. Or you can tell *what factors caused it to change.* Here's a page to take some
10   notes on, OK? *[hands her some paper]*

DINAH: *[writes down "how = ways" and "how = causes"]*

By examining possible meanings of "how," they refine their understanding of the assignment phrased as a practical question. Having done this, one alternative Reed considers is to use some techniques we described in Chapter 3. He could capitalize on Dinah's oral fluency by asking her to talk about her neighborhood: Who lived there in 1965? In 1985? What old businesses have disappeared? What new ones have come? What buildings have been torn down? Built? And so on. He could help her list, group, and map her responses, or they could use a double-entry list labeled "1965" and "1985." Because Dinah already has "something to say"—in fact, *too* much to say—Reed decides that using techniques of generating basic fluency would not be the best alternative strategy for this tutorial. What Dinah really needs, Reed knows, is a way to relate her observations to the various concepts of the course.

Consequently, in order to promote a more course-specific analysis of the assignment, especially with regard to the meaning of "how," Reed chooses a different alternative: problem-solving strategies. First, he helps Dinah to see this particular paper in its academic context:

REED: Maybe we can pin down the assignment further if you tell me something about what's been going on in the course.

DINAH: OK. Lately we've talked about how the growth of suburban office parks
15   affected the inner cities and how rent control affects who rents or owns property.

REED: Hmmm. You say "affects." Which of your possible meanings of "how" does that apply to?

DINAH: One thing we learned is that office parks caused big businesses, as well
20   as the small businesses that support them, like restaurants and suppliers, to leave the inner city. So I guess it sounds like *causes*.

REED: So your paper can't just describe *ways* your neighborhood changed. It also has to say what *caused* the changes. Could you add these ideas to your notes?

25   DINAH: Right. *[circles "ways" once and "causes" twice on her note page and jots down "business movements," "who owns housing?" and "who rents?"]*

REED: Why do you think the professor assigned this topic?

DINAH: She wants to see if we can apply the concepts about urban sociology to our own experiences. It's kind of like a test, to see if we understand the
30   course.

REED: Then let's make a list of the concepts you've been studying. You'll want to see if some of them apply to your neighborhood. What else have you talked about besides business movements and rent control?

DINAH: Just a second. I'll look at my notes.

By establishing the academic context, Reed's first problem-solving questions help Dinah to clarify the meaning of "how" and to construct a checklist of concepts in urban sociology (most likely entailing practical questions of relationship such as correlation, causation, probability, and perhaps, policy), some of which she can apply to her neighborhood.

Since Reed wants to make certain that Dinah carries away from their hour-long tutorial a piece of writing that her final essay can include, he needs to decide how best to use the remaining forty-five minutes or so. Several alternatives are available. To help Dinah see the paper not only as an academic "test" but also as a real communication aimed at doing something, Reed could ask some questions about the audience who might be interested in reading her paper:

35   REED: Besides your sociology professor, who else might be interested in knowing how the neighborhood has changed?

DINAH: Susan, my best friend in high school, who hasn't been back to the old neighborhood in all these years. We still send Christmas cards, though.

REED: Why would she want to know?

40   DINAH: Nostalgia. *[pauses]* Also, she might be interested in real estate, since she

knows that her great-aunt plans to leave her a house there. She might wonder whether to sell it or rent it, or even live in it herself.

REED: How might she decide which to do?

45 DINAH: Money—what she could sell or rent it for. I guess if she thought of living there herself she'd want to know about the neighbors, how they keep up their homes. I guess the concept of cultural relativity would interest her. And she'd need to think about getting a job. And that would involve transportation.

REED: You're really rolling now. How about listing these questions, so you don't
50 forget them?

DINAH: Sure. *[writes the list, elaborating as she goes]*

nostalgia—how have the old haunts changed?

prices of real estate? ('65 v. '85)

rental rates? ('65 v. '85)

55 who are neighbors? (Asian influx)

home maintainence? (improved)

jobs in neighborhood? downtown? in suburbs?

public transportation? parking?

REED: If Susan came back home tomorrow, what might she think?

60 DINAH: She'd be really surprised! The old furniture store is still right where it was, but the other businesses are all different. *[adds "new businesses" to her list]*

Thinking about why Susan might read her essay helps Dinah connect the abstract sociological concepts with the neighborhood changes she has observed in economics (real estate values, jobs, new businesses) and cultural changes (old haunts supplanted, new Asian neighbors); the application of sociological concepts becomes less abstract. In their continuing dialogue, Reed might help Dinah ask similar questions about other people who might be interested in her paper: she might suggest the retired high school principal ("She saw the high school as a microcosm of social change") or a recently arrived "urban homesteader" interested in the area's earlier cultural character; by considering questions like those above, Dinah could identify issues of interest to various real people. As time allows, Reed could then ask about other practical concerns, such as the following:

For whom is this a problem?
  "Who disliked the changes you've described?"
  "Why did some businesses move out?"
  "Why did some neighbors leave?"
What groups had interests in solving the problem? How?
  "Why did the old furniture store stay?"
  "Why did some of the old neighbors stay?"
  "Why did the Asians move into the neighborhood?"
  "Who were neighborhood leaders?"
  "What kinds of improvements did they work for?"
  "What government agencies outside the neighborhood helped?"

Dinah's responses to questions like these would provide her with additional material to include in her essay. She would probably not answer each of them, but would select a few (perhaps by using the technique of "mapping" described in Chapter 3) as particularly useful for analyzing the change in the neighborhood by using sociological concepts from her course. Which of these alternatives Reed actually selects depends on cues Dinah gives him about the contexts of course readings and class discussion and the directions of her own interests. We need not present the alternative dialogues and their potential products here. In the process of generating material, Dinah might also discover a good way of organizing it. If there is time for another tutorial meeting, she could ask Reed's help in organizing (using techniques we will describe in Chapters 5 and 6). Even if the paper she writes after this first session leaves something to be desired, Dinah's acquisition of some nonlinear analytical and problem-solving processes makes her a stronger, more independent writer.

Summary

Writers may lack fluency because they have been taught to compose in an artificially linear way that interferes with the natural, recursive composing process. Linear writers have been told that they should proceed from planning to organizing to drafting and finally to editing, a sequence that obstructs necessary shuttling among various writing activities. Some linear writers try to plan everything before writing; others try to outline before they have anything to say. These writers become confused and frustrated when their tactics do not produce fluent results. You can help writers discover the desirability of following rather than fighting their recursive instincts.

To discourage linear writing and promote critical analysis, you can, in addition to introducing methods described in Chapter 3, encourage a writer to think dialogically by analyzing the language of assignments. If he learns to circle key concepts, he can begin to state relationships among them. If he identifies an assignment's imperative and interrogative language, he gains understanding of his tasks and can construct lists, diagrams, and matrices that accomplish his purpose. You can also help writers discover what language carries out an assignment's directives, what "signal words," for instance, follow the instruction, "compare and contrast." You can further help writers abandon linear composing if you introduce problem-solving strategies that make writers see writing as purposeful communication. They can learn to rephrase assignments as problems concerning an assignment's objective and audience. Finally, you can reassure writers that fluent, critical writing develops slowly, that ideas must incubate if they are to flourish.

SUGGESTIONS FOR JOURNAL ENTRIES

1. Watch yourself in the process of composing a first draft, and write about the extent to which you may or may not resemble one of Perl's "shuttling" writers.

2. Recall the kinds of formal writing instruction you have received, and write about how one particular feature has influenced your composing processes.

3. If you keep a diary, or if you enjoy letter writing, write about the similarities and differences you notice between those kinds of composing and the composing processes you use for academic papers.

4. What do writers with whom you are working or have worked say about outlining? Why and how do they use it or not use it?

5. If you are working or have worked with a linear writer, describe how you realized that linear processes might be interfering with fluency and critical analysis.

SUGGESTIONS FOR FURTHER WRITING

1. For each of the following, write a short dialogue in which you help a writer analyze the language of the assignment; then write a paragraph explaining your strategy:

    a. Write an essay about a personal experience in which memory—failed, guilty, happy, sad, any kind—played a role.

    b. How can a major symphony orchestra fulfill its responsibility to encourage *avant garde* compositions and yet satisfy its subscribers' desire to hear the old favorites?

    c. Compare and contrast the benefits and disadvantages of attending a liberal arts college and a vocationally oriented college.

    d. Why did the National Football League adopt the rule against "spiking" in the end zone? What were the effects of the rule?

2. For each of the following, write a short dialogue in which you help a writer analyze the practical purposes and possible audiences; then write a paragraph explaining your strategy:

    a. Write a critical review of a film you saw recently.

    b. Why did the National Collegiate Athletic Association adopt the rule that makes college freshmen eligible to play varsity sports? What are the effects of the rule? How successful has it been?

    c. Should the federal government provide flood insurance to homeowners who build houses on barrier reefs?

3. An art major returning to school after a naval career, Kent took Economics 101 to fulfill a distribution requirement and a convenient slot in his class schedule. Assigned to "Write an essay on significant economic developments in an industry or business that is important to an area in which you live," he feels both bored and anxious, so he puts off working on the paper until after the due date. When his professor offers him a one-week extension on the condition that he consult a tutor, Kent brings the following outline of his paper to a conference with you:

The Textile Industry in New England, 1955–85

      I. Introduction of topic
     II. Body
          A. Lawrence
          B. Lowell
          C. Manchester
    III. Conclusion

Construct a dialogue in which you help Kent analyze the language of the assignment. Then write a short paper (500 words) explaining why you chose the particular strategies your dialogue illustrates.

SUGGESTIONS FOR CLASS ACTIVITIES

1. Read aloud several short dialogues about one of the writing assignments in exercise 1 or 2 above, and compare the various rationales used by members of your class.

2. Discuss the strategies you devised to help Kent analyze the language of the assignment and apply problem-solving strategies in exercise 3 above.

3. Supposing that a member of your class asked you for tutorial help in order to write the 500-word paper about Kent (exercise 3 above). Discuss how you would analyze the language of the assignment and what problem-solving strategies you, as a tutor, would employ.

SUGGESTIONS FOR FURTHER READING

Adams, James L. *Conceptual Blockbusting.* New York: W. H. Freeman, 1974.

Arrington, Phillip K. "Tropes of the Composing Process." *College English* 48 (1986): 325–338.

Bruner, Jerome S. *Toward a Theory of Instruction.* Cambridge, MA: Harvard University Press, 1966.

Donlan, Dan. "Teaching Writing in the Content Areas." *Research in the Teaching of English* 8 (1974): 250–262.

Draper, Virginia. "Formative Writing: Writing to Assist Learning in All Subject Areas." In *Teaching Writing: Essays from the Bay Area Writing Project.* Ed. Gerald Camp. Montclair, NJ: Boynton/Cook, 1982. 148–183.

Emig, Janet. *The Web of Meaning: Essays on Writing, Teaching, Learning, and Thinking.* Montclair, NJ: Boynton/Cook, 1983.

Flower, Linda. *Problem-Solving Strategies for Writing.* New York: Harcourt, 1981.

——, and John R. Hayes. "The Cognition of Discovery: Defining a Rhetorical Problem." *College Composition and Communication* 31 (1980): 21–32.

Freire, Paolo. *Education for a Critical Consciousness.* New York: Seabury Press, 1973.

——. *The Politics of Education.* Trans. Donaldo Macedo. South Hadley, MA: Bergin and Garvey, 1985.

Hawkins, Thomas A. *Group Inquiry Techniques for Teaching Writing.* Urbana, IL: ERIC/NCTE, 1976.

Kutz, Eleanor. "Between Students' Language and Academic Discourse: Interlanguage as Middle Ground." *College English* 48 (1986): 385–396.

Murray, Donald M. *A Writer Teaches Writing.* 2nd ed. Boston: Houghton, Mifflin, 1985. 17–40.

——. "Writing and Teaching for Surprise." *College English* 46 (1984): 1–7.

Odell, Lee. "Piaget, Problem-Solving, and Freshman Composition." *College Composition and Communication* 24 (1973): 36–42.

Perl, Sondra. "A Look at Basic Writers in the Process of Composing." In *Basic Writing: Essays for Teachers, Researchers, Administrators.* Eds. Lawrence N. Kasden and Daniel R. Hoeber Urbana, IL: NCTE, 1980. 13–32.

Peterson, Linda. "Repetition and Metaphor in the Early Stages of Composing." *College Composition and Communication* 36 (1985): 429–453.

Pfister, Fred R., and Joanne F. Petrick. "A Heuristic Model for Creating a Writer's Audience." *College Composition and Communication* 31 (1980): 213–220.

Raymond, James C. "Rhetoric: The Methodology of the Humanities." *College English* 44 (1982): 778–783.

Tedlock, David, and Paul Jarvie. *Casebook Rhetoric: A Problem Solving Approach to Composition.* New York: Holt, Rinehart and Winston, 1981.

Toulmin, Stephen A. *The Uses of Argument.* Cambridge: Cambridge University Press, 1958.

Walvoord, Barbara E. Fassler. *Helping Students Write Well: A Guide for Teachers in All Disciplines.* New York: MLA, 1982. 57–85.

Young, Richard E., Alton L. Becker, and Kenneth L. Pike. *Rhetoric: Discovery and Change.* New York: Harcourt, 1970. 71–118.

PART THREE

Composing Processes: Shaping Ideas

5

Helping Writers
Form Concepts

Writers who have learned ways of generating ideas may not yet have learned how to shape an essay into a unified whole (see Chapter 4). Inexperienced writers need to learn that early formulations are tentative, that they provide some sense of an essay's possible direction but probably need to be reformulated as each writer critically analyzes the possible relationships between his initial proposition and his groups of details. Experienced writers speculate about the materials they have generated, experiment with various ways of fitting them together, and set aside some which seem not to fit at all. This chapter considers strategies tutors can use to help writers shape the still amorphous material of preliminary drafts by forming concepts. Whereas Chapters 3 and 4 present tutorial techniques for helping writers to generate ideas with fluency and to analyze their parts with some critical depth, Chapters 5 and 6 present strategies for helping them to select and shape ideas.

The Nature of Concepts

A "concept" is a statement that "predicates" and that requires demonstration. By "predicates," we mean that it says something *about* something by naming one or more relationships between or among parts. The papers of inexperienced writers often announce a purpose, usually to "write about" or "discuss," instead of naming relationships. For example, the statement, "This paper will discuss Henry Kissinger," does not name a relationship between "Henry Kissinger" and anything else, so it is not a concept. The statement, "This paper will discuss the influence of Henry Kissinger on Ronald Reagan," is a little closer to being a concept because the word "influence" vaguely names some kind of causal relationship between the two parts, "Kissinger and Reagan." The author of such a statement may have identified the parts of an essay—Kissinger, Reagan, and perhaps a few policies or events—without having grasped their relationships; thus, this statement, like the first, may invite the writer merely to present information about the parts. In contrast, a much stronger concept might say, "This paper will show that Kissinger influenced Reagan to distinguish his administration's handling of the hostage crisis in 1985 from that of the Carter Administration during the Iranian hostage crisis in 1979." This statement predicates: it relates the two major parts, Kissinger and Reagan, by specifying "influenced . . . to distinguish . . . from," and it subordinates other parts of the statement (the Carter Administration and the two hostage crises of 1979 and 1985).

Verbs are often the words that name relationships in a concept. The relationship may be very general, such as "A differs from B" or "A and B belong to category C," or much more specific, such as "A contradicts B," "A makes B irrelevant to C," "A embodies B," "A prevents B," and so on. Logical connectors may complement the work of the verbs, for instance, "A did not only this but also that" or "Although A did this, X and Y made that happen." Finally, as you may already have noticed, concepts less often use the vague "This paper will discuss" than the more definite "show that," "demonstrate that," or "argue that"; they often simply name the relationship directly. The relationship named in a concept indicates the kind of development a paper requires; that is, it indicates what kinds of subordinate paragraphs or groups of paragraphs the writer will need in order to persuade readers to accept the truth of the asserted relationship. Whereas Chapter 4 suggests analytical strategies for identifying what subordinate paragraphs writers need to produce, this chapter will employ the reciprocal question: "What does this paragraph in a preliminary draft *do* to help demonstrate the concept?"

The second defining characteristic of a "concept" is that it requires "demonstration" by a writer. A statement of fact, such as "Henry Kissinger served as secretary of state," requires no demonstration and thus is not a concept. However, statements such as "This paper will show that Kissinger influenced Reagan to distinguish his administration's handling of the hostage crisis in 1985 from that of President Carter during the Iranian hostage crisis in 1979" or "Henry Kissinger was the most powerful American statesman in the latter half of the twentieth century" or "Henry Kissinger's policies unintentionally prolonged the Arab–Israeli conflict," are statements about which well-informed readers might hold differing views. Thus, they all require writers to demonstrate the truth of the assertions they make. The papers of inexperienced writers often make factual assertions in place of concepts; with nothing to demonstrate, such papers merely ramble along, accumulating and presenting facts purposelessly.

Why Writers Have Trouble Forming Concepts

In Chapter 7 of *Errors and Expectations,* Mina Shaughnessy describes essays "in incubation," essays revealing the writers' minds at work, as they alight on initial ideas, but then hop off into other notions. A diagram of their composing process might look like this:

```
PLAN        o
GENERATE    o o o o o o o o o o o o o o o o o o o o o o o o o o o   DONE
DESIGN
EDIT
            - - - - - - - - - - - - -  TIME  - - - - - - - - - - - - - - ->
```

They may have attained a *kind* of fluency—the ability to think of more things to say—yet they ramble on, unable to develop any one idea for more than a few sentences. Thus, even though they *seem* to be able to "think out loud on paper" and are seldom detained by questions of correctness, their fluency is deceptive, because their "thinking" is very superficial, lacking any focus and depth of analysis.

Shaughnessy explains why beginning writers often fail to develop an idea. They are not yet used to asking themselves questions such as, "What information did I use to arrive at this opinion?" "What further information do I need to support my contention?" "What am I assuming?" "How am I defining this term?" Without such questions, once they express the kernel of the idea, they go no further. When told to "be specific" or to "develop this idea," they add *bulk,* which most often consists of personal reflections and anecdotes, extra details and information, and platitudes. While forestalling early closure, this bulk does not answer the specific questions given in an assignment.

Nancy Sommers offers a complementary explanation ("Revision Strategies of Student Writers and Experienced Adult Writers"): some writers assume or have mistakenly been taught that writing is the transcription of speech in a mood of inspiration. (They seem to recall Wordsworth's definition of poetry as emotion but to forget his qualification: "emotion *recollected in tranquility.*") Seizing inspiration from a word in the assignment (without pausing to analyze the whole assignment), they skip from one thing to the next to the next as long as inspiration lasts, seeing no need to recollect and reflect upon what they have written. They often speak quite volubly, in a sprightly, chatty style, and they "write like they talk," but like nervous chatter at a cocktail party, their volubility often disguises the nagging anxiety that if they slow down to examine an idea in more depth, they may run out of information or encounter an exception or contradiction. Somehow, they fear, their ideas will not pan out. Yet the suggestion that they seek help from tutors may come as a surprise, since their papers may have gotten by for a long time on charm and correctness. While the writers in Chapters 3 and 4 often think they "can't write," these writers often think, or at least claim to think, that they write quite well.

Forming Concepts through Freewriting

Freewriting, as Peter Elbow describes it in *Writing Without Teachers,* is recursive. Because many people misunderstand freewriting as the random, unrevised generation of sentences, they fear that freewriting will make them write "garbage." In fact, however, freewriting always consists of two phases, which Elbow calls "tidal": the *uncritical* flow of sentences, followed by the *critical* reflection on them (to ask "What have I said?" and to locate patterns, contradictions, digressions, or points of special significance), followed by another uncritical flow, and so on. Writers' problems often arise because they overemphasize one of the two phases: self-censoring writers criticize without giving themselves enough chances to generate, whereas associative writers generate "bulk" without enough critical reflection. Very inexperienced writers (like Carol, author of "My Job" in Chapter 3) who have great difficulty in framing sentences might find freewriting too discouraging or too time-consuming to use during a tutorial session; their tutors might be wiser at least to begin promoting fluency through listing and mapping with single words and short phrases. However, these tutors might wish to recommend that the writers experiment on their own with freewriting, because it can help self-censoring and linear writers to form concepts and to order paragraphs in their essays so as to develop them.

In general, freewriting encourages writers to start anywhere and write about anything, including how boring/impossible/silly the writing assignment is and how frustrated/anxious/hopeless they may feel about ever completing it. Encouraging writers to spend a few minutes at the beginning of a session just freewriting about such feelings gives you an opportunity to acknowledge that dissatisfaction with assignments and anxieties about completing them are understandable feelings (even familiar to tutors!). (As Chapter 1 explains, airing feelings can enable writers to get beyond them and address the task at hand.) After helping writers to analyze the language of the assignment and/or apply some of the problem-solving strategies, you can ask writers to spend ten minutes or so during the tutorial session generating sentences about an item they have listed: a key idea or an academic, rhetorical, or practical issue they have identified. Then you can ask them to locate a central concern or kernel idea that appears in their freewriting. If writers have formed several concepts that could be developed, they may agonize over which issue to choose. If this happens, you can simply suggest, "Just choose *any* one," and wait for the writer's subconscious to make the choice. This procedure helps people write their way through to a concept that will form the basis of an essay.

Writers who hesitate to freewrite might try letter writing as a "real" kind of communication, in Freire's sense. Letters *do* something to their readers—entertain, inform, request, win assent or sympathy, chastise, and so on. Whereas writers who write to themselves in journals and diaries may be quite comfortable with freewriting, others may resist "talking to themselves" and need a "real" audience to communicate with. Your rapport with a writer makes you a good audience. Writers can also address their freewriting to relatives, friends, or classmates—to anyone who might conceivably be interested in their views on the subject of the assignment. If an assignment instructs a writer to imagine an audience for the essay, for instance, "As head of your neighborhood association, write a proposal to the mayor recommending rehabilitation of a particular six-block area," a tutor could try to "stand in" for the mayor. Any of these relatively "real" audiences would replace the abstract "reader" (for an equally abstract essay) with a real person with whom a writer could more genuinely communicate.

Forming Concepts by Glossing Ideas

Renaming various ideas by glossing helps writers form concepts and develop them throughout a series of paragraphs, as Ann E. Berthoff explains in *Forming, Thinking, Writing* (112–187). A *gloss* is a label (such as the labels written beside paragraphs in textbooks or beside the stanzas of Coleridge's "Rime of the Ancient

Mariner'' or at the top of each page in the Bible, telling what the verses on that page are about). In Chapter 3, we spoke of listing details, of sorting them into groups, and of naming each group according to the feature shared by all its members. Similarly, glossing names the feature shared by a group of sentences. A gloss can be a single word, a phrase, or a sentence, through which the writer names the concept or describes the rhetorical function in a passage. By teaching writers to gloss their paragraphs, tutors can help them develop the analytical, dialogical habits of mind that underlie all writing (as Chapter 2 explains). By helping writers to name the connections between glosses through HDWDWW (from Chapter 3), tutors can help writers to focus on the specific terms of assignments and to relate paragraphs to each other and to the essay's concept, thus developing the essay rather than merely adding bulk.

Whether a piece of freewriting is drafted at home or during a ten-minute segment of a tutorial conference, a tutor can ask a writer to reread the passage (perhaps aloud, in order to hear as well as see patterns, key words, and so on) and to write in the margins in a number of ways. A novice writer's paragraph may consist of one group of sentences that can be glossed with one name. More often, however, a novice's paragraph contains several clusters of sentences, and similar clusters may be strewn throughout the paper, as the writer shuttles back and forth, elaborating points made earlier. Tutors could ask some of the following questions to help writers gloss, elaborate, and shape their papers:

"What have I said?"

"How many ideas are in this passage?"

"What is the gist of what I've written?"

"What does/should this paragraph do?"

What have I said?"

Tutors can ask writers to question their freely generated passages and write descriptive labels in the margins. If a writer names her ideas, "Here I talk about how jogging helps people overcome mental depression. Here I say joggers can become physically addicted to endomorphins released by the body in pain," the tutor could suggest writing the names "overcome depression" and "physically addicting" in the margins. If she names rhetorical functions, "Here I'm *contrasting* the benefits and disadvantages of jogging," the tutor could suggest that she write "contrast" in the margin and then that she generate some more sentences about that particular contrast or other contrasts. After she glosses the whole passage, you might suggest she write some more sentences, perhaps elaborating on one of the glosses or pursuing a new direction suggested by one of them. A second round of glossing could similarly analyze the new passage and, perhaps, connect it with the first.

"How many ideas are in this passage?"

This question helps writers locate related sentences, to cluster and then to gloss them. Resembling listing, grouping, and mapping (Chapter 3), this technique can help writers recognize that clusters of sentences reveal parts of an issue, parts that can be further subdivided, consolidated, or related in a variety of other ways. Clustering is especially useful in tutoring associative writers, because it helps them notice both how many different subjects their strings of associations produce and how rapidly—perhaps in only two or three sentences—they move from one thing to the next. You can ask writers to separate each cluster into a miniparagraph that they gloss; then writers can select some clusters for full elaboration into paragraphs. A paragraph indentation is a typographical sign that says, "these parts go together"; thus, indentations can stimulate writers to consider possible relationships within and between clusters. As William F. Irmscher quotes Paul Rodgers, "To compose is to create; to indent is to interpret" (98).

"What is the 'gist'?"

In "looping," a variation on freewriting developed by Peter Elbow in *Writing Without Teachers* and Cowan and Cowan in *Writing,* the writer freewrites and then loops back to state "the gist." Whereas "What have I said?" and "How many ideas?" enumerate all the parts, stating the "gist" necessitates selecting or generalizing. Linda Flower uses the acronym WIRMI (for "What I really mean is . . .") (39) to help writers phrase the "gist," which may in turn serve as a point of departure for the next flow of ideas. Tutors may find that stating the "gist" reassures linear writers that they have "gotten somewhere" through freewriting. This is particularly true when, with tutors' help, they find that the "gist" is connected to their analysis of the language of the assignment or to the subproblems identified through their problem-solving analyses.

"What does/should this paragraph do?

These two questions help writers produce prescriptive outlines, working plans for articulating parts of papers. When tutors help writers ask these questions about passages of freewriting, writers explain to themselves what particular paragraphs should *do* to further the solution of a problem posed by an assignment. Typically, formal introductions announce topics rather than articulate propositions. They say, for instance, *"In this paper I will discuss* the use of steroids in weight training" or "The use of steroids in weight training *is very interesting."* More productively, a prescriptive outline might say, "This introductory paragraph should answer these questions: What are steroids? Why are they used in weight training? Who uses them? To whom are they 'interesting'—or better yet, 'controversial'?" and so on. By asking writers "What is this paragraph doing?" or "What purpose does this paragraph serve?" you can help them discover subtopics ("this paragraph is explaining why some athletes refuse to be tested for steroids"), dead-end digressions ("this paragraph tells about a racehorse disqualified for having been injected with steroids"), and irrelevant "filler" ("this paragraph gives the chemical structure of some steroids"). Once several tasks have been identified, writers can be asked to jot each task in a phrase or sentence on an index card or square of paper; these can be moved around, enabling linear writers to experiment with various arrangements without becoming overburdened by complexity.

This **storyboard** technique borrows the method by which screenwriters plan scenes by using a piece of board on which 3-by-5 cards bearing a few words or lines about the story can be pinned and rearranged in various ways. By moving the cards around, the writer can decide the best dramatic order, and the director can envision the various kinds of shots that should be made (DeNitto, 13–29). You can help writers pin to a storyboard squares of paper each bearing a gloss ("steroids harmful") or a sentence naming a task ("Write a paragraph telling why athletes using steroids were ejected from the Olympics"); they can then use these squares as a movable outline that promotes critical analysis of concepts and eventually leads to forming and developing a concept.

Another kind of movable outline is the *"issue tree"* made during the critical phase of freewriting (Flower, 88–102). These are hierarchical diagrams with top-level ideas branching or "rooting" downward into subsystems; they help generate ideas because, unlike traditional outlines that are made *before* one begins writing, they diagram *emerging* ideas and, therefore, are useful in spotting "runaway" branches (digressions that have taken over the paper) and missing concepts. They also help unify papers by adding an extra top level that renames all the parts. It really makes very little difference whether writers use traditional-*looking* vertical outlines or Flower's horizontal "issue trees," so long as they are willing to change, to rearticulate their plans as they "shuttle" among concepts in the course of problem solving. (Since "issue trees" resemble the diagrams in Chapter 3, we will not include an illustrative dialogue here.) All of these verbal and visual descriptive outlines help writers "talk to their writing," promoting the dialogical thinking that helps them transform fluency into critical analysis.

Freewriting, A Sample Tutorial Session

Joni wrote "My Florida Vacation" in response to this first-semester college English assignment: "Describe an experience that changed the way you think." Her professor commented, "This paper does not fulfill the assignment. Please make an appointment with Tran." Before you read our analysis, please take a few minutes to write your observations about the paper, guided (but not necessarily limited) by these questions:

- According to Chapter 4's ways of analyzing assignments, what does this assignment call for explicitly? Implicitly?
- What "experience" does the paper describe?
- How does the "experience" change Joni's thinking?
- What might be Joni's attitudes toward writing? Toward working with a tutor?
- On which passages might Joni try to focus critical analysis?

MY FLORIDA VACATION

It was five o'clock p.m. on Tuesday, April 27th when Cathy and I decided that we needed a vacation. Within ten minutes we had packed our bags and were on our way to Daytona Beach, Florida, with seventeen cents in our pocket. We informed a

few friends of our plans, so that no one would worry, and we left. The hitchhike
itself was an interesting experience and it was fun. We met some really nice people.
One of the rides was from two people from California. They gave me a gold pocket
watch I will always wear. The worst part of the trip was getting stuck in the Bronx
at nine o'clock at night in the pouring rain. We were terrified. It took us only twenty-
six hours to get to Daytona Beach, which was really good time. That night we slept
in a stairwell because we had no money for a hotel, and it was too cold outside. The
next day I got to play on the beach, swim in the ocean and get a great sunburn.
Sunburns can be really dangerous and also very painful. I looked like a lobster.
When I think back to this vacation I remember the fear that had overwhelmed both
of us. Daytona Beach was not a nice place at night, but during the day it was
beautiful. We returned to school five days later, after visiting a few people on the
way home. We returned to warm hugs and a good meal. We told our story of the
trip that evening and we realized we were glad to be home amongst friends. It was
so nice to feel safe and warm.

. . .

Particularly in contrast with the papers of the reticent and self-censoring writers
we analyzed in Chapter 3, this paper *appears* fluent. Although it has no problems
with correctness, its fluency is deceptive. What Joni submitted to her professor as
a "finished" paper is, in reality, merely first-stage freewriting: freely, uncritically
generated associations. One word in the assignment, "experience," propels her
along a chronological string of associations ("we did this . . . we did that"); she
does not pause to think analytically about them. She leaves the reader wondering
many things: Why did they leave so abruptly? Why with so little money? What
do the labels "interesting," "fun," and "nice" mean (line 5)? Why would someone give them a *gold* pocket watch? Moreover, because no event seems more
important than any other (a terrifying night in the Bronx receives no more attention than getting a sunburn), a reader wonders what "experience" the events all
add up to, what it means, and how it changed the writer's thinking. The clichéd
"happy ending" could just as well fit a trip to Oz as to Florida: it does not grow
out of the particularities of her experience. (Later in this chapter, we will examine
a different kind of problem with cliché, which distracts the writer of "Kevin"
from what he wants to say).

Joni's tutor, Tran, faces a challenging task in helping her transform chatter into
genuine fluency by showing her the second stage of freewriting:

TRAN: Hi. I'm glad to meet you.

JONI: Hi. I wish I could say the same. Nothing against you personally, you understand, but I've just never had any trouble with English before this and I
never had to see a tutor before now or anything and I just don't know what
I'm going to do. I mean, in high school my teachers just *loved* my writing
and I even did profiles on the cheerleaders for the school paper and everything, and now all of a sudden I can't write. I mean that's what my professor says. He's so *learned* and so serious, and I mean, I know he just hates
me!

Clearly, Joni "writes the way she talks": volubly. Tran wisely lets her vent her
frustration and anxiety. But if he allows their dialogue to become entangled in
interpersonal issues (Joni's anecdotes of her high school writing and writing teachers

and of her professor's disregard for both), it will never get around to focusing, to forming a concept. Tran can reassure her briefly and then help her see why her professor wrote, "This paper does not fulfill the assignment":

10 TRAN: What does the assignment ask the paper to do?

JONI: Let's see . . . tell an experience that changed my thinking.

Analyzing the assignment begins to help Joni and Tran understand the professor's comment. The imperative "describe" is deceptively simple. Whereas Joni seems to notice only one imperative and one key term, "describe an experience," a writer forming a concept about this assignment needs to relate "experience," "change," and "way you think." What this assignment calls for, then, is not a retelling of a series of events constituting an "experience," but rather a more complex response: to describe a change in thinking that occurred, to define what constitutes "an experience," and to explain how—by what means and/or in what manner—the experience brought the change about. An experienced writer would probably know how to read between the lines and identify the unasked question in this poorly worded assignment. Inexperienced writers, however, cannot readily answer questions that are not explicitly asked. Thus, one of Tran's challenges will be to help Joni identify the assignment's implied questions:

TRAN: So, we need to figure out what "an experience" means.

JONI: Easy! It means something that happens to you.

TRAN: Did you hear the phone ringing next door just now?

15 JONI: Sure!

TRAN: Would you call that "an experience"?

JONI: Sort of . . . , but I think I see what you're getting at. "An experience" has to mean something to the person it happens to. Like, if that phone call was for me, telling me I had won the lottery, THAT would be an experi-
20 ence, for sure!

TRAN: How do you mean?

JONI: Because I'd be rich and I could travel and everything.

TRAN: So would the phone call itself be "an experience"?

JONI: Only because that was how I found out. I mean, when I would tell my
25 friends about it, I'd say, "I'll never forget the day I was working on this English paper when the phone rang, and. . . ."

TRAN: [interrupting] OK. So what makes an ordinary event, like the phone ringing, "an experience"?

JONI: When it makes an important change in your life.

At this point in the dialogue, Tran has helped Joni to distinguish "an experience" from a series of events: "an experience" involves a significant change. This is a perfect moment for Tran to address the other major term in the assignment: change.

TRAN: Good. What does the assignment say about change?

30 JONI: Hmmmm . . . it says, "that changed the way you think." I'm supposed to say *the way* my thinking changed?

TRAN: OK. Now I think we're getting closer to what the paper is supposed to do.

JONI: Oh no! I don't know what way my thinking changed!

TRAN: Well, don't worry. We can talk it out. What might "how?" mean?

35 oni: It could mean "in what manner?" Like, "suddenly"?

TRAN: OK, we'll talk about that. Anything else?

JONI: *[pauses]* What made it change? You know, causes?

TRAN: Good. We'll look at the change that way too.

Gradually and patiently, Tran is helping Joni slow down, focus on the key words "experience" and "changed the way you think," and think more analytically about what her paper is supposed to do.

Since Joni seems very anxious about the paper she has brought with her, Tran decides that setting it aside in order to engage in problem-solving strategies might overtax her patience. Instead, he decides to help her to reflect critically on her paper, *as if* it were the first, generative phase of freewriting:

40 TRAN: As I read what you have written, I see a whole lot of different events. But I'm left wondering what "experience" they all add up to, why they're important.

JONI: Oh.

TRAN: What question does your paper answer?

45 JONI: I guess . . . what happened when I went to Florida?

TRAN: Right. Just a couple of minutes ago, you said the assignment asked. . . .

JONI: Yeah, I know . . . tell an experience that made an important change in the way I think. *[pauses]* So instead of just telling what happened, my paper has to answer the question, *"How did my Florida vacation change the way*
50 *I think?"*

TRAN: Good. Would you please just write that down at the very top of the page? *[She writes.]*

Tran asks Joni to restate the assignment using *reciprocal questions:* "What question does the assignment ask?" and "What question does the draft answer?" Tutors often find that reciprocal questioning helps writers identify some essential boundaries—what the artist Ben Shahn calls "finding the outer shape" (70) and what Donald Murray calls "sketching" (35)—for their freewriting.

Now Tran could continue helping Joni analyze her paper by asking her to find clusters of sentences on the same idea:

TRAN: OK. How about reading through the draft very slowly and seeing *how many*
55 *ideas there are in this paragraph.* You could just put a slash mark between different subjects.

JONI: I don't get it.

TRAN: OK. What do the first sentences talk about?

JONI: Let's see . . . about how we left?

TRAN: OK. What comes next?

60 JONI: Then I talk about hitchhiking and the people from California. Boy, were they something else. I mean, they were so laid back and everything. . . .

TRAN: *[interrupts]* OK, so put a slash mark where you shift from talking about leaving to talking about them.

JONI: OK . . . I see what you mean. *[makes the following divisions]*

65

line 4	and we left. /	The hitchhike
line 7	always wear. /	The worst part
line 8	terrified. /	It took us
line 12/3	like a lobster. /	When I think
line 15	beautiful. /	We returned

70   Jeepers! Would you look at that! Now what?

At this point in their dialogue, Tran has used "how many ideas are in this paragraph" to help Joni realize that she is indeed talking about a great many different things and moving very rapidly from one association to the next. Once clusters are identified, Tran can ask *"What is the gist?"* or use *WIRMI* to help Joni decide which are most relevant to the assignment:

TRAN: Next, I'm going to ask you to write, OK? First, reread what you wrote at the very top of the page, about what the paper should so. Then, finish this sentence: "What I really mean is. . . ."

JONI: Sure. Let's see. *[rereads "How did my Florida vacation change the way I*
75   *think?", then looks over her list of slash marks]* I think the fear was the most important thing. It changed the way I thought about home, like I didn't take it for granted any more, not as much at least. Right here *[points to lines 13–14]* I'm starting to say it.
      [She writes, "What I really mean is, the fear I experienced on my Florida
80   *vacation made me appreciate the security of home instead of taking it for granted."]*
      How does that sound?

TRAN: What would you say? Does it answer the question?

JONI: Yes, it shows how the vacation changed the way I think about home.

85 TRAN: I think so too. That's great. Some of what you've written could connect with that. . . .

JONI: Sure. The night in the Bronx. I could write a book on that! And how cold we were sleeping in that stairwell.

TRAN: Before you start to write, let's just take a few more minutes to think about
90   what paragraphs you're going to need in order to enable a reader to understand your idea.

JONI: OK. *[pauses]* I need some paragraphs about how I used to take home for granted—you know, think the security was boring and stuff like that.

TRAN: Good. . . .

95 JONI: Let's see. I have to say what changed. So, I'll need some paragraphs about how now what used to seem boring seems kind of nice, you know, comforting.

TRAN: Yes. . . . *[pauses]* Anything else?

JONI: Well of course! How the Bronx changed my attitude—I mean that was
100   certainly not boring, but it wasn't that great either!

TRAN: OK. How about spending the next five minutes writing about the Bronx
and the security of home? Then we'll read over it, as we did the original
paper.

The sequence of Tran's tutorial dialogue—analyzing the language of the assignment, identifying the clusters of sentences and noting the number of different
ideas in her draft, deciding what she really means, forming a working concept
(which she will probably need to refine as she composes), and considering the
groups of subordinate paragraphs she will need to develop the concept—helps Joni
begin to focus her paper. Tran and Joni will meet further challenges if and when
Joni starts to "write a book" about the Bronx. Tran might decide to help her
make a descriptive outline or a storyboard with "scenes" from her vacation and
how each contributed to a change in her thinking. But voluble writers like Joni do
not become critical analysts overnight, and Tran will probably have to repeat this
sequence with Joni more than once before she internalizes it and learns how to
analyze her associations more critically. However, even though Tran has not used
the term "concept," Joni now knows the difference between "discussing" a topic
and forming a concept about it.

Forming Concepts by Glossing Ideas, A Sample Essay

As you will recall from Chapter 4, the writing assignment about "The Brown
Wasps" is quite specific: "Explain the metaphor of the opening paragraph and its
relation to Eiseley's main idea." The following essay, written by Maxine in response to the same assignment, shows that she has obviously achieved fluency.
But she has something to learn both about forming a concept and relating para-
➤ graphs to one another and to the specifications of the writing assignment. After
you read this essay, take a few minutes to write down your observations, especially about these concerns:

- What does the writer see as "Eiseley's main idea"?
- What personal responses does Eiseley's idea evoke?
- Where does the author seem to be adding bulk?
- What conclusion does the writer offer? To what extent is it related to what
she has already written?

THE TRAIN STATION

In his essay "The Brown Wasps," Loren Eiseley describes some old men sitting
every day in the train station, always looking for "their" same seat because it seems
familiar to them. He says they are like wasps that return to die in the thicket near
their hive. The train station is like the hive because it is always buzzing with activity,
5   night and day.

This winter I have seen a lot of old men—and some young ones—sitting in South

Station. In Boston there are always homeless people trying to get a warm place. But the cops come along and say, "Move along, you can't stay here." Because otherwise they bother the travelers, asking for money or just looking dirty and talking
10 funny. Nobody wants to see them. Nobody really cares.

There are shelters like the Pine Street Inn and the Salvation Army where homeless men can go. But a lot don't want to go there because they feel like they're taking a handout or they don't like standing in line to get a ticket for the night. A few weeks ago when it got real cold, some people were lining up at 7 A.M. to get a ticket for
15 the night and then selling it. The government ought to take better care of them.

. . .

Unlike the writers who engage in shuttling (as we discussed in Chapter 4), the writer of "The Train Station" never looks back to connect her wandering observations with the specifics of the writing assignment. She recognizes the central comparison between the old men in the station and the wasps in the hive (lines 1–4). But instead of elaborating it by analyzing other comparisons and relating them to Eiseley's main idea about the nature of "home," Maxine thinks in a straight line, going farther and farther away from the assignment. Eiseley's train station reminds her of South Station (line 6), with its cadre of homeless men who would rather exploit each other (line 15) than accept charity from a shelter (line 11). She adds bulk: personal reflections (lines 8–10), additional information (lines 12–15), personal anecdotes (lines 6–7), and platitudes ("nobody cares" and "the government should do something" [lines 10, 15]). While forestalling early closure, this bulk does not address the specific questions given in the assignment. The conclusion (that the government should help) has nothing to do with Eiseley's notion of "home." No matter how accurate and authentic Maxine's view of the men in South Station may be, it leaves the writing assignment in the dust. However, the preliminary draft offers hope: Olga, her tutor, can use glossing to help Maxine notice the repetition of "homeless" in paragraphs two and three. "Homeless" names an idea the writer sees as important; it may be the seed of a coherent, controlled paper that does focus on the assignment. The direction a dialogue takes depends on Maxine's understanding of the assignment. Imagine two alternative versions of the assignment:

OLGA: What is this assignment asking you to do?

MAXINE: (1) Explain the connection of the wasps and men to Eiseley's main
5 idea.   (2) Write about old men in train stations, like Eiseley does.

Obviously, the first response shows a better grasp of the assignment than the second does. Olga's strategy would be guided accordingly:

OLGA: (1) Good. I see that too. What connection do you see?   (2) Well, let's look at it again. What's Eiseley's main idea?

MAXINE: (1) In the first paragraph I say that they are alike because the station
10 and the hive are buzzing with activity.   (2) That people and animals like to go back to a familiar place, someplace they call "home."

OLGA: (1) Yes. How does that connect with Eisley's main idea? What is his essay about? (2) How does that relate to his comparison? The one you mention in paragraph one?

15 MAXINE: (1) He writes about how all creatures return to familiar places they call "home," where their activity goes on. (2) The hive, and even just a seat in the train station, can be "home" if that's where your activity goes on.

The first response shows that Maxine accurately understands the specifics of the assignment. All Olga needs to do, then, is help Maxine name what connects the incidents, that is, to articulate the relationship of the details with her essay's concept: "home is where one's activity goes on." On the other hand, the second response shows a misunderstanding of the assignment. Olga could therefore begin by helping Maxine reexamine the exact wording of the assignment and attune her responses to it, instead of straying immediately into anecdotes. At this point in the dialogue, both responses have renamed the point of the first paragraph, and Maxine is ready to start connecting the second and third paragraphs to it. Because the concept—that "home" *means* the center of men's or wasps' activity—now

➤ controls more of the details, the paper is becoming more unified. Before you read further, imagine a third response Maxine might have given and write an appropriate series of questions and answers.

. . .

This kind of analysis—glossing and questioning—may help Maxine begin to see the possible connections between her personal responses and the specifications of the assignment. Olga then could help her connect these to Eiseley's general point. She might ask, for instance, "How do the old men in South Station resemble or differ from those Eiseley describes? How does each group feel about 'home'?" Or, "Why don't shelters like the Pine Street Inn fit Eiseley's definition of 'home'?" In this way, she could help Maxine make use of personal reactions to answer the assigned question, a much more honest and successful strategy than the intimidating task she may have given herself: "guess what answer the teacher has in mind." By showing writers how to work within the constraints of a specifically formulated assignment, tutors can help them fulfill assignments and still say what they genuinely want to say.

Some of the techniques for promoting fluency, which we presented in Chapter 3, might be used to help Maxine elaborate her idea, that "all creatures return to familiar places they call 'home,' where their activity goes on." Olga might now ask Maxine to make a *list* of the questions that she asked herself about Eiseley's first paragraph and add further questions, such as "Why do the men seek the same seat in the station?" and "Why do the wasps return to the hive?" These questions could form a *matrix* for analyzing the other homecomings Eiseley describes in the rest of his essay. Maxine could control her analysis of the various "homes" by asking the same questions about each of them. Or she might ask a more general question—"What is the opposite of home?"—and construct a double-entry list about the opposition. These techniques can help Maxine to avoid generating mere bulk and instead to discover more points relevant to her essay's concept (some of which she could develop in subordinate paragraphs).

Forming Concepts: Naming Connections through "HDWDWW," A Sample Essay

The language of the assignment on "The Brown Wasps" ("Explain the metaphor of the opening paragraph and its relation to Eiseley's main idea.") identifies the central idea to be developed; it directs the writer to explain and specifies exactly what to explain. Sometimes, however, an assignment may appear deceptively open. For example, it may say "Explain a change in the personality of someone you know well," leaving the writer free to choose the "someone." Yet this assignment specifies very firmly: in order to fulfill it, the writer must form a concept relating two key terms: "change" and "personality." In the draft of "Kevin" below, Brian generates a lot of bulk without yet having decided on a concept. Read the essay, then spend five minutes or so writing down your observations about the main point(s) it seems to be making. As you observe, consider these questions:

- To what extent does Brian understand and address the assignment?
- How does Brian feel about Kevin now? To what extent have his feelings changed? To what extent do they change during the writing?
- Where do you see Brian in the process of shuttling? Where does he arrive (at least tentatively) at a focus?
- What glosses might Brian use to label each paragraph?
- What, if any, glosses recur from paragraph to paragraph? How might Brian group the recurring glosses?
- How might Brian rename these groups?
- How could Brian relate these names using HDWDWW?

Only when you have finished writing your observations, continue reading our analysis. (The letters in parentheses beside the essay refer to our analysis, which follows the dialogue.) Then we will consider how HDWDWW can not only encourage fluency (as in Chapter 3) but also identify the controlling idea in a preliminary draft:

KEVIN

(a)   Kevin is as Irish as the four-leaf clover and possesses all the traits that go along with his nationality. Traits such as freckles indiscriminately dotting his face and body, the strawberry blond hair, and also the temperament. His temperament is as

(b)   flightly as a blue jay and as explosive as a stick of dynamite. There were fights that

5   I recall where logic and reason never entered the picture. Like the time when he and

(c)   his elder brother Steve, after an afternoon of football and a few hearty beers, fell into an argument over who was stronger. After push came to shove and shove went

(d)   to punch, the two of them after a moment lay practically unconscious on the living room rug exhausted. Neither would give in. The Irish are well known for their fool

10 (e)   hearted pride and their knack for flying off the handle.

    He was an energetic adolescent and could not sit still long enough to accomplish anything productive. Teachers tried endlessly to harness his strength, but found it difficult. Instead of offering understanding they enforced discipline, which of course he rebelled against. Kevin is the type of person who disrespects authority and I

15 believe that it stems from the lack of personal attention he needed from his father and also teachers. It seemed no matter how hard Kevin tried to gain his father's approval he found fault. This progressed to a point where eventually he gave up trying all together. Instead negative actions were introduced to obtain the greatly needed attention. If he couldn't do it the right way, why not find another way. After
20 many years of teacher against student, the school system finally threw in the towel and asked him to leave school. What a shame that this endless source of energy could not have been directed in a positive stream.

Kevin is now actively employed as a construction worker and enjoys it. The energy released through hard labor enables him to calm down and enjoy life. He started
25 attending night school and does quite well. TIme and age work wonders to mature a person. Hopefully Kevin with the years of hard work will find his niche in life.

. . .

If we looked at several tutors' written observations about this essay, they might resemble the proverbial blind men's descriptions of the elephant: the reactions vary according to where you touch it. As it stands, the paper includes a lot of information, but it is hard to see how the details fit together into any coherent whole. The reader winds up doing the writer's job of focusing and connecting the parts of the idea. Arnie, the tutor, needs to help Brian discover what he wants this essay to say about the topic, "how Kevin's personality changed."

Arnie could begin the tutoring session by helping Brian identify the many points the paper is making. He could try asking Brian to name the major ideas. Of course, Arnie could not give Brian his own glosses. But without prescribing answers, he could ask Brian to "gloss" each paragraph, renaming each point it makes. (If you have not already done so, please take a few minutes to write your own glosses of each paragraph.) Brian might gloss the first paragraph with something like one of these:

(a) Kevin is Irish in nationality and temperament.
(b) Kevin's typically Irish appearance indicates typically Irish temperament: flighty and explosive.
(c) Fights resulted from Kevin's Irish temperament.
(d) In a fight, neither brother would give in.
(e) Stubbornness and pride are Irish traits.

As you glossed the rest of the paper, you might have used terms such as "Kevin's energy," "Kevin's attitude toward authority," and "Kevin's feelings about work." You might have noticed that what initially absorbed so much of Brian's attention—Kevin's ethnicity—simply vanishes: it is not what Brian was really interested in after all. As this preliminary draft illustrates, a writer's focus often changes during drafting. A good tutor helps a writer notice such changes and choose his own focus. Ethnic and racial stereotypes do present an ethical problem, and later on, our tutorial dialogue will suggest one way of dealing with them. But in this paper, the problem takes care of itself as Brian gradually forms a more important idea.

➤ Once Brian has made a list of glosses, Arnie can help him sort it. Referring to your list of glosses, write down some questions you could ask the writer about them. If Arnie's first question were, "Why are you so prejudiced against Irish people?" he would certainly risk embarrassing and antagonizing Brian instead of helping him. If it were, "Are strawberry blonds as hot-tempered as redheads?" Arnie would risk evoking only a monosyllabic "yes" or "no" answer. And if it were, "What is the connection between Kevin's having *chosen* his job as a construction worker and his having been *forced* to go to school against his will?" Arnie's question would be prescriptive, that is, it would assume a connection that Brian has not made. If he reconsidered the dialogues in our earlier chapters and the questions listed above, Arnie could refine his strategy. Then the dialogue might go this way:

ARNIE: What's this essay supposed to be about?

BRIAN: About how somebody's personality changed? I'm writing about my friend Kevin.

ARNIE: Well, that says who the somebody is. What else does the assignment call
5   for?

BRIAN: I have to say how his personality changed?

ARNIE: Right. What do you think that means?

BRIAN: I have to say what he was like and what he's like now.

ARNIE: Yes . . .

10   BRIAN: Well, we've been friends for a long time. We were part of the same confirmation class, and we went to school together at St. Monica's. He liked shop and phys. ed.

ARNIE: You did a lot of things together. But I'd like to know more about what kind of guy he was. How did he act in school?

15   BRIAN: He would go to the classes, but not really pay attention. He would be fooling around, watching the clock, you know.

ARNIE: Sort of. What kind of person would you call him?

BRIAN: I'd say he was a person who got into trouble because he couldn't obey rules.

20   ARNIE: Yes, well, let's find the sentences that talk about that.

BRIAN: OK. The second paragraph starts off by telling how Kevin had trouble in school because he was too active and how he rebelled against the teachers' discipline.

ARNIE: Good. Now in the margin write a phrase than names that idea.

25   BRIAN: [writes "rebels against school authorities" beside lines 11–12.] Oh, yes. Right after that I tell about how Kevin's father neglected him and wouldn't approve of anything Kevin did. [writes "rebels against father's authority" beside lines 13–19]
       And finally, I say that Kevin just decided to get himself thrown out of
30   school, just to get some kind of attention, even bad attention. [writes "wanted negative attention" beside lines 20–22]

ARNIE: That's really good. Now I know what his personality used to be. Was there a connection between the school and his father?

BRIAN: Right here [points at line 15] I say Kevin didn't respect authority because

35   his father and teachers didn't pay enough attention to him to figure out his problems. You know. He was hyperactive. But they just called him "bad."

ARNIE: That's interesting. You say he was hyperactive. Is there a connection between that and the first paragraph?

BRIAN: Well, he used to get into a lot of fights.

40   ARNIE: This first paragraph really shows that. Let's jot down in the margin some labels for what the paragraph is talking about, OK? What would you say first?

BRIAN: Well, first I talk about his Irish looks. And then I tell about the fight, about how he just flew off the handle rather than give in.

45   ARNIE: Is there a connection between his looks and the fight?

BRIAN: Well, I guess some people think it's easier to call somebody a "typical Irishman" than to find out why he acts a certain way.

ARNIE: I get it. How could you change the first paragraph so it would state that idea more clearly?

50   BRIAN: I guess I should say something like, "My friend Kevin had a lot of trouble because of what some people call an 'Irish temperament,' but he really was hyperactive."

We are going to interrupt the dialogue here in order to examine the tutor's strategies for helping Brian form the concept of the paper. In this conversation, the tutor and writer go back to the assignment's specifications, enabling Brian to see that choosing Kevin as the subject is only the beginning. He must also explain the meanings of "personality" and "change." And he must interpret the language of the assignment: does "how" mean "in what manner" or "for what cause"? Arnie adopts the following strategy:

1. helps Brian form a concept about Kevin's personality;
2. takes Brian back to the draft to find passages that talk about that concept (paragraph two);
3. helps Brian gloss those passages;
4. in order to help Brian form a concept, asks if there is a connection among the three glosses;
5. for the same reason, asks if there is a connection between the concept formed in item 4 (rebelling against authority) and the first paragraph.

When Brian adds the new information that Kevin was hyperactive, he not only clarifies his perception of the nature of the teachers' and the father's lack of attention to Kevin, but also recognizes and rejects the ethnic stereotype that "some people" employ to explain what they do not understand.

We interrupted the dialogue before completing the assignment. The writer now needs to probe the idea of change. As the conversation continues, Arnie could ask, "Who has authority over Kevin at work? How does he feel about that? Is there any connection between school and work? What is it?" Arnie and Brian could experiment with versions of HDWDWW, adding an extra "W" column for "to whom." They could select from their dialogue some important terms and see

➤ how they could fit into various slots. Before reading further, take a few minutes to see how HDWDWW can help relate the key words "energy," "authority," and "work."

HOW	WHO	DOES	WHAT	TO WHOM	WHY
1.	energy	caused	problems	authority	
	work	provided	outlet		
2.	authority	could not channel	energy		
	work	enabled	to channel	him	
3.	Kevin	could never win	approval		
	he	rebelled		authorities	
	he	is	independent and mature		
	he	has chosen	to return		

From this speculative process, Brian could use verbs and logical connectives to relate the key terms in a predicated concept, perhaps like one of the following sentences about Kevin's traits:

1. Kevin's energy *caused* problems with authority *in* school, *but* work *provided* a constructive outlet.
2. The authority of his father and of his teachers could not *channel* Kevin's energy, *but* work has *enabled* him to channel it himself.
3. *Because* Kevin could never win his father's approval, he *rebelled against* school authorities; *however, now that* he is *more* independent and mature, he has *chosen* to return to school.

From the large amount of material Brian generated in his preliminary draft, Arnie has helped Brian use HDWDWW, specific verbs (e.g., "caused," "has enabled," "has chosen"), and logical connectors (e.g., "but," "however," "because," "now that") to express how the key terms are related in a concept both requiring and worthy of demonstration.

Heuristics and Speculative Play

Earlier we said a "heuristic" is a tool. But it is less a shovel than a tennis racket or a pool cue. It is an implement of intellectual play. *Playing* is a means to discovery. Experienced writers turn ideas over in their minds before settling down to see how one idea works out, and even then the working out is tentative. Another, more interesting one may pop up when the writer least expects it, just as Isaac Asimov shows in his widely anthologized essay, "The Eureka Phenomenon." But the less experienced writer, anxious for the paper to be worked out and finished, may be reluctant to play, to try various ways of shaping his paper. Writing has to be, everyone knows, *work!* And by refusing to play, by trying—too hard, too soon—to grasp a workable idea, the inexperienced writer may short-circuit his own discovery processes. The result may be insincere and superficial, a cliché instead of an idea the writer cares about. On the other hand, speculatively playing with various heuristics both helps shape meaning from a writer's preliminary thinking and reduces anxiety.

Summary

Writers who can generate ideas may not yet have learned how to shape an essay into a unified whole. Often they ramble instead of developing an idea in depth. In their essays, you may find kernels of ideas scattered amid extraneous bulk. These writers need to learn how to shape the still amorphous material of preliminary drafts by forming concepts, statements that require demonstration and that name relationships among ideas. The relationships named indicate the kind of development an essay requires.

You can help a writer learn how to form concepts by freewriting and by glossing. A writer who is uncertain about how to discuss a given topic can generate ideas associatively, randomly, and then can identify kernel ideas or patterns among his sentences. These ideas can become the bases for developed essays. That second, reflective step in freewriting resembles glossing, in which a writer reads his preliminary draft, names central ideas and connections among ideas, discards digressions, and unifies his essay. You can recommend that when writers gloss, they ask themselves such questions as, "What have I said?" "How many ideas are in this passage?" "What is the gist?" "What should/does this paragraph do?" and "HDWDWW?" By suggesting that writers reflect on their initial thinking, you help them give form to their essays.

SUGGESTIONS FOR JOURNAL ENTRIES

1. If you are about to begin writing a paper, construct a movable outline (a descriptive outline, storyboard, or issue tree) for it. To what extent does this technique help you generate and analyze ideas?

2. If you have introduced someone to freewriting, describe your presentation of both the generative and critical stages. What does the writer seem to have learned from your instruction?

3. If you have worked with someone who resists freewriting, explain how you have attempted to address this resistance.

4. If you have used glossing and HDWDWW to help a writer form a main idea and shape an essay developing it, describe your strategies and comment on which worked best for your tutorial.

SUGGESTIONS FOR FURTHER WRITING

1. Collect the observations you have just written about "Kevin," "The Train Station," and "My Florida Vacation." Gloss your own observations to discover HDWDWW—"How have you observed what about which essay and why?"

a. Make a list of the kinds of observations you have made about each paper.

b. Now rename and group your observations and write some sentences about the patterns you find.

c. How does one set resemble and differ from others? What changes do you discover as you progress through your observations on the three sample papers? Write three paragraphs about the resemblances, differences, and kinds of progression you find.

2. Write a completion of one of our two opening dialogues for tutoring the writer of "The Train Station." Or write a third complete dialogue of your own, following different initial responses. Exchange your dialogue with other tutors and write a paragraph analyzing the strategy you observe in operation. Write another paragraph in which you imagine what could go wrong with that strategy and suggest alternatives.

3. Here is another paper in search of an idea. The assignment is the same as before: "Explain a change in the personality of someone you know well." After you read it, spend ten minutes writing your observations about it, looking for the main ideas and considering the questions we provided to guide your observations on "Kevin." Do not try to begin planning strategies for tutoring yet!

NANNA

Nanna is a weak eighty-eight years old. Her real name is Mary, but the generation I come from grew up calling her Nanna. When I was growing up Nanna was a character seen often playing ball with the kids, or telling scary stories by the roadside. Of course, Nanna and myself go back a long way.

5 As I said in the opening, Nanna is eighty-eight years old. In more recent months her health has been deteriorating rapidly. It is really a bad feeling to know that one of your "oldest" friends has already lived her life and is all but waiting around to die.

Years ago, Mary's smile would have spread from cheek to cheek, yet today a smile only comes with great effort. I can remember her laugh which would echo in my ears and make me laugh. The
10 more Nanna laughed the more we all would laugh, and soon find ourselves with sore stomachs and watery eyes.

I can remember when Nanna caught me smoking, I must have been thirteen or fourteen years old. She sat me down and lit two cigarettes, and asked me if I wanted one. I respectfully thanked her anyway. As Mary stared at me I could tell by the look in her eyes that she really did care for
15 me. Before she could say one word I told her that I would never smoke again. But, Nanna corrected me by saying that I should never smoke until I could fully understand the dangers of the act. Here was an eighty-year-old lady talking to a fourteen-year old boy, as I look back, today, into her staring, caring eyes I can truly appreciate what a wonderful lady she really is.

When I come home from work, I frequently see Nanna sitting at her window watching TV, watching
20 the kids play, and I suppose, watching life go ever so slowly by. On many occasions, I have gone over to her house, which is right across the street from my own, and offered my company, which is always gratefully accepted. On Sundays, when Nanna is in the yard I often will go over and reminisce with her about times of the past, present, and times still to come. She is always a great one to talk to. She likes baseball in general, but loves the Celtics, and could make any preacher late for
25 mass talking about them.

I'm sorry to think that someday, in the not too distant future, Nanna's window will be empty, except for my memories of her. But now, while I have her I will continue to cherish her, for not too often in life does one find a true friend.

Now that you have completed your written observations, here are some questions to help you tutor Nicholas, the author of "Nanna," by applying some of the strategies discussed in this and earlier chapters.

i. Answer the following questions:

a. To what extent does Nicholas understand and address the assignment?

b. Where do you see Nicholas in the process of shuttling? Where does he arrive (at least tentatively) at a focus?

c. What glosses might Nicholas use to label each paragraph?

d. What, if any, glosses recur from paragraph to paragraph? How might Nicholas group these glosses?

e. How might Nicholas rename these groups?

f. How could Nicholas use HDWDWW to experiment with relating them?

ii. Make a list of questions you might ask in a tutoring session.

iii. Frame a dialogue, alternating your questions with the responses you expect from Nicholas. If you anticipate more than one possible response, let your dialogue branch (like the one between Olga and Maxine about "The Train Station").

4. Supposing that Joni comes to you for help with her assignment, but that she has not yet written anything. Write a dialogue illustrating how you might use problem-solving strategies to help her "shuttle" among concepts. Then write a paragraph explaining your rationale for asking the questions in the order you have devised.

SUGGESTIONS FOR CLASS ACTIVITIES

1. Compare your dialogue for tutoring Nicholas with those of your classmates.

2. Compare your dialogue and rationale for tutoring Joni (exercise 4 above) with those of your classmates.

3. Write a dialogue showing how you might help either Joni or Dinah (in Chapter 4) to construct a movable outline *before* beginning to write. Compare your strategy with those of your classmates.

SUGGESTIONS FOR FURTHER READING

Berthoff, Ann E. *Forming, Thinking, Writing.* Rochelle Park, NJ: Hayden, 1978. 46–79, 112–187.
————. *The Making of Meaning.* Upper Montclair, NJ: Boynton/Cook, 1981. 61–84.
Brannon, Lil. *Writers Writing.* Upper Montclair, NJ: Boynton/Cook, 1982. 76–100.
Cowan, Gregory, and Elizabeth Cowan. *Writing.* Glenview, IL: Scott, Foresman, 1980.
DiNitto, Dennis. *Film: Form and Feeling.* New York: Harper and Row, 1985. 13–29.
Elbow, Peter. *Writing Without Teachers.* New York: Oxford University Press, 1973.
Flower, Linda. *Problem-Solving Strategies for Writing.* New York: Harcourt Brace Jovanovich, 1981.
Fulwiler, Toby. "The Personal Connection: Journal Writing across the Curriculum." *Language Connections.* Urbana, IL: NCTE, 1982. 15–31.
Horton, Susan R. *Thinking Through Writing.* Baltimore: The Johns Hopkins University Press, 1982. 69–77.
Irmscher, William F. *Teaching Expository Writing.* New York: Holt, Rinehart and Winston, 1979. 94–106.
Murray, Donald M. *A Writer Teaches Writing.* 2nd. ed. Boston: Houghton, Mifflin, 1985.
Schwartz, Mimi. "Revision Profiles: Patterns and Implications." *College English* 45 (1983): 549–558.
Shahn, Ben. *The Shape of Content.* Cambridge, MA: Harvard University Press, 1957.
Shaughnessy, Mina P. *Errors and Expectations.* New York: Oxford University Press, 1977. 226–274.
Sommers, Nancy. "Revision Strategies of Student Writers and Experienced Adult Writers." *College Composition and Communication* 31 (1980): 378–387.

6

Committing Oneself to a Concept

Specifically formulated writing assignments (like those on "The Brown Wasps" and on personality change in Chapter 5) challenge writers to fulfill very definite goals. But assignments are often more open-ended; they may merely announce a general topic, such as "Write a five-paragraph paper about a problem you have observed and a solution you propose for it" or "Write a six-page paper describing an educational experience." As we saw in the dialogue between Tran and Joni in Chapter 5, the *apparent* freedom from specifications has a catch: choosing one's own specifications is absolutely necessary but seldom easy. As we explained in Chapters 4 and 5, experienced writers know how to use terms in an assignment in order to form a concept that controls or unifies the essay. Less experienced writers, however, may simply fill the paper by aimlessly "discussing" and "describing" for six pages or may half-heartedly assert one concept here and another there, leaving the reader wondering just what the writer does think. That is, the discussion or description asserts no overall point, substantiates no *central* position. Chapter 6 will treat the major problem writers experience with open-ended assignments: failure to form a concept requiring and deserving the writer's intellectual commitment.

Predication and Intellectual Commitment

In Chapter 5, we explained that a concept is "predicated," that it says something about something by asserting a relationship between or among parts. We also said that a concept, unlike a factual statement, requires the writer to demonstrate the truth it asserts. Thus, a concept requires a writer to take a stand and to substantiate it through subordinate paragraphs developing a series of relationships among ideas. For instance, "Many college students in the 1960's opposed U.S. intervention in Vietnam" is a bare fact—expressing no point of view, asserting no relationship between ideas, hence receiving and indeed *requiring* no intellectual commitment from the writer. In contrast, the sentence, "Economic security enabled college students in the 1960's to spend their time demonstrating against the war in Vietnam instead of studying" does treat facts—the fact of relative economic security, the fact of student antiwar demonstrations—from a point of view. It asserts a relationship between them: security *enabled* students to demonstrate. This assertion is arguable. For instance, some people would object, "Antiwar activists sacrificed their careers to the cause of political justice." Whoever asserts either of these concepts must take a stand, must defend the point of view it expresses.

Before we turn to specific papers, we need to examine some causes for writers' lack of willingness to take a stand, for we believe that it does *not* come from intellectual laziness or irresponsibility. William E. Coles has argued that educational institutions teach people to write impersonally and to be wary of taking a definite stand on an issue; he believes particularly that open-ended assignments themselves are unengaged, and that in response to them writers produce writing with the least possible personal engagement. Be that as it may, tutors can change institutions very little and very gradually. Meanwhile, when you converse with writers, you can immediately address what we see as two causes for lack of engagement, one external and one internal: the wording of open-ended assignments themselves, and the writer's diffidence.

Why Open-Ended Assignments Make Commitment Especially Difficult

The wording of open-ended assignments

Even with the clearly specified assignments we have dealt with in earlier chapters, writers can produce unpredicated papers. But the more open-ended an assignment is, the less it specifies its terms and their relations, the more the writer must do so. The simplest way for a tutor to find out more about an open-ended assignment is to ask the professor to provide more direction. You might ask, "Could you tell me what you had in mind for this assignment?" Such a question prevents the sort of conflict that can arise if you independently alter a topic. Further, this kind of tactful question can be helpful to instructors who may not be aware that their students are stymied by general assignments. Most importantly, what you can do by using the strategies in this chapter is help writers learn how to limit a topic, how to predicate, and thus, how to respond effectively to open-ended assignments.

The writer's diffidence

The writer's diffidence is harder to deal with than the wording of the open-ended assignment. By "diffidence," we mean reluctance to take a stand, to assert an idea that *needs* to be substantiated. Sometimes diffidence arises out of the feeling that one lacks the authority or expertise to take a position. For instance, a student in an economics course might be assigned a paper assessing the Federal Reserve's monetary policy during the first Reagan Administration. The student could present plenty of bare facts about how the Fed's control of the money supply affected interest rates. But she might feel unqualified to take a stand on so complex and widely debated a question as the extent to which the Fed's policies benefited or harmed the national economy. She might say to herself, "If all those expert economists at the White House can't figure it out, how can I?" Sometimes diffidence arises from seeing several sides to an issue and not knowing which to take. Another student writing on this assignment might see the "national economy" from several perspectives: a carpenter was laid off when high interest rates slowed housing starts; a young couple hoping to buy their first house could not qualify for a mortgage; an investor increased her tax shelter through higher mortgage interest deductions; an American in Europe enjoyed the increased buying power of the dollar, and so on. The Fed's policy harmed some people and benefited others. The writer might ask himself, "How can I add up all these individuals' losses and gains? How can I take a stand on how they affected the national economy?" Diffidence, whether from lacking expertise or from seeing several sides, can make writers cling to the facts and avoid taking stands, forming concepts.

Diffidence may also result in indecision about choosing an appropriate subject. Writers may prefer to be told what to write about rather than to face the anxieties of choosing their own subjects. Selecting a subject for an open-ended assignment, such as "Write a paper about a problem and solution," may seem easy at first. But Leslie, a management major, told her tutor how she had tried several subjects in the process of searching for one she felt relatively comfortable in writing about. She happened to save her first attempt at drafting a paper about a personal problem. It illustrates what can happen when a writer lacks confidence to take a stand:

> I can't get enough time in the computer lab. In the morning, I have to get my kids to school. Then my classes meet back to back, and then I have to hurry home to meet my daughter's school bus. On the weekends I have a part-time job, so my only chance to get at a computer terminal is if I come back to campus in the evenings.
> 5   And that's the only time I get to spend with my family. I'm going to flunk this math course!
>
> I don't actually want to become a computer scientist, but I think knowing something about programming will help me in management. A manager needs to be able to talk with the computer department, to explain the kinds of information the clients need,
> 10   etc. Even in my part-time job entering data at the bank. . . .

Leslie abandoned the draft here, because she didn't know what to say next. She hesitated to air her personal problems to a relative stranger like her professor, who (she surmised) never had similar worries. She also felt anxious about reading her paper aloud in class: the other students might think she was just asking for sympathy. Although assumptions are often erroneous (like her assumptions that professors always live on Easy Street and that classmates are heartless competitors), they often discourage writers from revealing themselves in writing about their personal problems. Finally, she rejected what she had written because it did not fit the assignment: she had no solution (see line 5). Like many writers, she felt that unless she could offer a simple, clear solution to the problem, she had better not bring it up. Writing about personal problems seemed to be a dead end.

Then she began to ask herself, "What does the *professor* think is an important problem?'' Since Leslie hardly knew her professor, it was hard to say. He would probably be interested in something like, ''Did Shakespeare really write *Hamlet?*''—but that was not a problem she had observed, nor could she even begin to propose a solution. The professor was, she thought, probably also interested in the subjects of recent class discussions, but it would be hard to say something that other students had not already said. So writing about the professor's interests was another dead end. This time, she had not even begun a draft.

Finally, she grasped at a familiar social problem she had often heard discussed and had herself observed: urban violence. Unlike the subjects she had already considered, it was not too personal, not too trivial, not too scholarly, and not already ''used up'' in class discussion. Leslie showed her tutor, Kim, the following draft. Spend a few minutes writing down your observations about what it seems to be saying. As you observe, consider these questions:

- To what extent are the problem and solution ''canned''?
- How, and how clearly, does the writer define ''violence''?
- Exactly what happened on the train? What is the point?
- What solution(s) is/are proposed?
- How do ''statistics'' relate to the proposed solutions?

Only when you have finished writing your observations, continue reading our analysis.

VIOLENCE IN THE CITIES

(a)   Violence in the cities today is very common. Some is due to crime both organized and unorganized. Other violence occurs naturally in the streets. Frequently, such violence results in severe injury or even death. In order to control this growing problem it is necessary to reinstitute capital punishment.

5   (b)   Frequently, violence gets out of hand. For instance, I was on my way to work one morning on the train, right beside me there was a vacant seat, so this elderly person got on the train and made an attempt to occupy the seat, but before doing so someone else got there before he did and took the seat. Instead of getting out of the seat and let the elder person have it, when he was asked to do so by another man who saw the incident. The man who was holding the seat refused. This then started
10   the issue of who should have the seat. The argument then led to a fight, and the use of knives in the crowded train.

(c)   Innocent people got hurt, and one person was killed. I feel that if these young men knew that they would be punished for this crime, they would have controlled
15   their temper.

(d)   Statistics show that states that have reinstituted capital punishment have a thirty-percent lower crime rate. On account of this there are less crimes in the streets.

(e)   People are more willing to conduct themselves in an orderly manner when they are faced with a difficult situation. These things are hurting organized crime because
20   people are aware of this law.

. . .

In this essay, Leslie avoids taking a stand. Stating a bare fact, the opening sentence portends a string of paragraphs on murder, child abuse, rape, armed robbery, mayhem. In response to the open-ended assignment to write about a problem and solution, the first paragraph tries to *cover* a lot of possibilities without taking a stance or defending a choice. This attempt to consider many kinds of violence may indicate that Leslie recalls hearing discussions of "organized crime" and "street crime" but has not thought them through in relation to the incident she experienced. She thinks that if some crime is "organized," then some crime must be "unorganized," but that it differs from "other" violence occurring in the streets. Leslie offers no justification for recommending *capital* punishment, as distinct from some other kind of punishment. Feeling that she lacks expert knowledge *and* seeing the issue from so many sides, the writer feels diffident and fails to commit herself to a concept of her own.

Such a failure is practically unavoidable in topics like urban violence and other social problems. Because they *are* so important, they have been discussed from every conceivable angle by experts and laypeople alike. So before putting a single sentence on paper, Leslie has *received* ready-made, "canned," but conflicting lines of argument. Each of these is powerfully persuasive (which is one reason why social problems remain perennially unsolved). Anxious because the assignment lacks very specific terms, she resorts to a safe but intellectually unengaging—for her—problem and solution. A clichéd response, illustrated by her personal anecdote of the incident on the train, becomes her refuge.

But the incident also raises questions: "Who used knives on whom?" and "What caused the person's death?" It is not clearly related to "organized" crime. Moreover, it is not connected to the first of the two proposed solutions: before telling the incident, Leslie recommends reinstitution of *capital* punishment (line 4), but after telling the incident, she recommends certainty of *some kind* of punishment (lines 14–15). Indeed, she seems unaware that her proposition changes. "Statistics show" (line 16) vaguely claims that capital punishment reduces the "crime rate," but does so without identifying the kinds of crime, without explaining how, when, and where the rate has been measured, without saying what is being compared in the phrase "lower than," and without supporting the claim that "less crimes in the streets" (line 17) actually results from reinstitution of capital punishment. Appealing to "statistics" or various anonymous experts is one way in which diffident writers may try to compensate for their lack of expertise and authority and to avoid taking their own stands on issues.

Salvaging an As-Yet-Uncommitted Draft

A tutor's problem is to help a diffident writer like Leslie to get beyond the "canned" social problem and clichéd response. If a writer has not succeeded, a tutor's first impulse might be to set aside the draft on the "canned" problem and start all over again. But to do so can be highly demoralizing to the writer. It tells her that she has wasted her time, that she has produced nothing of value. It might also imply that only drafts prepared with the tutor's help are worthwhile, and this idea might consequently undermine her confidence. Unless the draft is completely off the track, a tutor is much wiser to try to salvage something, to use some of the ideas that the writer has already expressed, to discover if one of them can be reformulated as a concept, or if several can serve as amplification of an as-yet-unarticulated concept.

Taking a Stand by Glossing and Dramatizing

Glossing

Glossing (see Chapter 5) can help a diffident writer to name the main idea expressed in each paragraph of a draft, to examine ways in which those ideas might be related, to identify the major proposition(s), and as a result to choose which proposition to substantiate as the essay's concept. In short, choosing one concept and taking a stand can help a writer to abide by I. A. Richards' admonition: know the proposition and stick to it (25). Leslie might gloss each paragraph of her draft something like this:

(a) Capital punishment deters violent crime.
(b) Even a trivial argument can lead to violence.
(c) Certainty of punishment deters violent crime.
(d) Statistics show capital punishment reduces street crime.
(e) Awareness of capital punishment hurts organized crime.

This list reveals that Leslie does not take a stand. Instead, she loosely strings together five statements. The list also reveals a shift in the proposition: paragraph (a) says that *capital* punishment deters crime, but in the course of drafting Leslie modifies this stance, saying in (c) that *certainty* of punishment deters crime. In tutorial dialogue, Kim could help her first to recognize the shift and then to decide what to do about it:

KIM: *[referring to gloss (a)]* Here you seem to say that capital punishment is a deterrent. Why is that?

LESLIE: Because it's so severe. I mean, the guy is afraid he'll die if he gets caught.

KIM: How is that related to what you are saying here? *[referring to gloss (c)]*

5   LESLIE: Well, here *[referring to (c)]* I guess it's not so much that he's afraid of dying. He's just pretty sure that he *will* get caught and punished.

So far, by figuring out how the glosses of paragraphs (a) and (c) might be related, Leslie more clearly recognizes the two propositions she has implied: that *severity* of punishment deters violent crime (dialogue line 3), and that *certainty* of punishment deters violent crime (lines 5–6). Having identified her two different options, she may choose which to substantiate (or seek another if neither seems worthwhile to her).

Dramatizing

Dramatizing is the technique of asking writers to imagine what people, institutions, and even nations might think, say, and do in given situations. Because it helps writers test hypotheses about interests and motives and about the probable results of alternative courses of action, dramatizing helps people decide whether or not to adopt a stand. This strategy could help Leslie test hypotheses about the incident on the train. Kim might continue the dialogue by helping Leslie speculate imaginatively about what motives might have prompted the actions on the subway.

KIM: Which do you think those guys on the subway thought?

LESLIE: They probably thought they could do whatever they wanted and nobody would dare to stop them.

10 KIM: Yes . . .

LESLIE: Yes. They knew they could get away before the transit cops got there.

Having helped Leslie to imagine what motivated the actions that actually did occur, Kim might now continue dramatizing to help her speculate about what could be done to change their actions:

KIM: So what do you think would keep them from doing something like that again?

LESLIE: They probably wouldn't worry much about capital punishment if they
15   thought they were going to get away. So I guess that certainty of punishment would be the deterrent.

KIM: Certainty of punishment would be the deterrent. That sounds sensible. Let's imagine the situation. What could the transit authority do to make sure that guys like that did get caught?

At this point, Leslie recognizes that her original proposition (that "capital punishment deters violent crime") does not really fit the situation she observed (lines 14–15). Hence, she does not want to commit herself to developing it. Instead, she decides that the second proposition (that "certainty of punishment deters violent crime") is the one she really believes in (lines 15–16). Kim repeats the proposition to help her remember it (line 17) and gives some encouragement (lines 17–18). Then, by asking what would improve the situation, Kim helps her imagine ways to ensure "certainty of punishment" (lines 18–19). Dramatizing helps the writer choose among alternative actions:

20 LESLIE: The transit authority could increase the number of transit cops. Give them better walkie-talkies. Have guards at each station. Have the city police monitor their communications, so they could get to the scene fast. Of course, all that would cost a bundle. . . .

KIM: Well, don't worry about that right now. What other people besides the transit
25   authority would have to cooperate to make sure they got caught and punished?

LESLIE: The courts! Everybody knows that by the time the lawyers are through plea-bargaining and stuff like that the guys are going to get off with a suspended sentence.

30 KIM: So the certainty of punishment depends both on the police and on the courts.

LESLIE: Yes.

KIM: Then let's draw a chart to help us keep track of each problem and who can

do what to solve it. Right across from each problem we can write what the
police and the courts could do to solve it, as you've just suggested. The
35   chart can help you substantiate your main idea.

[They begin to draw a chart.]

PROBLEMS	SOLUTION: CERTAIN PUNISHMENT	
	police	courts
kids lack self-control	make arrest certain	make jail mandatory
kids escape arrest	walkie-talkies more guards monitors	
kids escape punishment		no plea-bargaining no suspended sentences

Now that Leslie has a firmer grip on her real proposition, she can probably refine
and expand the chart on her own. In this part of the dialogue, Kim helps her
imagine how the kids (lines 12–16), the law enforcers (lines 18–23), and finally
the courts (lines 26–28) might behave. By focusing on the incident dramatically,
Leslie imagines ways of making punishment more certain, thus developing her
second proposition. Kim avoids "leading the witness" and instead simply helps
Leslie record on the chart the potential solutions she has imagined, prevents premature editing (line 24), and repeats Leslie's proposed solution to the problem
(lines 30–45). The writer's intellectual engagement now helps her avoid falling
back on platitudes.

Perhaps you have noticed that the tutorial dialogue has not yet addressed what
actually happened on the train. Leslie's account provides data about faceless people in a passive and anonymous way. She leaves the reader wondering about her
own role:

> Where was she during the fight?
>
> How did she respond?
>
> Why didn't she give her own seat to the elderly person?

Her phrase "the use of knives" (lines 11–12) makes it hard to tell exactly what
happened: if Kim were to use HDWDWW, Leslie could ask herself:

> Who used knives on whom?
>
> What exactly was the result?
>
> Did the victim die of knife wounds or other causes?
>
> How were the "innocent" people harmed?

Kim wisely helped Leslie commit herself to a proposition *before* inviting elaboration on these questions. If Leslie had begun to generate additional circumstantial
detail before making her choice, discerning the propositions and choosing between
them would have been much harder. However, having chosen which to defend,
she is now ready to clarify these other questions:

KIM: I'd like to find out more about what happened on the train.

LESLIE: Well, the man who wanted the young guy to give up the seat to the old man was wearing a three-piece suit and carrying a briefcase. He kind of ordered the young guy to mind his manners, if you know what I mean. Like
50   the young guy and his friend were scum.

KIM: Yes. . .

LESLIE: He was really pushy. So the young guys just wanted to give him a run for his money, at first. But you know how those things go. Pretty soon they all started taking the argument too seriously. That's when the guy in the suit
55   grabbed the young guy by his collar and tried to drag him out of the seat. So then his friend pulled a knife and stabbed the guy. Then they split.

In this portion of the dialogue, Leslie not only clarifies HDWDWW but also reveals her attitudes toward those involved in the incident (e.g., her dislike of the would-be rescuer's arrogance, her sympathy for the younger man). This revelation of attitude enables Kim to ask an important question directly:

KIM: Yes. Where were you all this time?

LESLIE: Right next to the young guy! At first I wasn't paying attention, but when they started to argue, you know, I just didn't want to get involved. *[pauses]*
60 KIM: *[sits quietly]*

LESLIE: You know . . . when I thought about it later, I knew I could have done better myself. I resented the way the guy in the suit talked to the kids, and I was sort of enjoying their resistance. If I hadn't been so scared of taking sides, I could have just given the old person my seat and the thing might
65   have quieted down. It just all happened so fast.

At this delicate spot in the dialogue, the tutor wisely avoids offering interpretation or judgment and instead listens as the writer examines her own responsibility:

KIM: Hmmm . . . . What do you think about it now?

LESLIE: Well, maybe by paying more attention to the people around me, I could have given the older man my seat and avoided the whole incident.

KIM: I see . . .

70 LESLIE: And if I hadn't been scared of getting involved, I might have been able to get the kid and the man in the suit to calm down.

KIM: I see what you mean. How does that relate to what you said before about the police and the courts?

LESLIE: What do you mean?

75 KIM: If I remember correctly, you said that police should make sure criminals get caught and that courts should make sure they get punished. What could a private citizen like you do?

LESLIE: Oh, yes. I should pay attention to potentially violent situations and try to prevent them. I guess avoiding incidents makes the deterrence by police and
80   courts less necessary.

Glossing and dramatizing can work reciprocally to help writers. Once glossing has helped this writer take intellectual responsibility for substantiating the assertion that "certainty of punishment deters crime," the tutorial dialogue uses dramatizing to explore and clarify the incident (lines 46–56) and *to help the writer relate it to that proposition.* By explaining her own role (lines 57–65), the writer recognizes the importance of avoiding violence. Then, by conversationally glossing their dialogue, the tutor helps her to formulate the connection between avoidance and deterrence (lines 70–80). A new proposition, that "avoiding incidents makes deterrence unnecessary" (lines 79–80), begins to emerge from the dialogue.

Applying What Has Been Learned about Commitment to Concepts

As we have said in earlier chapters, the goal of tutoring is not to *fix* a particular *product* but to help writers attain *independence* in all phases of their writing *processes.* Because it is important for writers to observe their own thought processes, there is one further step that in the long run might be even more helpful to this writer than what the dialogue has already accomplished. Even though the formulation of the new concept might seem to be a good place for Kim to end the already long tutorial conference, to become independent Leslie needs to apply what she has learned about predication to the paper as a whole. By helping her to recognize that the shift between propositions (a) and (c) is one of several shifts in her paper, Kim could alert her to a tendency in her writing and help her deal with it independently. A short dialogue could help Leslie recognize a shift in definitions resembling the shift between propositions she has already addressed:

KIM: Well, you've made your main proposition much clearer now. Do you see any other shifts in the paper?

LESLIE: Not right off. *[reads paragraph (d) aloud]* Oh-oh. I'm shifting my terms again, like before when I went from "capital" to "certain" punishment.
85   First I'm talking about the crime rate in general, but then I talk about street crimes.

KIM: Yes.

LESLIE: I feel like a dummy!

KIM: I don't think a dummy would have noticed that shift, let alone connect it
90   with the shift from "capital" to "certain." The important thing is that you're getting the idea now.

LESLIE: Yeah, I guess. You know, I don't think I ought to be using statistics. I mean, I really don't know much about them in the first place. And anyway, with my new proposition I'm not even talking about capital punishment
95   anymore.

KIM: Yes, your paper really doesn't need them now. Let's talk about how to use statistics some other time. We've done enough for one day.

LESLIE: You can say that again!

The tutor has alerted the writer to a pattern in her thinking: she tends to change terms without realizing it. Since this tendency to blur the terms and shift the proposition confuses her and the reader, Kim has helped her develop a strategy for guarding against it. (The relation between intellectual responsibility and the need for documenting the sources of these statistics will be discussed in Chapter 12.)

We would like to look back over the whole tutorial dialogue now, in order to identify the strategies by which a tutor can help a writer to work within the invisible constraints of an open-ended assignment:

SALVAGING:	Instead of setting aside the draft on a "canned" problem, the tutor searches for what is salvageable beneath its clichés.
GLOSSING:	The tutor helps the writer to use glossing to name the main point(s) of each paragraph. The tutor helps the writer to compare glosses in order to reveal the shift of proposition.
DRAMATIZING:	The tutor helps the writer imaginatively speculate on the motives and behavior of the kids, police, and courts in order to test the proposed solutions in "real life." Only after establishing this framework from what the draft already says, the tutor probes further into HDWDWW in the train incident. The tutor helps the writer to refine the proposition about "certainty of punishment' by considering her own behavior in the incident.
APPLYING WHAT HAS BEEN LEARNED ABOUT COMMITMENT TO A CONCEPT:	The tutor helps the writer find other examples of her tendency to shift terms, thus reinforcing the major point of the tutorial session: asserting and substantiating a concept.

Taking a Stand by Using Sentence-Paradigms

In "Violence in the Cities," the author's failure to take a stand on one concept can be attributed to her diffidence. However, even a writer who can establish limits for open-ended assignments and can take a stand privately may still find difficulty in expressing that concept in any essay that someone else will read. Some reasons for this reluctance may be deeply rooted in personality. But, as our colleague Neal Bruss reminds us, tutors (and writing teachers) are not qualified psychoanalysts or therapists and should avoid interpreting aloud to a writer what may or may not be the psychological motives and explanations for the writer's behavior. Such amateur interpretation does not help a person write better, and it might even be frightening or offensive. We believe that tutors do need to listen sensitively and to take silently into account the psychological factors that might underlie a writer's reluctance to take a stand. The social relations among the writer, tutor, and teacher (like the anxieties Leslie felt in writing about her personal problems and in speculating about which problems the professor might find interesting) are an example of such factors. But tutorial dialogue is most effective when it uses strategies that focus directly on writing. Sentence-paradigms are one such strategy.

Sentence-paradigms

Sentence-paradigms are helpful because they can help writers to postpone choosing which concept to substantiate. Meanwhile, they can experiment with several different ways of relating their ideas in fairly comfortable, nonthreatening ways. Paradigms drawn from familiar literary forms are particularly comfortable. The premise of Marie Ponsot and Rosemary Deen's *Beat Not the Poor Desk* is that *all* writers know literary forms. Their experiences as children listening to fables and fairy tales, as kids telling jokes, as adults enjoying folktales and family lore, all make literary forms very familiar, even if writers may not *think* they know anything about "literature." For Ponsot and Deen, the "oral tradition of literature, the seminary of structures, where the forms of written literature come from in the first place" provides writers with "whole structures" that help them shape and control the "plenteousness" of their materials (4–5). Literary "seed sentences" abstracted from these literary forms enable writers to imagine their own completely formed (though not yet completely developed) essays. Some "seed sentences" coordinate ideas:

> "Once I was _____, but now I am _____."
>
> "They say that _____, but my experience shows that _____."
>
> "You can do it another way, but you can also do it this way."

Other "seed sentences" subordinate one idea to another:

> "When I saw the fork just ahead in the road, I saw this instead of that."
>
> "In this dilemma or crisis, I turned to this tradition or principle."

This list is by no means exhaustive. Perhaps you may want to take a few minutes and write out some of your own "seed sentences" from oral or written literature—fairy tales, fables, folktales, romantic quests, or tragedies or comedies.

Experimenting with sentence-paradigms can help writers reach decisions on issues about which they are deeply perplexed, and it can ease their misgivings about how readers may respond. Lawrence's paper, "School and Me," written in response to another open-ended assignment, "Write a paper describing an educational experience," illustrates how both indecision and doubt may interfere with a writer's commitment to a concept. After reading it, please write down your observations, taking the following questions into consideration:

- What does the topic's phrase, "an experience," invite a writer to describe?
- How does this writer interpret "an experience"?
- What problem did he encounter at school? Where does he name it?
- What attitude(s) toward the other students does the paper express?
- What does the writer say he has learned?

Please read our analysis only after you have finished reading the paper and writing your observations.

SCHOOL AND ME

It can be thought of as a learning experience when an individual experiences a situation where he can benefit or learn a lesson from a particular situation. The situation that I experienced or that I was involved in concerned "prejudice" in grade school.

5   First I will present an overview of grade school and how the people were like there and that I will discuss experience and ideas in dealing with prejudice.

Most of the students functioned the same way. They thought the same way. They performed certain activities in the same manner. Also, everyone was somewhat fast-paced which was difficult for me. I had to do the same thing everyone else did,
10   which seemed easier for them, but somewhat harder for me.

At one time a couple of students in my fifth grade class were fighting. This always happens sooner or later since boys like to be tough. Whether it concerned me or not (and it never did), I always tended to my own affairs when a dispute was in session. I was very attentive and hardworking. This is what distinguished me from some of
15   the disruptive or noisy pupils. Everyone liked me and liked them. However, there always existed a few bullies who found me rather unacceptable or they just didn't like my being around. The main reason why these bullies didn't like me was because of the fact that I was different. Different in terms of being darker than they were. I was black and therefore I was offended and intimidated against by the use of slang
20   or vulgar language. I thought that such distasteful language was unforgivable, and I imagine that some of the nicer people in class who knew me well didn't enjoy hearing the vulgarities either because they knew who was being offended.

Nevertheless I tried to ignore bad comments that were made against me. Apologies were made to me by those who seriously offended me.
25   Looking back at the terrible experiences I had to put up with I felt extremely unpleasant. I just couldn't bear such terrible words that were insulting to me.

Now that I think about the traumas and tribulations I experienced, I learned that I would undergo similar events as I did in grade school time and time again. I also learned that prejudice is everywhere and there is no way you can possibly control it.
30   There's no way you can prevent a person from expressing the way he or she psychologically feels about you. There are people who think this way who are everywhere and you have to accept them one way or another. They are a part of society, in a way, and they are not. They are part of society in that they exist. However, I like to think of such people as not being part of society simply because of the way in
35   which they prejudge different people.

At any rate, prejudice is everywhere and it will never go away.

As far as prejudice furthering my development as a person is concerned, I've come to understand the impact of this bias. How? I recall some of the bad experiences I had as a child and some that I have had recently and I've learned to cope with them.
40   All these pressures stick in my mind and I will never forget them. That is how much of an influence, a psychological influence, it has had none. Another influence I've had is thinking or hoping that someday prejudice would fade away or suddenly become extinct. Prejudice has made me believe that hatred toward another human being is in itself an unforgiveable feeling to have in oneself.
45   In conclusion, as I look back at all my classes in grade school, I would not think of them as a forgive and forget situation. I only hope that I run into people like that less often and that someday prejudice will be stopped completely.

· · ·

This draft offers much to be salvaged. It already begins to form a concept about the open-ended assignment by implicitly defining "educational experience." While some people might restrict "educational" exclusively to "book-learning" and formal education, Lawrence focuses on the lessons learned informally through all kinds of experiences. And while "experience" could mean a particular event (such as donating blood or hitchhiking to Florida), a customary activity from which one learns something (like stamp collecting or reading the sports page), or an ongoing series of events (such as taking sailing lessons or working in a political campaign), he clearly chooses an ongoing series of events in school. Having chosen his definitions of "educational" and "experience," Lawrence nevertheless stops far short of taking a definite stand. Readers wonder, "What did he experience in the course of those events? And what did he learn?"

➤ Helping Lawrence define the "what" requires special tact from David, his tutor. Please take a few minutes to write down some reasons you think might account for the fact that although he mentions prejudice early (line 3), it takes him nearly one-third of the draft just to name it, and even then he approaches it very obliquely in three sentences:

> because of the fact that I was different. Different in terms of being darker than they were. I was black and therefore I was offended and intimidated against. . . .
>
> (lines 18–20)

. . .

Perhaps the reluctance to say directly "I learned about racial prejudice" indicates that the whole experience is still too painful, too "hot" for Lawrence to touch. After all, any of the commonly discussed social problems may be particularly painful for a writer who has experienced them personally. He might also be wary: how does he know whether or not the teacher and tutor are racists too? David might try to assess Lawrence's willingness to express his private feelings publicly, in writing that will be read by relative strangers:

DAVID: It sounds as if you've really had a tough time with this problem.

LAWRENCE: Well, sort of.

DAVID: You must have been about ten or eleven at the time those bullies were after you. *[points to line 11]* How do you feel about them now that you're
5   older?

LAWRENCE: *[after a long pause]* You mean *you* think I ought to get over it?

David has tried in the dialogue to elicit a statement about what Lawrence learned from the experience, but the attempt has failed. Despite David's supportive restatement of the "tough time" and interest in further information, Lawrence seems defensive, as if he expects David either not to care or not to understand. Lawrence's tone of voice, facial expression, body language, as well as the kind of rapport that has been established between them will all influence David's decision whether or not to pursue this topic now or to set it aside until some time when Lawrence may feel less sensitive about it. The continuing dialogue might use strategies we have discussed in earlier chapters to build rapport and assess the writer's commitment to writing about this experience now:

DAVID: No, I don't mean that. Who am I to say how you ought to feel? I don't know if I would get over it. I remember how I felt when kids picked on me because I was short. I just wonder what that experience is like for you now,
10   when you look back on how they acted.

LAWRENCE: Well, part of me wants to just forget it. I'm out of that school now. I haven't seen any of those guys in ten years So it seems kind of useless to be carrying around a lot of bitterness.

DAVID: I can see that. How about the other part of you?

15 LAWRENCE: Well . . . I don't know.

DAVID: *[pauses]*

LAWRENCE: I'll bet they haven't changed. They're probably going around making other people just as miserable as they made me. You know, making remarks, intimidating people on the job, protecting their "property values,"
20 getting ready to teach their kids to hate. So when I think about that, I get mad all over again. Who do they think they are, anyway?

DAVID: Yes, I think I can understand that.

David's strategies for salvaging—giving support, probing the writer's current attitudes toward his experience, sharing similar experiences of his own—help Lawrence overcome his reluctance to name the problem. If these strategies had not worked, David might help Lawrence select a different, less touchy subject. But the dialogue above shows that this is an experience with which the writer feels strongly engaged and able to talk about freely with the tutor. It need not be put away for the future.

If such a writer were able to overcome his reluctance, glossing could help him choose among possible concepts. David could ask him to gloss each paragraph (as Leslie and Kim did in their dialogue about "Violence in the Cities"); Lawrence could readily identify these contradictory propositions in his paper:

(a) Prejudice is everywhere and it will never go away (line 36).
(b) Someday prejudice will be stopped completely (lines 46–47).

Sentence-paradigms used heuristically could help him break the stalemate. But David must use care to avoid making the paradigms prescriptive. For example, if he were to select a paradigm arbitrarily and urge Lawrence to draft an essay to fit it, he would be putting the form before the function. The resulting paper might appear completely formed, but only by chance would it express genuine commitment. However, the draft of "School and Me" already contains some stories: Lawrence shows himself vaguely trying to keep up with others' "somewhat fast-paced" activities (paragraph three), avoiding fights and suffering insults (paragraph four), and receiving apologies (paragraph five). The dialogue could explore these stories by using "seed sentences." The tutor might begin by asking the writer to elaborate on the contradictory propositions he has identified:

DAVID: Well, would you say some more about those two ideas?

LAWRENCE: *[pauses]* I guess I *hope* prejudice will go away, but I don't really
25 *think* it will. I used to hope that somehow prejudice would disappear. Maybe somebody like Martin Luther King would persuade people that it was wrong, you know. But the more I experienced it, the more I realized that some people would never change. So I was just going to have to cope with it.

Hearing the familiar "seed sentence" in which the writer tells his story, the tutor uses that sentence-paradigm to help him try taking one stand:

DAVID: You say you used to hope prejudice would disappear, but now you know
30 it won't entirely, so you'll have to cope with it. Maybe if we get that idea down, it can help you figure out how you changed your mind.

LAWRENCE: *[writes, "I used to hope prejudice would disappear, but now I know I'll have to cope with it."]*

DAVID: That sounds like a basic storytelling form.

35   *[writes "Once I . . . , but now I . . . ."]*

Maybe you could use it to express the various ways in which you've changed your mind. Are there other "once I was" or "once I thought" ideas in the paper?

LAWRENCE: Yes, I guess there are. I mean, I used to try to keep up with the fast
40   kids. *[points to lines 8–9]* And I used to try to avoid fights. *[points to lines 12–14]*

DAVID: Right. How about writing them in a chart?

LAWRENCE: OK. *[He makes the following chart.]*

	Once I _____,	but now I _____.
45	hoped prejudice would just disappear	know I have to cope with it
8–9	tried to keep up with fast-paced kids	
12	tried to avoid fights	

50   Let's see . . . I used to hope hard work would make people like me. *[points to line 14]* And that vulgar language was a terrible thing. *[points to line 20]* I've changed my mind about both now that I'm older. *[adds these to his chart]*

14	hoped working hard would make people	
55	like me.	
20	thought vulgar language was unforgive-able	

DAVID: Good. Each of these tells about "before" your learning experience. How might you fill in the "after"?

60 LAWRENCE: It was the language that really expressed the racial prejudice. Let's see, "Once I *thought vulgar language was unforgiveable,* but now I . . . ."

DAVID: *[after a pause]* How do you feel now when you hear racial slurs?

LAWRENCE: Now I just think, "I pity anybody who has to carry around all that
65   hatred." Hey! I said that here. *[points to lines 43–44]* That's the other half of the sentence: ". . . , but now I feel sorry for those who use vul-garities." About work, I could say, ". . . , but now I know people like me for myself and not just for my grades." I get it.

[fills in the chart]

70	hoped working hard would make people like me	know people will like me for myself, not my grades
20	thought vulgar language was unforgive-able	feel sorry for those who express hatred by using it

Wow, thanks a lot. That really helped. I'll just continue filling this chart
75   in at home and write it up.

While Lawrence's statement of *what* he learned might seem to be a conclusion to the session, we can think of two good reasons for not ending the dialogue yet: (1) he has not yet fully formed his concept, and (2) he has not fully enough explored sentence-paradigms and their uses.

This writer is now feeling what writers often experience: happiness at having solved one part of a problem often makes people overlook remaining problems, makes them want to rush ahead and "get it over with." Whereas Lawrence once did not commit himself to one concept because of perplexities, he now does not do so because he mistakenly thinks he has solved all his problems. Therefore, David's decision to end the tutorial session now might encourage Lawrence to short-circuit the whole process.

In order to help him fully address the assignment by relating *how* he learned to *what* he learned, David could ask questions about the experiences that made Lawrence change his mind about the various "before and after" sentences he has listed in his chart. For instance, David could ask, "Why did you realize that people wouldn't like you just for your high grades?" or "What made you start feeling sorry for people who use racist slurs?" These questions would expand the "once . . . , but now" sentence-paradigm used earlier: "Once I _____, but now I _____, because _____." Lawrence might add a "because" column to the chart he has already begun. Since Chapters 3 and 4 have already presented ways of generating ideas, we will not include further demonstrations here.

The second reason for continuing the dialogue, either immediately or at another session if time is running short, is to allow fuller exploration of sentence-paradigms and their uses. This exploration is crucial. No *one* paradigm is appropriate to every assignment; the only way to assess which form most satisfactorily relates the ideas the writer is working with is to try out a few. We know of writers who have learned to use one paradigm and who cling to it ever after, no matter how inappropriate it might be to a given assignment or how unrewarding its repetition might become. For example, some people feel very comfortable writing in the fable form (see Ponsot and Deen, Chapter 2), a dramatic dialogue followed by an aphorism:

> Two people/creatures were having this dialogue _____, when this change/crisis interrupted them _____; afterwards, their dialogue continued _____: the moral of the story is _____.

While this paradigm would be useful for paper assignments requiring writers to draw generalizations based on events, fable enthusiasts might try to convert every assignment into an anecdote with a moral. In their hands, a paper assignment requiring analysis of commuter rail service might become a personal anecdote:

> Our train was inching along the track when we saw a terrible automobile accident, and *we realized we would rather arrive late than not at all.*

The "moral" of this fable (italicized) falls short of the analysis required by the assignment. The fable paradigm would not help a writer to generalize, perhaps augmenting the sentence this way: ". . . not at all: commuter rail service is slow, but relatively safe.'' Clearly, any sentence-paradigm can hinder as much as help. Moreover, unless writers have a number of paradigms in their repertoire, they are likely to misuse paradigms as empty rhetorical forms to be filled mechanically, instead of as heuristics to help in choosing among several possible predications. Since exploring two or three paradigms is time-consuming, tutors might want to avoid introducing just one near the end of a session and instead try to devote a whole session to introducing several of them.

Assuming that enough time remains in their session, David could help Lawrence to address the whole assignment and refine the central concept to which he will commit himself in the essay. They might also explicitly examine the heuristic value of paradigms:

DAVID: We *have* made a lot of progress. But since we still have some time left to work together, why don't we try a couple of other storytelling forms? We might find one that's more appropriate than this one.

LAWRENCE: You think this one's no good?

80 DAVID: No, I don't think that. But how do we know there isn't a better one unless we shop around a little? You can always come back to this one.

LAWRENCE: Well, OK.

DAVID: Speaking of shopping around makes me think of stories about making choices. You know this one, I'm sure.

85 [writes ''When I saw this fork in the road _____, I saw this _____ instead of that _____''

LAWRENCE: Hey, I could use that one too. It really expresses why avoiding fights was so important to me.
[writes, ''When I saw that I could fight the bullies or ignore them, I saw that
90 fighting would be degrading while nonviolence would maintain my self-respect'']

DAVID: How would that idea look if you wrote it in the ''Once . . . , but now . . .'' form?

LAWRENCE: [writes ''Once I just avoided fights, but now I'm totally committed to
95 nonviolence as a way of life'']

DAVID: Which expresses the relationship of your ideas better?

LAWRENCE: Well, I guess ''once/now'' just expresses the *fact* that I changed, but the ''fork in the road'' really gets at the reasons for choosing. So the ''fork'' is better. Wow, this is great. What other stories have you got?

Lawrence now realizes that trying a second or third paradigm does not endanger the results of his work with the first. Moreover, he now sees the value of shopping around in order to find a means of relating his ideas that is not merely adequate (as the ''once/now'' paradigm now seems) but precise and forceful (like the ''fork''). The tutor might offer one or two more ''seed sentences,'' depending on time available and the writer's interest. However, laying out a large array might tempt the writer to ''fill in the blanks'' with lots of new ideas, instead of using the paradigms as heuristics for relating ideas already in the draft. Either of the two sentences Lawrence has come up with could be used as the basic concept for a paper about his "educational experience." Other paradigms could be introduced at subsequent tutorials.

Many papers, of course, combine storytelling with other modes. The second half of "School and Me" (lines 27–47), for instance, analyzes the narrative of the first half. For analytical papers, sentence-paradigms that use logical rather than narrative connections might be more useful. Such "workhorse sentences" (Berthoff, 79–83) use logical connectives to relate single words or groups of words:

LIST   AND   RENAME   "_____, _____, _____:
_____."

Pizza, tacos, croissants: I adore ethnic calories.

We shovel snow, we hack ice, we chop wood for the stove: the Minnesota winter keeps us in shape.

CAUSE/EFFECT   "If _____, then _____."
"Because _____, _____."

If you pass the final security clearance, then you'll get an exciting job in North Africa.

Because you went to the Russian embassy to practice for the language exam, you made the security interviewers suspicious.

COMPARE/CONTRAST   "Just as _____, so _____;
but if you consider_____, then _____."

Just as dance movies depend on music, so they enrich record companies; but if you consider how popular TV videos have become, then you'll realize that movies are less important to the record companies than they used to be.

Just as musicians often depend on social contacts to find gigs, so they form a tight-knit community; but if you consider how competitive the music business is, then you'll understand why they also experience a lot of isolation.

DIFFERENCE/LIKENESS   "However _____, _____."

However individualistic cats are, they all love bossing people around.

SPECIFIC/GENERAL   "_____; _____."

My jade plant looks overwatered; succulents thrive on benign neglect.

ADDITION/AUGMENTATION   "Not only _____, but also _____."

Not only do star athletes like Magic Johnson and Kareem Abdul-Jabbar get fans out of their armchairs and into the basketball arenas, but also they make the networks compete for TV coverage.

Instead of exploring more "seed sentences," David might want to help Lawrence form some concepts by using these "workhorse sentences":

100 DAVID: Let's look over the glosses you made for the rest of the paper and see whether there are any other contradictions like the one you found earlier, about whether prejudice would fade away or last forever.

LAWRENCE: OK. [rereads] Yes, here [points to lines 31–35] I say that prejudiced people are part of society, and then I say they aren't.

105 DAVID: Yes. What did you mean by saying that prejudiced people aren't part of society?

LAWRENCE: I guess I meant that society depends on people trying to get along together, trying to accept each other's differences. If you play by the rules, then you're really part of society. They exist in society, but they aren't
115   really part of it.

DAVID: OK, I get it now. Could that "If . . . , then . . ." sentence pattern express any of your other ideas?

LAWRENCE: Let's see. *[tries sentences on scratch paper]*

IF	THEN
you accept others	you belong to society
you're prejudiced	you're "outside" even though you exist

115

Well, I guess it could straighten out the part about whether prejudice is forgiveable or not. *[points to lines 43–44]*

you hate people	
you forgive prejudice	

120

I guess I haven't written the "then" parts down yet. But I think I'd say, "If you hate people, you're going to carry around a lot of bitterness." And for the last one, I'd say, "If you forgive prejudice, you can be happier with yourself."

In order to make sure that Lawrence has plenty of paradigms to work with, David might want to introduce one or two more "workhorse sentences." You have probably noticed that there is a lot of overlap between the literary "seed sentences" and the logical "workhorse sentences." A tutor's own sense of what each writer works comfortably with is the best guide. We know of writers who, after using the "seed sentences" to help them write one narrative, were quite comfortable moving into the more straightforwardly logical connections.

The strategies of salvaging, glossing, dramatizing to test alternatives, and using sentence-paradigms heuristically can help both experienced and inexperienced writers to set their own limits when assignments are open-ended and to reduce the anxiety that such assignments often produce.

Summary

As Chapter 5 points out, inexperienced writers often have difficulty forming concepts that control or unify essays. Open-ended assignments are particularly problematic for novices because, in the absence of specific direction, they themselves must decide how to select and relate items for discussion. Beginning writers tend to be diffident: they are uncertain as to what constitutes an appropriate subject, and they are reluctant to take stands on many-sided or much-debated issues. Consequently, the writers may compose clichéd, unfocused, or disjointed responses instead of committing themselves to a concept, by which we mean taking and developing a stand.

A writer can salvage an as-yet-uncommitted draft if you help him learn to gloss or to dramatize. In glossing (see also Chapter 5), a writer names the main idea of each paragraph, decides how these ideas should be related, in so doing formulates the controlling concept, and discards unrelated ideas. Dramatizing helps writers test stands that they have adopted or are considering: you can ask a writer to imagine specific stituations to which her proposition applies so that she can see what it implies or how it would work and whether it holds up.

To help diffident writers experiment before choosing a concept to substantiate, you can suggest various sentence paradigms. These provide writers with syntactical structures that shape and bridle ideas.

SUGGESTIONS FOR JOURNAL ENTRIES

1. Looking back over some open-ended writing assignments you have worked on in your own writing, write about your processes of setting limits and taking a stand.

2. Record in your journal (as accurately as your memory allows) a tutorial conference in which you helped a writer set limits on an open-ended assignment and figure out how ideas were related. What strategies did you use? If you had it to do over again, which would you repeat and which would you alter? Why?

3. Identify "seed sentences" and "workhorse sentences" in several essays that are included in an anthology of essays used by a writing class. Write about how these function in the overall structure of the essays in which they occur. Can you identify certain paradigms with certain major sections of an essay? How many different paradigms can you discern in the overall structure of any one essay?

SUGGESTIONS FOR FURTHER WRITING

1. Write a dialogue in which you use "seed sentences" to help the writer of "Violence in the Cities" form a concept.

2. Write a dialogue in which you use "workhorse sentences" to help the writer of "Violence in the Cities" form a concept.

3. Using "School and Me," write a new complete dialogue of your own. Imagine that Lawrence gives different answers to your early questions than he did to ours. Try to employ as many of the strategies presented in this chapter as you can. Exchange your dialogue with other tutors and ask them to write their responses to your strategies.

4. "Basic Training" was written in response to the same assignment as "School and Me": "Write a paper describing an educational experience." The writer has not yet taken a stand. After you have read it, write responses to the following questions:

    a. How does this writer interpret the key terms of the assignment: *educational* and *experience?* What did he learn? How?

    b. Where do you see the writer attempting to "cover" many possible ways of limiting his subject?

    c. How might the writer gloss each paragraph? To that extent are the propositions consistent with one another? to what extent do you see shifts?

    d. What patterns of failure to take a stand can you find?

BASIC TRAINING

    The Army National Guard is a strict outfit designed to protect the United States. It is a high moral organization with a lot of discipline and honor. Whenever someone enlists in the Army, Army Reserve or Army National Guard, they go through eight weeks of vigorous training. This is called Basic Training or "Boot Camp." While at Basic, the training starts at 4 A.M. and ends at 9 P.M. It is rough, both physically and mentally.

5

Recently, I went through that experience. Fort Dix is the biggest place I've ever been. Most of the recruits, including me, had not been away from home much, except for summer camp. Fort Dix is no summer camp. I felt lost in the crowd.

During my Basic at Fort Dix, I had the honor of being trained by one of the most dedicated men in the United States Army today. He was my drill Sergeant, Sergeant First Class Joe Martin. S. F. C. Martin's role in the Army is to use any means to prepare trainees to become soldiers. This is a difficult task. The training consists of physical conditioning, drill and ceremony, weapons qualification, first aid, combat maneuvers and reaction to chemical agents.

I feel that Sgt. Martin did an excellent job in training my platoon. His dedication and outstanding code of honor makes him an extremely honest and trustworthy person. Most of the day, the expression on his face reminds you of the "Old man of the mountain." This serious face is a sign of concentration. At night when training was over, he would joke and laugh in a cynical fashion. But he never really cared about us.

One thing Sgt. Martin ingrained in us is that a soldier does not question his commanding officer. Some of the things we had to do in training seemed either foolish or brutal at the time. But if someone asked why we had to do them, Sgt. Martin just said he was the commanding officer and so long as he knew why we were doing it, it didn't matter if we knew or not.

Sgt. Martin has been very successful in his military career. He joined with a grade school education. In 16 years he went on to get his high school diploma, a college education, along with many medals and awards achieved through his outstanding duty. He was the right man to train us. Every man should have the experience of basic training.

5. After completing your written observations, apply some of the strategies discussed in this and earlier chapters to tutoring the writer of "Basic Training":

a. How could dramatizing help the writer test hypotheses about basic training? About Sgt. Martin?

b. What "seed sentences" might be most useful in helping this writer commit himself to a concept?

c. What "workhorse sentences" might be most useful in helping this writer commit himself to a concept?

d. Make an ordered list (possibly branching) of the questions you might ask in a tutoring session.

e. Frame a dialogue, alternating the questions you would ask with the responses you would expect from the writer. If you anticipate alternative answers, let your dialogue branch (as in Chapter 5).

6. Collect the observations you have just written about "Violence in the Cities," "School and Me," and "Basic Training." Gloss your own observations to discover HDWDWW—"How have you observed what about each essay and why?"

a. Using several of the "seed sentences," try out some predications you might make about (1) the composing processes the writers seem to be using, and (2) your own processes of observation.

b. Using several of the "workhorse sentences," try out some predications you might make about the relative usefulness of "seed sentences" and "workhorse sentences" in working with the writer of "Basic Training."

SUGGESTIONS FOR CLASS ACTIVITIES

1. Distribute to your fellow students copies of a paper in which the writer is undecided about what stand to take among several alternatives. Role play a dialogue in which a "tutor" helps the "writer" to test hypotheses through dramatizing.

2. Distribute to your fellow students copies of an as-yet-uncommitted paper. Divide the class into two groups, one for "seed sentences" and one for "workhorse sentences." Ask each group to devise questions and to role play a tutorial session for the class. Afterwards, discuss which paradigms most effectively helped the writer take a stand.

SUGGESTIONS FOR FURTHER READING

Berthoff, Ann E. *Forming, Thinking, Writing*. Rochelle Park, NJ: Hayden, 1978. 79–83.
Burke, Kenneth. "On Human Behavior Considered 'Dramatistically.' " In *Permanence and Change*. 3rd ed. Berkeley: University of California Press, 1984. 274–294.
Coles, William E. *The Plural I: The Teaching of Writing*. New York: Holt, 1978.
—— "The Teaching of Writing as Writing." *College English* 29 (1967): 111–116.
Deen, Rosemary, and Marie Ponsot. *The Common Sense*. Upper Montclair, NJ: Boynton/Cook, 1985.
Miles, Josephine. *Working Out Ideas*. Berkeley: Bay Area Writing Project, 1979.
Ponsot, Marie, and Rosemary Deen, *Beat Not the Poor Desk*. Upper Montclair, NJ: Boynton/Cook, 1982.
Richards, I. A. *The Philosophy of Rhetoric*. London: Oxford University Press, 1936.

7

Tutoring Revision
through Paper Comments

Because writing is a recursive process, writers constantly make conceptual and editorial revisions (see Chapters 3 and 4). A different occasion for revision is provided by the comments teachers (and workplace supervisors) write on drafts and papers. These can help writers and tutors assess writing needs and set priorities for tutoring sessions. By working closely with faculty mentors, some tutors learn the contexts in which writers are composing: how the goals of each writing assignment fit into the general designs of courses, and what readings, lectures, and discussions a writing assignment refers to. For these tutors, assessment and planning are fairly clear-cut tasks. Other tutors, however, may work less closely with particular mentors and, consequently, may lack knowledge of contexts. They may be assigned to help students from several different courses, or they may work in drop-in writing centers in schools, workplaces, and community-based educational programs that afford little or no direct contact with whoever makes the assignment. For these tutors, who must quite independently assess writing needs and set priorities, comments written on papers are invaluable guides.

The Nature of Paper Comments

All comments teachers write on papers are meant to help writers improve their writing. However, in order to use paper comments effectively, you must be aware that on any given paper there are likely to be two quite different kinds: *conceptual* and *editorial* (Sommers, ''Responding''). Conceptual comments address the ideas in a paper as if it is a work-in-*process,* but editorial comments treat surface errors as if a paper is a finished *product.* Through conceptual, process-oriented questions like the following, teachers respond as readers, talking *with* writers about ideas:

What does this passage say explicitly? Implicity?

What unanswered questions does it raise?

How might the point be supported more fully?

How might the writer develop the argument?

How could this point be connected with others in the paper?

However, even process-oriented comments can sometimes seem aimed at remaking a writer's ideas into teachers' ideal responses to assignments (Brannon and Knoblauch, "On Students' Rights"); such comments might prescribe rather than inquire about the writers' processes: "You could have cited Humphrey and Gibson to support this argument," or "Why didn't you use such and such a line of reasoning?" Usually, though, process-oriented comments like those listed above enable teachers to function as writers' "other selves" and thus to help writers develop dialogical thinking (see Chapter 2).

On the other hand, through editorial comments teachers respond as correctors, and sometimes as judges, of finished products; they talk *at* writers from the opposite side of the desk. Such comments say that sentences are "awk," that "sp," "p," and "s-v agr" are wrong, that diction is faulty. Some teachers even insert corrections, improving the paper-as-product at the cost of intervening in the writer's revision process and making her dependent on a teacher who has volunteered as proofreader. Some comments satisfy teachers' needs to demonstrate dedication through thoroughness; a teacher may be thinking, "I spent hours marking every error in your paper." Others assess writers' application of class discussion ("We went over that in class last week; you shouldn't be making that mistake any more!") and account for the grade ("Good analysis, but grammar problems and weak paragraph coherence are holding your grade down to a C + ."). No matter how "open" a grading system is, teachers (or supervisors)—unlike tutors—sooner or later *do* judge: Is the paper acceptable? Is the writer ready to pass the course? Can the administrative trainee send the vice-president for personnel this version of the recruitment report?

A combination of process- and product-oriented comments may confuse and frustrate a writer, who might think, "if the paper is finished, it is too late to revise, but if the paper is in process, it is too early to edit." Besides needing to be reminded of the constructive intentions of even the most judgmental-sounding editorial comments, writers need to learn how to distinguish between conceptual and editorial comments, to set priorities for addressing them, and ultimately to integrate both the conceptual and editorial comments into their own ongoing composing processes, so that by revising one particular paper they acquire understanding that can be applied to many compositions.

How Writers Misinterpret or Are Confused by Paper Comments

Before most writers take time to read the comments, they naturally look at the letter grade. If it satisfies them, they may not bother to read the comments; if it does not, they may feel too frustrated or discouraged to read them. For several reasons, even when they do read the comments, writers often have difficulty in understanding and applying them. First of all, whether grades are good or poor, people *do* tend to take grades and comments personally. Even though paper comments are *ipso facto* comments about a particular paper, not about all of the writer's work or about the writer himself, many writers are likely to think, "I wrote an 'A' paper; ergo, I am smart and successful!" or "I wrote a 'D+' paper, so I must have a hopelessly D+ mind and will probably have a D+ life." People less often say "My essay got a B+ " than *"I* got a B+." Telling writers, "Don't take the comments and the B+ personally," will neither soothe nor enlighten them. Because writing is so intimately tied to each writer's language, experiences, and values, paper comments are bound to be taken more personally than, say, comments on chemistry reports or accounting problems. Nevertheless, writers need to learn how to set aside their personal responses in order to attend to the instructional intent and value of paper comments.

Writers may feel that comments challenge their control of their papers. Some teachers write quite long, letter-style comments at the ends of papers, or they try to converse with writers by means of extensive comments along the margins. These conceptual comments do avoid the stultifying effects of overemphasis on editorial issues. However, they may also be overwhelming, making writers think, "My teacher wrote more than I did" or "She saw so many other things my paper could have included." Long comments may also bring confusion; a writer may think, "I read all her questions, but I'm still not sure what to do in my revision"). Ironically, plentiful commentary can subvert the dialogue between teacher and writer, because comments that grow into minilectures can imbalance the give-and-take characterizing genuine communication, leaving the writer feeling that someone else has had the "last word" about what he has tried to say.

The writers may be visually and intellectually dazzled. Even experienced writers know the perplexity of confronting a page on which a teacher has, probably with all good intentions, marked the paper extensively, mixing together both conceptual and editorial issues until both the writer's eye and the mind suffer what Richard H. Haswell calls "information dazzle" (601). No wonder less experienced writers often receive the individualized instruction provided by teachers' plentiful commentary with dismay. Sometimes the sheer quantity of red ink or smudged No. 2 pencil means ironically opposite things: to the teacher, it betokens hours of dedication and thoroughness; to the writer, however, it betokens a hopeless welter of error and, perhaps, even the teacher's anger (a writer might think, "Boy, she really tore up my paper!" or "It took me four hours to type this and now look! It's all so scrawled and smudged, she really trashed it! Well, maybe it *is* trash."). The comments on a single page may include questions of fact and inference, suggestions for extending the argument, abstract commands and queries such as "trans?" or "clarify," and rhetorical expressions such as "really?" along with assorted editorial symbols and handbook abbreviations. Writers may be so overwhelmed that they read none of the comments, avoiding anticipated criticism at the cost of missing out on praise. They need to learn ways of sorting out the conceptual from the editorial issues so that they can approach substantive problems before working on surface errors.

Some comments may leave them guessing. If plentiful comments can present difficulties, so can scanty ones. A teacher may intend to praise a writer by writing "aha!" in the margin, but the writer may be baffled: does "aha!" mean "this is a good point," "at last you got around to making your point," "now you are clarifying an earlier confusing statement," or something else? Because "aha!" expresses an emotional rather than intellectual response, the writer wonders "aha!—what?" Faculty and workplace supervisors who do not teach writing regularly may mean a great many different things when they comment, "'Work on your grammar": writers reading this comment might find themselves guessing whether "grammar" means syntax, agreement, pronoun reference, punctuation, and so on. Empty margins and a brief end comment like "A—fine work!" do not convey to writers what qualities made their papers "fine." Writers of "A" papers do not always know what the strengths of their papers are, and they sometimes mistakenly assume that their "ideas" are good but their "style" is not, or vice versa. Some writers may become overly modest, making up self-denigrating explanations such as "This paper got an 'A' only because it was longer/had more quotations/was more neatly typewritten than the papers other students submitted." Others may become overly confident, thinking "Since this paper got an 'A,' there's no way it could be improved! I have nothing further to learn about writing." Likewise, empty margins and end comments like "See the tutor!—F" imply that the problems are self-evident and, perhaps, that the teacher does not want to be bothered with so hopeless a paper and writer. Writers may explain such comments to themselves by thinking, "My paper must be so hopeless he doesn't even want to talk to me about it himself" or "I might as well drop out of school. I'm too dumb to learn."

Another problem arises when a teacher's desire to communicate encouragement conflicts with the necessity to evaluate fairly; the result can be a mixed message: "C+—good for you." The writer may wonder, "If the paper is 'good,' why is the grade only a 'C+? Maybe it is good for *me*, but not so good for somebody who is smart/talkative in class/friendly with the teacher?" Writers in all three of these situations need to be encouraged to confer with their teachers in order to eliminate guesswork and to identify strengths and problems in their papers. You can encourage writers in all of the above situations to consult their teachers as a first step. If for some reason such conferences are not possible, and if you cannot consult directly the comment-writers, you can of course use your own knowledge to make assessments and set priorities (as Chapter 1 explains).

Brief comments using abstract code words and editorial abbreviations can also confuse writers. Sommers finds that *"most teachers' comments are not text-specific and could be interchanged, rubber-stamped, from text to text"* ("Responding," 152). Probably because of time limitations, teachers write "example?" or "clarify" instead of writing out questions specifically directed to the writer's text, like "what example could you give of 'oppressive tactics'?" or "I'm not sure whether 'oppressive tactics' means 'restraining' or 'punitive' or something else in this paragraph. How could you clarify?" Moreover, as Mimi Schwartz (in "Response to Writing") finds by comparing comments written by faculty in various disciplines, stylistic code words do not have universally agreed-upon meanings among readers; what one reader finds "specific" and "clear" another may find "wordy." Consequently, a writer may have difficulty in interpreting just why a reader comments "clarify" or "be specific" or "wordy" in the margins. Furthermore, current research in discourse analysis reveals that writers in various professions and faculty in different disciplines have different stylistic criteria. Whereas humanities faculty often labor to eradicate the passive voice (because, for instance, sentences like "Executions were ordered" obscure moral responsibility), science faculty find the passive voice indispensable (biophysicists seldom write, "I focused my laser on her retina . . . ," but rather "A laser was focused on the retina. . . ."). In addition, editorial abbreviations (such as "sp," "fs," "agr") may look unfamiliar to writers. Even though in the first week of class teachers often distribute lists of commonly used editorial abbreviations, writers may pay little attention to these because it is not yet time to use them; the lists are tucked away and forgotten. These abbreviations, as well as checks in the margins (for each error in each line) and "theme rating blanks" listing criteria for numerical scoring of various aspects of "style" and "content" all *look* objective and clear. Nevertheless, these methods of commenting may be confusing, because writers may not know what some abbreviations and terms mean.

For these and other reasons, many writers may resist or ignore editorial comments. Some scorn them as trivia of interest only to nit-picking academics but unworthy of the writers' attention because, they believe, such matters do not interfere with communicating meaning; they may think, "Who cares if I used a comma or a semicolon? Who cares if I misspelled the author's name? You understood what I said, didn't you?" Some writers may interpret certain kinds of editorial comments as racially or ethnically prejudiced. For instance, beside the sentence, "He walk down to the beach every day," a teacher might write "s-v agr" (indicating the need to add the final -s to the present tense, third person singular verb). Assuming that he knows the meaning of the abbreviation, a speaker of Black English Vernacular (in whose dialect this -s is not pronounced) might assume that the teacher thinks he lacks the concepts of singular and plural, and worse yet, that the teacher is asserting the superiority—not just the difference—of Standard Written English (Chapter 10 will say more about tutoring writers for whom Standard Written English is a second dialect).

Perhaps the most pervasive kind of misunderstanding involves the nature of real revision. Rewriting a paper may seem like a punishment for error instead of an opportunity for growth. Many writers think revision involves merely "fixing up" surface errors pointed out in editorial comments; they do not realize that revision literally means "re-seeing," that is, rethinking the ideas in response to the conceptual comments. Because inexperienced writers often think of writing as transcribing speech, they tend to see revision of their first drafts almost entirely in lexical terms, substituting a "better word" from the thesaurus for the more casual word their inner speech provided for the first draft (Sommers, "Revision Strategies"). We have observed these writers responding to teachers' paper comments by "fixing up" errors and tinkering with sentence structure that a teacher has marked "awk" or "wdy," and then resubmitting what amounts essentially to the same paper. Such cosmetic tinkering is counterproductive for writers because they often neglect to "fix" unmarked errors which are identical or similar to those that are marked, and it is frustrating to teachers, who realize that they have wasted hours doing nothing more than proofreading on writers' behalf.

In contrast, Sommers finds that more experienced writers revise their first and second drafts in conceptual terms—discovering what they want to say, fashioning an argument, rearranging points—and only much later in syntactical and lexical terms. They understand that revising most often means seeing a subject afresh, literally re-seeing. More experienced writers we have observed know that they must set aside editorial comments in order, first of all, to attend to conceptual comments. By using the strategies explained below, you can help inexperienced writers learn how to interpret comments as objectively as possible and how to sort and interpret conceptual and editorial comments on particular papers. Moreover, you can help writers to generalize and integrate these sets of comments into their usual composing and revising processes.

Comments May Raise Issues of Fairness and Responsibility

Writers sometimes claim to find comments and grades "unfair." In some instances, "unfair" is a face-saving way of saying, "I don't like these comments." Sometimes writers feel that, for some reason, their papers are being held up to scrutiny that is not being applied to other students in a class, or that the teacher is using comments and grades to penalize them for lateness, absence, or some personal conflict. Of course, you can remind writers that grades often *do* reflect missed instruction (due to lateness or absence), since applying the lessons of class discussion depends on *remembering* to apply them. Writing instruction is highly interactive: it depends on writers' taking very active roles, asking themselves and their teachers why a particular aspect of writing is worth studying and how it answers their own needs. Without sacrificing neutrality, you can help writers assess the fairness of comments by ascertaining to what extent they are related to class assignments, or more generally, to aspects of writing which writers in a particular class might legitimately be expected to know. When you ask questions like "When did your class study logical transitions?" or "Let's look at your discussion notes on 'The Communist Manifesto,' " or "Didn't you work on pronoun reference in the course prerequisite to this one?" you help writers assume responsibility for remembering to apply class lessons when they sit down at home to write their papers. You might help writers use their class notes to construct a checklist—a homemade "theme rating blank"—of whatever editorial and conceptual aspects of writing they have been studying in class. Together, you could read through drafts to make sure that the items on the checklist are addressed. You might also suggest that writers ask their teachers to show them an example of an "A" paper written by a classmate or to explain what it would take to turn the "C+" or "F" paper into an "A" paper. "What do I have to do to get an 'A'?" can be asked in a constructive, nonadversarial tone. If you help a writer to identify the criteria by which his writing is being evaluated, he will be more likely to acknowledge his writing problems and to address them instead of complaining about "unfairness."

Sometimes, however, teachers *do* make mistakes. Even with the best intentions, teachers can misinterpret, can overlook connections writers have made, can ask writers to provide evidence that is sitting right there on the page, can misspell words, and (in the spirit of casual conversation) can break the rules of sentence structure and punctuation. Sometimes teachers hurriedly address comments to the writer as a person (for instance, ''You must work harder!'') without actually having any idea of how hard she worked, what other responsibilities she carries, or what crises she may be facing. Without implying that such factors justify lowered standards, you can rephrase such comments, making them neutral yet supportive. ''You must work harder!'' could be rephrased in several ways: ''How did you go about reading 'The Communist Manifesto'?'' or ''How long did you spend writing your paper?'' or ''Did you proofread?'' or ''Before you wrote this paper, did you review the comments the teacher wrote on your previous papers?'' You can remind writers that teachers' errors are not malicious attacks, but honest mistakes that can be straightened out in conferences so that positive communication can be restored.

Some tutors wrongly interpret paper comments as reflections upon the success of their tutorial conferences. Tutors are justifiably proud of their growing skill in helping other writers. Therefore, it is understandable that, occasionally, some take comments on their tutees' papers as criticisms of their own tutorial priorities or effectiveness. Frequent contact between tutors and their mentors can help keep priorities straight and can keep teachers up to date on the work going on in tutorial sessions. Teachers know that writing instruction is a very long-term process, with predictable backsliding. Perhaps the best way for tutors to avoid taking paper comments as reflections on their own knowledge of writing is to recall that the product of tutoring is not good *papers* but stronger, more independent *writers*.

Relating Comments to Writers' Composing Processes

As an experienced writer, you are familiar with many methods teachers use to write editorial and conceptual comments, and you understand the constructive purposes of the comments. Just as you can promote dialogical thinking by standing in for a writer's ''other self'' (see Chapter 2), so you can interpret comments, helping writers comprehend them, use them constructively to revise particular papers, and eventually integrate them into their habitual writing processes. Several tutoring strategies are useful.

Reclaiming the writer's authority over the text

Authority can make the difference between long-range learning and short-range fixing. That is because writers who see revision as a means of more effectively expressing what *they* want to say are likely to invest greater intellectual energy in the process than are writers who feel as if they are merely obeying orders, ploddingly ''fixing'' marked problems but ignoring similar problems that the teacher has not commented upon, grudgingly acceding to someone else's ''last word.'' Tutors, in helping writers reclaim authority, do not, however, become writers' advocates against teachers. They do help writers to *incorporate* teachers' purposes into their own habitual writing processes.

Choice distinguishes art from accident. Teachers grant authority to authors, that is, they assume that authors *choose* to present, withhold, or purposefully confuse information, whereas they assume—probably correctly—that most student writers simply stumble into vagueness, incompleteness, and ambiguity. What might be seen as an author's stylistic subtlety might be seen as a student writer's need to "clarify" and "be specific." One way for you to help writers maintain authority is to ask them to articulate and explore the reasons for their choices. Writers usually decide to accept the advice given in paper comments, but if they choose not to, they can recognize the need for justifying that decision in their papers. For instance, a fairly advanced writer who finds "frag" written in the margin might explain, "I wrote that fragment on purpose, for emphasis." If "frag" recurs several times, the tutor could ask in each instance, "Did you deliberately phrase the idea this way?" Once the accidental fragments, if any, have been revised, the tutor might ask questions probing the writer's notion of emphasis: "What might happen if you use one emphatic device very often? Will emphasis be lost? Might repetition of fragments suggest to your teacher that the fragments you include are deliberate?" Such questions would help the writer refine her understanding of the use of sentence fragments and of emphatic devices in general. Similarly, supposing that Sabrina shows Rob, her tutor, a graded and annotated music history paper bearing this end comment: "When you revise, be sure to include Gershwin in your analysis of American composers of opera." Rob could help her explore her choices:

ROB: What do you think about including Gershwin?

SABRINA: Well, obviously *Porgy and Bess* is probably the best known American opera in the world. But in the course readings, historians kept calling it a "folk opera." In my paper, I was writing about composers of serious opera like Douglas Moore, Virgil Thomson, and Roger Sessions. I deliberately excluded Gershwin in order to avoid getting all mixed up in defining "folk opera."

ROB: I can understand your strategy. Definitions can be very difficult. Now that you think it over, though, what might have made your teacher write that comment?

SABRINA: For one thing, we've studied Gershwin in the course. And we've talked quite a lot about how hard it is to distinguish "serious" from "folk" music.

ROB: Could you tell me some more about that?

SABRINA: Well, serious compositions like Sibelius's *Finlandia* and Smetana's *Moldau* include folk melodies.

ROB: That's interesting. So what might your paper gain by including Gershwin?

SABRINA: Hmmmm. . . . By analyzing "folk" and "serious" elements in *Porgy and Bess*, I could show how imprecise the definitions are—just by showing how one work fits into both categories.

ROB: Do any of the composers you classify as "serious" resemble Gershwin?

SABRINA: Yes, come to think of it, Moore's opera *The Ballad of Baby Doe* has some folk elements too.

ROB: That's good. Sometimes you can deepen an analysis by not trying to make the issues too black and white.

25 SABRINA: OK. Instead of trying to make the definitions clearer than they really are, I'll use Gershwin to demonstrate their complexity.

Such questions help writers distinguish accident from choice in their writing. When they retain authority over their texts, most writers are quite willing to revise to redress oversights, render information more complete and persuasive to readers, because doing so enables them to express *their* lines of reasoning and thus facilitate *their* communication.

A writer's first recognition that her English, chemistry, and sociology teachers may use stylistic code words like "clear" and "wordy" quite differently may prompt her to dismiss all of their comments as petty academic bickering and as completely irrelevant to communicating in the world at large. She might think, "If my English professor hates passive voice but my chemistry professor insists that I use it, why can't I just write any way I want?" By helping writers recognize that in everyday life they adjust their language to the people they are addressing, be they golf partners or union brothers on the picket line or elderly relatives at a family reunion, you can help writers realize that different stylistic norms and vocabularies are not confined to academic communities, but are part of everyday communication.

We have already mentioned the value of your encouraging writers to ask their teachers for conferences. In even a short conference, comments and grading criteria can be clarified and personal misunderstandings may be straightened out, clearing the way for more positive communication. You may also request three-way conferences, in which teacher, writer, and you can converse as equal partners. Such three-way conferences minimize authority struggles between a novice writer and an expert by demonstrating, in George Held and Warren Rosenberg's words, "communication as a *negotiated way* rather than *the right way*" (819). Negotiated communication often results in students' writing more genuine and more lively papers because (as Chapter 4 explains) their academic reading "audience" of one is better known, more "real." By helping writers identify accidents, weigh choices, and imagine the responses of various readers, you can help writers revise without relinquishing authority over their papers.

Sorting comments and setting priorities

In order to minimize the problem of visual and intellectual "information dazzle," you can help writers sort the conceptual comments from the editorial concerns. Unless teachers specifically indicate other priorities, you and writers wisely begin by addressing the important conceptual issues in revising. If a teacher writes a long letter-style comment, you can help a writer to gloss the issues it raises (see Chapter 5 on glossing), then list them and decide priorities. If, for instance, a long comment refers several times to differing definitions of a key term, you might suggest that the writer work first on clarifying that definition and postpone other kinds of queries (say, about evidence or about other sources of information) and editorial matters. You can also help writers translate abstract code words into text-specific questions like those in the following partial list:

IF THE COMMENT SAYS:	TUTORS CAN INTERPRET:
trans?	What is the logical connection between these two sentences or paragraphs?
ref?	To what word does this pronoun refer? What is "this"? "It"? "They"?
def?	What does this word mean?
ex? be specific	What example could you give to support or illustrate this assertion?
wdy	How could you say this idea more directly? What words are dispensable?
vague	What example or definition could you provide to make the meaning of this word or assertion more precise?

If several marginal comments call for examples by asking "for instance?" or "illustrate," the writer can make a list of passages for which he needs to supply examples; if several comments say "frag" or "fs," the writer can copy out the sentence fragments or fused sentences in a list (Chapters 8 and 9 will present strategies for tutoring sentence-level problems and punctuation). Listing and clustering comments enables you and a writer to identify the more serious, or at least the more recurrent, problems and to set priorities for addressing them, perhaps over the course of several tutorial sessions.

Some teachers aid writers in sorting comments by placing in the margins numbers referring to a list of end comments; for instance, the numbers 3 and 4 written here and there in the margins might be keyed to end comments saying "3—these spots all need examples to support assertions," and "4—these spots all need to move the main idea into the main clause of the sentence." Alternatively, some teachers mark a certain type of error only on the first page, asking the writer to locate and correct more examples of the same problem on subsequent pages. These two methods of commenting greatly simplify the tutors' and writers' work of identifying and setting priorities. Whoever does the mapping, this strategy enables writers to identify problems and to address them one at a time; writers are thus not visually and mentally overwhelmed.

Undertaking revising tasks immediately

Writers can maintain their authority and integrate particular lessons into their usual writing processes by beginning immediately to work during their tutorial sessions on one significant problem. Suppose, for instance, that a teacher's comments repeatedly ask for examples. A tutor might scan the paper looking for one passage that does give an example. By asking the writer, "Why do you give an example at this point but not at that point?" and "What difference do you think it makes?" the tutor can build upon what the writer has done "right," can name the technique the writer has used ("giving an example"), and can help the writer consider how examples strengthen assertions. Then a writer might generate examples to add to the passages where the teacher comments "for instance?" Similarly, if "ref?" haunts the margins, a tutor can locate one clear pronoun–antecedent reference, explain the relationship, and then ask the writer to practice the same thing—locating, or more probably, supplying antecedents—in the various passages marked "ref?" By identifying whatever writers have done well and helping them to revise weaker passages to resemble stronger ones, you not only reassure writers that their papers—no matter how heavily annotated—are not hopeless, but also that writers can go beyond making merely local repairs and can generalize comments to apply to all their writing for a particular discipline.

Comparing comments on successive papers

One of the most effective means of helping writers identify recurring problems as well as eliminate them is to set successive papers side by side and note the persistence or disappearance of certain kinds of comments. If, for instance, the margins of early papers have many comments of "cs" or "frag," but these no longer appear in, say, the fourth or fifth paper, a writer can see that he now knows how to avoid comma splices and to write complete sentences. If the teacher begins noting "cs" or "frag" on, say, the third paper, tutor and writer can look back at the first two papers to find other unmarked examples of these problems and can use them as self-made exercises. (You may sometimes notice errors that teachers have left unmarked; these may simply be oversights, but it is safer to assume that the teacher is choosing to postpone drawing the particular error to the writer's attention.) When comments like "be specific" give way to "good example!" or "sound data!" writers can see their writing becoming more concrete. Teachers' end comments often take note of such improvements, but because tutors work with fewer writers, they can make such comparative analyses more frequently and in greater individual detail. Writers can gain enormous encouragement by recognizing that their dialogues—with their papers and with their teachers—are working!

Helping a Writer Revise From Comments: A Sample Tutoring Session

Joshua, a student in an introductory college literature course, wrote the following paper in response to the assignment, "Write a paragraph explaining the relationship between the townspeople and Emily in Faulkner's "A Rose for Emily." (You may wish to read this frequently anthologized story, but you need not in order to understand the dialogue below.) When the paper was returned, he brought it to conference with Earlene, his tutor. Please read the annotated paper with these questions in mind:

- How could the various marginal comments be categorized?
- What issues seem to be most important to the professor?
- What seems to be the professor's attitude toward the writer?
- What might be the writer's attitude toward revising?

. . . .

The comments written on this essay illustrate Sommers' observation that teachers tend to mix editorial comments, treating the paper as a finished product with

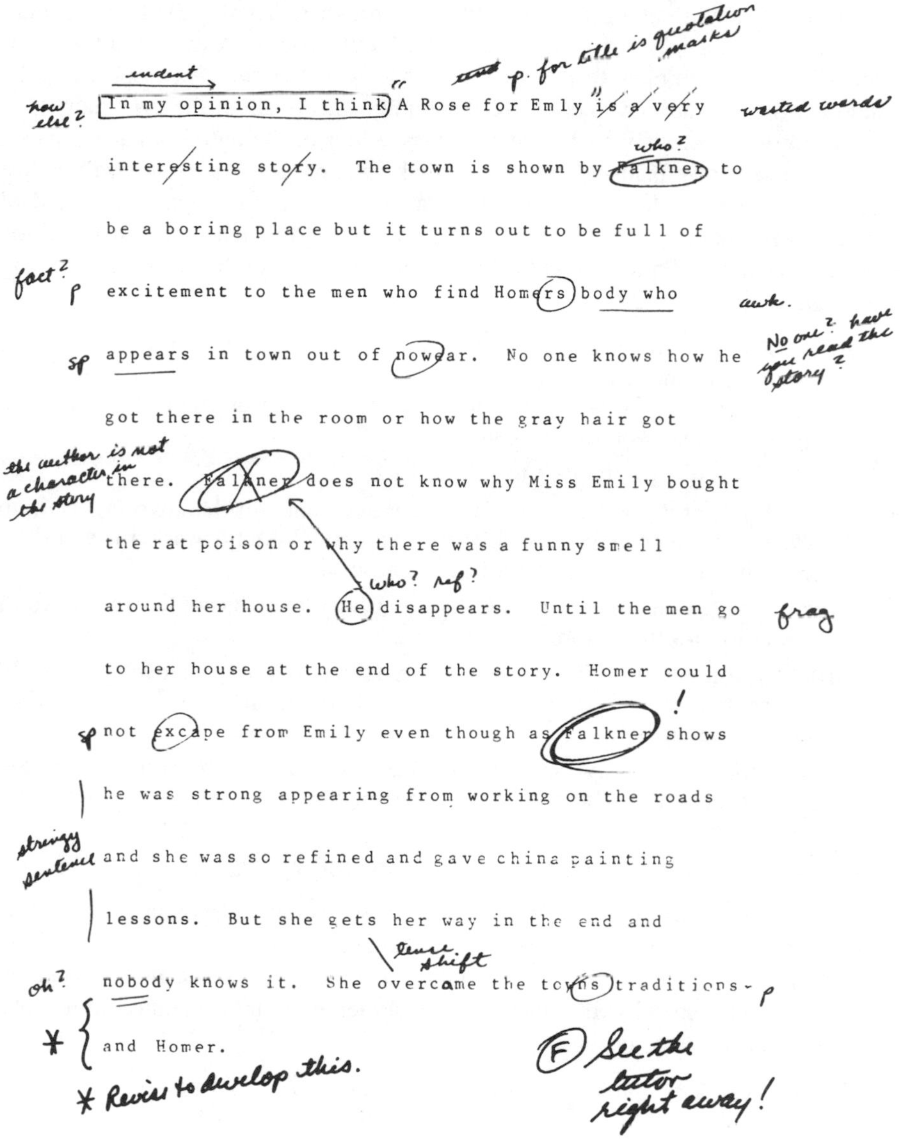

1   *how else?* | indent → | " | *use p. for title is quotation marks* | [In my opinion, I think] A Rose for Emly is a very | *wasted words*

2   interesting story. The town is shown by (Falkner) *who?* to

3   be a boring place but it turns out to be full of

4   *fact?* ¶ excitement to the men who find Home(r's) body who | *awk.*

5   *sp* appears in town out of nowear. No one knows how he | *No one? have you read the story?*

6   got there in the room or how the gray hair got

7   *the author is not a character in the story* there. (Falkner) does not know why Miss Emily bought

8   the rat poison or why there was a funny smell

9   around her house. (He) *who? ref?* disappears. Until the men go | *frag*

10 to her house at the end of the story. Homer could

11 *sp* not (excape) from Emily even though as (Falkner) *!* shows

12 | he was strong appearing from working on the roads

13 *stringy sentence* and she was so refined and gave china painting

14 lessons. But she gets her way in the end and

15 *oh?* nobody knows it. She over came the to(wn's) *tense shift* traditions~ ¶

16 ✱ { and Homer.

✱ *Revise to develop this.*

(F) *See the tutor right away!*

Figure 15

conceptual comments treating the paper as a work in process. This professor points out editorial errors in syntax—the redundancy (1), the sentence fragment (9), the "awkward" sentence (4), the stringy sentence (12–14)—as well as spelling errors (5, 11) mistakes in indenting (1), punctuating the story's title (1), and using apostrophes (4, 15); confused pronoun reference (9); and an arbitrary shift in verb tense (14–15). Her comments also address conceptual issues: the "wasted words" (1), questioning the writer's recall of facts (4, 5, 15), distinguishing author from character (7), and calling for development through revision (16). Her frustration is obvious: she asks sarcastically "how else [could you think except in your opinion]?" (line 1); implies that anyone who had read the story—except a hopeless student like Joshua!—would realize that Emily knows about the gray hair (5–7); circles more vigorously each recurrent misspelling of the author's name (lines 2, 7, 11); and finally banishes the writer, making him seek someone else's help to revise: "Grade = F. See the tutor right away!" Since Joshua might understandably be overwhelmed or upset by the number, variety, and increasingly frustrated tone of the comments, Earlene might try to counter his reaction by focusing on sorting the various revision tasks:

JOSHUA: This is a mess! I read the story—how else would I know about the rat poison and the smell?—but it just came out all wrong. How could I write "Falkner" all the way through, when his name was right there in the assignment? No wonder she's so mad.

5 EARLENE: How did you happen to misspell it?

JOSHUA: My roommate typed the paper for me, and my handwriting isn't too clear. I guess it looked like I wrote "Falkner." And it was so late, I didn't take time to proofread. I feel like a real jerk!

EARLENE: Well, don't take it harder than you have to. I mean, you know you're
10   going to proofread from now on, right?

JOSHUA: Absolutely! Actually, I think I'm going to type my own papers. It's easier than conning my roommate into doing it and then having to check everything anyway.

EARLENE: And as you say, she must realize you did read the story, right? So I
15   don't think she's mad at you as a person. She just wants you to write with more care.

JOSHUA: I can relate to that! So, let's get going on revising.

Earlene wisely reassures Joshua that his professor is not angry with some personal quality that Joshua might not be able to change, but because of an external and, for him, easily changed factor: inattention to details. Since he readily acknowledges and suggests ways of remedying his carelessness, they can turn immediately toward positive steps in revising:

JOSHUA: Well, I'm supposed to revise that last sentence. I'll just fix up the spellings and reword the sentences and pass it back in, OK?

20 EARLENE: You certainly should fix up those things, but there's more to revising than that.

JOSHUA: Oh.

EARLENE: The final comment says "develop." Your teacher wants you to say some more about the ideas in that last sentence. What would you say are
25   the main ideas there?

JOSHUA: Hmmm. [reads] OK, I'd say "town's traditions," "Homer," and the fact that she "overcame" both of them.

EARLENE: OK, could you just write each of those ideas in question form?

JOSHUA: [writes]

30   What were the town's traditions?
                How did Emily overcome them?
                How did Emily overcome Homer?

EARLENE: Good. In a few minutes, we'll come back and talk about how you might
           answer those questions. By doing that, we'll be developing ideas, not just
35   changing words around. That's the main point of revision.

Noting the inexperienced writer's tendency to think of revision solely in lexical
and mechanical terms, Earlene focuses on the comment directing Joshua to "develop" the final sentence. She makes the abstract comment, "develop," text-
specific by asking Joshua to identify the key terms in the sentence and then to
turn them into questions, which can later help them generate more ideas. First,
though, they need to sort and order the remaining tasks of revision:

EARLENE: OK. Would you please take a piece of paper and draw a line halfway
           across? On top, we'll write the comments about the meaning of the story,
           and below we'll list the other kinds of questions. OK?

JOSHUA: Ok. Hmmm, first she says, "indent." *[writes it below the line]* Next,
40   "how else?" I'm not sure. . . .

EARLENE: I think it refers to the box around "In my opinion, I think." What
           could "how else?" mean?

JOSHUA: OK, I guess she means "how else can I think, except in my opinion."
           So that's just getting rid of words that repeat an idea. *[writes below the line,*
45   "extra words" and the phrase]

EARLENE: What about the comment "wasted words"?

JOSHUA: *[starts to write them under "extra words"]* Hey, wait a minute. If I
           cross out those words, I won't have a sentence. So how can they be wasted?

EARLENE: Right! They aren't redundant like "in my opinion, I think." In what
50   way are they "wasted"?

JOSHUA: Hmmm. I guess "a very interesting story" doesn't say much. She wants
           a beginning sentence that tells my main point. OK, that's a question about
           the story. *[writes "what's my point?" at top of list]*

After Joshua generates the complete list, Earlene helps him sort it into clusters of
similar problems:

QUESTIONS ABOUT STORY: what's my point?

                                        facts?—who thought town boring?
                                           who knows where Homer came
                                        from?
                                           who knows how Homer died?
                                           who knows Emily won?

                                        author is not character

                                        develop—Emily overcame tradi-
                                        tion
                                           Emily overcame Homer

MISTAKES:

extra words:	sentence structure:
in my opinion I think	fragment
	awkward sentence
	stringy sentence
punctuation:	spelling:
indent	Faulkner
possessives	escape
quote marks	nowhere
pronoun ref	
tense shift	

In the process of listing, Earlene helps Joshua translate abstract comments like "wasted words" and "awk" into text-specific comments. They can refer to these clusters of comments as guides to their revision strategy.

Since Joshua's analysis of comments identifies more issues than he and Earlene can address during one tutorial session, they need to set priorities. Because the end comment points to the final sentence as their priority, Earlene can use strategies such as HDWDWW, tree diagrams, or problem-solving techniques (see Chapters 3 and 4) to help Joshua to elaborate the last sentence—not just to reword it. Then, perhaps, she can ask him to consider ways of connecting what he has said about Emily's victory over tradition to some of the questions he wrote on the top half of his list of comments. He might choose from the "fact" cluster the question, "Who knows Emily won?" and begin to consider how and to what extent the townspeople eventually realized Emily had had her way. Joshua could write down some of these ideas so that he can refer to them when he writes his revision. By making the general comment "develop" into text-specific questions, Earlene could help Joshua not only to solve the particular problems of this short essay but also to incorporate the more general lessons—the need to provide support for assertions, to make his evidence explicit, to relate various assertions to one another—into his usual writing processes.

Before their session ends, they might also decide to work on one of the clusters of "mistakes" Joshua listed at the bottom of his page of comments. Earlene might ask which ones still seemed puzzling:

JOSHUA: OK. These misspellings were just sloppy. For the fragment, I can just add
55   it to the one before, "He disappears, until the men go to her house. . . ."
        But I don't get what's "awk" about this sentence.

EARLENE: It's hard to understand the connections between the ideas, like the town's being boring and Homer's body and where he came from. How many ideas does that sentence express?

60 JOSHUA: One: the town is boring. Two: it's exciting to the men who find Homer's body. Three: Homer came to town out of nowhere.

EARLENE: What connects them?

JOSHUA: The contrast between "boring" and "exciting" connects the first two, but the third is different. I guess I should separate it. *[writes]*

65   The town was boring, but the men who found Homer's body found excitement along with it. Homer came out of nowhere, . . .

I just realized something. You know, the men thought Homer had left town years before. So it was only when they found the body that they realized Emily had managed to prevent him from leaving. *[writes]*

70   Homer came out of nowhere, but instead of vanishing to some distant place, he vanished right in their midst. All the while, they pitied Emily; all the while, she had won.

Yes, I like that.

Earlene translates the abstract comment "awk" into text-specific questions, "How many ideas?" and "How are they connected?" These questions help Joshua recognize what makes this sentence awkward: he has tried to include an unrelated idea. In the process of writing the two new sentences, he realizes a new connection between them and the issue of "Who knows Emily won?" That is, by reflecting on what he had written, he engages in further critical analysis and generation of ideas (see Chapter 4 on "shuttling"). Referring to the other editorial problems Joshua listed on the bottom half of his page of comments, Earlene could ask these two questions about the other members of the category "sentence problems," the sentence fragment and the stringy sentence. The cluster of punctuation problems would probably be postponed until another session.

In this tutorial session, Earlene helps Joshua avoid taking the paper comments personally and helps him to understand that revision entails not simply lexical and mechanical corrections, but further development through rethinking and elaborating ideas. She shows how to manage an array of tasks by sorting and then setting priorities. Through her interpretation of the abstract comment "awk," he learns two text-specific questions to ask himself the next time he sees "awk" written in the margins. By revising this particular paper, Joshua learns some procedures and skills that, in the long run, he can integrate into his usual composing processes.

Summary

Mentors' written comments can help writers and tutors assess needs and set priorities. While all comments are constructively intended, the mixture of process-oriented conceptual comments and product-oriented editorial comments with which most papers are annotated can confuse writers, who may wonder when, how, and even whether to apply either kind. Writers may feel personally criticized, may lose authority over their texts, and may be overwhelmed by the lengthiness or baffled by the scantiness of comments. Therefore, writers may resist or ignore them. Inexperienced writers need to learn that revising is more than cosmetic tinkering, that it means seeing a subject afresh, literally re-seeing. You can help them learn how to interpret a comment as objectively as possible and to use it constructively in deciding where to begin "re-vising."

If sometimes writers complain about the unfairness of comments, you can help them identify the criteria by which their writing is evaluated and can then help them acknowledge and address problems. If mentors have commented inadvisedly, harshly, or hastily, you can rephrase their ideas neutrally, supportively, and specifically. You should not interpret comments as reflections on the degree to which your tutoring has succeeded but should, instead, help writers use comments as part of the dialogical process of composing. You will thereby help writers maintain authority over their texts.

Writers who do retain such authority are more likely to integrate the lessons of comments into their usual composing processes than are those who grudgingly fix individual passages—and quickly forget why—because they feel that comments have taken their papers away from them. You can promote long-term learning by asking them to articulate (not only to change or reconsider) reasons for the choices they have made, by "translating" and making text-specific the code words, abbreviations, and perhaps cryptic comments written in the margins, by sorting conceptual from editorial concerns and setting priorities among them for revising, by undertaking some revisions immediately, and by gauging their progress on successive papers as reflected in comments.

SUGGESTIONS FOR JOURNAL ENTRIES

1. Examine side by side the comments written on several papers that you have submitted in the same course. What conceptual and editorial issues has your professor noted? What patterns of comments do you notice now? How and to what extent has your conception of "revision" changed in response to comments written on your papers?

2. Examine several drafts you have written of one paper. Have your revisions consisted more often of lexical substitutions and crossing out of repetitions, like those made by the student writers Sommers observed? Or have your revisions, like those of the adult writers she observed, reconceptualized?

3. If you have received a long, letter-style comment on one of your papers, how have you used it to revise that essay or to compose subsequent essays?

4. If you are working closely with a faculty mentor, to what extent do the comments he or she writes on student papers relate directly to topics of current class discussion?

5. If you have tutored someone who was dazzled by the quantity and variety of comments on a paper, describe how you helped him or her use the comments to revise.

6. If you have tutored someone who mistook constructive comments as personal criticisms, describe how you have addressed the problem.

SUGGESTIONS FOR FURTHER WRITING

For a beginning college composition class, Hamid submitted the following paper on this assignment (Figure 16): "Write a paper of 200–300 words introducing yourself to other members of our class." After you have read the paper and comments, carry out the following exercises:

1. Make a list of the conceptual and editorial issues addressed in the paper comments.

2. Arrange the items on the list into a map of revision tasks (such as that constructed by Joshua). Write a paragraph explaining why you would give certain tasks priority and postpone others.

3. Using your list from exercise 1, translate general comments into text-specific comments.

4. Write a paragraph explaining how you might make the end comments dialogical. Write a brief dialogue illustrating your plan.

5. Do you find some comments that seem to usurp the writer's authority over the text? If so, write a paragraph or brief dialogue showing how you might help the writer regain and maintain that authority.

6. Do you find some comments that the writer might take personally? If so, write a paragraph or brief dialogue showing how you might handle the writer's responses and refocus attention on the writing itself.

SUGGESTIONS FOR CLASS ACTIVITIES

1. Discuss your responses to exercises 4–6 under "Suggestions for Journal Entries."

2. Discuss your responses to exercise 3 under "Suggestions for Further Writing" with other members of your class, paying particular attention to exactly how various people formulate each text-specific question.

3. Role play some of the dialogues written in response to exercise 5 under "Suggestions for Further Writing." What alternative strategies do they illustrate? What pitfalls do they avoid?

4. Role play some of the dialogues or discuss some of the paragraphs written in response to exercise 6 under "Suggestions for Further Writing." What patterns of personal response and of tutorial intervention do they illustrate?

Who Am I?

Maybe true -- but this is not the assignment + not important enough to be the first sentence in your essay.

To tell you who I am is somewhat difficult to **awk. sentence** pinpoint in a sentence or two. My interests covers a **s-v agr.** *exaggerated?* vast spectrum. This reflects on the activities I do. I **ref?** have played two years of high school soccer for Newton North. I am also active in the Boy Scouts program where I proudly hold the eagle scout rank, the highest rank **me?** you can receive in scouting. Boy Scouts and playing *main point? give it a more emphatic spot in ¶* soccer gave me the chance to exercise leadership and responsibility. These are two major items important in a Boy Scout troop and among fellow players on the playing field. I had worked at Newton-Wellesley **tense shift** *These sentences are not connected to soccer + scouting. Relocate? New ¶?* **sp** Hospital as a volunteer, which I found very rewarding. *d.m.— awk* As a volunteer, it was a valuable experience as a career exploratory. It also made me more sensitive and *d.* respectful for the handicapped, the sick and the weak.

I also have my working experience to benefit from. As a worker in Burger King and now at Spinoff Skating Emporium, an efficient and pleasant environment has to **awk. sentence** be maintained. We are always in the public eye and any mistake of ours reflects on the business.

connect this idea with the rest of the ¶ When free time can be found I enjoy dancing at Boston's finest discoteques. But the interest that had **tense** *(impelled?)* *d.* compelled me more than half my life is my participation in competitive artistic roller skating. My skating *d.* experience has been more than generous. Out of the excitement of traveling and meeting new friends, my long hours of practice sessions and determination had made me **tense**

is this your main idea?

Figure 16

a four time national champion with several state and
northeast regional titles. I appeared on the front
cover of the Boston <u>Globe</u> magazine and a television
guest appearance on the nationally syndicated program
"Kidsworld." I have chosen to hang up my skates, at
least until I graduate. I believe that <u>the rich
experience and knowledge that I will be gaining in
college is worth much more</u> than a championship trophy or
medal. The transition to a "normal life" has not been
easy, but I know my decision is right and I will weather
the storm. *how has it been a "storm"? explain*

can you pin this down? in what sense?

This idea is worth a lot of development.
❋

The greatest asset that I have is my strong determination and <u>sense of humor</u>. I was Cupid during
Valentines, my senior year in high school. I admire
success and I am (ambitious.) Eventually, I wold like to
pursue a medical career. I can be industrious and
capable of (concentrated effort.) Criticism does not
affect me most of the time especially if they are bene-
ficial. I cherish the times when I am alone trying to
do something good for the present so as to lead me to
the bright future; however, I love to be with friends
and I look forward to meeting new ones.

awk

relate to other ideas? humor/scouts/hospital

sp

is there a connection between these qualities and skating?

ref? p-a agr?

I'm sure you will find some in our class.

① FOCUS — *what is the main thing you want us to know about you?*

② CONNECT — *how are the other ideas related to #1? For instance how is skating related to scouts? to hospital experience?*

③ DETAILS — *let us see what its like to skate competitively, then stop? say how you mean "storm".*

Congratulations!

wow!

Figure 16 *continued*

155

SUGGESTIONS FOR FURTHER READING

Beach, Richard. "Demonstrating Techniques for Assessing Writing in the Writing Conference." *College Composition and Communication* 37 (1986): 56–65.

———. "The Effects of Between-Draft Teacher Evaluation versus Student Self-Evaluation on High School Students' Revising of Rough Drafts. *Research in the Teaching of English* 13 (1979): 129–135.

———. "Self-Evaluation Strategies of Extensive Revisers and Nonrevisers." *College Composition and Communication* 27 (1976): 160–174.

Brannon, Lil, and C. H. Knoblauch. "On Students' Rights to Their Own Texts: A Model of Teacher Response." *College Composition and Communication* 33 (1982): 157–166.

———. "Teacher Commentary on Student Writing." *Freshman English News* 10 (1981): 1–4.

Flanigan, Michael C., and Diane S. Menendez. "Perception and Change: Teaching Revision." *College English* 42 (1980): 256–261.

Flower, Linda, John R. Hayes, Linda Carey, Karen Schriver, and James Stratman. "Detection, Diagnosis, and the Strategies of Revision." *College Composition and Communication* 37 (1986): 16–55.

Haswell, Richard H. "Minimal Marking." *College English* 45 (1983): 600–604.

Held, George, and Warren Rosenberg. "Student–Faculty Collaboration in Teaching College Writing." *College English* 45 (1983): 817–823.

Mallonee, Barbara, and John R. Breihan. "Responding to Students' Drafts: Interdisciplinary Consensus." *College Composition and Communication* 36 (1985): 213–231.

Murray, Donald. "Internal Revision: A Process of Discovery." In *Research on Composing: Points of Departure*. Eds. Charles R. Cooper and Lee Odell. Urbana, IL: NCTE, 1978. 85–104.

Polanyi, Michael. *Personal Knowledge: Towards a Post-Critical Philosophy*. Chicago: University of Chicago Press, 1962.

Schwartz, Mimi. "Response to Writing: A College-Wide Perspective." *College English* 46 (1984): 55–62.

Sommers, Nancy. "Responding to Student Writing." *College Composition and Communication* 33 (1982): 148–156.

———. "Revision Strategies of Student Writers and Experienced Adult Writers." *College Composition and Communication* 31 (1980): 378–387.

Sudol, Ronald A., Ed. *Revising: New Essays for Teachers of Writing*. Urbana, IL: NCTE, 1982.

PART FOUR

Composing Processes: Correcting

8

Sentence-Level Errors: Making Connections

1. Stepping around the broken wine bottles, my attention was drawn to the amount of rubbish on the street.

2. Rico Petrocelli has an inner ear problem in which he may not be able to play baseball anymore.

3. The adolescent is left to pull himself through the emotional breakup caused by his parents' divorce, proving they lack emotional support, which is a problem.

4. In these modern times of today, there is a sense of despair of people who live in anonymous conditions.

5. He has a feeling of fear about his father.

Sources of Difficulty

The writers of the sentences above share a common problem: they have improperly ordered or related words within the sentences. That is, these writers are having difficulty with written syntax. Because the sentences omit crucial language or misconnect ideas, the writers' intended meanings are obscured. Before we consider how to help these writers, we should examine some sources of syntactical problems.

Some arise from the differences between spoken and written English. Speech is extemporaneous; it is delivered spontaneously, whereas writing "withholds utterance to perfect it" (Shaughnessy, 51). Because people formulate ideas as they speak, because their minds are producing new thoughts while their tongues try to catch up, their statements are not as well ordered or articulated as they can be in writing. Speakers punctuate with "uhm's," "ah's," and "well's" to create an opportunity to think what to say next. They tend to string ideas together loosely, repeating ideas and linking them with "and" or "but" rather than with more complex connectives and structures that establish more precise relationships. Inexperienced writers may be unfamiliar with some structures simply because they seldom hear or use them in conversation. Few people today, for instance, would say, "That he is an accomplished mathematician is evident even when he computes a simple restaurant check," but the construction can be useful in writing.

Speaking and writing are further distinguished by the situations in which they occur. In conversations, speakers can tell from their listeners' verbal and nonverbal responses whether they are making themselves clear, whether they need to amplify or qualify their ideas. They also use gestures, facial expressions, and various tones of voice to show whether they are serious, joking, ironic, exaggerating, and so on. Their comments may not be very explicit because these gestures are at their command, because their audience's reaction indicates whether they have made their points, and because speaker and audience share an immediate context on which an utterance is based.

When writers compose, however, their readers are not present, so writers must anticipate their audiences' needs. This requires careful selection and arrangement of materials, a procedure for which there is less time (and less need) in conversation. Because their audience is not present, writers must, as well, use certain lexical and grammatical conventions "that enable a reader to narrow the meaning possibilities of a text sufficiently to convey the direction and limits of its meaning" (Hirsch, 29). Suppose that someone had an appointment to see a doctor who had a reputation for keeping her patients waiting, and the patient arrived to find an overcrowded reception room. He might turn to one of the other patients and say, "Late again." If, however, he were describing this experience in a letter to a friend, and he transcribed only the words above, his friend would be mystified. The writer would need to compose something like, "Dr. Thornhill kept me waiting again, this time for two-and-a-half hours." Experienced writers, then, use what has been called an "elaborated code," while speakers use a "restricted" one (Bernstein). Inexperienced writers often employ their oral or restricted codes in compositions. Unused to predicting their readers' questions, novices may therefore write elliptically.

The inexperienced writer's oral code, moreover, may include expressions that are considered nonstandard written usage or syntax: "He go to work every day on the bus" is a recognized construction of Black English Vernacular (BEV), but it is not an accepted form of Standard Written English. That is not to say that BEV is an inferior linguistic form, only that its conventions may not be comprehended outside the BEV speech community. For instance, a BEV speaker uses "He be sick" to mean that "he" is often sick, has a sickly nature. The speaker will use "He is sick" only in reference to a particular occasion. Members of other English dialect groups would not recognize this usage distinction. Similarly, "Where I am a woman, I understand Juliet's problem" could be used in some colloquial contexts in which "where" is understood to be "because"; but to many ears and eyes, "where" misconnects the ideas because it indicates a spatial rather than a causal relationship. Other speakers use "where" to mean "whereas" or "while," for example, "Where one historian thinks the war was caused by a weak economy, another says racism was to blame." In this sentence, the "where" is used to establish a contrast, usage that will make sense to some listeners but not to others and is not considered Standard Written English (see Chapter 10 for more on dialects).

Aware that their speech patterns differ from written ones, some beginning writers try to imitate written forms without understanding the relationships established by connectives like "where" or "because." This is the case in our second sentence at the beginning of this chapter, "Rico Petrocelli has an inner ear problem in which he may not be able to play baseball anymore."

Many writing errors occur, then, because writers cannot negotiate the transition from speaking to writing. This is so not only because they are inexperienced in forming complicated, embedded sentences, but also because they are unfamiliar with other necessary writing procedures. The very act of writing, the physical transcription of words, is awkward for those who seldom engage in it. Forming the letters, spacing the words, inserting the punctuation marks are not automatic actions, as they are for more practiced writers, and this sort of inexperience can lead to errors of omission, placement, spelling, and punctuation. Novice writers, as well, do not realize that well-connected sentences are crafted through addition, subtraction, and reordering. They tend "to think that the point in writing is to get everything right the first time and that the need to change things is the mark of an amateur" (Shaughnessy, 79). In other words, they are unfamiliar with the procedures of revision by which the experienced writers produce complexly related ideas. They do not know "how writers behave" (Shaughnessy, 75).

When the inexperienced writer attempts to consolidate her ideas in writing, she may falter because her vocabulary is limited and because she is unpracticed in "shifting word order to meet the demands of syntax" (Shaughnessy, 75). The sentence below illustrates what often happens when beginning writers try to connect ideas in the written code. As you read the sentence, try to enumerate the ideas contained in it:

> The adolescent is left to pull himself through the emotional breakup caused by his parents' divorce, proving they lack emotional support, which is a serious problem.

The sentence contains at least four ideas: (1) that adolescents have a problem; (2) that this problem is caused by their parents' divorces; (3) that adolescents must deal with the emotional aftermath of these divorces; and (4) that they must do so without emotional support. Having tried to establish some connections, the writer deserves credit for a valiant first attempt, but he did not manage to link the ideas syntactically. For instance, he has tried to forge a connection between "pull themselves through" and "lack of emotional support" by using "proving," but he is not "proving" or substantiating. If the writer meant that "lack of emotional support" describes *how* adolescents must "pull themselves through," the sentence could be revised as follows: "The adolescent is left to pull himself through the breakup without emotional support." This revision also eradicates the pronoun problem ("they" becomes "he"). Further, the revision omits a repetition of "emotional," on the assumption that readers will take for granted that "the "breakups" are, by their very nature, emotionally taxing; such a judgment requires a writer to evaluate his reader's sophistication, but inexperienced writers often do not think about their readers. Rather (as Chapter 2 explains), they write what Linda Flower calls "writer-based prose," in which the writer is writing to himself rather than to an imagined audience ("reader-based prose").

Finally, inexperienced writers' lack of confidence hinders their writing experience. Students assigned to basic composition classes often arrive with histories of academic misadventure. They have come to think of themselves as unintelligent, not because they are, but because they have been inadequately trained. Writing is especially painful for them because it ineradicably exposes their technical deficiencies and confirms their low self-esteem. Even many older students, made wise by experience, may not trust what they have learned as workers, spouses, parents, consumers, and voters. They may consider this experience different from and less valuable than what professors know and talk about.

A beginning writer's sense of inadequacy takes various forms in her writing. A person who is unsure of what she thinks, who hesitates to commit herself to an independent judgment, may compose overgeneral, vague, or ambiguous statements. Consciously or unconsciously, she does not wish to be found wrong, so she takes evasive action. In an essay about the advantages and disadvantages of moving into her own apartment, one inexperienced writer says, "My attitude toward these small units holds a sense of confinement." Did she mean that she felt confined by the meager spaces of the apartments she had looked at? If so, perhaps she hesitated to come right out with a negative statement. Many people have been raised to believe that we should not criticize, that we should make only positive statements. If this is not true of the writer, she may rather feel that she lacks the authority to make judgments about the relative desirability of various housing arrangements. Think about the ways in which your own speech or prose is affected when you feel threatened by your audience, and you may understand what was happening to this writer.

Diffidence may lead, as well, to wordy, pompous, garbled phrasing. This kind of writing, sadly enough, represents writers' efforts to write like academics. Conscious that their speech does not resemble the vocabulary and cadence of academic writing, and distrustful of their own voices, novices try to sound sophisticated without knowing how to control syntactical and lexical forms. For example, "In these modern times of today, there is a sense of despair of people in anonymous conditions," may mean that the anomie bred by contemporary living conditions produces despair. But to reach that conclusion, the reader must plough through the repetitious opening and must supply missing connections. Ironically, the sentence defeats the writer's wish to seem sophisticated.

Clearly, we need to encourage writers to value their own insights and to express them naturally, as in conversation, but we must also help them examine and sharpen their thinking through writing. This we can do by helping them learn how to use the syntactical forms of the written code, forms that relate ideas precisely and coherently when used appropriately.

Helping by Asking Commonsense Questions

How can a tutor do this when a writer arrives with an essay in hand, an essay riddled with the sorts of syntactic errors we have described? A conventional procedure would be to offer a grammatical analysis of the paper. By the time you see the composition, an instructor may already have dappled it with such comments as "misplaced modifier" or "awk passive." Unfortunately (as Chapter 7 explains), the writer probably lacks familiarity with grammatical terms and will not understand what the comments mean, let alone how to revise. If you yourself are not well versed in grammar, you might not be able to interpret the comments even if you felt it advisable to do so. However, whether or not the paper comments contain technical language, the writer may be confused and intimidated if you do use grammatical terms to describe what is amiss. Notice what happens in the following dialogue, in which Zack, the tutor, is trying to help Carolyn, the writer, improve the following sentence: "Stepping around the broken wine bottles, my attention was drawn to the amount of rubbish on the street."

CAROLYN: I don't get what's wrong with it. Sounds OK to me.

ZACK: Well, you have a dangling participle there.

CAROLYN: A what? Oh wow.

ZACK: No big deal. It's just a verb part, you know, a participle. The present ones
5   always end in "-ing" and the past ones usually end in "ed."

CAROLYN: Present what? I'm lost.

ZACK: Well, that's not so important right now. What matters is that a participial phrase always has to be next to the noun it's modifying.

CAROLYN: Uh, I don't get it. I mean, I'm no good at grammar and I don't know
10   what all these things are, like the thing you said, um, I forget.

ZACK: A noun?

CAROLYN: Yeah, well, I don't know what it is and I gotta turn this paper in tomorrow, so can you help me?

➤ Before reading further, write down your observations about this dialogue. What's good in the tutor's approach? How does he get himself into trouble? How might he have avoided it?

·   ·   ·

Introducing grammar can be risky. You can intimidate a writer who lacks familiarity with the terminology, and once you start using it, you may, like this tutor, have to spend a lot of time defining terms when the writer is eager to revise his essay. This tutor has tried to minimize the grammar discussion, but the writer remains confused and is slightly frustrated by explanations that, even though supportive, do not help her see a way to revise. Instead, you might respond as a reader, as someone who can't understand what was intended or who receives an impression that was probably not intended. Here are some general questions you might raise to help a writer see and correct a miscommunication:

1. What is the action and who (what) is doing it? Or, how does who do what? Or, simply, who does what?

2. How many ideas are in this sentence? How about listing them separately? What is the relationship (connection) between the first idea and the second idea?

3. When is the action taking place? Past? Present? Continuously? Future?

4. Who is speaking to whom? About what?

5. What's another way to say this? What's a single word that expresses this idea?

You will probably want both to tailor one of these by adding language or concepts from the writer's sentence and to provide a context for your question so that the writer knows why you are asking it. Consider the sentence earlier referred to:

> Stepping around the broken wine bottles, my attention was drawn to the amount of rubbish on the street.

"Who does what?"

ZACK: I'm having trouble figuring out who is doing what here.

CAROLYN: Me. When I was stepping around the broken wine bottles, I noticed the rubbish.

5 ZACK: How about writing it that way? It sounded before as if your attention was doing the stepping. Your sentence is clearer now. Look at the sentence you wrote above this one, "On my way to the bus stop, I realized how dirty the neighborhood has become." How does it differ from the original "Stepping" sentence?

CAROLYN: I guess it's clearer that I'm doing it, the realizing I mean.

10 ZACK: Yes, you have "Who does what" in that order, and readers have learned to expect to get information in that order. Now let's look through your paper. What other sentences do you see here that need the "Who does what" sequence?

➤ Before reading any further, analyze this dialogue. What are its pedagogical strengths? What did the session accomplish?

. . .

This time, Zack begins the conversation by establishing the context for his subsequent questions. He identifies the source of his difficulty by indicating what he could not comprehend. When Carolyn offers an improved version by using her habitual speech pattern, Zack encourages her to write the revision on the spot. Carolyn might not have remembered later what she had said, and she might also consider the session more productive if she actually wrote something during it. Notice also that Zack does not start by pointing out the specific error. What if he *had* said, "Well, it sounds as if your attention was doing the stepping, and you didn't mean that, did you?" By focusing on the error, the tutor would have risked humiliating the writer (as Chapter 2 explains), but by starting with "who does what?" Zack gives Carolyn an opportunity to revise without making her feel stupid. Once a writer has amended an original statement, she will probably feel less embarrassed if you then point out the error, as this tutor does. By choosing a good example from the paper (the sentence about the bus stop), Zack helps Carolyn discover the syntactical principle. This practice should help the writer see that she does write some clear sentences, and that she can use them as models when she revises. For further reinforcement, Zack then asks Carolyn to apply the principle elsewhere in the essay. If you encourage writers to apply a method you have used (in this case, asking "Who does what?") to make a successful revision, you increase the chance that they will use it independently at some future time.

In order to establish "Who does what?" you may at times want to write down the syntactical base and ask writers to fill in information taken from their sentences. In "He has a feeling of fear about his father," for instance, it is not clear whether "He" fears the parent or something that might happen to the parent. Filling in the pattern resolves the ambiguity:

ACTOR	ACTION	WHAT'S ACTED ON OR OUTCOME
He	fears	his father

"How many actions are there?"

If a writer has misconsolidated several ideas, one strategy is to get her to separate them, decide how they are related, and then to reconnect them. We can use the second sentence listed at the beginning of this chapter, "Rico Petrocelli has an inner ear problem in which he may not be able to play baseball anymore," to illustrate this procedure:

ALLIE: I can't quite figure out what's going on here. How many actions are there? Let's make a list.

BETTY: He has the ear problem is one, and he can't play is the other.

ALLIE: Good, write those down. Now, what's the connection?

BETTY: Well, he won't be able to play because of the ear problem.

ALLIE: OK, so one thing causes the other. How about writing it that way?

Allie asks Betty to extract the major actions in the sentence so that she can look at them without the connectives that have caused the problem. The writer then uses her habitual speech pattern to make the correction with "because." You might wonder why the writer didn't get it right the first time, since her speech pattern establishes the intended connection, but in the previous section we have pointed out several potential causes for such misconnections. Also, the tutor does not ask the writer directly, "Why can't Petrocelli play anymore?" Since "why" automatically cues "because," this question would have been more prescriptive than asking the writer to make the connection. If, however, the writer could not do so, the tutor might have become more directive. The more open-ended approach allows the writer to make her own revisions. If the tutor were next to highlight the procedure just followed, she would provide the writer with a method for making future revisions independently:

ALLIE: OK, let's review what we just did. What questions did we ask in order to make the revision?

BETTY: We figured out how many things were going on.

ALLIE: Right. Then what?

BETTY: Then we put them back together again.

ALLIE: Sure. Now how about reading some of the remaining sentences aloud to see if you can find spots where you need to do the same thing.

Here, the tutor has added oral reading to the procedure to encourage the writer to test her written phrases against her ear. Betty may not be able to identify similar errors immediately, but she may improve with time and practice. The last part of the dialogue, then, indicates what you might do when you think the writer can operate on her own.

Knowing that written codes often observe different conventions from oral codes, you might well ask why we suggest that the writer try to reproduce a speech pattern in writing. Often, however, spoken and written conventions are identical. Both establish causal relationships by words like "because" or "since." Alternatively, a speaker might not use a causal connective but might offer a pregnant pause instead; a writer uses a semicolon to achieve the same effect. If you think a writer might say an idea more directly or clearly than he has written it, "How would you say that?" then, is not a regressive question.

"When is the action taking place?"

This question is appropriate when the writer's verb tenses are inconsistent or illogical. The dialogue below suggests how you might avoid too much technical discussion and obtain a revision by means of asking "when?" The tutor is directing the writer's attention to this passage:

> As I started walking, I can feel that it's quite chilly out; it must have been around the fifties. Also, the air was very fresh and clean as though there are no traces of pollution. The roads are quiet now—only an occasional car goes by.

DON: I can't tell exactly when all these things are happening in relation to each other. For instance, when did you feel that it was chilly?

ALEC: When I started walking.

DON: But the "I can feel" sounds as if it's happening now. What can you do to
5   make me see that it happened earlier?

ALEC: Change it to "I felt"?

DON: That does it.

ALEC: But I sort of wanted to give the feelings and sights as they were then.

DON: Do you mean that you wanted to recreate the experience? Did you want to
10   write as if you were recording the experience while it was happening?

ALEC: Yes.

DON: So what in your original phrasing isn't going on in the present, and how should you change it?

ALEC: I don't get what you mean.

15 DON: Well, when does "the air was fresh and clean" happen, then or now?

ALEC: Oh, I see. In the past.

DON: How can you tell?

ALEC: Because of the "was." So shall I change it to "is"?

DON: Sure. What other changes to you need to make?

20 ALEC: "Started."

DON: Sure. We said that if you put all of the action in the present tense, the experience seems to be just happening. What happens if you put the action in the past?

ALEC: Well, it's over and I'm looking back on it. So doing it that way gives the
25   impression that I'm thinking about it and not doing it.

DON: Yes, that way you have more distance and are reflecting on the past. The other way makes the action immediate.

ALEC: Yes, the way I want it is that way, not reflective, I mean. It puts you there in the scene and I like that.

Notice how Don tries to discover Alec's intention. Once the tutor establishes it and has helped the writer revise (by asking a more specific question when the general one does not work [lines 12–15]), he tries to make the writer realize that his revisions involve more than mere technical correctness, that a writer has various options and that exercising one or another produces different effects. Once novices begin to grasp this idea, they gain more control as writers. Notice also that when Don rephrases Alec's idea ("you are reflecting on the past"), he provides vocabulary that the writer adopts in his next statement ("not reflective"). The idea is the writer's; the tutor just offers additional language with which the writer can describe what he intended. This expands the writer's vocabulary; it gives him more ways to talk about the composing process.

"Who is speaking to whom about what?"

This variation of "Who does what?" is useful when a writer produces a sentence like the following:

> Explaining cell division by means of a comparison to the reader is the idea in this paragraph by Lewis Thomas.

WILL: I can't figure out who does the explaining.

DAVID: Thomas is writing, so he's explaining.

WILL: OK, so how about starting that way, with what Thomas does.

DAVID: Thomas explains cell division by means of a comparison to the reader?

5 WILL: Who is he explaining this to?

DAVID: Well, the reader, of course. I said that. How come you ask?

WILL: Well, it sounded as if you meant that Thomas drew a comparison between the reader and cell division.

DAVID: No way. I better tell what he compares it to.

10 WILL: Great. So now where are you going to put in the "reader?"

DAVID: Let's see, where can I. . . . Thomas explains cell division to the reader by comparing it to—

WILL: That's a lot clearer.

Here, again, the tutor has avoided discussing grammar in favor of responding as a reader. He has indicated what confused him instead of pointing out syntactical errors. Observe, also, the sequence of questions. Will asks, "Who does the explaining?'' first, to determine who is talking. He then moves to the ''To whom?'' That discussion alerts David that he needs to complete the comparison, and he instinctively changes the form of the word, ''comparison'' to ''by comparing.'' The tutor's systematic, patient approach has let the writer revise broadly without too much prodding.

"What's another way of saying this?"
"What single word expresses this idea?"

Consider the lack of economy in these sentences:

> Erikson has the idea that there are definite stages in human development. They can be described in terms of a series of conflicts.

While they contain no grammatical errors, the writer could more concisely and precisely convey the ideas by substituting single words for ''has the idea'' and ''in terms of.'' As readers, we want to discover ''who does what'' as easily as possible, but the wordy phrases obstruct comprehension. Here is how one tutor, Sandro, addressed the first problem sentence by asking the questions above:

SANDRO: I think I get your point, but I think you can make it more effectively if you take fewer words to do it. Look at the phrase, ''has the idea that.'' What's another way to say that?

MARNIE: Like what?

5 SANDRO: Like some action. What is Erikson doing?

MARNIE: The idea is that this is what he believes, but you can't say that, can you? I was told to stay away from that because we don't really know what the man believes, only what he says. But ''says'' sounds so dull.

SANDRO: There may be times when a writer does express beliefs, and then I see
10 no reason to avoid ''believe''; however, if you don't think this is one of those times and you think ''say'' is blah, try to think of another action. You might try to imagine a scene with Erikson in it. What is he doing?

MARNIE: Well, you could say he's stating a position to a group of psychologists. That's it! He's stating, or maybe arguing.

15 SANDRO: Either of those will work, but now you need to decide how they differ and which one suits your purpose.

MARNIE: ''Argue'' sounds angrier, as if the people were disagreeing with him. I didn't mean that. I guess I'll take ''states'' because that's like a strong ''says.''

In this exchange, perhaps out of genuine confusion, the writer asks Sandro to make a revision for her (''Like what?''). However, Sandro wisely avoids doing so because he believes that Marnie can and should generate her own response. He also suggests a method to help her do so (''imagine a scene''); Marnie should be able to reuse this method, particularly if Sandro were to review the procedure at the end of the session. Finally, the tutor encourages the writer to consider the connotations of the words she has generated. Marnie should become more conscious, as a result, of the effects of her choices. We have deliberately omitted from the dialogue any discussion of the second sentence. Exercise 1 under "Suggestions for Further Writing" at the end of the chapter asks you to write a dialogue in which you help a writer work on this one.

Consolidating Ideas: Lexical Forms, Coordination, and Subordination

When a writer learns how to substitute a single word for a phrase, he may also learn ways to alter lexical forms so that he can consolidate ideas. Consider the following sentences:

ORIGINAL: Jane Addams says that the children of immigrants are embarrassed by their parents. Their parents have not become like Americans and don't live like Americans.

POSSIBLE REVISION: Jane Addams says that children of immigrants are embarrassed because their parents have not become Americanized.

In the original, the causal connection between children's embarrassment and parents' behavior is not explicit, so a tutor might ask, "What is the connection?" If necessary, he might subsequently ask, more prescriptively, "Why are the children embarrassed?" But there is more to be done here. Jane Addams describes naturalized parents, people who are, in fact, Americans, but who have not adopted the customs of their new country. Changing "Americans" to "Americanized" makes this point, but the writer may be unused to the "-ize" or "-ise" form and may be unaware of its meaning. In that case, there is little point in asking the student, "How could you change the ending of 'American'?" Instead, you might use a related example like the one below to illustrate the meaning and function of the suffix. Then, you could ask the writer to apply the principle to his essay:

1. The students felt that the conference on the nuclear freeze should appear on television.
2. The students wanted to televise the conference on the nuclear freeze.
3. The students felt that the conference on the nuclear freeze should be televised.

These three sentences make roughly the same point but use different syntactical forms. Ultimately, you and the writer might want to explore the differences in meaning, but the first task is to alert him to the function and meaning of the suffixes. You might ask how "televise" functions in sentence 2 (it is part of the verb, "wanted to televise"). You might then ask the student to define the meaning of "-ise" in the context of the original sentence. If he sees that the whole word means something like "the act or action of putting them on television," he has taken the first step toward discovering the meaning of the suffix. You could then ask him, "What other verbs use the two forms '-ize' and '-ise'?" Once he supplies these, he may see what they have in common and should be able to define the suffix ("to cause or to be formed into").

Sentence 3 can help a writer recognize that there is a related form of "-ize" and "-ise" that functions differently (it turns the base word into a modifier). If you ask him how "televised" functions in "a televised conference on the nuclear freeze," he will probably say it describes the conference or tells what kind of conference. Next, you could ask how the ending differs from the "-ize" or "-ise" suffix. Then, you could have him list other words that used "-ized" or "-ised" and ask him to explain how adding them to the base word changes its function and meaning (and position) in the sentence.

Illustrative examples help someone discover a principle inductively. This is a good approach because the writer remains actively engaged in learning; he is not a passive listener while you lecture. To borrow John Dewey's tenet, one learns best by doing. In general, we suggest that you avoid asking questions when you think the person with whom you are working lacks the knowledge or skill to provide an answer. Instead of giving it to him, you should, if possible, try to use an example or an analogy from which he can draw an applicative principle. You may not always have time to do this; you may have to give explanations if little time remains or the item at hand is not the focus of the session. Whenever it is feasible, however, we recommend that you help the writer make his own discoveries.

Sentences can also be improved through sentence combining. This technique uses coordinators and subordinators to connect related ideas. Writers unfamiliar with word structures such as roots, prefixes, and suffixes (as in the previous example) are relatively inexperienced in using the syntactical patterns of the written code. They may, as we have said, repeat words unnecessarily or string ideas together without showing their precise relationships. Besides introducing structures such as suffixes, you can help students learn how to improve their writing by using connective language that links or embeds ideas. This can be done in a variety of ways.

If a writer brings an essay to the tutoring session, you can select two conceptually related sentences and ask her to combine the two ideas in a single sentence. She may be able to do so without much coaching because, in preparing the draft, she may have been concentrating on getting the ideas down and may not yet have revised. Writers often have not reworked their sentences because they do not realize that looking back, or "re-vising," in Berthoff's language, constitutes an important part of the writing process. You can encourage students to see revision as an essential activity, as a way of making meaning, not just of editorially dotting *i*'s and crossing *t*'s.

Let's say the writer is trying to introduce the main point of an essay he has read: "The author of 'Confessions of an Erstwhile Child' says that children suffer because they cannot choose their parents. He grew up in an unhappy home himself." An experienced writer, if asked to combine these ideas, might write, "The author of 'Confessions of an Erstwhile Child,' who himself grew up in an unhappy home, says that children suffer because they cannot choose their parents." A less practiced writer might be unused to employing "who," and might revise this way: "The author of 'Confessions of an Erstwhile Child' says that children suffer because they cannot choose their parents. He says this because he himself grew up in an unhappy home." While the writer has not consolidated the ideas in a single sentence, he has added a causal connection. This shows progress. Sometimes a revision takes several steps. You could help this writer take the next one by asking what "this" stands for. Then you might ask him if he can get the cause and effect together with the cause coming first: "Because he himself grew up in an unhappy home, the author. . . ."

Sometimes you can encourage a writer to make more than one useful revision ("That's great. What's another way you could get these ideas together?"). You and the writer can explore the different effects achieved by each variation. This deliberation helps the writer to realize that he has options and that each one will produce a different result. For instance, let us look at the two revisions of the ideas on "Confessions of an Erstwhile Child":

> Because he himself grew up in an unhappy home, the author of "Confessions of an Erstwhile Child" says that children suffer because they cannot choose their parents.

> The author of "Confessions of an Erstwhile Child," who himself grew up in an unhappy home, says that children suffer because they cannot choose their parents.

Using "because" emphasizes *why* the author of the essays takes the position he adopts; using "who," on the other hand, gives additional information about the author of the essay, information that is interesting in light of the stand that he takes. The "because" makes the connection more explicitly, the "who" implicitly. The writer can decide on the basis of his intention which of the two he likes better.

Another way of teaching students how to combine ideas is to have them assemble a list of coordinators and subordinators from their own papers or from whatever they are reading. If necessary, you can supply missing words. The list might look something like the one below:

CONNECTING WORDS

1. Linking words that connect ideas of *equal* or *coordinate* emphasis (coordinating conjunctions):

and	but
for	yet
so	or

2. Embedding words that introduce *subordinate* ideas that give information about the action (subordinating conjunctions):

after	though	as if
although	unless	as long as
as	until	even though
because	when	in order that
before	whenever	so that
since	while	whereas

3. Embedding words that introduce more information about a subject or object (relative pronouns):

that	which
whom	whose
who	

The list indicates the general functions of the different types of connectives. Writers may revise more easily if they understand how the words they choose function in a sentence; as the writers revise, you can ask them what the changes accomplish. To demonstrate how connectives work, you might ask a writer to extract some sentences from a draft, check over the list of connectives, and select an appropriate one.

When writers are choosing connectives, you can ask them to construct alternative revisions so that they can see and explain how the meaning changes depending on the connective they use. You or a writer might discuss an example like the following and then move to the writer's essay:

1. He was tired. He went to bed. (original)
2. He was tired, and he went to bed.
3. When he was tired, he went to bed.
4. Because he was tired, he went to bed.

In the first example, the ideas are separate. We cannot assume a clear connection. In the second, "and" asks us to assume that two things occurred in either physical or temporal proximity, although it is not clear which. The third sets up a time sequence by using "when." The fourth establishes a causal relationship between the two ideas. You can set up similar sets of examples to help writers conceptualize the functions of connective words. In the following set,

> I like violent films, and he likes romantic ones.
>
> I like violent films, but he likes romantic ones.

the "and" links the two people's movie preferences while the "but" emphasizes the difference in their tastes. If you ask writers to analyze the differences, they will probably begin to make choices more consciously and carefully.

Another way of helping writers gain control over written syntactical forms is to construct blank patterns and have writers fill them in with ideas from an assigned topic. For instance,

ACTOR   ACTION

_____ _____ because _____ .

ACTOR   ACTION   ACTION

_____ , who _____ , _____ .

ACTOR   ACTION   ACTOR   ACTION

After _____ _____ , _____ _____ .

If a writer is taking a composition course, he may be using a text that offers exercises in sentence combining. Typically, these texts pair sentences that are implicitly related in meaning, and the directions ask the student to combine them by using coordinators and subordinators. You can use these exercises to good advantage, as *part* of your entire instructional plan. Correcting someone else's sentences is a different process from generating one's own, and at some point writers need to construct original written statements that use connective language. After the writer has gotten some practice through the text's exercises, you will probably want to ask him to make up his own sentences. Perhaps our best advice is to give writers practice of various kinds in hopes that they will begin to master and to internalize the syntactical forms of written English.

Summary

Inexperienced writers make syntactical errors for a variety of reasons, chiefly because of differences between spoken and written English. Often writers are unfamiliar with complex connectives and structures used to link written ideas. Further, because inexperienced writers are unused to anticipating an absent audience's needs, they tend to write elliptically. Their oral codes, as well, may not conform to the forms of standard written English. Many sentence-level errors occur, then, because writers cannot negotiate the transition between speaking and writing. They are hampered by limited vocabularies and inexperience in transcribing, transforming, and revising words. Writers' awareness of their technical deficiencies can lead to diffidence, which, in turn, produces vague, ambiguous, or garbled phrasing.

Rather than analyze sentence-level errors grammatically, a practice that confuses and intimidates inexperienced writers because they are unfamiliar with grammatical terms, you can respond in everyday language. Basic queries like "Who's doing what?" "How many ideas are in this sentence?" and "Who is speaking to whom?" help writers see and correct miscommunications. To make these questions text-specific, you can tailor them to include details from writers' sentences.

To help writers consolidate stringy, choppy, or misconnected ideas, you can, through illustration, introduce lexical forms like affixes. Examples help writers unfamiliar with these forms infer each one's meaning and semantic effect. You can also suggest various kinds of sentence-combining exercises in which writers use coordinators and subordinators to join and embed ideas. If you ask a writer to construct alternate consolidations of paired sentences, she will begin to see how meaning changes depending on the connectives used. Handbook exercises that invite writers to combine ready-made sentences can be useful, but writers also need to construct original ones that contain connective language. As writers amend syntactical errors in their essays, you can reassure them that consolidating two ideas may require several revisions rather than just one. Only through diversified practice in recognizing, manipulating, and generating the syntactical forms of written English, do writers internalize them.

SUGGESTIONS FOR JOURNAL ENTRIES

1. Ask a friend or classmate to tape unobtrusively conversations in a public place, conversations that you yourself do not observe. Transcribe the conversations. Discuss whatever uncertainties about meaning that you as a listener experience, and analyze the aspects of the speakers' language that account for your perplexity. If the recorder-observer were editing the tape for publication, what kinds of changes would she make to clarify meaning?

2. Write about how your speech changes when you lack confidence or feel anxious. How does your writing change under comparable circumstances?

3. List several expressions that you would use comfortably in speaking but not in writing, and vice versa. What characteristics does each group have in common? How do the two groups differ?

4. At what point in composing do you tend to craft syntax? What sorts of revisions do you typically make and why? How can your observations help writers with whom you work?

5. To what extent has formal instruction in grammar improved the syntactical clarity of your sentences?

6. What seems to be causing the syntactical problems of a writer with whom you are working? What strategies have you adopted and why? How well are they working? What will you try next?

SUGGESTIONS FOR FURTHER WRITING

1. Review our dialogue about the sentence: "Erikson has the idea that there are definite stages in human development. They can be described in terms of a series of conflicts" (pp. 168–69). Then write a continuation in which the tutor helps the writer revise the second sentence: "They can be described in terms of a series of conflicts."

2. Without using grammatical terminology, write out questions that would help the writers of the following sentences to recognize problems and to revise for clarity. Where appropriate, use the questions and strategies suggested in this chapter.

a. This truck was on Morse Avenue, it was repairing the sidewalks.

b. Have you every been brainwashed by evolution?

c. The tragedy of today is the injustice and blatant disregard we have for our elderly citizens.

d. Perhaps the rise of designer jeans can be compared to "The Emperor's New Clothes" by Hans Christian Anderson.

e. There are many holes in the evolution of man.

f. When the police took him to the station, they found a man was wanted for murder in another state that fit this man's description.

g. Another example of a judge who was incompetent at his job because of outside problems is a suicidal one.

h. This problem consists of a street which is located in your jurisdiction and with your support and consideration in the matter I see no reason why the problem cannot be overcome.

i. The anonymous writer refers to marriage as a psychological trap that was put there by people's misunderstandings as children that never got straightened out.

j. Pilar is considered by Hemingway as a simple peasant. Along with this description, her actions contribute to the enhancement of her personality.

k. Heller's reason for brutalization is not attributed to simply a war and a common cause. There is never any mention of a real enemy.

l. There is a feeling of distaste for the institution of slavery.

m. In the book, *The Politics of Experience,* R. D. Laing, the author, suggests that contemporary society of today is more interested in having normal average people who conform than imaginative unconventional people who want society's institutions.

n. Occasionally things happen that we can't explain with our present knowledge of natural laws. We call such things "supernatural." Sometimes we ridicule or deny these occurrences.

3. Read the sample of student writing below. List the kinds and possible sources of error. Given the pattern of errors that you have found, write a dialogue between you and the writer in which you address the problem or problems you would give priority. Explain your choices and the reasons for the strategies you adopt in the dialogue.

HYPERACTIVE CHILDREN

The true cause of hyperactivity is presently unknown. The problem has been studied for the past fifty years, and the number of remedies or solutions to the problem have evolved. There are many arguments about the safety of the treatments given to hyperactive children, and whether there necessary at all. The main concern of parents, since there is no present core is to try to shape their
5   hyperactive children into a normal state like their peers, so that they may expand and develop their personalities.

A large number of solutions have come about for the treatment of hyperactive children. The most comon and widespread is the use of stimulant drugs known as amphetamines. Other solutions are to control the childrens diet by restricting the types of food that they eat. The reasons for this was
10   because it was believed that additives such as synthetic colors, flavors, and salicylates affected behavior. The remaining possibilities of hyperactivity are psychological reasons. They relate the fact that if a child was confined to the home and limited in his outdoor activities, then he has narrowed his outlets for energy thus making himself hyperactive.

Each of the above solutions has its own set of problems related to it. The most common solution being the use of amphetamines creates the largest problem. There have been a number of tests
15   done in which both the good and the bad have resulted from the use of drugs.

Judith Rappaport of the National Mental Health Institute states "these drugs dramatically improve hyperactive children's behavior when the children take them for short periods of time. A physician quoted from the NY Times states "We give it (Ritalin) to one terrible little boy, and a few minutes later the child was actually taking out the garbage for his mother. She almost flipped out." These
20   are just a few examples of how the short term use of amphetamines have helped hyperactive children.

There are also some ill side effects to the use of the drugs. Robert Sprague from the University of Illinois through years of research has determined that if children take amphetamines the heart rate and blood pressure become increased, and if this is taken for many years then it may become
25   harmful.

4. Write a dialogue for a second lesson for the writer of the essay above. Decide what sorts of follow-up exercises would help reinforce what you had covered in the first session. Attach this second dialogue to the first one.

SUGGESTIONS FOR CLASS ACTIVITIES

1. Share with classmates your answers to the exercises in "Suggestions for Further Writing."

2. Bring to class copies of mispunctuated paragraphs written by people with whom you work. Lead a class discussion in which classmates analyze the errors and suggest tutoring strategies, or use the paragraphs for role-playing exercises.

3. Bring to class copies of handbooks and discuss the relative merits of the punctuation exercises.

4. As a class, make up some exercises that would address the punctuation problems of writers with whom you work.

SUGGESTIONS FOR FURTHER READING

Allen, Robert L. *English Grammars and English Grammar*. New York: Scribner's, 1974.

Bartholomae, David. "The Study of Error." *College Composition and Communication* 31 (1980): 253–269.

Bernstein, Basil. "Linguistic Codes: Hesitation, Phenomena, and Intelligence." *Language and Speech* 5 (1962): 31–46.

Berthoff, Ann E. *Forming, Thinking, Writing*. Rochelle Park, NJ: Hayden, 1978. 70–78.

Carkeet, David. "Understanding Syntactic Errors in Remedial Writing." *College English* 38 (1977): 682–695.

Chaika, Elaine. "Who Can Be Taught." *College English* 35 (1974): 575–583.

Christensen, Francis. *A New Rhetoric*. New York: Harper and Row, 1976.

Cooper, Charles R. "An Outline for Writing Sentence-Combining Problems." *English Journal* 62 (1973): 96–108.

Daiker, Donald A. "Sentence Combining and Syntactic Maturity in Freshman English." *College English* 29 (1978): 36–41.

Emig, Janet A., James T. Fleming, and Helen M. Popp. *Language and Learning*. New York: Harcourt Brace and World, 1966.

Faigley, Lester L. "Generative Rhetoric as a Way of Increasing Syntactic Fluency." *College Composition and Communication* 30 (1979): 176–181.

Fisher, John C. "Generating Standard Sentence Patterns and Beyond." *College Composition and Communication* 21 (1970): 264–268.

Fries, Charles Carpenter. *The Structure of English: An Introduction to Construction of English Sentences*. New York: Harcourt Brace and World, 1952.

Hartwell, Patricia. "Grammar, Grammars, and the Teaching of Grammar." *College English* 47 (1985): 105–127.

Hirsch, E. D., Jr. *The Philosophy of Composition*. Chicago: University of Chicago Press, 1977. 13–50.

Hoover, Mary Rhodes. "Community Attitudes toward Black English." *Language in Society* 7 (1978): 65–87.

Joos, Maertin. *The English Verb: Form and Meanings*. Madison: University of Wisconsin Press, 1968.

Labov, William. *Language in the Inner City: Studies in the Black English Vernacular*. Philadelphia: University of Pennsylvania Press, 1972.

———. *The Study of Nonstandard English*. Champaign, IL: NCTE, 1970.

Maimon, Elaine P., and Barbara F. Nodine. "Measuring Syntactic Growth: Errors and Expectations in Sentence-Combining Practices with College Freshmen." *Research in the Teaching of English* 12 (1978–79): 233–244.

Marzana, Robert J. "The Sentence-Combining Myth." *Educational Journal* 65 (1976): 57–59.

Mellon, John C. *Transformational Sentence Combining: A Method for Enhancing the Development of Syntactic Fluency in English Composition*. Urbana, IL: NCTE, 1969.

O'Hare, Frank. *Sentence Combining: Improving Student Writing without Formal Grammar Instruction*. Research Report 15. Urbana, IL: NCTE, 1973.

Roberts, Paul. *English Sentences*. New York: Harcourt Brace and World, 1962.

Shaughnessy, Mina P. *Errors and Expectations*. New York: Oxford University Press, 1977. 44–159.

Strong, William. *Sentence Combining: Improving Student Writing without Formal Grammatical Instruction*. Research Report 15. Urbana, IL: NCTE, 1973.

Waddell, Marie L., Robert M. Esch, and Roberta R. Walker. *The Art of Styling Sentences*. Woodbury, NY: Barron's Educational Series, 1972.

Wolfram, Walt, and Ralph W. Fasold. *The Study of Social Dialects in American English*. Englewood Cliffs, NJ: Prentice-Hall, 1974.

9

Punctuation

1. For leisure in that community men fool with cars and women play racquetball separately.

2. This writer made a good point about advertising. Although I don't agree with it.

3. Children are very observant, they know when their parents are unhappy.

4. He never had trouble making decisions, he always made fast decisions. The wrong ones.

5. The first point made by the book is, large government means more taxes.

6. I wanted the dinner to be a special occasion, however, my plans were ruined by constant interruptions.

7. Some people see psychologists, other people see their clergymen, it doesn't matter who they see, they just need to talk to someone when they are in trouble.

8. Because men and women differ due to the fact of their upbringing. Women are not as competitive in seeking jobs.

9. The author did not have a happy childhood, for example: his father beat him every Saturday.

The writers of the above examples may appear to have a different problem from that of the writers described in Chapter 8: the sentence-level errors previously discussed reflect conceptual problems, while the punctuation mistakes seem merely surface errors. Actually, however, both the writer who fails to punctuate correctly and the writer who uses "and" for "although" are having trouble expressing relationships among ideas precisely. Punctuation is as essential to making meaning as connective language, which it often functionally resembles. The confusion caused by the absence of a comma in the first example shows how necessary punctuation is: "For leisure in that community men fool with cars and women play racquetball separately." Because there is no comma between "can" and "and" to signal the beginning of a new idea, a reader might initially assume the writer means that dalliance is a community sport. Ambiguities and unintended meanings result from punctuation errors because the marks group words into units of meaning. Punctuation helps readers predict meaning by telling them when to expect an idea to continue and when to assume that it has been completed. Unfortunately, inexperienced writers and even some more practiced ones do not use punctuation discriminatingly.

Causes of Some Punctuation Errors

The types of punctuation errors represented in the examples above are not hard to recognize. Less apparent, however, are the causes of such problems. Some writers, it is true, are simply careless. They may not consider punctuation significant enough to bother with, or they may be too pressed for time to check for it in editing, but these explanations do not generally apply to inexperienced writers, who are unaccustomed to the conventions and do not use them as automatically as more practiced writers. Novice writers do not attend to punctuation because they are concentrating on other basic composing activities that they are just beginning to master. However, the writers need more than an advisory to proofread because they are not familiar with all of the punctuation marks, their various functions, or their appropriate placement.

Some writers, having received little instruction, try to punctuate by ear, that is, by recalling the cadence of spoken phrases. While this method can work to some extent for writers with a good rhythmic sense, it is only a partial and often a misleading approach because units of speech are often shorter or longer than a grammatical sentence. In a conversation, for instance, if someone were to ask, "Why were you so late for work?" the answer, "Because I missed my bus," would sound complete by itself because it derives meaning from the interrogative (rhetorical) context. In the written code, however, a "because" clause derives its meaning from a grammatical context, a main or independent clause; therefore, the "because" clause is not separated from it. The writer of the second example, "This writer makes a good point about advertising. Although I don't agree with it," may be unaware of this principle. On the other hand, he may have wanted the "although" clause to sound parenthetical, and because he did not know how to use parentheses, he set off the clause.

Writers who try to punctuate by ear may also have trouble distinguishing a partial from a full stop, as in the third example, "Children are observant, they know when their parents are unhappy." The comma suggests that the writer "heard" a pause between the two ideas, but the rhetorical connection between them may have decided him against using a period. The second idea illustrates the first, so a period might have seemed to create too wide a separation. A similar problem is reflected in the fourth example, "He never had trouble making decisions, he always made fast choices. The wrong ones." Since the first two clauses are closely related in meaning, a speaker would probably pause more briefly between them than before the phrase, "The wrong ones," where a long pause would underscore the sarcasm. This writer, like the previous one, uses punctuation in a way that makes rhetorical but not grammatical sense. The writer, in other words, does not know that punctuation hinges on grammatical rather than on rhetorical structures. Strictly speaking, the grammatical structure requires a period (or semicolon) after "decisions" and a comma after "choices." While a period before the phrase, "the wrong ones," could be justified by the claim that such punctuation heightens the irony, one would need to make such a choice deliberately, and inexperienced writers tend to be unable to distinguish justifiable from unjustifiable cases. They need to understand the grammatical principle before they can violate it selectively, to good advantage. Writers who punctuate by ear can also be misled because speakers often pause for dramatic effect or emphasis. If written, the sentences they utter would require *no* interior punctuation. The comma in "The first point made in the book is, large government means more taxes," signals a pause that a speaker might make for emphasis, as if to suggest a missing "that." Grammatically, however, the comma incorrectly separates subject from verb.

A writer's punctuation difficulties are compounded when she is neither aurally discriminating nor grammatically discerning. The sixth example, "I wanted the dinner to be a special occasion, however my plans were ruined by constant interruptions," suggests not only that the writer failed to "hear" a complete stop before "however" and a partial one after it, but also that she misunderstands its grammatical function. She probably assumed that "however" serves as a conjunction like "and" or "but." Thinking, therefore, that she was supposed to be linking rather than separating ideas, she acknowledged a pause by using a comma.

Besides being misled by their aural sense, some writers try to apply rules that they misremember or misunderstand. They know that punctuation can help them to connect and to separate ideas, but since they do not understand the underlying principles of the system, they do not know how to accomplish either aim. Two contradictory tendencies, as Shaughnessy points out (Chapter 2), appear in their writing as a result. On the one hand, they may ignore sentence endings altogether, stringing ideas together by omitting punctuation or by overusing commas, as in the seventh example, "Some people see psychologists, other people see clergymen, it doesn't matter who they see, they just need to talk to someone when they are in trouble." On the other hand, writers may break sentences into fragmented segments. Since the writers do not yet use embedding structures comfortably and have difficulty keeping in mind all that they want to include in a sentence, they separate elements that should be joined, as in "Because men and women differ due to the fact of their upbringing. Women are not as competitive in seeking jobs." Both impulses, the one to link and the other to separate, reflect the writers' efforts to form statements that are more syntactically and conceptually complicated than those they can extemporize as speakers. But just as their uncertain written use of connective language creates misimpressions, their punctuation produces ambiguities and unintended meanings.

Writers' unfamiliarity with certain punctuation marks further restricts their efforts to write more fully and complexly articulated statements. Inexperienced writers usually have seen colons, semicolons, parentheses and marks of ellipsis, but they do not have a clear enough sense of their functions to use them. Punctuation is, for novices, a way to link or separate ideas only in the simplest sense. They do not yet know that the marks themselves can operate semantically, that a colon, for instance, can be used to mean "for example" or "in the following way" or that a semicolon can implicitly express a "because." Consequently, when writers do begin to use these marks, they simply add rather than substitute them for the words for which they stand, as in, "The author did not have a happy childhood, for example: his father beat him every Saturday." Once writers learn how these marks work, they gain alternate ways of expressing their ideas. For writers to see the punctuation system as a way to make meaning rather than as a battery of arbitrary and confusing rules, they need to understand that the marks guide a reader's eye and voice by signaling rests and pauses that cluster or divide words into independent or subordinate units, and they need to know that what constitutes independence or subordination is grammatically rather than rhetorically defined.

Helping Writers to Punctuate: Reading Aloud, Reading Unpunctuated Passages

Because punctuation is part of a complex system of linking, embedding, and separating written ideas, you need not wait until a fragment or run-on sentence appears in a writer's essay before introducing the subject. You can, instead, include it while you are helping writers learn various ways of combining ideas, just as you can give them practice in using coordinators and subordinators when addressing punctuation errors. If you approach punctuation errors as an opportunity to help a writer explore alternate ways of relating ideas, not as an occasion for fixing up "mechanical" errors, as so many English handbooks do, you will be addressing her real need. As always, before selecting tutoring strategies, you will have to assess each writer's degree of understanding and the basis on which she uses the system. You will need to know whether a writer uses her ear, whether doing so leads her into error, whether she is acquainted with all of the various marks and with the grammatical system that governs their use, and at what point in the writing process she attends to punctuation.

Oral reading is a basic strategy useful both for assessing a writer's understanding and illustrating the functions of punctuation. When a writer misplaces or omits it, particularly at sentence endings, you can ask the writer to read some of the sentences out loud. Someone with a good ear may hear pauses or stops that he did not notice as he wrote and may correct the errors immediately. If he cannot distinguish pauses from stops, or if he pauses where punctuation is rhetorically but not grammatically called for, you will then need to introduce some of the principles of the system described later in the chapter. If, on the other hand, the writer's ear is reliable, you can suggest that he proofread orally or at least that he reread slowly as if reading aloud. You may, at times, wish to read a writer's sentence as punctuated to let him hear how he is misleading a reader, but this approach risks embarrassing the writer and should be adopted with caution. You could, instead, read the sentence aloud several times, each time delivering it differently. Next, you could ask which way the writer intended it to be read, and the two of you could then discuss the punctuation that would signal each version. If the writer has a "tin ear," oral/aural exercises like these will not work well. Just as some people have trouble keeping time to the rhythm when they dance or play a musical instrument, some writers cannot distinguish speech rhythms. In such cases, which are easy to detect, it is well to adopt an alternate strategy.

Both kinds of writers, those with reliable and those with unreliable aural senses, can, however, profit from an exercise in which they are asked to punctuate an unpunctuated passage aloud. This exercise is quite different from reading their own essays because they do not already know what the author intended to say. Since they do not know how the words should be grouped, the readers typically pause at the wrong places, discover their errors, and have to reread a line to regroup the words so that they make sense. The ambiguities and illogicalities that follow from the absence of punctuation are often amusing, and the object of the exercise is inescapable. If you are tutoring in a writing center, such exercises may already be on hand, but it is easy enough to reproduce a paragraph from a story or an essay without its punctuation. You might, alternatively, use literature that is deliberately unpunctuated, such as an e e cummings poem or a passage from Don Marquis' *Archy and Mehitabel,* in which the absence of punctuation functions rhetorically or dramatically. Writers can then be asked to punctuate these passages by ear or by rule depending on their level of understanding. As a prelude to a discussion of punctuation, these passages can be helpful because they reveal a writer's problem, dramatize the need for punctuation, and lead to lively discussion.

Introducing Some Punctuation Conventions by Asking Questions

When writers do not have reliable ears, or when they are learning new punctuation conventions, they need to understand the rationales behind them. However, you need not use a lot of grammatical terminology to explain them. Instead, when discussing a writer's sentences, you can usually use everyday language and ask questions like those we have suggested in Chapter 8. The only grammatical grasp required is that writers know how to recognize subjects and verbs, that they know what a sentence is, what coordinators and subordinators are, and how they function. If you find, as the tutor in the following dialogue does, that a writer does not understand the necessary terms or concepts, you can introduce them in the process of asking questions about the writer's punctuation. The questions that help a writer discover and correct punctuation errors include the following:

For eliminating fragments:
1. "Who's doing what?" or "who is what?"
2. "Can this idea stand by itself?"
   (This often works better if you cover up the preceding and following sentences.)

For eliminating run-ons and for punctuating compound sentences:
3. "How many ideas (actions) are there?" and "Which ones can stand by themselves?"

For adding commas around nonessential embedded phrases, nonrestrictive and introductory subordinate clauses:
4. "If you take away this idea, will the sentence still make sense?"

In the dialogue below, Joyce, a tutor, has detected some sentence fragments in Tony's essay. The first lines that concern her are: "It took him five minutes to get to the drugstore. Running all the way." As you read the initial portion of the dialogue, which we have broken into two sections, please notice the sequence of questions and speculate as to why Joyce might have begun the session as she did. Include in your response answers to these specific queries:

- What does Joyce accomplish by first asking Tony to read aloud?
- What does she accomplish by helping Tony recognize sentence elements before she discusses his punctuation?

JOYCE: *[Points to "running all the way"]* How about reading this aloud?

TONY: Running all the way.

JOYCE: Hear anything?

TONY: Is there something wrong with it?

5 JOYCE: Well, who's doing the running?

TONY: The guy who's running to the drugstore. Isn't that clear?

JOYCE: Well, I see what you're trying for, but by using a period, you set the second part off as if it could stand alone, and by itself it doesn't tell who's doing the running. How can you make the second part say who's running?

10 TONY: I guess you have to have a "he" there.

JOYCE: Good. Write that down.

TONY: *[writes]* "He ran all the way."

JOYCE: Good. Do you know what "he" would be called?

TONY: Is that the subject?

15 JOYCE: Right, the "who" is the subject. Now let's figure out what else a sentence has to have besides a subject. Think about my question, "who does what?"

TONY: I guess the "does" is like a verb.

JOYCE: Good, Try saying in your own words what a verb is.

TONY: An action?

20 JOYCE: Yes, that's one kind of verb. So subject and verb are important parts of a sentence. What other kinds of verbs are there?

TONY: Let's see. "He ran," "he talked," "he sang." All of those are actions though. I can't think of anything else.

JOYCE: OK, try these: *[writes]*

25   Ivy is a good houseplant.
    He feels tired.

    Where are the verbs there?

TONY: I guess "is" is the first one. It's not an action though.

JOYCE: Right. That's exactly the point. Some verbs aren't actions. They tell what the subject *is*. You could call them "state of being" verbs. Can you think

30   of any others like "is"?

TONY: "Are"? "Was"? I guess you could say, "The Ivy was pretty."

JOYCE: OK. Now what about "He feels tired." Where's the verb?

TONY: Um, "tired"?

35 JOYCE: Not really. Try substituting "is" for "feels" and you may see why.

TONY: Well, in that sentence, "is" would be the verb.

JOYCE: Right, and "feels" works just like "is." You could say that a state of feeling is a state of being. Can you think of other verbs like that?

TONY: "I *was* tired"?

40 JOYCE: Right. How have you changed it?

TONY: Well, "is" is now and "was" is past.

JOYCE: Right. There are other state-of-being verbs, "seems," for instance, but for now, let's look at the differences between "He ran all the way" and "Ivy is a good houseplant." What does "ran" tell?

45 TONY: What he did.

JOYCE: Good. So it tells what the subject did. And "is"?

TONY: That's different. It just sort of tells you, um, I don't know, what he is.

JOYCE: That's right. Notice that you could shift the sentence around to "A good houseplant is ivy." The "is" works like an equals sign in math. It lets you
50 describe ivy. Ivy equals houseplant. So whatever follows the "is" will describe the subject. Now how is that different from "he ran all the way"?

TONY: Hmm, that sort of describes him too, but it's different.

JOYCE: Try to explain the difference.

TONY: Well, it does talk about what he *did*. I guess it describes the action, not
55 the person so much.

JOYCE: That's great. That's a good distinction between the two main kinds of verbs and what they do. How about writing that down and also what you said about what's in a sentence?

TONY: You mean subject and verb? *[Joyce nods; he writes.]*

60 JOYCE: Right. OK, so far, you've said that a sentence has a subject and a verb. Now here are a few more examples to help you get a more complete definition: *[writes]*

He ran all the way.
Because he ran all the way.

65 How are those different?

TONY: Um, the second one adds a "because."

JOYCE: Do they sound any different?

TONY: I don't know.

JOYCE: Well, when you see "because," what else do you want to know?

70 TONY: You mean, because what?

JOYCE: Good. Go on.

TONY: Like, where's the rest of it?

JOYCE: Super. That's it. The "because" makes it sound as if something is coming or was already said. Now, with the "because" do you think it's a sentence?

75 TONY: Well, the one without "because" is. It has a subject and a verb. So does the one with "because," but, I don't know; somehow it doesn't sound complete.

JOYCE: That's right.

TONY: So does that mean it's not a sentence? I mean with the "because"?

80 JOYCE: Exactly. So what do you have to add to your definition of a sentence?

TONY: That it's gotta be a complete idea.

JOYCE: Right, and what you're sensing is that the "because" keeps the idea from being complete. Now let's go back to what you wrote:

Running all the way.

85 Let's apply the definition and see if it works. Does this have a subject, a verb, and a complete idea?

TONY: Well, the "running" looks like a verb, but there's no subject, so it can't be a real sentence.

JOYCE: That's right. So you can't set it off with punctuation that says it is. Now
90 let's see if "running" is a complete verb. Try using it in a sentence.

TONY: He was running all the way.

JOYCE: Good. Now what did you add?

TONY: Oh, I see. I added a "was." Does that mean that "was" is a verb?

JOYCE: "Was running" is the whole verb. Here the "was" is helping tell when
95 the running took place. When it's by itself, it's a state-of-being verb like "is" in "Ivy is a good houseplant." So let's review. To make your "running" idea into a sentence, you need to add what?

TONY: Add "he was," subject and verb, I mean the rest of the verb.

JOYCE: Great!

"Who does what?"

We interrupt the dialogue here to point out what Joyce has accomplished so far. When she realizes that Tony's ear does not help him punctuate, she asks a "Who does what?" question (line 5) to begin a discussion of sentence elements. If she had merely identified the error by saying, "This is a fragment. It can't stand by itself," she would merely have labeled the error without helping Tony see what grammatical principle he violated. Her introduction of sentence elements helps him understand why the phrase is incomplete and gives him a vocabulary for talking about what he has written. Still, Joyce uses only a few grammatical terms, avoiding "participial phrase" and "adjectival function" in order not to confuse and overburden him with too many concepts at once. Since the primary objective of the session is to help Tony with punctuation, she probably wants to move on to that topic as soon as possible, so she abbreviates the discussion of verbs and does not get into the subject of subordination when she uses "because" in her example (line 82). We return now to the dialogue:

100 JOYCE: That's a good first step. Try writing it that way.

[Tony writes, "It took him five minutes to get to the drugstore running all the way."]

Now, who's doing the running?

TONY: He is, you know, the guy who went to the drugstore.

105 JOYCE: But if you put the "running" idea next to "drugstore," what might a reader think?

TONY: You mean they'd think the drugstore was running? But the drugstore couldn't possibly run.

JOYCE: That's true, but strictly speaking that "-ing" word, "running," is going
110 to describe whatever it's next to. So what can you do to avoid the problem?

TONY: Well, I have to put it next to the guy. Let's see: *[writes]*

It took him running all the way five minutes to get to the drugstore.

That sounds awful.

JOYCE: How about trying it another way?

115 TONY: *[writes]*

Running all the way he got to the drugstore in five minutes.

JOYCE: Great. Now let's see if some punctuation is needed.

TONY: Well, I know I can't have a period after "way."

JOYCE: Right. Would you put anything else?

120 TONY: Should there be a comma?

JOYCE: Yes. Why did you think so?

TONY: I just figured there had to be something.

JOYCE: Your instinct is good. Try reading the whole thing out loud.

TONY: *[reads, pausing at "way"]* "Running all the way he got to the drugstore
125 in five minutes."

JOYCE: How many pauses do you hear?

TONY: None really.

JOYCE: Well, actually, you paused before the "he," but you may not have heard the pause. Why might someone want to pause there?

130 TONY: Well, the first part isn't the main idea. The main idea is the subject and verb, right?

JOYCE: Right. When a sentence starts with phrases that aren't the main idea, we tend to pause right before we get to the subject, sort of to tell the reader or listener that the main idea is coming. So that's what the comma says: pause.

135 TONY: OK.

JOYCE: See if you can think up another sentence that starts with an introductory idea before the main idea.

TONY: Gee, I don't know.

JOYCE: Try starting with the main idea and adding to it.

140 TONY: OK. *[writes]* "He sang." Um, "Walking to work, he sang." And I'd put a comma after "work."

JOYCE: Great. Now try putting the "running" phrase in your original sentence somewhere else. You didn't like it after the "he," but you can try substituting "Dan" and see if it sounds any better.

145 TONY: OK, lemme try it: *[writes]* "Dan running all the way got to the drugstore in five minutes." But how do I punctuate it?

JOYCE: Well, think about where it comes in the sentence. Where are the subject and verb now?

TONY: The "running" idea separates them.

150 JOYCE: If you took it out, would you still have a sentence?

TONY: Sure. It has a subject and a verb, and it makes sense.

JOYCE: So if you can take that phrase away, it's not really essential, and since it interrupts the subject–verb sequence, you need to put commas around it to tell the reader that you're interrupting. So there are really two reasons for
155 enclosing the phrase in commas. Got 'em?

TONY: I think so. The "not essential" idea. I mean, you can take out the "running" stuff. And separating the subject and verb.

JOYCE: Good. How about writing that down so you can refer to it when you proofread?

"If you take away this idea, will the sentence still make sense?"

Once Tony understands the basic elements of a sentence, he can better see why a period before his "running" phrase won't do. By suggesting that he place the participial phrase at different points in the sentence, Joyce teaches him syntactical variations while explaining the punctuation convention. She also wisely suggests that he generate sentences that illustrate a principle he has just learned (lines 114, 136). Another good strategy she uses is to ask him to write a new sentence that begins with an introductory phrase: she suggests that he start with a "kernel" sentence and then that he supplement it, which he does by joining "walking to work" to "he sang" (line 140). This is a basic method of helping writers to expand an idea, a method that can be used when they need to elaborate as well as when they are learning punctuation. Finally, Joyce asks "If you took [this idea] out, would you still have a sentence?" (line 150) to help Tony understand that interruptive, nonessential phrases must be set off with commas.

By the end of the session, Tony has learned quite a bit: that a sentence contains a subject, a verb, and a complete thought; that a participial phrase can be positioned either before or after the noun it describes, and that commas should be used after introductory phrases and around nonessential phrases. Without getting too technical, Joyce has introduced some sophisticated ideas that should help Tony phrase as well as punctuate his ideas more effectively.

"How many ideas are there?"

This question can be asked when writers produce run-on sentences, or when they mispunctuate compound sentences (two main clauses linked by a coordinating conjunction) and complex sentences (one main clause and one or more subordinate clauses). In the following dialogue. Thad helps Senta, the author of the first example at the beginning of the chapter, learn to punctuate a compound sentence. As you read the dialogue, notice how Thad introduces the idea of coordination as they discuss the sentence.

THAD: How about reading this sentence? *[points to it]*

SENTA: *[reads]* "In that community men fool with cars *[pauses]* and women play racquetball separately."

THAD: The way you read that makes sense, but it could be read a different way.

5 SENTA: I don't get what you mean.

THAD: OK. First, let's see how many ideas there are.

SENTA: Two: what the men do and what the women do.

THAD: OK. Now when I first read this, I had a hard time seeing what you meant.

SENTA: How come?

10 THAD: Well, when I read it at first, I thought the men liked two things.

SENTA: You mean the men liked, oh golly, I see, to fool with women.

THAD: That's the problem. Can you think of a way to solve it?

SENTA: Get rid of "and" and make two sentences?

THAD: You could, but you don't need to. You can change the punctuation.

15 SENTA: I don't see how.

THAD: Well, where do you want your reader to pause?

SENTA: Between the ideas. I guess before the "and."

THAD: That's it, so what could you put there?

SENTA: A comma?

20 THAD: Yes.

SENTA: But I thought I didn't have to if I put the "and" in.

THAD: That raises an interesting issue about how words like "and" work. Look at these examples for a minute, and then we'll get back to your paper. *[writes]*

25   Joe and Marcia went to the movies.

He's stingy and suspicious.

She whistled and tapped her feet.

She likes steaks and burgers and Tom likes vegetarian food.

OK, so what is the "and" doing in each example?

30 SENTA: In the first one, "and" puts the two people together.

THAD: Good. How about the second one?

SENTA: The "and" connects two things that describe "he." The third one has two ideas. She did two things; she "whistled," and she "tapped."

THAD: But if we mean by two ideas that there's a subject and a verb in each, try
35   finding both pairs.

SENTA: Well, there are two verbs. OK, there's only one "she." There's no second subject. So it's only one idea.

THAD: So what is the "and" doing?

SENTA: I see. It connects the two things she does. One subject does two things.

40 THAD: Terrific. OK, look at the last one. Try reading it out loud.

SENTA: [reads] "She likes steaks and burgers and Tom." No. "She likes steaks and burgers [pause] and Tom likes only vegetarian food." It get it. It's the same problem I had before.

THAD: Right. So what do you need to do?

45 SENTA: Add a comma after "burgers." But it's weird. The first "and" doesn't need the comma.

THAD: Right. Now maybe you can figure out why, if you go back over the list and see what "and" can link.

SENTA: Gee, it seems to be able to link two of anything, you know.

50 THAD: Right, it can link two subjects, two verbs, two descriptions, and even two ideas. Why should there be a comma when it links two ideas?

SENTA: I don't know. I guess to avoid the mix-up I got into.

THAD: That's right. Since "and" can link so many things, you want to signal your reader that a whole new idea is coming, a whole new subject and verb
55 pattern. That's like a whole sentence. So it's a way of helping a reader know when to pause and to expect this new idea.

SENTA: OK.

Varying the sequence of questions

We have interrupted here to draw your attention to several features of the dialogue, first to the difference between Joyce's (the tutor in the previous dialogue) and Thad's sequences of questions. Joyce, as you may remember, does not raise the issue of punctuation until Tony understands what a sentence is and can therefore grasp the reason for the punctuation convention. Thad, on the other hand, can begin to introduce punctuation earlier because, unlike Tony, Senta recognizes the confusion her punctuation creates even before she grasps the grammatical structure. The contrast suggests that you need not always introduce the grammar first and that your sequence of questioning must depend on the kind of error a writer has made and what she discovers by looking at her sentence. As we resume the dialogue, Thad expands the discussion of "and" to a general consideration of coordination so that Senta can learn to apply the punctuation convention in all of the appropriate cases. Notice what happens when Senta unwittingly brings up subordination. How does her error affect the course of the discussion?

THAD: There are other words that work just like "and." Do you know what they're called?

60 SENTA: Um, conjunctions.

THAD: Right. Can you think of any others?

SENTA: I guess "but" is one.

THAD: Good. Write it down with "and" and keep going.

SENTA: "Because"?

65 THAD: That's a different kind of conjunction. Write it in a different column and we'll get back to it in a minute.

SENTA: I don't get it. There are different kinds of conjunctions?

THAD: Yes. We can talk about that now if you want to. Let's look at the difference between "and" and "because." In your sentence, you said the "and" linked
70 two separate ideas. Could each be a sentence?

SENTA: Sure, I guess. Each has a subject and a verb, and they make sense.

THAD: OK. Now see what happens if you substitute "because" for "and."

SENTA: *[writes]* "The men fool with cars because the women play racquetball separately." That's not what I meant. I mean it sounds as if the men do
75 their own thing because the women shut them out.

THAD: Sure, but could we just use this for a minute as an example of how "and" and "because" work? What you said is useful. You said, in effect, that one action happens because of the other. So could the second idea, what the women do, stand by itself?

80 SENTA: You mean, "because the women play racquetball separately"?

THAD: Yes.

SENTA: That doesn't make sense by itself. It doesn't sound like a sentence.

THAD: That's right. With the "because," what does the second part of the sentence explain?

85 SENTA: Why the men fool with cars.

THAD: Exactly. Now can the first part stand alone?

SENTA: Yes.

THAD: Good. Why?

SENTA: It's a sentence. It's got all the parts.

90 THAD: So that becomes the main idea, and the "because" part just helps out the main idea. It gives information about the action. That's called "subordination." This is one kind of subordinate clause, and "because" is called a "subordinator." So put that word at the top of the column with "because." Try to guess what the other column would be called.

95 SENTA: I really can't.

THAD: Well, let's go back to the idea that "and" was linking two ideas. Those ideas are separate, as you said, and the "and" just links them the way a plus sign in math adds numbers. Do you think the two ideas are equally important, or does one seem more important than the other?

100 SENTA: It's equal.

THAD: Right, because the two parts are both main ideas. The "and" helps them stay that way. We call it a "coordinating conjunction." Let's look at the difference between the two prefixes, "sub" and "co."

SENTA: "Sub" means under, I get it, and "co" must mean equal.

105 THAD: Good. They cooperate, like equal partners. Let's see what other conjunctions there are. Try listing some.

When Senta mistakes "because" for a coordinator and then expresses confusion about conjunctions ("I don't get it. There are different kinds of conjunctions?"

line 67), Thad alters her planned sequence of questions. While she had intended to introduce subordination only after she and Senta had completed their discussion of coordination, she decides that adapting to the writer's reasoning process will be more productive than maintaining a predetermined course. She can still accomplish her goal, perhaps more easily than if she tries to control the direction of Senta's thinking. By making this adjustment, by varying the sequence of questions, Thad acknowledges that different people may reach identical conclusions in various ways. Requiring writers to answer to predetermined sequence of questions, no matter how intelligent or artful the plan, may obstruct their independent thinking (see our discussion of "branching" in Chapter 14).

Legitimate uses of "yes/no" questions

Another feature of the dialogue you may have noticed is that Thad's questions are not always open-ended: she poses several "yes/no" questions (lines 59, 70, 78, 86) and once presents Senta with a choice of alternatives (line 99). Although we have said in Chapters 1 and 2 that such questions risk stifling a writer's thinking, they are appropriate in this context because Senta is trying to understand a given system, not to generate or elaborate ideas. Sometimes the only way Thad can find out if Senta can identify the system's parts and understand its operations is to ask quite directly. A "yes/no" question, when paired with a follow-up question such as "Why?" or "Could you explain your reasoning?" does not close off a writer's thinking. On the contrary, the sequence can encourage a writer to analyze her own reasoning process. For example, Thad asks, "Can this stand alone?" and then "Why?" (lines 86–88). If Senta had responded incorrectly to the first question, Thad could still have asked "Why?" in order to discover and help Senta correct her assumptions.

Using concrete comparisons

One other feature of Thad's approach is worth remarking: she draws concrete, familiar comparisons in order to explain abstract concepts. Like Joyce, she equates a grammatical function with a mathematical operation in order to explain the former. Thad's comparison of "and" to a "plus" sign (line 98) and Joyce's of "is" to an "equals" (line 51) are simpler than abstract explanations such as " 'And' conjoins identical grammatical elements." Whether comparisons are drawn from mathematics or other sources, they should offer a quick, uncomplicated way for a writer to conceptualize a sophisticated concept.

Using diagrams

Like concrete comparisons, simple diagrams can also help explain grammatical principles and punctuation conventions. To see how this visual aid can be used, let us now return to the dialogue. When we interrupted, Senta was about to list coordinating and subordinating conjunctions; here is the final version of her list:

COORDINATORS	SUBORDINATORS
and	because
but	although
for	when
or (nor)	since
yet	after
so	before

THAD: Now that we've listed coordinators and subordinators, let's figure out the punctuation. We've said you need a comma with a coordinator under what conditions?

110 SENTA: If it's linking two main ideas.

THAD: OK. Let's diagram that. I'll use a square to stand for the coordinator. *[writes]*

$$S\ V,\ \square\ S\ V$$

How about when the coordinator links just two verbs? Try diagramming 115 that.

SENTA: That wouldn't have the comma. So it would be like this:

$$S\ V\ \square\ V$$

THAD: Good. Let's do the same kind of thing with subordination. We haven't talked about the punctuation for that, but you'll probably be able to figure 120 it out from the diagram. Let's use a triangle for a subordinator. *[writes]* "He rubbed his knee because he had bumped it." Now put the S, V, and triangle over the right places.

SENTA: *[writes]*

$$S\ \ \ \ V\ \ \ \ \ \ \ \ \ \ \ \triangle\ \ \ S\ \ \ \ V$$
He rubbed his knee because he had bumped it.

125 THAD: Good. Can that second part, the subordinate clause, be positioned any-where else in the sentence?

SENTA: Um, I guess you could put it at the beginning.

THAD: OK. Write it out and then diagram it.

SENTA: *[writes]*

$$\triangle\ \ \ S\ \ \ \ V\ \ \ \ \ \ \ \ \ S\ \ \ \ V$$
130 Because he had bumped his knee he rubbed it.

THAD: Good. Look at where the subordinator is.

SENTA: It's way over at the beginning.

THAD: Right. So how is a reader supposed to know when the subordinate clause stops and the main idea begins?

135 SENTA: I get it. You need a comma to tell the reader. So I'll put that in. It'd look like this. *[writes]*

$$\triangle S\ V,\ S\ V$$

THAD: Good.

SENTA: What about when it's in between?

THAD: What signals the reader that a new idea is coming?

140 SENTA: Oh, I see. The subordinator. So you don't need a comma.

THAD: Right.

SENTA: But with the coordinator, you did. I mean, up above we have a comma before the "and," and it's between the clauses.

145 THAD: That's right, and it's good that you noticed that. But do you remember why we wanted the comma there even though the coordinator does signal the reader?

SENTA: Um. Oh. Right. It can connect anything, like two verbs or two subjects or two descriptive words, so you need the comma to show you're starting a whole new idea.

150 THAD: That's right. How about writing some sentences that use the patterns we've just diagrammed. You can pick subordinators and coordinators from the lists we made.

In the session above, the diagrams help Senta understand the punctuation, and they suggest ways to form new sentences as well. By asking writers to make up sentences based on patterns they identify, you can simultaneously help them familiarize themselves with syntactical structures of the written code and with the punctuation that demarcates them. One pattern that Thad could have introduced as an alternative to S V, □ S V is S V; S V. She could, in other words, have brought the semicolon into the discussion as an alternative to the coordinating conjunction (as the tutor in the next dialogue does), and she and Senta could have considered the semantic distinctions between the two patterns.

Helping writers use apostrophes

So far, we have discussed ways in which punctuation helps to link, embed, and separate ideas, but it can also serve other functions. For example, it can indicate possession and contraction through use of the apostrophe. Inexperienced writers often misplace or omit this mark for a variety of reasons, chiefly because they do not know that it can express these concepts. Let's look first at why writers err with possessives. Novice writers do not know that an apostrophe followed by an "s" is a way of writing the genitive case; that is, they do not know that "the boy's keys" is a way of representing "the keys of the boy." As listeners, they would understand that the phrase means "the keys belong to the boy." As writers, however, they might transcribe the phrase as "the boys keys" or "the boys' keys." They would write in an "s" because they hear it, but they might misposition or omit the apostrophe because they have little sense of how the word should look (see also Chapter 13 on spelling problems connected to writers' lack of visual acuity). Since inexperienced writers tend neither to read much nor to observe words closely, they also do not know how to transcribe possessive pronouns. They often write "hers' " for "hers," or "its' " and "it's" for the pronoun "its." Writers may also err because they confuse possessives with plurals.

The "s" is used in forming each, but the writers aren't aware of the distinct functions of the letter and so may not know whether or where to place an apostrophe. It is not uncommon, for instance, to see such errors as "womens' " for "women's" or "telescope's" for "telescopes'."

Contractions are equally mysterious to beginning writers, some of whom do not realize that a word like "didn't" actually fuses two words and that the apostrophe stands for a missing letter. Inexperienced writers tend either to omit the apostrophe in these words because they do not consider them composites, or else they misplace it, as in "did'nt." In the latter case, they may assume that the apostrophe has something to do with the junction of the words instead of with the ellipsis.

Since the reasons for a writer's erroneous use or omission of apostrophes vary, you can begin by analyzing the kinds of errors that a writer makes and finding out what assumptions have guided his decisions (we will talk more about error analysis in the next chapter). Then you can help the writer discover both the functions of apostrophes and their appropriate placements by asking the questions listed below. You could also suggest that the writer make a checklist of these questions and the procedures he should follow:

FOR POSSESSIVES: Who is the owner?
Write the name of the owner; then add 's
example: keys belong to the boy = *boy*'s keys

FOR CONTRACTIONS: What letter is missing?
Place the apostrophe where the letter should be.
example: did not = didn't

You and a writer can refer to such a checklist in going over his essay, and he can also use it when practicing with exercises, like those contained in English handbooks. The most helpful of these ask the writer to transform a phrase into one that uses an apostrophe:

POSSESSION: prize of the department _____
prizes of the department _____
prizes of the departments _____
CONTRACTION: did not see _____
is not coming _____

A brief caveat: during a conference on possessives, you may have to spend some time exploring the concept of "ownership" if you ask "Who is the owner?" That word does not always precisely state the relationship effected by the apostrophe. Look, for example, at "the government's obligations." The government does not "own" or "possess" obligations. However, in cases like these, you can ask direct questions like, "Whose obligations are these?" The writer would probably say, "The government's," and you could then say, "So let's call the government the owner." Also, if you begin a discussion of possessives by using examples in which "ownership" or "possession" really do describe the relationship established by the apostrophe, writers will probably not be troubled by a later, less precise application of the term.

Combining strategies

At times you may want to combine several of the strategies we have mentioned for helping writers use punctuation to link, embed, and separate ideas. To illustrate how this can be done, we offer two dialogues, one in which a tutor helps a fairly inexperienced writer whose essays contain run-on sentences, the other in which a tutor helps a more advanced writer learn to punctuate relative clauses. In the first, Michael, a college sophomore, has written an essay that contains errors like the following: "The villagers heard that a war was likely, therefore they were afraid of running out of food, consequently they began to hoard supplies." As you will see, Michael thinks "therefore" and "consequently" are conjunctions, but in fact they are not. Like "meanwhile," "nevertheless," "moreover," and "furthermore," they are conjunctive adverbs, words that establish semantic links between ideas but do not function grammatically as connectives, a distinction that
➤ Michael's tutor, Blake, makes during the conference. As you read the dialogue, try to identify the strategies that we have described and speculate above why Blake chooses the sequence he follows.

MICHAEL: I don't see what's wrong with this sentence, but the professor made a check in the margin here. *[points to the lines quoted above]*

5 BLAKE: OK. Let's see now. How many ideas have you got here?

MICHAEL: Two. No, three, really.

BLAKE: OK. Would you list them, please?

MICHAEL: *[writes]*

> The villagers heard a war was likely.
>
> They were afraid of running out of food.
>
> They began to hoard supplies.

10 BLAKE: OK. Could each one be a sentence?

MICHAEL: Yes, they're all complete ideas. Do you mean I should keep them separate?

BLAKE: Not unless you want to. My question is about how you connect them. Try reading your original sentence out loud to see if it sounds OK.

15 MICHAEL: *[reads the original]* Yes. I think it makes sense. I don't see what's wrong with it.

BLAKE: There isn't anything wrong with it as far as the logic goes. It's the punctuation that needs a bit of work. Let's figure out why. First of all, you said that each of the ideas could be a sentence. So how come you didn't use
20 periods?

MICHAEL: Because I used "therefore" and "consequently" to get the ideas together.

BLAKE: I see. Well, let's look at how "therefore" works. I'll write the last part. *[writes]* "Therefore they began to hoard supplies." Can "therefore" be
25 placed anywhere else in the sentence?

MICHAEL: I don't get what you mean.

BLAKE: Try moving it around. Can you position it anywhere else?

MICHAEL: I guess you could say, "They therefore began to hoard supplies."

BLAKE: Good. Anywhere else? *[long pause]* How about at the end?

30 MICHAEL: I guess that will work too. I don't see what you're driving at.

BLAKE: Well, hang in there for just a minute, and it may get clearer. Can you think of some other word you could use instead of "therefore," a word that means the same thing?

MICHAEL: Hmmm. "So"?

35 BLAKE: That's a good one. Now try moving that around in the sentence the way you did with "therefore."

MICHAEL: *[writes a few lines, scratches them out, tries again, scratches out the new lines]* No, I can't move it.

BLAKE: Right, you can't. OK, you can move "therefore" around but not "so."
40 Let's figure out what this difference means.

MICHAEL: It's gotta mean that "so" and "therefore" aren't the same kinds of words.

BLAKE: So even though they mean pretty much the same thing, as you said, there's still a difference. How would you describe the difference?

45 MICHAEL: I can't quite say it, but I see they are different.

BLAKE: Well, you said you used "therefore" to connect two ideas. Where do you normally find a word that connects?

MICHAEL: Between the things it's connecting. *[pause]* You mean, if you can move the word around, it's not a conjunction?

50 BLAKE: Right. Glad you can see that. Even though "therefore" means pretty much the same thing as "so," it doesn't work the same way in the sentence. Since you can move it around, it really doesn't have the same function as "so." It's not a conjunction in the real sense of the word, even though it does link the ideas a bit. OK. So if "therefore" isn't a conjunction, how are you
55 going to punctuate the sentence?

MICHAEL: I can't use a comma anymore.

BLAKE: Good. Let's figure out why. How about setting up a diagram like the one we did last week, only this time let's use a star for "therefore." You can still use the S V pattern. Make a diagram of the sentence with "therefore"
60 coming after "they."

MICHAEL: OK. It would look like this: *[writes]*

> S   *   V
> They therefore began to hoard supplies.

BLAKE: Good. Now put the preceding one next to it.

65 MICHAEL: *[writes]*

> S   V
> They were afraid of running out of food,
> S   *   V
> they therefore began to hoard supplies.

70   So it's S V, S * V. No, wait! I've got two sentences stuck together with a
      comma, and I know that's wrong. So do I use a period?

BLAKE: You could. That's one option. You have others.

MICHAEL: You mean go back to "so" and keep the comma?

BLAKE: Good. That's another. There's still one more.

75 MICHAEL: I can't think of one.

BLAKE: How about a semicolon?

MICHAEL: I never know how to use those. What do they do, anyway?

BLAKE: They're sort of like periods but not quite as strong. You can use them
      instead of a period when you want your reader to see that the next sentence
80   is closely related in meaning. So now try writing it.

MICHAEL: *[changes the comma to a semicolon]*

       S   V
       They were afraid of running out of food;
       S   *   V
85   they therefore began to hoard supplies.

BLAKE: Good. Now try reading it out loud.

MICHAEL: *[reads with a definite pause before "therefore" and a slight pause after
      it]*

BLAKE: Do you hear any pauses?

90 MICHAEL: I stopped before "therefore."

BLAKE: Any others?

MICHAEL: I don't think so.

BLAKE: I thought I heard you pause a little, after the "therefore." You'd use
      commas around "therefore" if it were in the middle of the sentence to show
95   the reader that you are breaking into the main idea, interrupting it sort of.
      Also, when you begin a sentence with a word like "therefore," you use a
      comma after it to tell a reader to pause before the subject and verb appear.
      Why don't we set up some diagrams, one for each of the patterns we've
      talked about?

100 MICHAEL: Sure.

Here are the patterns that Michael wrote with Blake's help:

1. S V, □ S V   They were afraid of running out of food, so they began to hoard sup-
               plies.

2. S V; *, S V   They were afraid of running out of food; therefore, they began to hoard
               supplies.

3. S V. *, S V   They were afraid of running out of food. Therefore, they began to
               hoard supplies.

4. S V; S, *, V   They were afraid of running out of food; they, therefore, began to
               hoard supplies.

They next discuss the semantic differences among these variations and then move
back to Michael's sentence to work on punctuating around "consequently." Finally, they assemble a list of words like "consequently" and "therefore" (con-

junctive adverbs), words that can be variously positioned within clauses and must be distinguished from conjunctions. By the end of the session, Michael has learned a good deal more than just how to correct a run-on sentence: he has learned several different ways of relating ideas.

A similar combination of strategies can help writers who have begun to use more advanced syntactical structures but who do not yet know how to punctuate them. Such is the case with Warren, a junior executive at a glass manufacturing company, who has sought help from Julio, a writing consultant hired by the firm. Warren does not make basic punctuation errors, but he is eager to perfect his writing and is confused about when to use commas with "who" clauses (relative clauses). The explanation rests on a relatively sophisticated grammatical distinction: the difference between restrictive and nonrestrictive clauses. These terms themselves often confuse writers, but the dialogue suggests how you can introduce the grammatical concepts and punctuation without using the terms "restrictive" and "nonrestrictive." Even when you work with advanced writers, using everyday language to explain grammatical concepts can be advantageous. As you read the dialogue, try to identify the strategies that we have described and speculate about why Julio has adopted the sequence he follows:

WARREN: I never know whether I'm supposed to use commas or not with those "who" clauses. I always do, for safety's sake, but then my boss tells me I'm wrong, and I don't know what the rule is. I'd really be grateful if you could clear that up.

5 JULIO: Let's see if this example will help you a bit. *[writes]*

> Pilots who are nearsighted seldom reach old age.
>
> Pilots, who are nearsighted, seldom reach old age.

What's the difference between the one with commas and the one without?

WARREN: I guess the commas do something, but I don't quite get it.

10 JULIO: Try reading them aloud.

WARREN: OK. *[reads each one]* I'm still not sure what the difference is.

JULIO: Suppose I read it to you. *[reads the first one without pausing, then the second one, pausing dramatically before the "who," dropping his voice as in an aside, and resuming his normal tone once the relative clause is ended]*

15 WARREN: The second one sounds different because of the pauses. You made it sound like something you'd say under your breath.

JULIO: That's right. That's an important idea and a good way of saying it. If you'd say the idea under your breath, that is, if it's sort of parenthetical . . . *[waits]*

WARREN: *[nods]* I know what parenthetical means.

20 JULIO: If it's almost parenthetical, then how essential is it to the main idea?

WARREN: I guess not very.

JULIO: Right. So you can take it out. Cross it off for the moment. Now what does the sentence say?

WARREN: That pilots seldom reach old age. Oh, I get it. That means *all* pilots. In

25   the first one, we're talking about all pilots, but the second one is talking
      about the nearsighted ones.

JULIO: Very good.

WARREN: The first one, the one without the commas, makes sense, but the second
      doesn't. I mean, obviously, not all pilots are nearsighted.

30   JULIO: Excellent. In the first, it's as if the writer is saying, "nearsighted pilots do
      not reach old age." The "who" clause there works to limit the identity of
      the subject. So how essential is the clause?

WARREN: I see now that it is essential. It has to be there or else you think the
      writer is talking about all pilots.

35   JULIO: Right. Now what tells us that this clause is essential?

WARREN: I don't get it.

JULIO: Which of the two ways to punctuate tells you that the "who" clause is
      part of the identity or the name of the subject?

WARREN: You don't use the commas if it's part of the name.

40   JULIO: Right. And you do use commas when . . .

WARREN: When it's not essential. I get it.

JULIO: You are catching on to this very quickly. Now look at this one for a
      minute. *[writes]*

      Men who have beards suffer less from sunburn than men who are clean-shaven.

45   WARREN: I get it—bearded men versus clean-shaven men.

JULIO: Right. So how would you punctuate?

WARREN: I wouldn't. I'd leave it alone because the "who" clauses tell us *which*
      men, and that's crucial here.

JULIO: Exactly. Otherwise, if you used commas, you'd be comparing all men with
50   all men, which doesn't make sense. One way to help you think about this
      is to put brackets around what's being compared. That helps you to see each
      entity.

WARREN: *[puts brackets around "men who have beards" and around "men who
      are clean-shaven"]*

55   JULIO: Exactly. So the name of each item in the comparison includes the "who"
      clause. Now let's work on the sentence you wrote in your report on affir-
      mative action. *[points to the following sentence]*

      Women, who had been denied access to executive positions in this company for
      many years, are now being hired for such positions.

60   I know you said you always used the commas, but now that you understand
      when to use them, let's see whether in this case you need them. Does the
      "who" clause seem essential? Does it limit the name of the subject?

WARREN: I'm not sure.

JULIO: Let's use the same technique we used before. If you take away the "who"
65   clause, does the sentence still make sense?

WARREN: Let's see. *[reads]* "Women are now being hired for such positions." I *am* talking about all women, and the "who" clause just gives additional information. That *is* the point I was making, I mean, that women are now being hired.

70 JULIO: Good. So now how would you punctuate?

WARREN: I'd need the commas.

JULIO: Good. What happens if you don't use them? What's the subject of the sentence? Try using brackets again.

WARREN: *[puts brackets around "women who have been denied access to execu-*
75 *tive positions"]*

JULIO: OK. Now how does that change the meaning?

WARREN: I don't know, exactly. It sort of sounds as if the same women that didn't get the jobs in the first place are getting them now. I see why I need the commas.

80 JULIO: That's very good. OK. Let's go through the rest of your report now.

In this dialogue, Julio combines oral/aural exercise, questions, and diagrams to help Warren grasp the grammatical principle and the punctuation conventions. He does not need to use the terms "restrictive" and "nonrestrictive." Instead, he uses everyday language to get across the grammatical idea: "Is the clause part of the name of the subject?" If Warren were a college student enrolled in a composition course, Julio might introduce the technical language because Warren might need to know it: his professor and text might use it. The extent to which you employ grammatical terms should depend on the writer's need and on his interest in the language. If he wants to learn it and you think you have time to discuss it, there is no reason to avoid it. After all, it is not a secret code.

Helping writers learn to punctuate may seem, to the uninitiated, a trivial and boring chore, not half so much fun as helping writers generate ideas. But if you approach the task as a way of assisting a writer's efforts to make meaning, to relate ideas with greater clarity and precision, we think you will find the work substantive and enjoyable.

Summary

Punctuation is a way of making meaning. Like connective language, it helps to link, embed, and divide ideas into signifying units. Unfortunately, many writers do not use punctuation discriminatingly. They may not consider it important, may be concentrating on other composing activities, may not distinguish pauses from stops, may not understand the grammatical principles that underlie punctuation conventions. Some writers misapply rules they half remember; others are unfamiliar with them and with the semantic functions of punctuation. For writers to see the punctuation system as a way of making meaning rather than as arbitrary rules, they need to know that the marks signal rests and pauses that cluster or separate words into independent or subordinate units. They must also learn that independence and subordination are grammatically rather than rhetorically defined.

If you address punctuation errors as an opportunity to help a writer explore alternate ways of relating ideas, not as an occasion to fix up mechanical errors, you will address her real need. Oral reading is useful for assessing a writer's understanding and for illustrating the functions of punctuation. By asking "Who does what?" "Can this idea stand by itself?" and "How many ideas are there?" you can introduce punctuation conventions and underlying principles without getting too technical. Your sequence of questions will vary: sometimes writers will need to grasp a grammatical principle before they can understand a punctuation rule; sometimes, working on the convention first provokes discussion of its basis. Concrete comparisons and diagrams also help writers understand how to use commas, periods, and semicolons.

Writers can learn appropriate use of other marks like apostrophes if you help them develop checklists consisting of questions to ask themselves and procedures to follow when editing or practicing with exercises. You may want to combine several of these strategies to help familiarize writers with the punctuation system and its rationale.

SUGGESTIONS FOR JOURNAL ENTRIES

1. What problems, if any, have you experienced with punctuation, and how did you solve them? How could your experience help a writer with whom you work?

2. Observe your punctuating habits: In the composing process, when do you punctuate? Do you do so automatically, while drafting? Do you have to stop and think about it or refer to a handbook? When you proofread, are you merely looking for typographical errors, or do you, at this point, try to remember punctuation conventions?

3. What kind of instruction in punctuation did you receive? What was helpful? What was not?

4. Describe the punctuation problems of writers you are working with. Speculate about the causes for their problems. Describe what you are doing to address the problems and explain your rationale.

SUGGESTIONS FOR FURTHER WRITING

1. Assuming that the writers of our examples 2–9 on the first page of this chapter do not have reliable ears, select at least two examples and plan a sequence of questions that would help each writer. You may create imaginary dialogues if you like. Then explain the rationale for your approach.

2. When Thad taught Senta how to punctuate a compound sentence, she might also have taught her how to use a semicolon as an alternative. Write a dialogue in which you do so.

3. Write a dialogue in which you help the writer of the passage below learn how to use apostrophes. Then explain the rationale for your approach.

> The dog was wagging its' tail as I opened the gate. As soon as I reached the door, it started growling. I rang the bell and looked in the windows' but didnt see anybody. Then the dog began to bark angrily, showing it's teeth.

4. What punctuation problems is the writer of the following paragraph experiencing? What might have caused them? Next, write a dialogue in which you address them. Finally, explain the rationale for your approach.

> I was thinking, that another place to use for the assignment for my English class, like the elevator or the lobby of Wheatley Hall, would have been better than this one particular place, such as, this cafeteria. I was angry at being in this cafeteria, because I could not eat, I had to work. Another reason, for my disliking this cafeteria, in this building, was that I had been here, only once before and the surroundings still felt strange to me, and I do not like new places. I was a new student, and did not know many other college students.

SUGGESTIONS FOR CLASS ACTIVITIES

1. Share with classmates your answers to the exercises in "Suggestions for Further Writing."

2. Bring to class copies of mispunctuated paragraphs written by people with whom you work. Lead a class discussion in which classmates analyze the errors and suggest tutoring strategies, or use the paragraphs for role-playing exercises.

3. Bring to class copies of handbooks and discuss the relative merits of the punctuation exercises.

4. As a class, make up some exercises that would address the punctuation problems of writers with whom you work.

SUGGESTIONS FOR FURTHER READING

Since much of this chapter considers sentence-combining techniques, we refer you to the bibliography for Chapter 8. In addition, we include the following:

Bartholomae, David. "The Study of Error." *College Composition and Communication* 31 (1980): 253–269.

Kline, Charles R., Jr., and W. Dean Memering. "Formal Fragments: The English Minor Sentence." *Research in the Teaching of English* 1 (1977–78): 97–110.

Laurence, Patricia. "Error's Endless Train: Why Students Don't Perceive Errors." *Journal of Basic Writing* 1 (1975): 23–43.

Shaughnessy, Mina P. *Errors and Expectations.* New York: Oxford University Press, 1977. 14–43.

Wiener, Harvey S. *The Writing Room: A Resource Book for Teachers of English.* New York: Oxford University Press, 1981. 172–183.

10

Working with Dialects and Patterns of Error

Speakers of vernacular English (or nonstandard speakers) and speakers for whom English is a second language (or ESL speakers) have different problems in *learning* to speak and to write standard English, but these problems may *manifest* themselves in the same or similar ways and may respond to similar tutorial techniques. For American-born nonstandard speakers, such as residents of rural Appalachia or urban black ghettos, English *is* the native language; they know the fundamental rules of sentence formation (though probably not the grammatical terminology for analyzing sentences). In certain speech contexts (for instance, questions like "Are you coming?" and emphatics like "Black is beautiful!" or "I am somebody!" or "Allah is God!"), they may use words that in other contexts they produce less readily (such as in the black English vernacular sentences, "He sick" or "She have three sister."). Nonstandard speakers must also learn the letters that are silent in their dialects (such as -*s* and -*ed*) and which mark grammatical functions in standard written English. ESL speakers, in contrast, must learn both the markers and the language functions particular to English. Even when ESL speakers have more or less mastered the functions, they may still err in using these markers; at that point, they might be considered to have become nonstandard speakers. It is important for tutors to keep the two groups' differing learning processes in mind, even though some of the same tutorial strategies may help both.

The similar manifestations of ESL and nonstandard speakers' problems led Mina Shaughnessy to describe some American-born students as having a "quasi-foreign relationship" to standard written English (92). It is "quasi-foreign" for two reasons. First, their spoken dialects differ from standard spoken English, the language commonly spoken in public transactions in the United States (Bailey and Robinson, 16–19). Second, whereas even those who use standard spoken English (sometimes informally called "TV network English" or "Walter Cronkite English") must employ at least some new linguistic forms when they write, speakers of nonstandard English, and to a much greater extent ESL speakers, must learn a great many. As Shaughnessy observes, some American-born students (her examples are three students with twelve years' education in New York City schools, one from a Yiddish-language background, an Irish-American, and a Chinese-American) "are clearly colliding with many of the same stubborn contours of formal English . . . that are also troublesome to students learning English as a second language" (92). Despite important differences between the language-learning problems encountered by intermediate and advanced ESL speakers and by American-born speakers of nonstandard English, many of the same tutoring strategies can help both groups to learn Standard Written (sometimes called "standard edited") English.

Because the field of teaching English as a second language (TESOL) is so broad, this chapter will make no attempt to "cover" it. ESL teachers, researchers, and theorists share our concerns with the processes of composing and with writing as meaningful communication, and they often refer to the work of Perl, Flower, Murray, Sommers, and others cited in our earlier chapters. However, ESL writers also need help with aspects of English with which native-language teachers (and tutors) who have not worked in multicultural settings seldom concern themselves:

QUANTITY WORDS: some, many, much, little, a few, several, etc.
>   I bought a few soap.
>   I cooked many rice.
>   He carried several furnitures.

DETERMINERS WITH COUNTABLE OR UNCOUNTABLE NOUNS: a, an, the
>   He drank a milk.
>   I lost knife.

THE -s INFLECTION ON NOUNS AND VERBS:
>   The childrens are here.
>   Apes lives in families.
>   The grass need water.
>   Pieces of cake is on the platter.
>   The value of yen have risen.
>   By the looks of thing, you are pretty busy.
>   Ten dollar were stolen from my purse.

PARTICIPLES AND AUXILIARY VERBS:
>   If you walked to school, you can walked home.
>   We are suppose to call her after the meeting.
>   She does a wonderful job, but she has does even better.
>   They have study for a month to pass this exam.
>   She will read our revise papers next week.

THE USE OF NEGATIVES: not any, no, hardly any, few, not much, not many, none
>   We don't need no tickets.
>   He didn't see hardly no sea gulls on the pier.

SHIFTS IN PERSON:
>   A serious student does their work.
>   I waited at the corner because that's where you catch the bus.
>   Anyone can find a job if they try hard enough.

POSSESSIVES:

> This city youth need summer recreation programs.
> The chemistry book is her's.
> The emergency teams nurse's were working overtime for there
> third night.

This short list of examples can alert tutors to the kinds of problems inexperienced and ESL writers most often encounter; for more complete taxonomies of problems than this chapter can present, we urge tutors to consult Chapter 4 of Mina P. Shaughnessy's *Errors and Expectations* and David Bartholomae's "The Study of Error." Instead of providing exercises, we will simply refer tutors to Ann Raimes' excellent ESL textbook, *Focus on Composition*. Tutors in multicultural settings may find valuable insights into such matters as nonverbal communications, time and space patterns, and personal values in Deena R. Levine and Mara B. Adelman's ESL textbook, *Beyond Language: Intercultural Communication for English as a Second Language.*

What this chapter will do, then, is to explain the kinds of problems you may encounter in helping both inexperienced and ESL writers to acquire proficiency in Standard Written English. Because teachers usually must present lessons to groups of writers with diverse language backgrounds, the instruction you provide can be especially effective in helping students to learn through individualized conversations about their own writing. We will concentrate on tutorial strategies for understanding the nature of "standard" and "nonstandard" dialects, for establishing rapport, for understanding the nature of "error," and for using the process of language acquisition (especially the hypotheses about language that each learner forms and gradually refines throughout the learning process) to help writers observe their own writing and solve problems independently as they acquire Standard Written English as a new dialect. Perhaps the most important principle we can voice is that because nonstandard and ESL speakers have the same *composition* (as opposed to linguistic) problems as other writers, the strategies presented in this chapter should be used in addition to, not instead of, those presented elsewhere in this book.

Psychological Aspects of Language Change

Our experience shows that tutors who have studied foreign languages (or whose native language is not English) may find themselves better prepared to help ESL writers than those who have not. Whether or not they happen to find opportunities to converse in their tutees' native languages, tutors who have studied other languages—for instance, the genders of nouns and the importance of accents in Spanish, or the German syntax which suspends "meaning" by delaying separable verb prefixes until the ends of sentences, or the ninety-six Japanese kana or the countless Chinese ideographs—are less likely to take English for granted as "common sense" and to become at least somewhat more aware of its many peculiarities. These tutors may be more likely to understand why features they have never given a moment's thought, such as the use of the definite articles *(a, an,* and *the),* present particular problems to an ESL writer. They may see why the illogic of English inflections, in which final -s makes most nouns plural but makes verbs singular (consider for instance, "She sells seashells"), causes frustration.

Even classroom instruction in foreign languages cannot afford you the ESL speakers' wearying experience of trying to communicate about daily necessities in an unfamiliar language (for instance, buying a can labeled with a picture of chicken, but finding it contains only Crisco shortening). And such practical frustrations are often much less serious than the psychological stresses of language learning. For many ESL writers who attend American universities but plan to return to their native countries, acquiring standard English is primarily a professional goal; it will not interfere with their resuming relationships when they return home. On the other hand, inexperienced American-born and ESL writers who live permanently in the United States may worry that acquiring standard English will inevitably estrange them from their original speech communities. In *Hunger of Memory,* Richard Rodriguez, the son of Mexican immigrants, eloquently examines the conflict between being a good student and a good son: the more he excelled in formal education (which necessitated his withdrawing from the family hearth to the quiet concentration of his room or the library), the more he sacrificed warmth and intimacy with his Mexican-born parents. He felt ashamed of their language and their self-deprecation before his teachers—and then guilty for feeling ashamed. Proud of his accomplishments, his parents seemed to understand his language, his books, his ideas less and less. However, many ESL writers experience the sacrifices without achieving Rodriguez's brilliant academic success. The resentment sometimes expressed by parents, children and spouses of adults who come to college relatively late in life may focus on and inhibit the acquisition of standard spoken and written dialects.

Shaughnessy (92) describes important differences in the ways ESL and American-born students learn and use Standard Written English:

> [the native-born students] have usually experienced little or no success with written English in school, which is often not so of foreign-born students in relation to their native language; they have not identified the real reasons for their lack of success in writing, having usually perceived themselves (and having been perceived by teachers as well) as native speakers of English who for some reason use "bad" English; and finally, perhaps most importantly, they have been functioning in English for years, understanding the English of people in their communities and being understood by them in the full range of situations that give rise to speech, and managing, although usually in more restricted and restricting ways, to hold jobs, get diplomas, and talk with a variety of "outsiders."

These differences notwithstanding, inexperienced American-born writers may undergo estrangement in learning the spoken and written language of the academic world. When friends ask, "What are you studying?" they may feel more comfortable in vaguely answering, "math," than in trying to explain why anyone pays serious attention to Pascal's triangle or imaginary numbers. Lively class discussions on questions like "If you were standing on a frictionless disk, how could you get off?" or "How do I know the rock I'm looking at is really there?" may suddenly seem hopelessly eggheaded. When academic language crops up in conversation, family may feel patronized: "What do you mean 'infer'? Who do you think you are, all of a sudden?"

When working with both inexperienced and ESL writers, you are wise to keep the psychological ramifications of language change in mind and to be alert for anxieties that might distract your tutees from the learning process. Later in this chapter, we will say more about how understanding something about dialects can help you and writers establish trusting relationships conducive to learning.

"Standard Written English" as Everyone's Second Dialect

Virtually all writers acquire, as it were, a second dialect: the standard English that is *written* for academic and professional purposes. *It is a dialect that nobody speaks.* However, most people think of dialects as differences in speaking, primarily as regional differences in pronunciation and vocabulary. For example, many longtime Bostonians rhyme "pot" with "bought." Also, when Midwesterners, who say "She brought some pop over *to* my house," hear some Bostonians say, "She brought some tonic over my house" (omitting the "to"), they may envision a Chagall-like figure floating "over my house" and carrying "tawnic," whatever that is. Spoken dialects also vary in vocabulary, syntax, and idiom, according to occupations and to economic and social classes. Fluently *spoken* standard English that students, professors, and supervisors use appropriately in classrooms and workplaces is full of fragmentary sentences and ellipses, which are considered "errors" in standard English *written* in academic papers as well as in workplace reports and proposals. Standard spoken English consists more often of simple or compound sentences, whereas Standard Written English sentences are apt to contain more subordinate clauses, more qualifiers (as Chapter 8 explains). Such constructions, along with words like "virtually," "as it were," "whereas," and "nevertheless," which do not seem labored or pompous in writing, may seem so in ordinary conversations. Nevertheless, the Standard Written English of academic and professional writing demands more complex syntax and different choices of vocabulary (not to mention concern for conventions particular to writing, such as spelling and punctuation) than does standard spoken English.

The kinds and amounts of tutorial help writers need in order to learn Standard Written English depend on the proximity of their spoken dialects to it. For ESL speakers, of course, learning standard English is more than learning a second dialect. As Alice Roy (440) observes,

> People who speak standard English as their native dialect, . . . and have reading competence in written standard, normally do not have very far to go, linguistically speaking, in acquiring standard written English. Native speakers of nonstandard and non-native speakers of English, on the other hand, have farther to go and are both, in effect, learning language. Acquiring a second dialect is a subset of acquiring a second language, differing at the outset in degree but not in kind, and differing even less when the second-language learner has reached an intermediate level.

The spoken dialect of middle-class Americans resembles Standard Written English more closely than do, say, Black English Vernacular (BEV), dialects spoken by residents of remote Appalachian communities, or dialects spoken by Asian-, Hispanic-, and Native Americans. Even though some nonstandard speakers may have heard "network English" all their lives, passive TV watching never requires them to produce standard spoken English. For ESL speakers, who need to acquire both the functions and the forms of English, TV watching actually has an isolating effect. We know Southeast Asian families in which the older relatives who remained at home learned neither to understand nor to speak English, even though TV was turned on all day long; however, these families' young adults in the workplace and their children who played and talked with English-speaking children in the neighborhood learned English quite rapidly. Racial and ethnic attitudes, going hand-in-hand with economic deprivation and social isolation in urban or rural ghettos, limit the occasions in which speakers of nonstandard and nonnative dialects and speakers of standard English converse.

Linguistic isolation from standard spoken, not to mention Standard Written, English is often broken first in schools and colleges, and the individualized conversation that takes place in tutorials may be a key factor. Researchers in second-language acquisition know that learners of a new language must have opportunities to hear and assimilate its forms in ways that *matter* to them psychologically and socially, for instance in getting acquainted with new friends, in obtaining useful information about the new language and culture, not to mention solutions to daily problems, and in attaining the spoken, and eventually written, fluency for academic and occupational use. Furthermore, so long as the learner's psychological and social needs are being met solely by members of their native-language communities, little learning of the new language will occur (Roy, 443). In our experience, the same kinds of social and psychological factors apply to inexperienced writers' second-dialect acquisition. In the process of helping both nonstandard and ESL speakers acquire Standard *Written* English, the intensive conversational opportunities provided by tutorial conferences do provide incentives and rewards for their *speaking* as well as writing standard English. The more frequently they converse in standard English, the more closely they approximate Standard Written English. By helping people enter a new, wider speech community, you may often find yourself at the forefront of linguistic, hence social, change.

Establishing Rapport by Explaining Dialects

In order to establish rapport with nonstandard and ESL speakers and to help them learn Standard Written English, you need to help them understand something about dialects. In particular, you need to dispel two commonly held misunderstandings: one is about "inferiority," and the other is about "getting rid of" dialect.

The first misunderstanding is the assumption that any dialect that is not "standard" must be "*sub*standard," inferior both linguistically and socially to the "standard." In fact, the "standard/*non*standard" dichotomy confers no linguistic superiority upon the standard dialect, because all dialects are equally valuable means of communication to those who fluently speak and understand them. "Standard" English simply describes what Mina Shaughnessy calls "the language of public transactions—educational, civic, and professional" (125) in this country (a language that, incidentally, differs from the "standard" English of Great Britain). Nonstandard and nonnative dialects are no less effective as languages, but they are spoken and understood by smaller speech communities than are the standard dialects in which the nation carries out its public transactions. As Basil Bernstein has argued, adult speakers of nonstandard dialects do not earn their livings by manipulating language, and they therefore do not teach their children those manipulations. Instead, they choose other manipulations, particularly the use of language for social solidarity within their particular community. Solidarity notwithstanding, because those who speak and write standard dialects can carry out public transactions more readily than those who do not, people who speak and write *only* nonstandard dialects are often placed in economically and socially inferior positions—relegated to low-paying jobs and poor housing, subjected to more than usual frustration in communicating with schools, public utilities, government agencies, and so on. Furthermore, as natural language processing and voice synthesis by computers (both of which call upon the computer to recognize standard syntactical, grammatical, and lexical patterns) come to be used in the public transactions of the wider culture, those who add standard spoken and written forms to their repertoire of dialects will expand their educational and professional options. The "inferiority" of their dialects is not, then, a linguistic aspect of the dialects themselves, but rather a set of social attitudes toward them.

You can explain to writers that, although Standard Written English is in one sense even standard speakers' "second dialect," in another sense it is not a dialect at all. As E. D. Hirsch explains, no nationally normative (or "standard") written language is a dialect in the same way that the purely oral language of a speech community is. Such a written language is a "different kind of language system," one that is isolated from any class or region, "transdialectal in character, an artificial construct that belongs to no group or place in particular, though of course it has greater currency among those who have been most intensively trained in its use" (44). This transdialectal, artificial language is called a **grapholect,** "a normative language in ways that cannot be attributed to any dialect" that is spoken: its grammatical and phonological standards are more fixed and more widely promulgated than those of any spoken dialect; its vocabulary is more extensive than that of any spoken dialect; and because it is written down in standardized spelling, punctuation, and syntax, "a grapholect [whether of established or of newly formed nations] serves as a norm by virtue of its actual or potential *stability through time*" (44). One need only reflect upon the ways in which India's many dialects hamper the conduct of national affairs to realize the usefulness of a national language. It is the normative qualities of the grapholect that enable its users to carry out public transactions in a society as large and diverse as the United States. To those who argue that teaching a standard grapholect is an elitist act of linguistic imperialism, diminishing "students' rights to their own language," Hirsch points out that "the normative status of a grapholect is an historical-linguistic fact which no ideology can overcome or evade" (45): a fact is a fact, and argument is beside the point. Moreover, Hirsch argues that "the elitism of the written form entirely disappears with the advent of the little red schoolhouse," that a stable written norm, which mass literacy (and we would add, the democratization in higher education since the mid-1960s) can make available to all people and which can make all people mutually intelligible to one another, is in fact egalitarian. It in no way diminishes the correctness of oral dialects, because correctness "is an internal feature of a particular dialect, not an arbitrary standard which exists outside of the dialect" (40). To be sure, you may prefer not to burden writers with the linguistic term "grapholect," but you can (as will be demonstrated later in this chapter) nevertheless help writers to understand the distinctions between spoken and written norms and, more important, to replace notions of "inferiority" with the realization that "the foundational assumption of modern linguistic science is that of the *linguistic equality* of all dialects" (41).

The second misunderstanding that you may need to clear up is that one must "get rid of" a nonstandard or nonnative dialect in order to attain the standard. This misunderstanding can create psychological conflicts that impede the learning process. On the one hand, the nonstandard and ESL speakers with whom you work may aspire to attaining standard spoken and written dialects that they hope will enable them to succeed academically, politically, and professionally. On the other hand, they may simultaneously fear that doing so will estrange them from their home speech communities, may in Bernstein's terms give them a linguistic power they cannot share. By using a simple analogy, you may help writers avoid this conflict: all the tools in a toolbox are equally useful instruments for accomplishing particular tasks, and some of them (such as a ratchet, a Phillips screwdriver, or a plumber's snake) have more specialized uses than others (say, a claw hammer). But nobody uses a ratchet to pound nails if a hammer is available, and nobody gets rid of the ratchet in order to drive the nails. Just as the ratchet works best for a specialized task, nonstandard or nonnative dialects work best for particular speech communities. In fact, standard English speakers are often called upon to learn the dialects of particular speech communities (for instance, political organizers working in ethnic neighborhoods or technical writers working in various high-tech environments). (Richard Rodriquez and others advance strong arguments against bilingual education, but tutors are seldom in positions to influence policy decisions or to enter directly the debate about bilingual education.) By openly discussing with writers the functions of various dialects in society, you can help them realize that knowing nonstandard and nonnative dialects *in addition to* the standard spoken and written dialects of English may often be an advantage: the standard does not *necessarily* threaten the nonstandard.

A variation on the notion that one dialect threatens another is the argument that learning "standard" English interferes with writers' self-expression and robs them of their authentic voices. Students enter a university speaking the language of a Philadelphia streetcorner or a West Indian island, which (so goes the argument) Freshman English teachers proceed to homogenize into anonymous mush in the name of standards. Those who hold this view ignore an important question: when a student cannot go home again linguistically, cannot talk the way he or she did before school, is it the fault of the language, or has the student changed identifications, changed as a person? We have known writing instructors who claim to detect "poetry" in the accidental ellipses and misfired diction of inexperienced and ESL writers. Such sentimental views ignore the difference between art and accident: choice. Shielding nonstandard and ESL speakers from exposure to standard forms preserves their "character" (as some writing teachers perceive it) but deprives them of choice among languages appropriate to their own various purposes—personal, educational, civic, and professional, as well as perhaps poetic. Only writers who know a variety of dialects can choose for themselves when to sound like Jimmy Breslin and when to sound like a corporate chief executive officer. You can reassure writers that acquiring standard forms enlarges, rather than threatens, their means of choosing many ways of expressing their ideas.

In addition to clearing up these two misunderstandings about dialects, you may need to make special efforts (beyond those described in Chapter 1) to encourage nonstandard and ESL speakers to converse with you as equals. These students may ascribe to tutors a much greater degree of authority than is realistic. They may also assume that nonstandard and nonnative dialects establish great social distances between them and their tutors, the models of a "standard" of speech and writing they hope to acquire. Dialects that have been perfectly adequate to communicating successfully with friends and family suddenly seem not "good enough" for use in academic and workplace speaking, not to mention writing. The tendency of some basic composition and ESL courses to emphasize correctness at the cost of excluding other aspects of composition serves to reinforce their assumption that their dialects are "inferior." Imagine that after the introductions and a few pleasantries, the first meeting between Linda and Reg, who speaks BEV, goes awry:

REG: Well, I sure do hope you can help me get rid of my dialect, Ms. Walker.

LINDA: Call me Linda. Why do you want to get rid of it?

REG: Shouldn't I call you Ms. Walker? You the tutor and all.

LINDA: No, really, Linda is just fine. Tutors are students too, you know. Just like
5   you. We're in the same boat.

Linda, who may have grown up in a middle-class ghetto, fails to acknowledge the social distance between her and Reg, a novice aspiring to attain the expertise that her status as tutor confers upon her. Her well-intended but naive assurance that as fellow students they are "just alike" and her taking for granted the job, good grades, and privileged status that society confers upon those with "standard" dialects are patronizing. He is probably too polite to say what he may be thinking: "*Just* like? You got to be kiddin'! You a tutor, with a job and all A's, most likely. You got yours, and I got mine to get." Suppose instead that Linda focuses on Reg's expressed goal:

REG: My teacher sent me to you, so I could get rid of my dialect and talk right.
        And write right, too. Just like it say on this sheet the teacher pass out the
        first day, *[handing her the syllabus, he reads]* "Standard Written English."

LINDA: You seem to be assuming that dialects are either "standard" or "substan-
10   dard."

REG: You hear right.

LINDA: Well, that's not true. Dialects that aren't "standard" are just different, not "substandard" or inferior.

Linda starts to clarify the often held misunderstanding that nonstandard dialects (belonging to the immigrant and minority groups who are most often victims of economic and social discrimination) are *linguistically* inferior. Her assertion alone is not, however, enough to convince Reg:

REG: Yeah? I still want to get rid of my dialect.

15   LINDA: Why? Your friends and family understand you, right? What if you walked in the house tonight talking exactly like Peter Jennings on ABC news talks?

REG: They say, "Two weeks in that University and he a big shot. Can't talk right no more."

LINDA: Right. So your dialect is just right for home. Learning a different dialect
20   to use when you write your papers for college courses doesn't mean you have to give up your old way of speaking or talk to your friends in a different way.

REG: No?

LINDA: Look, everybody has different dialects for different situations. I don't talk
25   to my brothers at home the way I talk in class. And when I write, my language is different than what I use in class.

REG: You do? Like how?

LINDA: OK. a minute ago I said "different *than.*" I really would have been more correct to say "from" instead of "than," but in our informal conversation
30   that's not so bad. In a paper, though, I'd be sure to write "different from," because that's Standard Written English.

By sharing her own experience of using for academic papers a written dialect that differs from her spoken one, and by acknowledging differing levels of formality in speaking, Linda increases her rapport with Reg and convinces him that her assertion that "nonstandard" means "different," not "inferior," is true. She can clarify the distinctions between speaking and writing standard English:

LINDA: Know what else? Nobody *speaks* "Standard Written English."

REG: Nobody? Then why am I suppose to?

LINDA: You're not. Maybe after a while your speaking will sound more like the
35   speech of your teachers and friends from other backgrounds. Usually people who talk together a lot begin to trade dialects somewhat. But none of us will ever talk "Standard Written English," because that's only for writing, not for speaking conversationally.

REG: OK. Let's look at my writing then.

Sociolinguists like William Labov know that as nonstandard and ESL speakers have opportunities to converse with speakers of standard English, their speech more nearly resembles standard forms (Roy, 443). Thus, by reassuring Reg that through conversation he can gradually acquire standard spoken English to whatever extent he wishes (without worrying about trying to speak the written standard), Linda removes some of his self-conscious and ambivalent desire to "get rid of" his supposedly inferior dialect and refocuses attention to his writing, where it belongs.

The Nature of "Error"

Some inexperienced writers, as well as the intermediate and advanced ESL speakers with whom composition tutors are most likely to work, speak English fairly fluently. They know the language, but when they write it, they run into trouble. Chapters 9 and 13 explain why native speakers of English have problems with punctuation, spelling, and vocabulary, and they present tutorial techniques for addressing these problems. Now we want to consider some of the kinds of errors that tutors most often help very inexperienced writers and ESL writers to address—errors to which tutors who are speakers and writers of standard English have seldom given much thought.

What is an "error"?

Pedagogy has been influenced by linguists' and sociolinguists' explanations of what causes "error." An overview of some major explanations can help tutors to understand various textbook and classroom pedagogies and, more important, to choose some tutorial strategies that are preferable to others. The first explanation, that error is evidence of the learner's lack of concepts, has serious limitations for most tutorial situations (except for certain cognitive disabilities that are beyond the scope of this book). The second, that error is evidence of the learner's incomplete acquisition of linguistic habits, is more useful. The third, that error is evidence that the learner is continually constructing, testing, and refining an intermediate system of hypotheses (or an "interlanguage"), underlies a pedagogy that is in our view not only the most effective for learners, but also the most challenging and interesting for tutors.

Errors and concepts

Thirty or forty years ago, it was thought that error betokened lack of concepts; this explanation can create serious problems for tutors. In their study of the Hopi language, Edward Sapir and Benjamin Lee Whorf hypothesized that failure to use certain surface features of language indicated lack of the concepts underlying them (Traugott and Pratt, 106–110). For instance, because Hopi has no equivalent *word* for our future auxiliary "will," they thought that the Hopi lacked the *concept* of future time. Similarly, some researchers of ghetto speech patterns (who were usually white and middle-class) thought that BEV lacked ways of expressing fundamental concepts such as negation and past time; for instance, they thought that because speakers of BEV do not join sentences with "if," they lack the concept of conditionality (Dillard). However, in both of these examples, the ease of "translating" Hopi and BEV expressions into standard English expressions indicates that the concepts are there, even though the surface expressions are not. Thus, the notion that errors betoken lack of concepts has largely been abandoned today.

Even now, though, certain comments can unintentionally imply that writers lack concepts and can thus damage the trust and rapport that are are so helpful to language acquisition. Some comments may make nonstandard and ESL speakers feel that their tutors think they are too stupid to understand everyday concepts like tense, conditionality, and number. For example, an error of subject–verb agreement may not arise from the writer's confusion about the concept of *number,* but simply from confusion about the written code. If after reading the sentence, "My sister were proud of my high school graduation," a tutor were to ask, "How many were proud?" the BEV writer might feel belittled, as if the tutor thought she did not know how many sisters she had. If the tutor were to ask, "Why didn't you make the subject *sister* plural to match the plural verb *were?"* the writer might (assuming she understood the grammatical terminology) feel that the tutor was implying that she did not know the difference between singular and plural, whereas in BEV she has indeed made subject and verb agree (since if she were speaking about only one sister, she would write "My sister *was* proud . . ."). In this example, the tutor would be wise to focus on the contrasts between spoken and written codes, noting the presence of *-s* on most plural nouns in Standard Written English. She could help the writer make a chart showing when to add the *-s,* and together they could locate some instances in the paper where the writer has done so successfully.

Errors and habits

Another way to view "error" comes from the behavioral psycholinguists, who think that "error" is evidence that the learner has not yet acquired the information about and habits of the new language or dialect. The behavioral model suggests teaching language by two methods: intensive correction of oral and written error, and drill of vocabulary and sentence patterns. (One of us, who took German 101 in 1960, recalls the tedium of memorizing a twenty-sentence lesson about "Das Grossfeuer im Lackfabrik," tedium assuaged only by the confidence that, should she on a visit to Germany encounter "a conflagration in a varnish factory," she would be prepared—to throw in the German textbook.) Intensive correction proves inordinately time-consuming for teachers and discouraging for writers; since corrections seldom say to a writer, "How well you made your subjects and verbs agree!" the only news is bad news. Moreover, as Chapter 7 explains, error correction tends to pick up every error, an unsystematic approach that not only undermines confidence but also confronts the writer with a confusing welter of detail.

The behavioral view gives rise to textbooks emphasizing drills and models by means of which inexperienced and ESL writers can practice standard forms. These techniques seem to work well with beginning students of a second language, who need to acquire basic information and internalize sentence patterns. However, for nonstandard and intermediate ESL speakers, there are serious objections to the use of models and drills: some require almost no writing; all risk boredom because they are detached from the students' own writing; and many pattern manipulations (such as transforming declarative into interrogative sentences) "produce entirely unnatural discourse that no [standard or] native speaker would ever produce" and thereby subvert the communicative purpose of writing (Watson-Reekie, 100–101). These objections do not mean that you should entirely abandon the use of drills, particularly since many writers are assigned such exercises in their writing courses. Instead, you can use them as adjuncts to the students' own writing. If a writer has done a textbook exercise on subject–verb agreement, you can locate some sentences in her paper that handle agreement correctly and others that do not; together, you can examine the differences and correct the written code in the writer's own paper. By using the writer's sentences to make up exercises, you can avoid the pitfalls of boredom and noncommunication and can sharpen the writer's eye for editing her own work.

You can use the same technique to expand inexperienced and ESL writers' knowledge of sentence connectives. For example, as Vivian Zamel explains, many textbooks present lists of cohesive devices categorized according to function (for instance, transitions that qualify: but, however, although, though, yet, except for) without explaining "what relationships [the individual words] express and which ones are appropriate in which contexts" ("Teaching Those Missing Links," 111–113). Zamel recommends that textbooks offer completion exercises, sentence-combining exercises, scrambled paragraphs which writers are asked to rearrange according to the signals given by the cohesive devices, and paragraphs for which writers are asked to restore cohesive links that have been deleted. (Besides Ann Raimes' *Focus on Composition,* we suggest the exercises in Janet Ross and Gladys Doty's *To Write English: A Step-by-Step Approach for ESL* or Jann Huizenga and colleagues's *Basic Composition for ESL: An Expository Workbook.*) You can help writers integrate these exercises with their own writing by drawing writers' attention to how their paragraphs use cohesive devices and by considering the options for connecting some of their own sentences. By helping writers drill on sentences from their own compositions, you can help them acquire standard forms without sacrificing the vitality of communication.

Errors and "interlanguage"

In contrast to the behavioral approach, which conditions learners to acquire the habits that will correct errors but pays no attention to the etiology of error, a newer approach called "error analysis" seeks the reasons for a particular writer's making a particular error. One early hypothesis of error analysis was that a learner's first language (or dialect) could interfere with the acquisition of the second. Supposing that LiFang, an exchange student from Peking, asks her tutor Paul to explain the comment "plural?" written in the margin of her paper beside the sentence "Ten dollar were stolen from my purse":

PAUL: How should you show that an English noun is plural?
LIFANG: Oh, I forgot! You have to add -s usually.

PAUL: Could you find an example in your paper?

LIFANG: Hmmm . . . *[reads]* OK, here I write, ''We have to wait for an hour to
5   buy the tickets.'' The *-s* on ''tickets'' means more than one.

PAUL: Right! So that time you formed the plural correctly. Does Chinese show
       plurals that way too?

LIFANG: Oh, no. Chinese characters don't make plurals.

PAUL: I see. So it must be hard to remember to be extra careful when you're
10   writing plural nouns in English.

LIFANG: I keep trying.

Paul begins by finding out whether or not LiFang knows the information about
how English nouns usually form plurals. If she had not known, he could simply
have told her. However, since she knows the rule and has applied it correctly in
writing ''tickets,'' he surmises and she confirms that her first language has a
different way of expressing plurals. If they had time, Paul might ask LiFang to
explain the Chinese system to him, thus showing his interest in her culture. In any
case, they now know that ''first-language interference'' is a partial explanation for
her having written ''ten dollar.'' LiFang understands enough grammatical terminology to make the explanation quite readily, but writers who lack the terminology can nevertheless explain their choices in ordinary language (as Chapter 8
illustrates). Rest assured that you can identify ''first-language interference'' without knowing the native languages or nonstandard dialects of the writers with whom
you work: all you have to do is ask.

A more general approach to error analysis focuses less specifically on how the
first-language system compares with the new system but more broadly upon the
process of language acquisition. Whoever has heard a child learning English as a
first language knows that (no matter how many rules a parent *teaches*) the *learning*
depends on the child's formulating general rules and then gradually refining them
through experience. For instance, a child we know said (referring to an Old English sheepdog named Lord Peter Wimsey): ''Wimsey haves him's bone.'' His
sentence reflects his having formulated two general rules: add the sound of *-s* to
show ownership and to form present tense verbs that go with ''he.'' He continued
listening and eventually distinguished ''has/have'' and ''him/his.'' Similarly, nonstandard and ESL speakers can learn by associating with standard speakers. But
because these adult learners already know at least one language, you can help
them much more effectively by adopting a strategy Mina Shaughnessy pioneered
for basic writers: seeing apparently haphazard fluctuations in form not as results
''of carelessness or irrationality but of *thinking*,'' sometimes imitating first languages and sometimes overgeneralizing rules:

> There is no point in discouraging a learner from making these premature formula-
> tions. He will make them anyway, sensing that mastery lies in the direction of gen-
> eralization rather than memorization. . . . Part of the task of helping [nonstandard
> and ESL writers] . . . depends upon being able to trace the line of reasoning that
> has led to erroneous choices. . . . (105)

Taking up Shaughnessy's challenge to reconstruct the line of reasoning that has led the learner into error, more recent theorists such as Kroll, Schafer, and Bartholomae focus their analyses upon "interlanguage." This term means "an 'intermediate system,' an idiosyncratic grammar and rhetoric that is a writer's approximation of the standard idiom" (Bartholomae, 257). This "intermediate system" consists of the changing set of hypotheses about the new language that each learner progressively constructs and tests. Because "interlanguage" sees errors as "clues to inner processes, as windows into the mind" (Kroll and Schafer, 136), it is particularly useful for tutors, who have constant opportunities to analyze the verbal and written hypotheses of each individual, either to figure out or to ask directly which hypotheses each writer might have constructed, and to help each writer state these hypotheses and test them for accuracy. Supposing that Paul tries to find out whether LiFang's omission of the final -s on dollars was merely accidental or if it reflects an hypothesis:

PAUL: You could just have forgotten this time to add -s. I'm wondering, though, if there was something else going through your mind that made leaving off the -s seem logical?

15 LIFANG: I thought "ten" already said that "dollar" was more than one. It was "ten dollar."

PAUL: I see what you mean. It does seem kind of silly to say the idea of plural twice, doesn't it. But that's what English does.

LIFANG: OK. But I hear someone say, "That was a ten-dollar book." Now I don't
20 know when to put -s.

PAUL: I think I understand. It *is* pretty confusing. I never actually thought about this before, but let me try to explain.

LIFANG: OK.

PAUL: Hmmm . . . *[pauses]* OK. Let's write out two sentences:

25   (a) That was a ten-dollar book.

    (b) I paid ten dollars for that book.

Where does "ten-dollar" or "ten dollars" appear in each sentence?

LIFANG: Hmm. In (a), it comes just before book. In (b), it comes after the verb.

PAUL: What difference does that make?

30 LIFANG: In (b) it names.

PAUL: And how do you show that a name, or noun, is "more than one"?

LIFANG: Oh yes! Add -s. I should write, "Ten dollars were stolen from my purse."

PAUL: That's good. Let's look at (a). What word names something?

LIFANG: "Book"?

35 PAUL: Right. So what does "ten dollar" do in (a)?

LIFANG: It tells about the book. Like, "That was a red book." "Ten dollar" describes, like "red."

PAUL: Good. "Ten dollar" is only describing. There is no rule about adding -s to describing words, OK?

40 LIFANG: OK. I understand. Let's practice.

PAUL: OK, let's make up sentences about the size of an oil tank. Do you know the word "gallon"?

LIFANG: Yes, OK. *[writes]*

    (a) My house has a one-hundred gallon oil tank.

45   (b) I bought fifty gallon*s* of oil.

PAUL: Good, you're getting it. Do you watch football? *[She nods yes.]* OK, write two sentences about a long pass.

LIFANG: *[writes]*

    (a) He threw a seventy-yard pass.

50   (b) The pass went seventy yards.

PAUL: Good. You've got a name that ends in -*s* already. What would you say if he did it two times?

LIFANG: I know. I add -*es* to make "pass" plural: "He threw two seventy-yard passes," and "The two passes went seventy yards."

55 PAUL: You've got it.

Instead of merely correcting LiFang's errors, as might a tutor who sees error as lack of a concept or as imperfect formation of a habit, Paul employs the concept of "interlanguage" to help him imagine what rules LiFang may be constructing in the process of refining her understanding of English. Surmising that her error was not simply a slip of the pen, he asks her to explain her line of reasoning. When she brings up an apparent contradiction that Paul has not considered previously, he does not become flustered or try to give a fancy linguistic explanation; instead, he constructs a commonsense, descriptive explanation and offers practice. Thus, instead of seeing the error as a "bad" use of language, they view it as a "good" opportunity for learning, in this example for learning about hypothesizing a false rule (about not repeating the concept of plurality) and learning a rule restriction (not adding the -*s* to nouns when they are being used descriptively). Their further practice aids Lifang in refining her hypotheses and in approximating the target language.

American-born inexperienced writers form "interlanguage" too, and, like ESL writers, once they know a rule, they may tend both to overgeneralize it and to hypercorrect. In David Bartholomae's words (254),

> They get into trouble by getting in over their heads, not only attempting to do more than they can, but imagining as their target a syntax that is *more* complex than convention requires. The failed sentences, then, could be taken as stages of learning rather than the failure to learn, but also as evidence that these writers are using writing as an occasion to learn.

If an inexperienced writer learns that verbs add -*ed* to form past tense, he may overgeneralize the rule and hypercorrect: "Did you work*ed* all day?" If he learns that -*s* makes nouns plural, he may write, "I watched the childrens play ball," even though that doesn't sound right. Shaughnessy points out the irony: "[Basic writers'] intuitions having proved wrong in so many instances, they may even conclude that 'sounding wrong' is a sign of being right'' (99). Tutorial sessions are especially useful for helping writers refine their general rules, because you can use your understanding of ''interlanguage'' to help writers identify their reasons for using a particular rule—or hypothesis—in a particular situation and can then either reinforce the rule or explain its restrictions. Even though writers might not always use hypercorrections systematically, their systematic basis enables you to address them theoretically instead of simply correcting individual manifestations.

Not all errors, though, are aspects of ''interlanguage.'' Some may be merely accidental, or ''performance errors'' rather than ''competence errors.'' For example, Carol, the writer of ''My Job'' in Chapter 3, may be seen to be forming two hypotheses about capitalizing the word ''job'' in the title when it reappears in the first paragraph: ''. . . my job. My Job . . .'' (line 1). On the other hand, the ''J'' may be a slip of the pen; a tutor addressing this issue would be wise to rule out accident before launching into an examination of hypotheses. As David Bartholomae observes (259–263), the physical act of writing can produce accidental (or ''performance'') errors that have nothing to do with a writer's ''interlanguage'' or with ''competence'' in the new language; by asking a writer to read aloud what she has written, you can discover whether or not, for instance, missing -s and -ed are pronounced or missing words are added to make the sentences sound ''right.'' In such cases, the writer's readiness to supply the missing pieces shows ''competence'' in the language, which ''performance errors'' belie. The strategy for coping with most performance errors is teaching the writer to do very slow proofreading that is particularly attentive to habitual performance errors. The strategy for competence errors is more elaborate, calling for analysis of the writer's ''interlanguage.'' (Chapter 13 will say more about perceptual problems, proofreading, and ways in which tutors may use writers' reading miscues to help them solve problems of spelling and vocabulary.)

Setting Realistic Goals

Those with many years of experience in teaching Standard Written English to nonstandard and ESL speakers know that certain problems take a very long time to abate. Some ESL speakers may take years to handle the definite article correctly, yet these errors seldom interfere seriously with communicating. So too, some inexperienced writers who understand perfectly the uses of -s and -ed may nevertheless continue for a very long time making performance errors in writing. The persistence of such errors might make you feel frustrated and defeated; seeing them in the full context of language acquisition, though, might help you recognize that you do help writers in two ways. Directly, you help writers attain greater competence in Standard Written English, even though performance may lag behind. Indirectly, tutorial dialogue gives writers practice in producing more nearly standard spoken and written English, breaks through the linguistic and social isolation, and offers social and psychological incentives for acquiring new dialects. As long as you resist allowing concern for correctness to take all your energy and attention away from other important aspects of the composing process, you and the writers can concentrate on making progress toward, if not entirely attaining, the goal of using Standard Written English.

Summary

Nonstandard speakers and ESL speakers have different problems in learning to speak and write standard English, but these may respond to similar tutorial strategies. ESL speakers often need help with quantity words, inflections, verbs, negatives, shifts in person, and possessives. As nonstandard and ESL speakers acquire standard forms, they may feel estranged and anxious.

Standard Written English is a dialect that nobody speaks. It demands more complex syntax than and different choices of vocabulary from standard spoken English. The kind and amount of tutorial help writers need in order to learn Standard Written English depends on the proximity of their spoken dialects to it. To establish rapport with nonstandard and ESL speakers and to help them learn Standard Written English, you need to help them understand that their spoken dialects are not inferior and need not be abandoned: they need to know Standard Written English *in addition* to their spoken dialects.

Since errors are evidence that a learner is constructing an intermediate system of hypotheses about language (interlanguage), you can discover what they are and help writers to test them for accuracy and to refine general rules (error analysis). You can also use drills, sentence completion and combining exercises, and scrambled paragraphs to complement the primary work on writers' compositions. Because some problems take a very long time to abate, you need to set realistic goals and to recognize that you are helping nonstandard and ESL speakers by giving them the practice necessary for gradually mastering the standard spoken and written forms of English.

SUGGESTIONS FOR JOURNAL ENTRIES

1. If you have studied a foreign language, write about hypotheses you formed and the processes by which you refined them.

2. If you have used a language lab or have been assigned written drills, write about your learning experience. Which aspects of this kind of instruction were most productive for you, and why do you think they were?

3. If you have lived in a speech community differing from that in which you grew up, write about your feelings about speaking and writing the new language. How did native speakers' reception of your attempts to speak their language influence your attempts and success?

4. If you have worked with ESL students, write about the differences in helping those who were already fluent readers and writers in their native languages (such as many European and Mideastern students in this country) and those who were not (such as Southeast Asian children who spent many years in refugee camps).

5. If you have tutored speakers of Black English Vernacular, Native American dialects, or Hispanic dialects, write about the psychological and social aspects of your tutoring.

SUGGESTIONS FOR FURTHER WRITING

1. Our colleague, Vivian Zamel, has given us the following paper composed by a writer in an intermediate ESL course. After reading the paper, write your answers to the following questions:

- **a.** What patterns of error do you observe?
- **b.** What hypotheses might the writer have formed to account for the use of "the"?
- **c.** What hypotheses might account for errors of subject–verb agreement?
- **d.** What hypotheses might account for the writer's use of modifiers?

Whether human being is one of animals or not is a problem; physically, human being may belong to the group of animals. However, we also can recognize a lot of differences between human and animals, which may lead us to regard human as totally different creature on the earth. In this paper, I will discuss both view points explaining evidences.

5   Looking at our body, we can find a lot of similarity to most animals. For example, we have one head, four limbs, to eyes, one mouth, as all other animals do. Especially, apes looks like human; they walk with two legs, fingers are skillful enough to peel the rind of an orange. Moreover, they could use tools and fire, We, as same as animals, eat food, sleep, reproduce other generation. These behaviors are called the instinct which is the innate aspect of actions that is unlearned,
10   complex, and nor,nally adaptive.

However, what we also primary have gotten is the ability to control these instinct, which is the capability of reason. It has been biologically proofed that the brain of human is much more complex and delicate than that of other animals'. That makes us think, worry, and moreover, study to be an intelligent; we make an effort to enhance values of ourselves. No other animals trys to do these kind
15 of things, but they just live with their instinct. In terms of value, human being seems to establish a single group which is mentally very different from other animals on the earth.

It is very difficult to state whether human being belongs to the group of animal or not because both ideas can be proofed. Now, I would like to bring out Pascal's famous words "Man is a thinking reed," which means that a man is one of the living creature on the earth which has an ability to
20 think. I, myself, agree with Pascal. I think that human being is one of animals, and at the same time he has rational brain which intuitively lead human being manage the earth.

2. Write a dialogue in which you help the writer of this paper to address one or two of the patterns of error you have identified.

3. After reading the following essay by an inexperienced writer, analyze it to identify patterns of error and construct a dialogue you might have with the writer to help her address one or more errors.

HYPERACTIVE CHILDREN

The true cause of hyperactivity is presently unknown The problem has been studied for the past fifty years, and the number of remedies or solutions to the problem have evolved. There are many arguments about the safety of the treatments given to hyperactive children, and whether there necessary at all. The main concern of parents, since
5 there is no present cure is to try to shape their hyperactive children into a normal state like their peers, so that they may expand and develop their personalities.

A large number of solutions have come about for the treatment of hyperactive children. The most common and widespread solution is the use of stimulant drugs known as amphetamines. Other solutions are to control the childrens diet by restricting the

10 types of food that they eat, The reason for this was because it was believed that additives such as synthetic colors, flavors, and salicylates affected behavior. The remaining
possibilities of hyperactivity are psychological reasons. They relate the fact that if a child
was confined to home and limited in his outdoor activities, then he has narrowed his
outlets for energy thus making himself hyperactive.

15 Each of the above solutions has its own set of problems related to it. The most common solution being the use of amphetamines creates the largest problem. There have
been a number of tests done in which both the good and the bad have resulted from
the use of drugs.

Judith Rappoport of the National Mental Health Institute states "these drugs dramati-
20 cally improve hyperactive children's behavior when the children take them for short periods of time." A physician quoted from the NY Times states "We gave it (Ritalin) to one
terrible little boy, and a few minutes later the child was actually taking out the garbage
for his mother. She almost flipped out." These are just a few examples of how the short
term use of amphetamines have helped hyperactive children.

25 There are also some ill side effects to the use of the drugs. Robert Sprague from the
University of Illinois through years of research has determined that if children take amphetamines the heart rate and blood pressure become increated, and if this is taken for
many years then it may become harmful.

4. Write a second dialogue in which you employ some of the strategies suggested in
Chapters 8 and 9 to help the writer of this paper.

SUGGESTIONS FOR CLASS ACTIVITIES

1. Compare your response to exercise 2 under "Suggestions for Further Writing" with
those of your classmates. Which patterns were most often identified? What hypotheses
were suggested to account for each? What tutorial strategies were most often used?

2. Compare your response to exercise 4 under "Suggestions for Further Writing" with
those of your classmates. Which patterns were most often identified? What hypotheses
were suggested to account for each? What tutorial strategies were most often used?

SUGGESTIONS FOR FURTHER READING

Bailey, Richard W., and Jay L. Robinson. *Varieties of Present-Day English*. New York: Macmillan,
1973.
Bartholomae, David. "The Study of Error." *College Composition and Communication* 31 (1980): 253–
269.
Bernstein, Basil. *Class, Codes and Control*. Vol. 3. *Towards a Theory of Educational Transmissions*.
London: Routledge and Kegan Paul, 1977.
Carter, Candy, Ed. *Non-Native and Nonstandard Dialect Students: Classroom Practices in Teaching
English, 1982–1983*. Urbana, IL: NCTE, 1982.
Diederich, Paul, John French, and Sydell Carlton. *Factors in Judgments of Writing Ability*. Research
Bulletin RB-61-15. Princeton, NJ: Educational Testing Service, 1961.
Dillard, J. L. *Black English: Its History and Usage in the United States*. New York: Random House,
1972.
Fox, Robert P., Ed. *Essays in Teaching English as a Second Language*. Urbana, IL: NCTE, 1973.
Garcia, Richard L. "A Linguistic Frame of Reference for Critiquing Chicano Composition." *College
English* 37 (1975): 184–188.

Gray, Barbara Quint. "Dialect Interference in Writing: A Tripartite Analysis." *Basic Writing Journal* 1 (1975): 14–22.

Heath, Shirley Brice. *Ways with Words.* Cambridge: Cambridge University Press, 1983.

Hirsch, E. D., Jr. *The Philosophy of Composition.* Chicago: University of Chicago Press, 1977. 34–50.

Hoover, Mary Rhodes. "Community Attitudes toward Black English." *Language in Society* 7 (1978): 65–87.

Hughey, Jane B., et al. *Teaching ESL Composition: Principles and Techniques.* Rowley, MA: Newbury House, 1983.

Huizenga, Jann, Courtenay Meade Snellings, and Gladys Berro Francis. *Basic Composition for ESL: An Expository Workbook.* Glenview, IL: Scott, Foresman, 1982.

Kaplan, Robert B. "Cultural Thought Patterns in Inter-Cultural Education." *Language Learning* 16 (1966): 1–20. Reprinted in *Composing in a Second Language.* Ed. Sandra McKay. Rowley, MA: Newbury House, 1984. 43–62.

Kroll, Barry M., and John C. Schafer. "Error-Analysis and the Teaching of Composition." *College Composition and Communication* 29 (1978): 242–248. Reprinted in *Composing in a Second Language.* Ed. Sandra McKay. Rowley, MA: Newbury House, 1984. 135–144.

Labov, William. *Language in the Inner City: Studies in the Black English Vernacular.* Philadelphia: University of Pennsylvania Press, 1972.

———. *The Study of Nonstandard English.* Champaign, IL: NCTE, 1970.

Laurence, Patricia. "Error's Endless Train: Why Students Don't Perceive Errors." *Journal of Basic Writing* I (1975): 23–43.

Lay, Nancy. "Chinese Language Interference in Written English." *Basic Writing Journal* 1 (1975): 50–61.

Levine, Deena R., and Mara B. Adelman. *Beyond Language: Intercultural Communication for English as a Second Language.* Englewood Cliffs, NJ: Prentice-Hall, 1982.

McQuade, Donald, Ed. *Linguistics, Stylistics, and the Teaching of Composition.* Akron, OH: L & S Books, 1979.

Matalene, Carolyn. "Contrastive Rhetoric: An American Writing Teacher in China." *College English* 47 (1985): 789–808.

Nattinger, James R. "Second Dialect and Second Language in the Composition Class." *TESOL Quarterly* 12 (1978): 77–84.

Oster, Judith. "The ESL Composition Course and the Idea of a University." *College English* 47 (1985): 66–76.

Raimes, Ann. "Anguish as a Second Language? Remedies for Composition Teachers." In *Learning to Write: First Language / Second Language.* Eds. A. Freedman, I. Pringle, and J. Yalden. New York: Longman, 1983. 258–272. Reprint in *Composing in a Second Language.* Ed. Sandra McKay. Rowley, MA: Newbury House, 1984. 81–96.

———. *Focus on Composition.* New York: Oxford University Press, 1978.

Richards, Jack C., Ed. *Error Analysis: Perspectives on Second Language Acquisition.* London: Longman, 1974.

Rodriguez, Richard. *Hunger of Memory.* 1981. New York: Bantam, 1982.

Ross, Janet, and Gladys Doty. *To Write English: A Step-by-Step Approach for ESL.* New York: Harper and Row, 1985.

Roy, Alice M. "Alliance for Literacy: Teaching Non-native Speakers and Speakers of Nonstandard English Together." *College Composition and Communication* 35 (1984): 439–448.

Schwalm, David E. "Degree of Difficulty in Basic Writing Courses: Insights from the Oral Proficiency Interview Testing Program." *College English* 47 (1985): 629–640.

Selinker, Larry. "Interlanguage." *International Review of Applied Linguistics* 5 (1967): 209–231.

Shaughnessy, Mina P. *Errors and Expectations.* New York: Oxford University Press, 1977. Chapter 4.

Traugott, Elizabeth Closs, and Mary Louise Pratt. *Linguistics for Students of Literature.* New York: Harcourt, 1980.

Watson-Reekie, Cynthia B. "The Use and Abuse of Models in the ESL Writing Class." *TESOL Quar-*

terly 16 (1982): 5–14. Reprinted in *Composing in a Second Language*. Ed. Sandra McKay. Rowley, MA: Newbury House, 1984. 97–109.

Zamel, Vivian. "Teaching Composition in the ESL-Classroom: What We Can Learn from Research in the Teaching of English." *TESOL Quarterly* 10 (1976): 1–41.

———. "Teaching Those Missing Links in Writing." *English Language Teaching Journal* 37 (1983): 22–29. Reprinted in *Composing in a Second Language*. Ed. Sandra McKay. Rowley, MA: Newbury House, 1984. 110–121.

PART FIVE

Reading and Writing

11

Reading and Writing
across the Disciplines

Tutors of writing are also tutors of reading, surprising as that might seem given the prevailing separation of these two activities in higher education today. However, reading and writing are actually closely related, mutually reinforcing forms of verbal thinking. While this relationship has consistently been acknowledged in primary and secondary education, where instruction in reading and writing are integrated in language arts programs, reading is not often explicitly taught at the four-year college level (except for courses that offer training in literary analysis or programs that are designated as "developmental"). For many years, college instructors across the disciplines assumed that entering students could, in a general sense, read analytically and critically, that they could, for example, comprehend readings in sociology, history, or biology without guidance. Colleges recognized the need for more basic and extensive instruction in composition sooner than they identified a similar need in reading, and they have only just begun to consider ways of adjusting teaching methods and materials accordingly.

In English departments, the exclusion of reading instruction from freshman programs was also caused, in part, by the "influence of some literary theories that place their main emphasis on the elaborate analysis of the structures and meaning of a literary text" (Salvatori, 658–59). These theories led to the belief that the teaching of reading is antithetical to the teaching of writing.

More recently, this position has been challenged by psycholinguists, reader-response critics, and composition theorists who have convincingly defended the "integrationist" position by demonstrating that both reading and writing are "constructive" or "meaning-making" activities.

> When we read, we comprehend by putting together impressions of the text with our own personal, cultural and contextual models of reality. When we write, we compose by making meaning from available information, our personal knowledge, and the cultural and contextual frames we happen to find ourselves in.
>
> (Petrosky, 26)

Reading is not simply information retrieval, but a forming process. Just as writers must, in the process of composing, question their own texts (thereby becoming readers), readers must engage in a dialogue with someone else's text. The same analytical and synthetic acts of mind are required for reading as for writing. Not surprisingly, then, failure in writing is often accompanied by failure in reading, and improvement in one activity leads to improvement in the other.

Because reading and writing problems are often interconnected, tutors assigned to help writers with composing often find it necessary to help with reading. If writers do not understand assigned books and essays, they are not able to respond well to essay questions or to formulate their own topics. Teaching them to become better readers helps them to become better writers by promoting greater fluency and accuracy. Such instruction can also improve writers' rhetorical form and mechanics. Studies by Lunsford and Salvatori confirm the operating assumption of primary and secondary instructors, that as readers' consciousness heightens, they begin to adopt in their writing the conventions they observe in reading.

Typical Reading Problems Experienced by Writers

It is certainly true that many adult writers fail to analyze and synthesize reading materials, but it would be misleading to say that they need only be taught how to do so. The reading problems of college-level writers are, in some cases, more basic. Some adults have not mastered the elementary skills of decoding and word recognition. Writing tutors, however, are not usually called upon to help readers master such principles as phonics, syllabication, and word structure (except insofar as they relate to spelling and vocabulary, subjects that will be discussed in Chapter 13). These issues are normally addressed in reading programs or by reading specialists. While this ''separatist'' policy is under debate, it is current practice, and therefore this book discusses only those reading problems that writing tutors typically handle.

Some writers compose essays that reveal a lack of basic reading comprehension: the writer inaccurately summarizes what happened or what was said. Such a writer may have read too quickly, with poor concentration, or without looking up unfamiliar vocabulary. Other writers may be able to summarize accurately but cannot get beyond that activity to interpret what they have read (all reading can, in a general sense, be said to be interpretive, but the term is used here to distinguish commenting on the significance of a passage from reconstructing it). These readers do not recognize connections (be they causal, comparative, chronological, classificatory, or illustrative) among ideas within or between paragraphs, nor do they see the significance of a passage or a statement in the context of an entire work or a college course. A typical example is the student who, when asked to analyze a piece of literature, simply retells the plot. This sort of writer may not know what interpretive questions to ask of the text as she reads. She may not know what literary elements or topics she ought to consider. For instance, a naive reader is not apt to ask what an author gains or loses by choosing a particular narrative stance.

The same kind of difficulty is experienced by readers in other disciplines. These students are not aware of the typical concerns or methodologies of various forms of academic inquiry, so they do not know how to extract salient details or how to conceptualize large chunks of information. The information washes over them as they wait passively for meaning to take shape. Novice readers of history, for instance, are typically overwhelmed by the amount of data with which they are confronted. Some may try to memorize everything, but if they have no understanding of how to order or conceptualize the material, it becomes a formless list of inert facts. Were these people taught to think of history as a dynamic process of change, and were they to categorize these changes as political, social, or economic, they would have a preliminary means of thinking and writing about various events' importance.

While these readers do not know how to select or cluster details, other readers who venture beyond sheer summarization may hazard interpretation without substantiation. This often occurs not simply because they do not understand their obligation to their reader, but also because they are not sufficiently in command of a text's details. They may have formed vague impressions, but they cannot cite the evidence (even when it exists) on which their assertions are based.

Inexperienced writers also have difficulty describing a writer's apparent purpose, argumentative strategy, and tactics because they have not analyzed an author's rhetorical forms, structure, or usage. In addition, they are cowed by the "authoritativeness" of the printed page and do not question the validity of an argument's logic or evidence: who are they, lowly students, to challenge the wisdom of an expert in the field? Faced with intellectual controversy, a disagreement among specialists, these readers are stymied. Often, they will try to force agreement where there is none, as if they cannot believe that the so-called authorities would disagree or as if they must find concord because discord is unpleasant or morally wrong. Such readers have been characterized by William Perry as "absolutistic," developmentally unready to perceive or tolerate contradictions and ambiguities.

Short-Term Strategies for Improving Reading

Assessing problems and establishing priorities

The writers with whom you meet may experience one or more of the reading difficulties described. Most frequently, these problems become apparent when you look over someone's paper at the beginning of a session although they may also appear when a writer who is trying to get started on a paper discusses the reading on which the essay is to be based. If the problems are extensive or severe, you will probably need to make a judicious assessment of their nature and cause. You could ask how much time the reader devoted, what, if any, tactics he used, what dictionary work he did, at what point, and in general, what he found difficult about the reading. If a reader needs to adopt different reading procedures, you are then faced with a dilemma: should the session be devoted to an exposition and application of these procedures, or should it focus on the composition? That is, should you postpone discussion of the paper and teach the reader how to approach his text, or should you just ask questions that will help the reader correct the errors that appear in the essay? The choice need not be absolute, and the relative attention given to immediate and long-term objectives can be weighted according to the writer's preference, the nature and severity of his reading problem, and the demands on his time. He may be working under a deadline, so you might, accordingly, subordinate formal instruction in reading techniques to a discussion of the writers' essay. As you raise questions about it, you may find opportunities for teaching reading tactics. It is possible, then, to combine the two different kinds of instruction, that which helps the writer to discover and correct reading errors in his composition, and that which teaches him how to approach a text. In the following discussion, however, these strategies are separated for purposes of exposition.

Meeting immediate objectives: improving basic comprehension and interpretive ability by asking reconstructive, interpretive, and applicative questions

There are roughly three types of reading questions that you can ask when a reader's basic comprehension and interpretive ability need improvement: reconstructive, interpretive, and applicative. The ability to reconstruct (paraphrase or summarize) a text is necessary for valid interpretation. Similarly, readers must be able to interpret a passage in order to see its applicability to other contexts. You should therefore carefully assess readers' ability to reconstruct, interpret, and apply a text in order that you formulate sensible sequences of questions. Usually a mixture of the three types is appropriate in a conference, and when they are posed, the text should be available for reference, particularly since you may be unacquainted with the readings. Although you might feel ill-equipped to work on a text that you have not read, unfamiliarity can actually be an advantage: if you have not read the material, your questions will be genuine and open-ended. They cannot cue or give away answers. The reader will take on greater responsibility because you no longer simulate the role of naive audience. Rather, you will truly depend on the reader. To make certain that the reader has accurately reconstructed or interpreted a text, you can always ask the reader to point to the passages in the text where he got his ideas.

Reconstructive questions. These questions require a reader to state the text's ideas in her own language, that is, to paraphrase or summarize. They are the most fundamental of reading questions in that they determine whether a reader has comprehended basic meaning. It is often a good idea, therefore, to begin with reconstructive questions. You might also ask this sort of question when a reader needs to substantiate an assertion or to correct an erroneous statement. For example, suppose a writer has mistakenly suggested that Lady Macbeth is emotionally unaffected by Duncan's murder. You could ask, "What does Lady Macbeth do or say after her husband commits the murder?" The writer would have to recheck the play and summarize the action. On the basis of her textual reconstruction, she would probably revise her interpretation. Reconstructive questions, then, may ask the reader to state what happens in a text.

These questions may also require a reader to paraphrase a specific passage, phrase, or word. You might say, "What does this word mean? Say it in your own words," or "What is another word for this idea?" in order to ensure that the reader grasps the denotation (literal meaning) of the text's language. A question concerning connotation can be considered reconstructive insofar as it calls for generally accepted associations (as opposed to more subjective ones). If, for instance, you asked what the term "ratted" means in the sentence, "He ratted on his buddies," a reader might say, "It means he told on them." If you asked how "told on" and "ratted" differ, you could then determine whether the reader also understood that the term connotes a negative judgment. This discussion would probably lead to interpretive considerations: what ratlike characteristics are suggested or who would be likely to use language like "rat" as opposed to "tell," or in what context one would be likely to hear either word. It is often hard to separate reconstructive from interpretive activity. The point here is, however, that if a reader does not understand literal meaning or basic connotation, you will need to ask questions that promote fundamental comprehension.

Interpretive questions. These questions help a reader discover the significance of reading selections: what a statement implies, how one idea relates to another, on what unstated assumptions an idea is based, what an idea reveals about an author's values and attitudes. Since inexperienced readers seldom search for implications or underlying assumptions, you can ask questions that encourage readers to draw inferences from textual statements such as, "You said that this author considers human life sacred. What attitude toward capital punishment is implicit in this view?" or to induce tacit premises: "This author opposes capital punishment. What assumptions about the nature of human life might underlie this view? Which apply in this case?"

You can also help readers to identify an author's inferences and judgments and to distinguish them from factual statements. For example, you might ask, "When Erich Fromm says that the 'passiveness of man in industrial society today is one of his most characteristic and pathological features,' is he stating a fact or his own opinion? How can you tell?" Having identified conclusions or emotionally charged language that reveals an author's attitudes toward the subject, you can help readers begin to evaluate the strength, function, and legitimacy of such inclusions in particular texts. For example, suppose a text said, "In his report to the police captain regarding the picketers' behavior during the strike at the Widget plant, the sergeant said, 'Those picketers were troublemakers from the start. So my partner and I decided to set up the barriers as fast as we could, but they went crazy before we could stop them, so we had to use the tear gas.' " You could ask, "How useful is this as a report of the incident? How objective is it? What is the effect of words like 'troublemakers,' 'went crazy,' and 'had to'?"

Interpretive questions can also help readers assess an author's authority to write about a particular topic; for instance, you might ask something like this: "Can the

Senator from Wisconsin speak objectively about the Dairy Subsidy Amendment?'' ''Can the Senator from the Bronx speak knowledgeably about it?'' and ''Can Larry Bird speak about it at all, just because he obviously drank his milk?'' Since an author's authority may shift with time, after new discoveries or views have been accepted as valid, you can suggest that readers check publication dates.

Interpretive questions can also help a reader establish conceptual relationships among ideas, such as part to whole, general to particular, chronology, cause and effect, process, comparison/contrast, and definition. If readers can identify these relationships, they gain understanding of an author's vision of her material, her argumentative line and apparent purpose, how a particular passage functions in the whole selection, and so on. You can simply ask, ''How does this idea relate to the previous idea?'' or can help the student identify the language that establishes this relationship: ''What words in the text show that this idea contrasts with that?'' That is, the reader is asked to identify structure words (connectives, transitional and cohesive devices, verbs) that connect ideas. In the sentence, ''The rapid industrialization of Northern Ireland led to social unrest,'' the words ''led to'' establish a causal connection between ''industrialization'' and ''unrest.'' Reconstructive questions like ''What caused what?'' can reinforce such interpretive activity.

If readers fail to see that a particular detail is related to a main idea, you can ask questions like, ''You said that Jane Howard's main point was that since nuclear families aren't usually happy, people should create surrogate families using their friends as members of their 'clan.' What does her comment about how nuclear families behave at holiday gatherings have to do with this point?'' Similarly, when readers do not see what general idea can be derived from a specific point, your questions can call for generalizations: ''You said that Othello kills himself as well as Desdemona. What point does that make about the effects of jealousy?'' If the reader drew a hasty conclusion in answering this query, you could revert to reconstructive questions like, ''What does Othello do to make you think this?''

Sometimes, readers do not interpret reading matter because they do not know what kinds of questions are characteristically raised by different disciplines. While each of the conceptual patterns mentioned above appears in readings from all disciplines, some of the patterns tend to dominate in each field. For example, in historical writing, ideas are often causally or chronologically related; you can help readers to improve comprehension by asking questions based on these dominant conceptual patterns. Earlier in this chapter, we suggested some questions that you might ask novice readers of history; similarly, if you are helping anyone working in other social sciences, in natural sciences, and in the arts, you might consider the typical concerns of these fields and their specialized vocabulary in order to form questions relating to them. For example, biology students are often required to define phenomena, to identify steps in a biological process, or to distinguish one phenomenon or process from another. Questions like ''What does it look like?'' ''What does it do?'' ''What is it made of?'' ''In what ways does it change?'' ''What makes it change?'' and ''How is it different from?'' elicit useful information when the reader is approaching science texts. Having introduced such questions, you can encourage readers to make use of them in subsequent reading.

(For ways of deriving such questions from texts, see p. 240 on long-term strategies.)

Applicative questions. These ask readers to go beyond the interpretation of a text's explicit or implicit meaning. They can ask a reader to apply some idea to a new context, for example, "You said that Lewis Thomas thinks that we should allocate the majority of health care funds to basic biological research. Would he support Greengage's proposal to subsidize medical fees for the poor and elderly?" Applicative questions can also ask readers to test an idea against their own experience: "We said that this book argues that factory workers are alienated from their jobs. You have worked on an assembly line. How does that stack up against your experience?" Such questions may help a reader evaluate the merit or usefulness of an idea. You can also ask, more directly, "What kind of and how much evidence does this author provide?" "Is this true in your experience?" or "How valid does this idea seem in light of other evidence presented?" in order to encourage the reader to assess the strength of an idea or argument.

Applicative questions can also call for the reader's emotional responses to readings, for example, "How did you feel when David Copperfield's mother died?" The reader's reaction may be a combined result of dramatic or rhetorical effect and personal association, so it is usually wise, after raising such questions, to refer to the assigned topic to see whether subjective, associational comments are appropriate. It is also a good idea to follow up a "How did you feel about" question with "What made you feel that way?" for explanation or substantiation (often, this kind of question is reconstructive).

Intermingling the three kinds of questions

As we have already pointed out, all three types of questions are usually appropriate in a conference (unless the writer is simply asked to summarize), but one type may dominate, and sequencing will vary according to each reader's level of proficiency, the difficulty of the text, and that of the assignment. If a reader has not comprehended the fundamental meaning of a passage, it is essential to begin by emphasizing reconstruction so that he has a firm basis for making interpretations. With a reader who can reconstruct a text, you might begin with interpretive questions to see if he can draw plausible conclusions. If he cannot, you can ask reconstructive questions that will help him gather evidence. Even if the reader makes a useful interpretation, it is a good idea to follow up with reconstructive questions that educe substantiation. No set formula for intermingling the three types of questions can be offered because of the individual circumstances in each conference, but the following dialogue offers one example of how they can be combined.

Joanna, a student in an introductory literature course, has been given a passage to analyze from Joseph Heller's *Catch 22,* which her class has just read. In this passage, a corrupt medical doctor describes what happened to his practice when other doctors were drafted in World War II. She is asked to respond to the following question: "Assuming that Doc Daneeka can be considered representative of

civilians during the war, what does Heller seem to be criticizing about their behavior?'' Below you will find the passage that Joanna is asked to analyze:

> "It [the war] was a godsend,'' Doc Daneeka confessed solemnly. "Most of the other
> doctors were soon in the service, and things picked up overnight. The corner location
> really started paying off, and I soon found myself handling more patients than I
> could handle competently. I upped my kickback fee with those two drugstores. The
> beauty parlors were good for two, three abortions a week. Things couldn't have been
> better.

Joanna writes:

> Doc Daneeka's practice improved because the other doctors were gone. He got more
> patients, did a lot of abortions. For him the war was a real plus because he got more
> business.

The paragraph does not address the question but instead merely summarizes some
of the character's remarks. It's possible that Joanna read the question hastily or
that she misunderstood it, but it is also likely that she did not approach the text
actively as she read it, nor, once given the question, did she know what follow-
up questions she needed to ask in order to respond. In the dialogue that follows,
a tutor, Phillipa, raises some of these questions. In the first half of the dialogue,
we have, for purposes of illustration, categorized the tutor's questions as recon-
➤ structive, applicative, and interpretive. When you get to the second half of the
dialogue, try to identify each of the remaining questions by type yourself.

PHILLIPA: What did the assignment ask you to do?   (reconstructive)

JOANNA: Tell what Heller criticizes about the doctor and others like him.

PHILLIPA: I can't really tell from your response what you think Heller criticizes.
What does that mean, he criticizes?   (reconstructive)

5   JOANNA: He thinks it's bad?

PHILLIPA: Sure. So what's bad about Doc Daneeka's behavior?   (interpretive)

JOANNA: Well, he shouldn't be doing abortions. I guess they were probably illegal
then.

PHILLIPA: OK, so why does he perform them?   (interpretive)

10   JOANNA: To make money. I guess if it's illegal, it's probably real expensive.

PHILLIPA: OK. When you think of someone who is a doctor, what reason do you
usually think he has for choosing that profession?
(applicative, to help Joanna see the ironic contrast)

JOANNA: They usually want to help people. But this guy doesn't care about that.
15   He's in it for the money.

PHILLIPA: Sure. What else does Doc Daneeka do or say that makes you think he's
interested in money?   (reconstructive, to support interpretation)

JOANNA: Well, he talks about getting more patients.

PHILLIPA: Yes. Anything else? . . . *[long pause]* What about kickbacks? Do you
20   know what that is?   (reconstructive)

JOANNA: I um, wasn't sure.

PHILLIPA: Oh, OK. It'd be a good idea next time to look up words you don't know, particularly when you're working on such a short passage. But this word is slangy; I'm not even sure it's in the dictionary. A kickback is a
25   payoff. The doctor makes a deal with a pharmacist to send patients to him if the pharmacist will give him a percentage of the profit. What he gets from the pharmacist is the kickback.

JOANNA: OK, I see, so this guy is really a crook.

PHILLIPA: Right.

30 JOANNA: He's supposed to be helping people but he's just interested in the money.

PHILLIPA: Sure, you could say that and use what we've discussed to back up that point. Is there anything else in the passage that you could use to support your idea that he's in it for the money?
35   (reconstructive, to support interpretation)

JOANNA: Maybe when he says things picked up!

PHILLIPA: Sure. What does he mean by "things"?   (reconstructive)

JOANNA: I guess the abortions and kickbacks and stuff—how he makes money.

40 PHILLIPA: Good. Now what makes it possible for him to make that money?
                              (type of question?——————)

JOANNA: The other doctors are gone. So the war, really.

PHILLIPA: Yes. Where in the passage is that made clear?
                              (type of question?——————)

45 JOANNA: When he says the war was a godsend.

PHILLIPA: Good. Let's look at that term for a minute. What does it mean, exactly?   (type of question?——————)

JOANNA: That it was a gift from God.

PHILLIPA: OK. When you think of gifts from God, that is, things you would think
50   of as being sent by God, what kinds of things would they be?
                              (type of question?——————)

JOANNA: Well, things that would be good for people. Helpful. Things that would make them happy.

PHILLIPA: Yes. So what is peculiar about calling war a godsend?
55   (type of question?——————)

JOANNA: You mean that it is weird that the war is making him happy and that he thinks God would send this as a gift like something good? God wouldn't send war as a gift.

PHILLIPA: Right. So if Doc thinks of it that way, what does that reveal about his
60   morals?

JOANNA: They're awful. I mean he's not moral at all.

PHILLIPA: Sure. What makes him immoral?   (type of question?——————)

JOANNA: He thinks of war as a gift, but war is bad, obviously. It kills people.

PHILLIPA: Right. But to him, what is war?   (type of question?—————)

65   JOANNA: It's a way to make money, so he's happy. He profits from it. I get it. To him, anything that makes money is OK even if it is illegal or immoral.

PHILLIPA: Good. OK. Now, the question asks you to see his behavior as representative: What does that mean?   (type of question?—————)

70   JOANNA: Typical?

PHILLIPA: Right. We know that all civilians were not doctors. So what in his behavior can be considered typical?   (type of question?—————)

JOANNA: I see what you mean. Not everybody did abortions, right? But maybe other people use the war to make money. Like that Milo character. Well, 75   he's not a civilian, but he's like a corrupt businessman. I mean, he bombs our own troops just to make money.

PHILLIPA: Great. Now you're really making connections. Maybe you can check back over the text later and see if you can find other examples like Milo that you could name. But for now, let's see if we can get back to the main 80   question, what is Heller criticizing?   (type of question?—————)

JOANNA: Well, he seems to be against moneymaking.

PHILLIPA: Yes. There's a word for making money from war. Are you familiar with it?   (type of question?—————)

JOANNA: Gee. I don't know. Exploitive?

85   PHILLIPA: That's a good one, but there are others. Try making "profit" into a verb. What can make it a verb?   (type of question?—————)

JOANNA: Profit—profitize?

PHILLIPA: That's a great guess. A lot of nouns become verbs when you add -ize, but not this one. I was thinking of "profiteering." You can write that word 90   down and see if it comes in handy when you write your paper. Now, let's see if we can pull together the ideas you've had. I've been jotting them down. Let's look at the list.

Here is the revised paper that Joanna turned in to her instructor:

> In *Catch 22* Heller is criticizing civilians for profiteering. Doc Daneeka is one of those people. Doc made out while the other doctors were away. He was only interested in making money, not in helping people. He thought of the war as a godsend, which tells you how corrupt he was. It doesn't matter to him that doing abortions or taking kickbacks is wrong and illegal and he doesn't care about people getting killed in the war. All he cares about is profit. He exploits people. Like Milo Minderbinder, Doc sees the war as good business.

➤   Before reading further, jot down some observations about the dialogue: What did the tutor's primary objective seem to be? What do you notice about the sequence of the conversation? What functions do the applicative questions have? What is your reaction to the tutor's having explained a word ("kickback") and having provided a word ("profiteering") for the writer? Next, comment on Joanna's second draft. In what ways is it an improvement over the first draft? Judging by this later draft, to what extent does the tutor seem to have accomplished her objective?

· · ·

Since Joanna's first draft does not get beyond summary, Phillipa's primary objective is to help her form interpretations. To accomplish this, she sometimes calls for interpretation and then asks for substantiation (lines 9,16). At other times, she reverses the sequence, helping Joanna to assemble details that allow her to draw a conclusion (16,54). In other words, Phillipa moves from general to specific or from specific to general questions. Regardless of whether the tutor's sequence is inductive or deductive, Joanna must connect textual details and interpretive propositions. At first, Joanna is unable to make a broad interpretation: in response to the question, "What's wrong with Doc's behavior?" she offers an overly specific response: "He shouldn't be doing abortions" (7), yet the answer is still interpretive; it does draw a minor conclusion that stays fairly close to the text. Phillipa then asks another interpretive question so as to build on Joanna's first conclusion. When Joanna asserts that Doc is out to make money (10), Phillipa asks her to gather more evidence for this claim and uses Joanna's interpretation to help her form a more abstract conclusion regarding Doc's moral character (54). Finally, she helps Joanna generalize the moral issue by asking what is typical about his behavior (70). In other words, she has prepared Joanna to make increasingly broad conclusions.

Along the way, the tutor has asked two applicative questions (11,48). Both require Joanna to consult her experience in order to recognize Heller's implicit criticism. Joanna needs to go outside of the text to understand it, to see the ironic distance between what Doc considers a "godsend," for instance, and what people normally associate with that term.

Asking questions about vocabulary

In the process of exploring the text, Phillipa also checks to see whether Joanna understands its vocabulary. When it is clear that she does not know what "kickback" means, Phillipa offers a definition. While this violates our general rule, "Ask, don't tell" or "Let the writer do the work," Phillipa's comment is, in this context, defensible. Her priority in the session is not to teach Joanna how and when to do dictionary work, so she does not sacrifice time to this. Alternatively, if she had said, "Go look this up when you get home," she would have lost the opportunity of making Joanna use the word to form an important interpretation about Doc's immorality, an interpretation that is central to the session's goal of helping Joanna identify what is being criticized. Furthermore, since Phillipa is not certain whether a "slangy" word like "kickback" appears in dictionaries (it does), her decision to volunteer a definition is even more justifiable.

While vocabulary building is not the session's central aim, it contributes to Joanna's basic comprehension of the text and therefore to her ability to interpret it. (Chapter 13 will say more about vocabulary.) Similarly, if a tutor can help a writer expand her own *working* vocabulary (as opposed to her reading vocabulary), the writer can enrich her understanding of the text. Phillipa helps Joanna conceptualize Doc's behavior by asking if she knows a word for people who profit from war (line 80). While her effort to elicit "profiteer" fails, Joanna at least comes up with an alternative ("exploit") that she incorporates in her second draft.

While her second guess, "profitize," show some understanding of linguistic structure and is therefore an intelligent error, it is an error nonetheless, so having
allowed Joanna to experiment, Phillipa offers "profiteering." Since she does not
tell the writer when to use the term or construct a sentence for her, she cannot be
said to be doing the writer's work. Rather, she enriches the writer's vocabulary
so that Joanna will put the term to her own use (which she does in the first
sentence of the second draft).

Reading the assignment

One other strategy that Phillipa uses deserves mention: her reading questions concern not only the excerpt but also the essay question itself. By asking what "criticize" and "representative" mean, she gets Joanna, in effect, to reconstruct the
assignment. In so doing, Phillipa ensures that Joanna understands and focuses on
the assigned task. Such reading questions about assignments make writers like
Joanna more responsive to topics. A tutor can ask questions that help a writer
determine whether summary, interpretation, application, or a combination of these
is required (as Chapter 4 suggests). For instance, if Joanna's topic had been,
"Social Criticism in *Catch 22:* What are Heller's targets? Support your answer
with textual evidence," Phillipa might have asked into how many parts the question could be divided. Joanna might have said two. Phillipa might have asked,
"What are your tasks?" Joanna might have responded, "Name the targets and
give examples." Since the first part of the question calls for interpretation (the
reader must decide from the textual evidence what Heller is criticizing) and the
second for summary (the writer must provide the evidence on which the conclusions are based), Phillipa might have then introduced the terms: "OK, so the first
part asks you for an interpretation, what *you* think the targets are, and the second
part asks you for a summary of the details that show what made you draw your
conclusion." In this way, a writer like Joanna might begin to learn to distinguish
the two kinds of writing activities. Her tutor might also suggest that the writer
gather and generate material for such a paper in two columns. Here is the kind of
list that Joanna might have made:

TARGETS (MY INTERPRETATION)	EXAMPLES (EVIDENCE)
Profiteering: money over human life	Doc does illegal abortions; Milo bombs troops
War: no rules, death makes no sense	Catch 22
Prostitution: anything for money; loss of feeling	Nately's whore

Long-Term Strategies for Improving Reading

Tutors often need to help writers to improve their concentration, to read more
actively, and to strengthen comprehension and retention through note taking.

Improving concentration

Sometimes readers do not absorb reading material because they are unable to concentrate. This may occur because they are studying in a distracting environment or because they are preoccupied with personal problems. Other readers do not concentrate well because they are overwhelmed by the amount of reading assigned. They feel that they will never finish the material, that there is too much to comprehend. Their anxieties rise and block their powers of concentration. These readers might be advised not to try to complete all the reading at once. They might schedule several well-spaced reading periods, or they might stop temporarily when they feel their concentration dwindling. Some students mistakenly believe that they should be able to read intensively for hours at a stretch and that there is something wrong with them if they cannot. They try to force themselves to stick with the reading instead of taking a break. By asking when and under what conditions readers normally study, how much time they allot to reading, when their concentration begins to fail, and what they are thinking about when it does, you can help readers discover what adjustments to make (see Chapter 1 for more ideas).

Activating the reader

Most often, college-level readers do not concentrate or comprehend well because they do not read actively, purposefully. As we commented earlier, they do not know what information to extract, nor do they question the logic of an argument or the validity of presented evidence. When they do not know what to look for, they often become bored, particularly if they are reading about a subject in which they are not particularly interested. One way of helping orient these readers to texts is to teach them to overview and skim expository or argumentative materials before reading them deeply (in Chapter 12 we will discuss approaches to literary narrative and to poetry). The overviewing process involves scrutiny of tables of contents, chapter headings, subheadings, italicized words, diagrams, and chapter summaries. Skimming for main ideas serves much the same purpose as overviewing. Readers can be taught to check chapter introductions and conclusions for central points, to locate places in paragraphs where writers typically place topic sentences, to spot repeated words or concepts, and to check for all these prior to a full reading. Books on college reading and study skills, which are readily available these days, contain more information about these reading tactics, and you can recommend that readers avail themselves of such texts as Walter Pauk's *How to Study in College*, Kathleen McWhorter's *College Reading and Study Skills*, and Shirley Quinn's and Susan Irvings' *Active Reading*. Tutorial sessions might then be devoted to some of the exercises provided by these texts, or you can make up your own.

Overviewing and skimming abet the constructive process of reading. Experienced readers make meaning out of texts by predicting how the words they are reading fit into some whole, be it a sentence, a paragraph, or an entire work. Words take on meaning in a context, and experienced readers infer that context in order to understand the words or phrases that they are decoding. Inexperienced readers, by contrast, have few expectations as to what a text will yield. When such readers fail to infer the frame into which a word or phrase fits, they divorce the textual fragment from its whole, so they often have to return to the fragment once they have read beyond it in order to make sense of it. Since overviewing helps provide a context for individual sentences or paragraphs and reduces the number of predictions that a reader must make, this preliminary survey promotes accurate and efficient comprehension.

Another purpose for overviewing and skimming is for readers to discover what they should look for when they read closely, what further information they should glean from the reading. Another way of saying this is that overviewing and skimming help readers see what questions they should ask of a text. Some college textbooks provide reading questions at chapter endings, and, although many readers rather moralistically assume that these should only serve as tests of comprehension, you can suggest that they be read first and used as study guides. You can also help readers turn what they learn from overviewing or skimming and what they know about a course's or instructor's special concerns into reading questions.

Let's say that in a history text, a reader finds a chapter on the Industrial Revolution with a subheading entitled, "Origins of the Revolution." A reader could transform that into the question, "What caused the revolution?" and could then search for agents of change. You might ask, "What organizational pattern would you predict from this subheading?" If the reader saw that "origins" is plural, she might realize that a list of causes was likely. You and the reader could then skim to see if signal words like "first," "another" "the third" and "a final" flag the places where causes are introduced.

With this reader, you might also want to review the course outline and lecture notes to see if the professor emphasizes some particular aspect of the field. If, for instance, the syllabus or recurring themes in the notes indicated a focus on economic rather than on social or political history, the reader could then approach the chapter on the Industrial Revolution with an eye to its economic aspects and could look for words relating to economic topics (for instance, "profit," "labor," "market").

More fundamentally, you can help readers uncover basic questions raised by various disciplines (as suggested on p. 232) so that they gain a way to conceptualize the material they are reading. Again, these questions can be derived from course outlines, notes from introductory lectures, and tables of contents of assigned texts.

Improving comprehension and retention through note-taking

You can foster increased comprehension and retention by teaching readers how and when to take effective notes. Many readers think they have accomplished the equivalent of note-taking by copiously underlining texts with magic markers. If this underlining is selective, it can be a useful first step, but often readers mark undiscriminatingly as they read, so true "highlighting" is not accomplished. What could be suggested is that a reader return to passages she has just completed, be they underlined or not, and that she write marginal glosses for each paragraph (or for whatever portions of the text, upon reflection, seem particularly significant). These glossings could be single words or phrases that either summarize the content or name its function (for example, "definition of courage" followed by "example of courage"). The glossings could be written up separately instead of in the book margins, a method particularly advisable when a long or borrowed text is in use. Even if a reader owns a text, however, he may need encouragement to write in it. Some readers hesitate to do so because they consider marking books a desecration. Others worry that the resale value of their college texts will drop if the books are not clean, but you can reassure people that most college bookstores pay a fixed used-book rate. The best way to demonstrate the value of glossing texts is to help a reader make use of her notations in writing her essays. By briefly characterizing a passage in the text margin, a writer creates a vocabulary for writing about that text, as we pointed out in Chapter 4, and this becomes apparent to the writer if you encourage her to refer to the glossing as she generates ideas for an essay.

Outlining is another form of note-taking, and some readers prefer it to glossing. These notes can be structural, that is, they follow the author's sequence, or they can be thetical, that is, they start with an author's thesis and reconstruct the argument's logic though not its linear sequence. In either case, you should encourage readers to make the notes brief, for purposes of quick review. Readers need not use full sentences and should abbreviate words wherever possible in order to save time. An indented numbering system, such as Roman numerals, can be useful, but it can also be cumbersome and is not necessarily advisable. An informal indented system often can be just as effective. You may want to suggest that writers experiment with different note-taking forms to see which is most usable for them.

Regardless of the choice, be it glossing or more formal outlining, note-taking has several advantages. Unlike underlining, it forces a writer to extract main ideas and to put them into her own language. This fosters greater comprehension and control over the material as well as fluency. It also promotes retention because it forces a reader to review what she has read. Note-taking, then, should ordinarily be done after reading, not during it. If a reader tries to write notes while reading, she may not be sufficiently selective, may copy sentences verbatim and therefore defeat the condensing and reviewing purposes of the activity. Also, readers who write as they read interrupt their concentration; they lose their place in the reading and must sacrifice precious time finding it and regaining their reading momentum.

Yet another form of note-taking can be introduced when readers must integrate ideas drawn from several readings: the synthesizing chart. After a reader has taken notes on individual articles, the major ideas in each can be transformed into questions that are applied to the remaining articles. Or, readers can simply jot down key concepts in one article and see if they are treated in another. The findings can be transcribed on a chart that establishes the connections among the articles:

MEDICAL TECHNOLOGY READINGS:			
	Illich	Knowles	Thomas
View of doctors			
View of Research			
Environment's role in health			
What solutions are proposed?			

This technique is particularly helpful to a reader like Joanna, who needs to learn how to move beyond summary, who needs to learn how to form interpretations.

Writing about Reading: Typical Problems and Some Solutions

Attribution failures

Novice writers often experience difficulty when incorporating into their essays ideas drawn from readings. Many of these writers are unaware of the need to attribute their sources, so they adopt an author's ideas without acknowledgment. This may occur, in part, because the writers do not understand the distinction between general knowledge, which does not require attribution (like historical dates such as 1789 for the French Revolution) and individual interpretations or research findings, which do. Typically, inexperienced writers assume that whatever they read can be taken as fact and as general knowledge. What they borrow from authors is, in their view, only what everyone besides them knows.

This confusion is compounded by their having been asked, in elementary and high school, to write informational reports that draw heavily on broad sources like encyclopedias. Inexperienced writers often copy passages from such sources verbatim (or close to it), either because they lack sufficient fluency or confidence to reconstruct the text in their own language or because the source itemizes information in a way that can be rephrased only with difficulty. For instance, the first part of the *New Columbia Encyclopedia*'s entry on Michelangelo reads, "Michelangelo Buonarotti, 1475–1564. Italian sculptor, painter, architect, and poet, b. Caprese Tuscany." A writer might understandably write, "Michelangelo was a famous Italian sculptor, painter, architect, and poet. He was born in Caprese Tuscany in 1475." This sort of adaptation is unavoidably close to the original because there is no easy way to rephrase Michelangelo's date and place of birth or the names of his vocations.

Someone who has written only such assignments, which almost encourage the adoption of the text's language, is likely to follow the same procedure when using ideas from less general sources or when writing different kinds of assignments. Such a writer may be accused of plagiarism when in truth he just does not realize that he should be quoting, or if he reconstructs the text, that he should give credit to the author in the body of his essay and/or in a footnote. If you identify unattributed quotations or reconstructions in a writer's essay, it is probably wiser and certainly more tactful for you to assume that the writer has erred unwittingly than to accuse the writer of deliberate wrongdoing. Arnie raises the issue neutrally and constructively in order to help Larry, the writer in the dialogue that follows:

ARNIE: Here, where you write about how people increase their capital, you say, "Whatever a person saves from his revenue he adds to his capital and either employs it in maintaining an additional number of productive hands, or enables some other person to do so by lending it to him for an interest, that
5   is, for a share of the profits." That's a good idea. Did you think it up yourself?

LARRY: No, I got it from that chapter from *The Wealth of Nations* that we had to read.

ARNIE: Well, your reader is going to think it's your idea, unless you say that it is
10   Adam Smith's.

LARRY: But it's a fact, isn't it? It seems common sense that you can increase capital by saving. So it's not just his idea.

ARNIE: That's true, but remember when this was written. When did Smith write this?

LARRY: Way back. I don't know exactly. Here's the book. It says on the cover
15   that he lived from 1723 to 1790.

ARNIE: OK. Now see if you can figure out what difference that makes.

LARRY: Um, maybe it wasn't so obvious then? Maybe he thought it up?

ARNIE: That's a good point. He could have been one of the first to articulate that
20   idea. So you need to give him credit. How can you do that?

LARRY: I don't know. Footnote?

ARNIE: Sure, but you also need to make it clear in the paragraph because of the way it's phrased. How did he say it and how did you?

LARRY: I sort of copied down what he said.

25 ARNIE: Well that's okay as long as you use quotation marks to show the reader that you are borrowing the author's language.

LARRY: OK. *[puts in the marks]*

ARNIE: Good. Now how is the reader supposed to know whom you're quoting?

LARRY: Oh. Well. That's where the footnote comes in.

30 ARNIE: Yes. You could also introduce the quote by naming its author. How could you do that?

LARRY: Um, *[writes]* In Adam Smith's *The Wealth of Nations* he says that . . . .

ARNIE: That's the right idea. How could you say it more briefly?

LARRY: *[writes]* In *The Wealth of Nations* Adam Smith says.

35 ARNIE: That's a lot better. Now if you didn't want to quote him, I mean if you
    wanted to say his idea in your own words, you wouldn't have to use the
    quotation marks. How about trying that?

LARRY: Let's see. *[writes]* People can increase their capital by employing it, no,
    he uses that. Um, by using it himself to hire people, no, hire more workers,
40   or by loaning it for interest.

ARNIE: That's good. Now what might be the advantage of using your own words?

LARRY: Well, it's shorter.

ARNIE: Yes, it's to the point. Anything else?

LARRY: I don't see it.

45 ARNIE: Well, it might sound smoother than chopping your essay up into just a
    string of quotations. It'll be more consistent in your own language, that is.
    Now if you did use your own words, what would you do to make the reader
    know it was Smith's idea?

LARRY: I don't know. I don't have to quote, do I, because it's not Smith's words,
50   right?

ARNIE: Right, but how did you let the reader know whom you were quoting when
    you did use his words?

LARRY: Oh. I put in the "Smith says" and the footnote. You mean I have to do
    that even if I don't quote?

55 ARNIE: You at least have to footnote. Now see if you can figure out why.

LARRY: I see. It's his idea even if I put it in my words so I have to give him
    credit.

ARNIE: Right. In this case, you could just footnote and not use the "he says"
    since you are writing an informational report on ways of expanding capital,
60   but you could introduce the summary by saying whose idea it is as you did
    with the quote. That's up to you.

➤ Before reading further, analyze the dialogue: How does Arnie react to Larry's
problem? What points about attribution does he teach Larry? What sequence does
his questioning follow and what is its advantage?

                                · · ·

   In this dialogue, the tutor's questions help the writer learn first why attribution
is necessary and then how to proceed. Initially, Arnie introduces the principle so
that Larry will understand why he must give an author credit. That way, when
Arnie teaches the formats, Larry can see some purpose for revising his essay. You
probably noticed that Arnie acts on the assumption that Larry's error was not
deliberate, and since it seems not to have been, the tutor has spared himself embarrassment and the writer humiliation. Arnie neither preaches nor criticizes. He
does not threaten Larry with the possible consequences of plagiarism because this
writer requires no such warning.

   While he does encourage Larry to consider summary as an alternative to quoting, Arnie might, as well, have introduced other forms of attribution such as the
indirect quotation (Adam Smith says that) or the partial quotation (Adam Smith
says that capital can be increased by using savings to hire more "productive hands"),

a method useful for highlighting some distinctive or telling language from the text. Whether or not you should introduce all of the alternatives at once depends on whether you think that would be likely to overwhelm the writer and on the extent to which teaching attribution is your primary concern in the session. It is, however, usually a good idea to give writers at least some indication of their options.

Overquoting

While some inexperienced writers do not refer to their sources, others use them to excess. So frequently does this occur that the "paste pot paper" has become a cliché. Although this sort of essay is often viewed as the work of a lazy or disinterested writer, it may be, instead, the product of one who is diffident or uneducated in documentation. Writers who are intimidated by the authoritativeness of printed material frequently feel that they dare not tamper with an author's work and must faithfully reproduce it. They may, it addition, lack fluency and, having seen an author's wording, cannot readily think of another way to phrase the idea. The author, in their view, has said it better than they could ever hope to. Additionally, student writers often inset lengthy quotations in their papers because they feel that extensive quoting is necessary to convince a professor that they have completed the reading. They take assignment directives like "please refer to the readings in your essay" to mean that they must quote heavily. Finally, writers may overquote in order to expand the length of an essay.

A writer, then, may rely too much on quoted material for a complex combination of reasons and may require considerable practice before he can reconstruct texts accurately and before he learns to use quotations sparingly and for specific purposes. You can, much in the manner that Arnie asked Larry to reword Adam Smith's sentence (lines 35–49), provide writers with opportunities to rephrase short passages and can discuss how various ways of incorporating an author's ideas (quoting, paraphrasing, summarizing) differ in their effects. In addition to using passages quoted in the writer's essay, you can bring in exercises from college composition texts such as Bazerman's *The Informed Writer* and Spatt's *Writing from Sources*.

Quoting and reconstructing without comment

Even when novice writers have learned to limit the number of quotations, they often have difficulty integrating ideas from sources into their essays. They may, like Joanna, hesitate to form their own interpretations and therefore merely paraphrase or summarize. Alternatively, they may present an author's view as evidence of some point without explaining the inclusion because, as we suggested in Chapter 2, they think it is self-evident. In either case, what is lacking is the writer's guiding voice, which should provide the context and thereby the meaning or purpose of the inclusion. The following dialogue illustrates how you can help writers who interject quotations or reconstructions without commentary.

Students in a women's studies course have been asked to write an essay on the social and historical circumstances that have led to women's secondary status in the workplace. They must base their discussion on several assigned articles. When Sandy, a student in the class, brings her first draft to a tutoring conference, Eileen, her tutor, notices that Sandy has not explained some of the passages from the articles to which she refers in her essay. Here is one of Sandy's paragraphs:

> Like the Lorber essay, Yankelovitch's article suggests that women get second place at work because of how they see themselves. He says, "Increasingly women accept the idea that both husband and wife may work, but the woman's economic role continues to be supplemental." Yankelovitch thinks this is changing but according to him, so far neither men nor women want total equality.

EILEEN: This starts well because you make a connection with what you said about Lorber and also you're sticking to the topic. But I can't tell from reading this what women's only earning supplemental income has to do with getting second status at work.

5 SANDY: Well, I thought that was obvious. If men are supposed to be the primary breadwinners, then they are going to get the better jobs.

EILEEN: That helps me understand a little better, but why will they get the better jobs?

SANDY: Because women see themselves primarily as wives and mothers. If the
10 woman only wants to supplement the family income she'll apply for part-time work so she can be home with the kids. Or full-time jobs that won't wear her out or keep her away from home too much.

EILEEN: Good, it's important to make that explicit. The quote about women supplementing family income may imply that women don't seek better jobs
15 because they want to be accessible to their families, but it was a lot clearer to me when you came right out and said it. If you do that in your paper your reader will know why you included the quote. How about doing that now?

SANDY: OK. *[writes]* "Like the Lorber essay, Yankelovitch's article suggests that
20 women get second place at work because they see themselves primarily as wives and mothers rather than as breadwinners. Yankelovitch says, 'Increasingly, women accept the idea that both husband and wife may work, but the woman's economic role continues to be supplemental.' Women will look for part-time jobs or undemanding jobs so they can be available to their
25 children and husbands. Yankelovitch thinks this is changing, but according to him, so far, neither men nor women want total equality."

EILEEN: That's better. But I'm still not sure why having a part-time or undemanding job gives women inferior status in the workplace.

SANDY: Maybe I should tell what kinds of jobs these would be, like secretaries or
30 even research assistants. I mean, after all, who gets the credit? Not them.

EILEEN: OK, so what are you implying about the two kinds of jobs you mentioned? I mean, what do they have in common?

SANDY: The women are working for someone. They're not in charge or anything. Maybe they think that if they were in charge, they'd have less time to be
35 with their kids, so they work for someone else.

EILEEN: How can you work that into the paragraph?

SANDY: What if I put something after where I talk about being available to the kids and husbands like *[writes]* "Women will look for part-time jobs or undemanding jobs so they can be available to their children and husbands. So
40   they end up working under someone else, which gives them lower status."

EILEEN: The idea is good. But now what happens to the last sentence, "Yankelovitch thinks this is changing" if you insert the new idea before it?

SANDY: Huh?

EILEEN: What does "this" refer to now?

45 SANDY: Oh I see, that women are in subordinate positions. I guess it looks like Yankelovitch thinks that what's changing now is that women are less likely to seek subordinate positions, and he didn't really say that. Maybe I better put the new stuff at the end.

EILEEN: OK, try it and let's see. Sometimes it takes a few tries before you get it
50   the way you want it.

Here is Sandy's next revision:

> Like the Lorber essay, Yankelovitch's article suggests that women get second place at work because they see themselves primarily as wives and mothers, not as breadwinners. He says, "Increasingly, women accept the idea that both husband and wife may work but the woman's economic role continues to be supplemental." Yankelovitch thinks this is changing, but according to him, so far neither men or women want total equality. Women therefore continue to look for part-time or undemanding jobs so they can be available to their husbands and children. In the jobs that they get, like secretary or research assistant, they are subordinates, not bosses, and thus they have lower status.

➤ Before reading further, please answer the following questions: what did Sandy fail to do and how did Eileen help her improve the paragraph? Compare the three versions of the paragraph and analyze the differences. What accounts for them? What do the dialogue and the revisions indicate about the revising process? How could the paragraph be further improved?

. . .

Eileen's skillful, patient questions gradually help Sandy revise her paragraph. After praising what Sandy has done well, always a good strategy, Eileen indicates that she is confused by the quotation because its relevance to the question is not clear—only she does not say that. Rather, she responds as a reader, which is, as we pointed out in Chapter 2, more constructive than talking abstractly about the composition or criticizing it because the writer is directly invited to supply what is missing from the essay: Eileen and Sandy's discussion concerns the essay's ideas (the connection between women's supplementing family income by working and their having lower status in the workplace). Eileen also wisely concentrates on one aspect of the revising process at a time. She seems to realize that revision involves several activities that cannot all be accomplished simultaneously, for she helps Sandy generate first one and then another new idea before assisting her in inserting the additional material into the paragraph. As Sandy revises, she repeats her newly formed interpretations but uses more sophisticated vocabulary ("subordinate positions" for "working under somebody"). This language appears in the final version of the paragraph. If Eileen had interrupted the discussion to suggest that Sandy make stylistic revisions, Sandy might have become distracted and might have had more trouble generating the missing interpretations. You can wait to see if writers will spontaneously amend phrasing, as often happens once they have formed an idea (notice that the last revision omits an unnecessary "jobs"). If they do not, you can, as a concluding step, ask how the idea could be phrased differently.

Sandy's interpretation of Yankelovitch's sentence could, of course, have been expanded to include some of its other implications (that since women are perceived as homemakers and mothers rather than as breadwinners, male employers are less likely to consider them competent for high-status jobs, for instance). Eileen could have taken the discussion further than she does, but perhaps she felt pushed for time.

Framing quotations repetitiously and awkwardly

Writers who are unused to writing about sources may not be aware of the variety of conventions for identifying the author of a quotation. Inexperienced writers will, when introducing quotations, often construct awkward, wordy frames for them as Larry did in writing about Adam Smith: "In Adam Smith's *The Wealth of Nations* he says." Larry's tutor, Arnie, prompted a concise revision simply by asking Larry to say the idea more briefly. If that had not worked, Arnie could have asked, "How many ideas are in this sentence and what are they?" a strategy explained in Chapter 8. The sentence actually misconsolidates several ideas:

1. Adam Smith wrote *The Wealth of Nations*.
2. He says, ". . . ."
3. He says this in *The Wealth of Nations*.

But it is likely that Larry would offer only two: "Adam Smith wrote *The Wealth of Nations*" and "In *The Wealth of Nations* Adam Smith says." Arnie could then ask why the first is necessary (it is not). In so doing, he would avoid a complicated discussion of nouns and pronouns. If Larry expressed concern that his second sentence did not identify Smith directly as the author of *The Wealth of Nations*, Arnie could ask what "Adam Smith says" indicates about the authorship of the quotation.

Inexperienced writers are usually unfamiliar with the different stylistic options available for framing quotations. Typically, they introduce a quotation with the author's name or a pronoun followed by "says." They vary neither the verb nor its placement in the sentence, and they separate quotations from clauses that comment on them. For instance, in response to the assignment on *Catch 22* ("Assuming that Doc Daneeka can be considered representative of civilians during the war, what does Heller seem to be criticizing about them?"), here is part of what another reader wrote: "Doc Daneeka is shameless in seeing the war as an opportunity to make money. He says, 'It was a godsend.' " As his tutor, you might explore with the writer several other ways of introducing this quotation. If the writer were overusing "says," you might ask what other verbs convey roughly the same idea. The writer might then generate a list of verbs like "states," "remarks," "announces," and could be asked to consider their connotative differences.

If the writer invariably sets the "he says" or its equivalent at the beginning of a sentence, you could ask if this language could be placed anywhere else. The writer would probably see the sentence's end as a possibility " 'It was a godsend,' he says.") but might not imagine it possible to interrupt a quotation (" 'It was,' he says, 'a godsend.' "). In this event, you could suggest that the writer place "he says" somewhere inside the quotation and could then let the writer experiment.

If the writer rarely combines commentary with a quotation in a single sentence, you could ask the writer to consolidate by using a colon or a partial quotation, as in "Doc Daneeka shamelessly sees the war as an opportunity to make money: 'It was a godsend,' " or, "Doc Daneeka shamelessly sees the war, which he calls a 'godsend,' as an opportunity to make money." Another way of introducing such stylistic variations is to provide the writer with brief examples (not based on the writer's essay) so that the writer can imitate the models.

Summary

Because reading and writing are mutually reinforcing forms of verbal thinking, failure in reading is often accompanied by failure in writing, and improvement in one activity leads to improvement in the other. Some readers comprehend poorly because they read too quickly, do not concentrate, or do not look up unfamiliar vocabulary. Others fail to read actively, analytically: they do not look for relationships among written ideas, for logical fallacies, and for authors' purposes and rhetorical strategies. When poor readers write about reading, they may misrepresent a text's ideas, may summarize although they are asked to analyze, and may not use or attribute sources appropriately. By helping people become better readers, you help them become more fluent and accurate writers.

You will probably want to combine short- and long-term strategies for helping readers. To address immediate problems, you can ask three types of reading questions: reconstructive questions (which ask readers to state what was said or what happened), interpretive questions (which ask readers to draw inferences or make judgments about what happened or what was said in a text), and applicative questions (which ask readers to apply what happened or what was said to a new context). In general, it is a good idea to intermingle these questions, but you should make sure that a reader has basically comprehended a passage before you ask interpretive or applicative questions. Most often it is advisable to move from specific to general questions, so that the reader has a basis for forming generalizations.

To improve reading comprehension and retention, tutors can also teach long-term strategies: overviewing and skimming; using a text's reading questions as a study guide; formulating questions for study from the structure of the text, the emphasis of a course, or that of an instructor; and taking various forms of notes.

To help inexperienced writers integrate ideas drawn from reading into their essays, you can introduce basic principles of and various formats for attribution. If writers use too many or overly long quotations, you can suggest how to paraphrase, summarize, and use quotations sparingly and for special effect. If writers fail to comment on ideas drawn from sources, you can ask questions that elicit the missing information. If writers introduce quotations awkwardly, you can, by questioning or providing models, suggest alternative ways of framing an author's sentences.

SUGGESTIONS FOR JOURNAL ENTRIES

1. Observe yourself as you read. Write down questions and comments that occurred to you as you were reading. What reading strategies do you use? How did these questions affect your comprehension and your overall response to the reading? Which seem most successful? Which would you recommend to readers with whom you work, and in what ways would they be particularly useful for them?

2. What kinds of notes do you take and when? How do your notes vary depending on the kind of material you are reading?

3. In responding to essay questions, how do you ensure that you answer the questions directly? How could you adapt your own methods to help the writers with whom you are working?

4. What experience have you had with individuals who have reading difficulty? How did you determine the nature of the difficulties? What did you do to help? How successful were your strategies? Would you adopt a different strategy another time?

SUGGESTIONS FOR FURTHER WRITING

1. Below is an essay by Bertrand Russell. Assuming that you are working with a student who has been assigned to read it in a Freshman English class, prepare the following:

    a. a list of five or six questions you would ask the reader to help him or her reconstruct the content of the essay.

    b. a list of questions you would ask to help the reader interpret it.

    c. a list of questions you would ask to help the reader apply ideas in the essay to his/her experience.

    d. a list of questions to help the reader approach the following writing assignments:

        i. Write a two- or three-page essay in which you explain Bertrand Russell's idea of what makes work satisfying and in which you evaluate your chosen occupation in Russell's terms.

        ii. Write a two- or three-page essay supporting or attacking Russell's assertion that "few things are so likely to cure the habit of hatred as the opportunity to do constructive work of an important kind."

        iii. Write a two- or three-page essay in which you explain an educational experience that you believe has helped prepare you for satisfying work as Russell describes it.

WORK

BERTRAND RUSSELL

Whether work should be placed among the causes of happiness or among the causes of unhappiness may perhaps be regarded as a doubtful question. There is certainly much work which is exceedingly irksome, and an excess of work is always very painful. I think, however, that, provided work is not excessive in amount, even the dullest work is to most people less painful than idleness. There are in work all grades, from mere relief of tedium up to the profoundest delights, according to the nature of the work and the abilities of the worker. Most of the work that most people have to do is not in itself interesting, but even such work has certain great advantages. To begin with, it fills a good many hours of the day without the need of deciding what one shall do. Most people when they are left free to fill their own time according to their own choice, are at a loss to think of anything sufficiently pleasant to be worth doing. And whatever they decide on, they are troubled by the feeling that something else would have been pleasanter. To be able to fill leisure intelligently is the last product of civilization, and at present very few people have reached this level. Moreover the exercise of choice is in itself tiresome. Except to people with unusual initiative it is positively agreeable to be told what to do at each hour of the day, provided the orders are not too unpleasant. Most of the idle rich suffer unspeakable boredom as the price of their freedom from drudgery. At times they may find relief by hunting big game in Africa, or by flying round the world, but the number of such sensations is limited, especially after youth is past. Accordingly the more intelligent rich men work nearly as hard as if they were poor, while rich women for the most part keep themselves busy with innumerable trifles of whose earthshaking importance they are firmly persuaded.

Work therefore is desirable, first and foremost, as a preventive of boredom, for the boredom that a man feels when he is doing necessary though uninteresting work is as nothing in comparison with the boredom that he feels when he has nothing to do with his days. With this advantage of work another is associated, namely that it makes holidays much more delicious when they come. Provided a man does not have to work so hard as to impair his vigor, he is likely to find far more zest in his free time than an idle man could possibly find.

The second advantage of most paid work and of some unpaid work is that it gives chances of success and opportunities for ambition. In most work success is measured by income, and while our capitalistic society continues, this is inevitable. It is only where the best work is concerned that this measure ceases to be the natural one to apply. The desire that men feel to increase their income is quite as much a desire for success as for the extra comforts that a higher income can procure. However dull work may be, it becomes bearable if it is a means of building up a reputation, whether in the world at large or only in one's own circle. Continuity of purpose is one of the most essential ingredients of happiness in the long run, and for most men this comes chiefly through their work. In this respect those women whose lives are occupied with housework are much less fortunate than men, or than women who work outside the home. The domesticated wife does not receive wages, has no means of bettering herself, is taken for granted by her husband (who sees practically nothing of what she does), and is valued by him not for her housework but for quite other qualities. Of course this does not apply to those women who are sufficiently well-to-do to make beautiful houses and beautiful gardens and become the envy of their neighbors; but such women are comparatively few, and for the great majority housework cannot bring as much satisfaction as work of other kinds brings to men and to professional women.

The satisfaction of killing time and of affording some outlet, however modest, for ambition, belongs to most work, and is sufficient to make even a man whose work is dull happier on the average than a man who has no work at all. But when work is interesting, it is capable of giving satisfaction of a far higher order than mere relief from tedium. The kinds of work in which there is some interest may be arranged in a hierarchy. I shall begin with those which are only mildly interesting and end with those that are worthy to absorb the whole energies of a great man.

Two chief elements make work interesting: first, the exercise of skill, and second, construction.

Every man who has acquired some unusual skill enjoys exercising it until it has become a matter of course, or until he can no longer improve himself. This motive to activity begins in early childhood: a boy who can stand on his head becomes reluctant to stand on his feet. A great deal of work gives the same pleasure that is to be derived from games of skill. The work of a lawyer or a politician must contain in a more delectable form a great deal of the same pleasure that is to be derived from playing bridge. Here of course there is not only the exercise of skill but the outwitting of a skilled opponent. Even where this competitive element is absent, however, the performance of difficult feats is agreeable. A man who can do stunts in an aeroplane finds the pleasure so great that for the sake of it he is willing to risk his life. I imagine that an able surgeon, in spite of the painful circumstances in which his work is done, derives satisfaction from the exquisite precision of his operations. The same kind of pleasure, though in a less intense form, is to be derived from a great deal of work of a humbler kind. All skilled work can be pleasurable, provided the skill required is either variable or capable of indefinite improvement. If these conditions are absent, it will cease to be interesting when a man has acquired his maximum skill. A man who runs three-mile races will cease to find pleasure in this occupation when he passes the age at which he can beat his own previous record. Fortunately there is a very considerable amount of work in which new circumstances call for new skill and a man can go on improving, at any rate until he has reached middle age. In some kinds of skilled work, such as politics, for example, it seems that men are at their best between sixty and seventy, the reason being that in such occupations a wide experience of other men is essential. For this reason successful politicians are apt to be happier at the age of seventy than any other men of equal age. Their only competitors in this respect are the men who are the heads of big businesses.

There is, however, another element possessed by the best work, which is even more important as a source of happiness than is the exercise of skill. This is the element of constructiveness. In some work, though by no means in most, something is built up which remains as a monument when the work is completed. We may distinguish construction from destruction by the following criterion. In construction the initial state of affairs is comparatively haphazard, while the final state of affairs embodies a purpose: in destruction the reverse is the case; the initial state of affairs embodies a purpose, while the final state of affairs is haphazard, that is to say, all that is intended by the destroyer is to produce a state of affairs which does not embody a certain purpose. This criterion applies in the most literal and obvious case, namely the construction and destruction of buildings. In constructing a building a previously made plan is carried out, whereas in destroying it no one decides exactly how the materials are to lie when the demolition is complete. Destruction is of course necessary very often as a preliminary to subsequent construction; in that case it is part of a whole which is constructive. But not infrequently a man will engage in activities of which the purpose is destructive without regard to any construction that may come after. Frequently he will conceal this from himself by the belief that he is only sweeping away in order to build afresh, but it is generally possible to unmask this pretense, when it is a pretense, by asking him what the subsequent construction is to be. On this subject it will be found that he will speak vaguely and without enthusiasm, whereas on the preliminary destruction he has spoken precisely and with zest. This applies to not a few revolutionaries and militarists and other apostles of violence. They are actuated, usually without their own knowledge, by hatred: the destruction of what they hate is their real purpose, and they are comparatively indifferent to the question what is to come after it. Now I cannot deny that in the work of destruction as in the work of construction there may be joy. It is a fiercer joy, perhaps at moments more intense, but it is less profoundly satisfying, since the result is one in which little satisfaction is to be found. You kill your enemy, and when he is dead your occupation is gone, and the satisfaction that you derive from victory quickly fades. The work of construction, on the other hand, when completed is delightful to contemplate, and moreover is never so fully completed that there is nothing further to do about it. The most satisfactory purposes are those that lead on indefinitely from one success to another without ever coming to a dead end; and in this respect it will be found that construction is a greater source of happiness than destruction. Perhaps it would be more correct to say that those who find satisfaction in construction find in it greater satisfaction than the lovers of destruction can find in destruction, for if once you have become filled with hate you will not easily derive from construction the pleasure which another man would derive from it.

At the same time few things are so likely to cure the habit of hatred as the opportunity to do constructive work of an important kind.

The satisfaction to be derived from success in a great constructive enterprise is one of the most massive that life has to offer, although unfortunately in its highest forms it is open only to men of exceptional ability. Nothing can rob a man of the happiness of successful achievement in an important piece of work, unless it be the proof that after all his work was bad. There are many forms of such satisfaction. The man who by a scheme of irrigation has caused the wilderness to blossom like the rose enjoys it in one of its most tangible forms. The creation of an organization may be a work of supreme importance. So is the work of those few statesmen who have devoted their lives to producing order out of chaos, of whom Lenin is the supreme type in our day. The most obvious examples are artists and men of science. Shakespeare says of his verse: "So long as men can breathe, or eyes can see, so long lives this." And it cannot be doubted that the thought consoled him for misfortune. In his sonnets he maintains that the thought of his friend reconciled him to life, but I cannot help suspecting that the sonnets he wrote to his friend were even more effective for this purpose than the friend himself. Great artists and great men of science do work which is in itself delightful; while they are doing it, it secures them the respect of those whose respect is worth having, which gives them the most fundamental kind of power, namely, power over men's thoughts and feelings. They have also the most solid reasons for thinking well of themselves. This combination of fortunate circumstances ought, one would think, to be enough to make any man happy. Nevertheless it is not so. Michelangelo, for example, was a profoundly unhappy man, and maintained (not, I am sure, with truth) that he would not have troubled to produce works of art if he had not had to pay the debts of his impecunious relations. The power to produce great art is very often, though by no means always, associated with a temperamental unhappiness, so great that but for the joy which the artist derives from his work, he would be driven to suicide. We cannot, therefore, maintain that even the greatest work must make a man happy; we can only maintain that it must make him less unhappy. Men of science, however, are far less often temperamentally unhappy than artists are, and in the main the men who do great work in science are happy men, whose happiness is derived primarily from their work.

One of the causes of unhappiness among intellectuals in the present day is that so many of them, especially those whose skill is literary, find no opportunity for the independent exercise of their talents, but have to hire themselves out to rich corporations directed by Philistines, who insist upon their producing what they themselves regard as pernicious nonsense. If you were to inquire among journalists in either England or America whether they believed in the policy of the newspaper for which they worked, you would find, I believe, that only a small minority do so; the rest, for the sake of a livelihood, prostitute their skill to purposes which they believe to be harmful. Such work cannot bring any real satisfaction, and in the course of reconciling himself to the doing of it, a man has to make himself so cynical that he can no longer derive whole-hearted satisfaction from anything whatever. I cannot condemn men who undertake work of this sort, since starvation is too serious an alternative, but I think that where it is possible to do work that is satisfactory to a man's constructive impulses without entirely starving, he will be well advised from the point of view of his own happiness if he chooses it in preference to work much more highly paid but not seeming to him worth doing on its own account. Without self-respect genuine happiness is scarcely possible. And the man who is ashamed of his work can hardly achieve self-respect.

The satisfaction of constructive work, though it may, as things are, be the privilege of a minority, can nevertheless be the privilege of a quite large minority. Any man who is his own master in his work can feel it; so can any man whose work appears to him useful and requires considerable skill. The production of satisfactory children is a difficult constructive work capable of affording profound satisfaction. Any woman who has achieved this can feel that as a result of her labor the world contains something of value which it would not otherwise contain.

Human beings differ profoundly in regard to the tendency to regard their lives as a whole. To some men it is natural to do so, and essential to happiness to be able to do so with some satisfaction. To others life is a series of detached incidents without directed movement and without unity. I think the former sort are more likely to achieve happiness than the latter, since they will gradually build up those circumstances from which they can derive contentment and self-respect, whereas the others will be blown about by the winds of circumstance now this way, now that, without ever arriving at any haven. The habit of viewing life as a whole is an essential part both of wisdom and of true morality, and is one of the things which ought to be encouraged in education. Consistent purpose is not enough to make life happy, but it is an almost indispensable condition of a happy life. And consistent purpose embodies itself mainly in work.

2. This exercise is designed to give you practice in assessing reading problems and formulating reading questions. The following paper was written by Joseph R. in response to the first essay question above (a two- or three-page paper in which you explain what makes work satisfying and in which you evaluate your chosen occupation in Russell's terms). Having read Russell's essay and Joseph's paper, make a list of his reading problems and their possible sources. Then write an imaginary dialogue in which you ask reconstructive, interpretive, and applicative questions that will help him improve his essay.

According to Bertrand Russell, he says that work is satisfying because it pays you so you can have extra comforts and can better yourself. You also get satisfaction by exercising skill or by doing construction work. He say that great artists and great men of science also do work which is delightful. Surgeons get satisfaction from their work. So do politicians.

5 Working can be a game like bridge where you compete. Work is also satisfying because it lets you do what you want according to your choice. If you didn't work, you'd be bored like the rich people he mentions.

In my job at the garage I am a mechanic. I get satisfaction in my work because I like to figure out what is wrong with a motor and then fix it. It is like doing a puzzle. I suppose some people would
10 think this is boring, dirty work, but I like working with my hands, fooling around until I find where the problem is coming from. Russell is right. It feels good to work.

3. Using a chapter from a college textbook used by you or by readers with whom you work, plan a session in which you teach a reader how to overview and skim. Write an imaginary dialogue.

4. Write a dialogue in which you teach a reader how to take notes on the same material.

SUGGESTIONS FOR CLASS ACTIVITIES

1. Do some role-playing in which you use questions you formulated for exercises in "Suggestions for Further Writing."

2. Discuss the dialogues you wrote for exercise 2 in "Suggestions for Further Writing."

SUGGESTIONS FOR FURTHER READING

Bazerman, Charles. *The Informed Writer*. Boston: Houghton, Mifflin, 1981.
————. "A Relationship between Reading and Writing: The Conversational Model." *College English* 41 (1980): 656–661.
Bleich, David. *Readings and Feelings: An Introduction to Subjective Criticism*. Urbana, IL: NCTE, 1975.
Falke, Anne. "What Every Educator Should Know about Reading Research." In *Language Connections: Writing and Reading across the Curriculum*. Eds. Toby Fulwiler and Art Young. Urbana, IL: NCTE, 1982. 123–138.
Gage, John T. "Conflicting Assumptions about Intention in Teaching Reading and Composition." *College English* 40 (1978): 255–263.
————. "Freshman English: In Whose Service?" *College English* 44 (1982): 469–474.
Gibson, Eleanor J., and Harry Levin. *The Psychology of Reading*. Cambridge, MA: MIT Press, 1975.
Goodman, Kenneth. "What Do We Know about Reading?" In *Findings of Research in Miscue Analysis: Classroom Implications*. Eds. P. David Allen and Dorothy J. Watson. Urbana, IL: NCTE/ERIC, 1976.
Hoetker, James. "A Theory of Talking about Theories of Reading." *College English* 44 (1982): 175–181.
Horning, Alice. "The Connection of Writing to Reading: A Gloss on the Gospel of Mina Shaughnessy." *College English* 40 (1978): 264–268.

Karlin, Robert, Ed. *Teaching Reading in High School: Selected Articles.* New York: Bobbs-Merrill, 1969.

Lunsford, Andrea A. "What We Know—and Don't Know—about Remedial Reading." *College Composition and Communication* 29 (1978): 49–50.

McWhorter, Kathleen T. *College Reading and Study Skills.* Boston: Little, Brown, 1980.

Pauk, Walter. *How to Study in College.* 3rd ed. Boston: Houghton, Mifflin, 1984.

Perry, William. *Forms of Intellectual and Ethical Development in the College Years: A Scheme.* New York: Holt, 1968.

Petersen, Bruce T. "Writing about Responses: A Unified Model of Reading, Interpretation, and Composition." *College English* 44 (1982): 459–468.

Petrosky, Anthony R. "From Story to Essay: Reading and Writing." *College Composition and Communication* 23 (1982): 19–36.

Quinn, Shirley, and Susan Irvings. *Active Reading.* Boston: Houghton Mifflin, 1986.

Rosenblatt, Louise. *Literature as Exploration.* New York: Noble, 1965.

Salvatori, Mariolina. "Reading and Writing a Text: Correlations between Reading and Writing Patterns." *College English* 45 (1983): 657–666.

Smith, Frank. *Psycholinguistics and Reading.* New York: Holt, 1973.

Spatt, Brenda. *Writing from Sources.* New York: St. Martin's, 1983.

Suleiman, Susan R., and Inge Crosman, Eds. *The Reader in the Text: Essays on Audience and Interpretation.* Princeton: Princeton University Press, 1980.

Wolf, Maryanne, Mark K. McQuillan, and Eugene Radwin, Eds. *Thought and Language. Language and Reading.* Harvard Educational Review 14 (1980).

12

Reading and Writing about Literature

In the previous chapter we suggested that inexperienced writers are also apt to be inexperienced readers who have not yet learned to approach texts actively. Since writing tutors frequently address reading problems of students engaged in literary study, we are devoting this chapter to a discussion of the kinds of questions that readers can learn to raise as they read and as they formulate topics for compositions about literature. Some of these questions (those that are particularly appropriate when college readers are asked to analyze literature in social science courses) help readers glean behavioral, historical, and cultural information from imaginative works, but most of the questions that we offer to tutors are not intended to help readers master a body of information, for that is not the primary purpose of reading literature. Rather, these questions aim to increase readers' *enjoyment* of literature by helping them to experience it fully.

To experience literature is to participate in an author's imaginative vision, to gain a sense of what a character, a place, an action, or a feeling is like, to respond emotionally and sensuously as well as intellectually to a text. Asking questions like those that we provide can heighten readers' responses and thus their pleasure. This end, however, is not always immediately apparent to readers who have not previously analyzed literature. When asked to do so, they may, at first, grouse a bit. "Why do we have to pick this apart?" they often say. "It spoils the book." Such reactions often reflect the readers' resistance to change, their fear of new territory, and their reluctance to rise to the new venture. You, therefore, may have to exercise patience until such readers become more comfortable with methods of literary analysis.

On the other hand, some readers have been exposed to literature in high school but have not learned how to enjoy the activity of reading. This is particularly true with poetry, for students may have been required to memorize poems with which they find no affinity, or they may have been asked to decipher lines of inverted syntax, archaic vocabulary, or highly abstract language without seeing any purpose or pleasure in the process. Reading poetry thus has become a terror, a bore, a chore. No amount of preaching on the moral or aesthetic value of poetic art will overcome these fears and prejudices, but helping readers learn how to approach poems may.

What is it, then, that we want readers to look for? What do we want them to gain from reading literature, and what can be done to demystify it? To say that we want to increase readers' "understanding" is not fully accurate. We do, but that is not all there is to experiencing literature. If we merely asked that readers paraphrase a poem to demonstrate their comprehension, for example, we would reduce the work to denotational statement. We would not be considering the effects of its language, its rhythm, its music on our senses and emotions. We would not, in other words, be asking *how* the poem means. And that is part of the fun, accepting the poem's invitation to play with it, to see how it works itself out. Most of this chapter, accordingly, is devoted to a discussion of strategies for helping readers enjoy literature by seeing how it works, how it means, but we begin with a section on reading for information, for there are occasions when this is perfectly legitimate (if not necessary). We then suggest formal, impressionistic, and evaluative questions that tutors can ask to promote reading pleasure, and, finally, we discuss typical problems that occur when readers write about literature.

Helping Readers Look for Behavioral, Cultural, and Historical Information in Literature

Finding Illustrations of behavior

College courses, particularly in sociology, psychology, and history, often utilize literary works to illustrate theories presented in textbooks. In such instances, tutors can use applicative questions (see Chapter 11) to help readers relate specific examples to general descriptions of behavior. If, for instance, *I Never Promised You a Rose Garden,* a fictional rendition of the experience of schizophrenia, were assigned in an introductory psychology course when abnormal behavior was being discussed, a tutor might ask a reader, "To what extent does the central character's behavior conform to the description of abnormalities identified by the psychology text?" The reader could be asked to list the behaviors manifested by the character. If various treatments for schizophrenia were discussed in the course, a tutor could say, "What kind of therapy does the character undergo, and to what extent does the novel present it as being effective?" Or, the tutor might ask, "What other forms of therapy might have been used?"

To suggest a similar example, let us say that a sociology course that studies group behavior introduces Gustav Le Bon's analysis of crowd behavior in *The Crowd* and illustrates the theory with William Faulkner's description of events leading to a lynching in *Light in August.* Elaine, a student in the course, does not understand why she must read the fictional excerpt; she wonders what it has to do with sociology. To help her make the connection, her tutor, Nicky, begins by suggesting that Elaine list the behaviors Le Bon identifies. Here is Elaine's list:

1. Crowds have a "docile respect" for force; they "bow down servilely" before a strong authority and "revolt against a feeble one."

2. Crowds like a strong leader and are awed by his "insignia," "authority," and "sword."

3. Crowds are conservative: they respect all tradition.

4. Crowds are capable of "lofty morality" as well as "low instincts."

Now that Elaine has compiled the list, Nicky can help her check the fictional illustration for evidence of these behaviors. A word about *Light in August* may help explain the dialogue between Nicky and Elaine that follows. In Faulkner's novel, Joe Christmas, who is presumed Negro because of his uncertain parentage and the spite of one of his caretakers, is wrongly accused of murdering a white woman in Jefferson County, Mississippi. When Joe is imprisoned in the local jail to await a grand jury hearing, Percy Grimm, a young state national guardsman, tries to persuade the local American Legionnaires to arm themselves and stand guard "to preserve order." Since the supposed murderer has already been caught and since there has been no talk of a lynching, such a step is unnecessary, as the Legion commander and the sheriff point out. Grimm, however, independently recruits a "platoon" of men, and, appealing in the name of his country's honor and principles, directs them to arm themselves and to appear in the town square. The sheriff tells Grimm to abandon the plan and to leave his firearms at home, but Grimm defies the order, dons a uniform, and carries his gun. The men "stand guard" for two nights, and the sheriff reluctantly deputizes the young man who disobeyed him. The novel continues (432):

> The town had suddenly accepted Grimm with respect and perhaps a little awe and a deal of actual faith and confidence, as though, somehow, his vision and patriotism and pride in the town, the occasion, had been quicker and truer than theirs.

It is this sentence that Elaine and Nicky are discussing in the dialogue below, as they begin to compare the story's events to the list Elaine has drawn from Le Bon:

NICKY: Which of the items on your list are related to this passage?

ELAINE: Like it says, he's patriotic and Le Bon says crowds are traditional.

NICKY: Are you saying that Grimm is part of a crowd?

ELAINE: Like, sort of. He's a nobody in the town, so he's like, just one of the
5   men. But when he, like, rounds up the guards, he becomes a leader. It says they have "confidence" in him.

NICKY: Sure. Why do the men follow him?

ELAINE: Because he wears a uniform? Like Le Bon said, crowds like insignia, and sure, in the same item on the list, it says crowds like forceful leaders.
10   *[writes notes]*

NICKY: What seems forceful in his behavior?

ELAINE: Like, he went around and got a bunch of men together and gave them orders to get their guns. *[writes notes]*

NICKY: Good! Anything else? *[pauses]* How about returning to your idea about
15   patriotism?

ELAINE: Yeah. Grimm keeps saying he wants to preserve order and show how the
government feels about things like murder, especially interracial murder.
So, like, maybe that's one reason that people look up to him. Of course,
they are really racists, but they feel they're being patriotic, I mean. *[writes]*.

LE BON	FAULKNER
1. Crowds have "docile respect" for force; they "bow down servilely" before a strong authority and "revolt against a feeble one."	Guns = force
2. Crowds like a strong leader and are awed by his "insignia," "authority," and "sword."	Grimm rounds up guards, becomes leader in town, orders men to get guns, gets "respect" and "confidence" of men.
	G's uniform = "insignia"
3. Crowds are conservative: they respect all tradition.	Grimm is "patriotic."
	Grimm wants to preserve "vision" of order, especially between races (racism/patriotism).
4. Crowds are capable of "lofty morality" as well as "low instincts."	

NICKY: I'm glad you're writing all this down. These are good ideas. Now let's
look at the list again. We've found correspondences with items 2 and 3.
How about the first one?

ELAINE: You mean, like, about crowds respecting force? I thought we did that.
35   The gun is a kind of force.

NICKY: Good, but keep going. Look at the rest of item 1.

ELAINE: They, like, revolt against "feeble authority"?

NICKY: Yes.

ELAINE: Well, Grimm isn't feeble.

40 NICKY: What about the other authority figures?

ELAINE: Hmmm. Oh, the sheriff!

NICKY: Anybody else?

ELAINE: The Legion commander.

NICKY: Good. How much force or authority do they exercise?

45 ELAINE: Not much. Like, I get it. The sheriff caves in and gives Grimm a badge
after he told Grimm to knock off the soldier routine. Grimm just, like,
ignored him and went ahead and did his thing.

NICKY: Anything else?

ELAINE: So, like, the men in town follow Grimm 'cause he's struttin' around with
50   his gun and his uniform while the old sheriff is home takin' it easy. But,
like, can you call what the guys do a revolt?

NICKY: Try asking yourself that.

ELAINE: Well, they disobey the sheriff and he's, like, the law, so I guess it's sorta
like a revolt. *[adds notes]*

LE BON	FAULKNER
1. Crowds have "docile respect" for force; they "bow down servilely" before a strong authority and "revolt against a feeble one."	Guns = force
	Sheriff and Legion commander are both weak authorities.
	Sheriff deputizes Grimm, who ignored his orders; rewards revolt with badge.

NICKY: Good thinking. We've covered all the terms on the list except the last one. Let's see if it fits.

ELAINE: Like, lofty morality? No way. Oh, well, the men I guess think they are being patriotic. But when Joe Christmas, the guy in jail, escapes and they go after him, and like butcher him. They're animals.

NICKY: Uh-huh. *[pauses]*

ELAINE: Oh! That's the "low instincts" Le Bon talks about. *[adds item 4]*

4. Crowds are capable of "lofty morality" as well as "low instincts."	Crowd butchers Joe Christmas.

NICKY: Great. You've got two useful columns here now, one for each author. How do the two fit together?

ELAINE: How?

NICKY: What can you say about the relationship between Le Bon's ideas and Faulkner's story?

ELAINE: Well, *[pauses]* they're real similar.

NICKY: Similar in what way?

ELAINE: Huh?

NICKY: How many crowds is each describing?

ELAINE: Faulkner has only one, but Le Bon is, like, talking about crowds in general.

NICKY: That's a useful word to describe Le Bon's article. If he gives a *general* description, what does Faulkner give? What's the opposite of "general"?

ELAINE: I get it. "Specific." He gives, like, a specific example.

NICKY: He sure does. How about looking through the course syllabus to see if your professor is using other readings as specific illustrations of general ideas in the course?

Not only does Nicky help Elaine find the textual details that correspond to Le Bon's general assertions; she also skillfully asks Elaine to identify the general-to-specific relationship between the two readings herself. When Elaine does not understand what Nicky means by "the relationship" between the two passages, Nicky asks a less abstract question ("How many crowds?") that helps Elaine see the point. Finally, Nicky asks Elaine to apply to a broader context what she has learned about the way readings may be related. Nicky makes tutoring look easy, but she has had a lot of practice, having served for several years. It takes time and experience to become fluent in the art of questioning. If you stumble, pause, and have to backtrack a lot at first, rest assured that there is nothing wrong with you and that you will become more adroit as you become more seasoned.

Gleaning historical and cultural information

Literature offers imaginative renditions of individual experience, often the felt experience of certain states of being. Thus, the reader of *I Never Promised You a Rose Garden* gains a sense of what it feels like to hallucinate, but this is not, strictly speaking, "information," while a psychology textbook's definition of "hallucination" is. The imaginative example, however, can deepen readers' understanding of behavior. Literature can, as well, offer information about how a particular historical moment or milieu affects individual lives. In fact, some historians plumb literary works as sources of this sort of information. For instance, Elizabeth Gaskell's novel, *Mary Barton*, written by an observer of the nineteenth-century industrial conflict in England, is often cited in historical descriptions of the acrimonious relationship between millowners and workers. Some writers of imaginative literature take as one of their purposes the evocation of a period or famous event. They may, like Mrs. Gaskell, record their firsthand observations and interpretations, or they may, like the contemporary novelist, John Fowles, who sets *The French Lieutenant's Woman* in Victorian England, make use of historical and cultural research to represent past eras. You can help readers analyze the represented historical environment and its impact on the characters. Doing so is especially helpful when readers are assigned literature in history courses. Suppose, for instance, that you are working with a student who is reading Dickens's *A Tale of Two Cities* for a course in French revolutionary history. You might ask, "What does the novel tell you about how individual lives can be affected by revolution?" or "What political, social, and economic conditions described by the novel seem to shape the characters' attitudes toward the revolution?" and the readers might also be asked to what extent the shaping factors correspond to those represented by other assigned materials.

Literature can also be used as a source of information about social organization, manners, and morals of a particular historical period or cultural milieu. Someone reading Jane Austen's *Emma*, for instance, might be asked about the Woodhouses' life-style and how it differs from that of contemporary people of the same or another class. His tutor might say, "How do the Woodhouses and Mr. Knightley spend their time? What do they do for fun?" "What is the purpose of marriage in the society Austen depicts?" "What kinds of social and economic roles do men and women play?" "To what extent are these patterns of behavior similar to today's?" Such questions, then, serve the dual function of developing readers' awareness of different historical and cultural beliefs and practices, and of stimulating readers' thinking about their own.

Further, recognizing the differences between contemporary and past values or between one culture and another can help readers understand the actions in their context. For instance, readers of Shakespeare's *Measure for Measure* need to comprehend the religious and social importance of virginity during the Renaissance in order to understand the significance of Isabella's refusal to accede to her brother's plea that she sacrifice her virginity in order to save her brother's life. Some inexperienced readers might not be alert to these attitudes and might say, "Why is she making such a fuss? Sure, Angelo has no right to bargain that way, demanding her virginity as the price of Claudio's freedom, but if she can save her brother's life by sleeping with Angelo, why doesn't she just go ahead and do it?" A tutor might ask questions that direct a reader's attention to speeches that reflect the dominant attitude of the period. The tutor and the reader might reconsider the play's justification for Isabella's refusal and then discuss the extent to which her action might have different moral significance if set in another historical or cultural context.

Helping Readers Enjoy Literature: Asking Formal, Impressionistic, and Evaluative Questions

Introducing formal elements of fiction, drama, and poetry

When inexperienced readers talk or write about literary works, they may try to reconstruct what they have read, but they tend not to analyze the substance and the craft of literature, so they do not experience its richness. Introducing formal elements of literature is one way of providing readers with new ways of responding to what they read, of deepening their understanding and increasing their enjoyment. Anthologies and handbooks designed for introductory literature courses typically contain the kinds of questions that we have in mind. Often they are arranged in sequences in which they may be asked. It is a good idea to help writers use such material when it is provided, but if it is not, you can refer readers to reference books like Holman's *Handbook of Literary Terms* or to texts that suggest ideas for writing about literature like Roberts' *Writing Themes about Literature*. Alternatively, you can help readers to develop their own lists and sequences of questions, which can also be used to create essay topics. Here are just a few of the kinds of questions that can be raised as readers approach literature. For more questions on each of the three major genres and ideas for sequencing them, we suggest that you consult an introductory text or handbook of the kind we have just mentioned.

Questions about the narrator or the speaker. These questions pertain primarily to fiction and poetry, but they may apply, to some extent, to certain characters in drama, like the Greek chorus, who summarize events that are not acted on stage. In analyzing poetry and fiction, it is often wise though not always essential to begin with questions about narrators or speakers, for it is through their lens that an author presents an imaginary world. Also, starting with questions such as "What sort of person is the speaker of this poem and how can you tell?" "Who tells the story and how would it differ if it were told from another perspective?" "What is gained and lost by the choice of narrator?" "How trustworthy is this narrator and what makes you think so?" will direct readers' attention to something other than plot, which they are all too prone to summarize. Consideration of other formal elements follows easily from discussions concerning speakers or narrators. If, for example, a tutor were to ask, ''How does the speaker of Shakespeare's Sonnet 18 feel about his beloved?'' she could move smoothly to questions regarding the character of the mistress: ''What qualities does he praise? What is she like and what makes you think so?''

Questions concerning plot. ''Plot'' means the sequence or series of actions in fiction, drama, and dramatic poetry. Inexperienced readers may not have too much difficulty reconstructing plots; in fact, that is all they may have been asked to do in high school, but they do find it hard to analyze them. You can encourage readers to interpret rather than to summarize action if you ask them to name conflicts and causalities. Such questioning invites readers to form concepts about the significance of action. The following questions can be raised: ''What external and internal conflicts can you list?'' ''Which conflicts seem major, which minor?'' ''What is the function of the major (minor) conflict?'' ''How is suspense created?'' ''What is the turning point of the action?'' ''Can any of the conflicts be generalized?'' ''Of what are they symbolic?''

Questions about structural divisions. Looking at structural divisions, be they scenes or acts in drama, chapters in novels, or stanzas in poems, enriches readers' experience of the dramatic or of the emotional movement of a work. Often, close analysis of the first structural section of a work can prepare readers to participate fully in the rest of it. Asking ''What has been established by the end of the first scene of *Hamlet?*'' for instance, invites a reader to name features of the setting, to identify major characters, to get some sense of the conflict that is to come, and to have the fun of seeing how all this is accomplished. Considering the rhyme scheme or the stanzaic division of a lyric poem is a way to help readers chart a speaker's emotional progress. You can ask what a division signals, what a break in the lines or a change of rhyme accomplishes; or, you can ask whether a speaker's voice or feeling seems to change and where the changes occur so that readers will notice the function of the divisions.

Questions about character. When inexperienced readers think about literary characters, they are likely to be more concerned with who *did* what than with who *means* what or with the ways in which one receives one's impressions. Asking such questions as ''How do you learn about the characters in this work? Through their actions? Speech? Thoughts? What the narrator or others suggest?'' alerts readers to the means through which they experience characters; it alerts them, to put it technically, to techniques of characterization. You might, additionally, ask whether the characters are fully drawn or one-dimensional, static or dynamic, and what their presence adds to the work. In raising these interpretive questions it is important to ask how the reader forms his conclusions; that is, you should follow these interpretive questions with reconstructive ones that call for the basis on which such an interpretation can be made (as we pointed out in the previous chapter).

Questions about setting. This is a very broad term that includes the cultural and historical context in which a work is set (which we have already discussed) as well as the immediate location, time, and emotional atmosphere. You can ask questions pertaining to the manner in which setting is established (light and sound effects, stage sets in drama, for instance) in order to help readers understand how they are experiencing setting and how setting affects their overall response to a work. Other useful questions ask about the function of setting in a work, whether it helps to describe character, to articulate theme, or to form the basis from which the plot is built.

Questions about language. Central to any literary discussion (be it impression-istic, evaluative, or formalistic), these questions ask how the work means, and what effect the language of a work has on a reader. They include such queries as, "What do we learn about the narrator (speaker, character) from the kind of lan-guage she uses?" "How does one character's language differ from another's in this work and what is the significance of the difference?" "How would the work change if a different word (words) were used?" "What patterns of imagery can you locate and what do they add to the work?" "How do the sentence structure and length affect your overall impression of the narrator (speaker, character, work)?" "How do the sounds, rhythms, and rhymes contribute to the sense of this poem?" Before asking the last question—in fact, before raising any questions about a poem—it is advisable to ask a reader to read it out loud (or at least a passage from a long poem) so that the reader can fully experience its sounds and rhythms. If a reader has difficulty pronouncing words or has a speech impediment, you may, instead, prefer to read the poem to the reader. Another procedure that you can recommend is that a poem be read more than once. Because poetry tends to compress ideas into short, figurative statements, each is usually richly suggestive. It usually takes more than one reading to uncover multiple meanings and connec-tions among words, sounds, rhythms, and structural divisions.

Questions about theme. A theme is a repeated motif or a central idea of a work. Usually represented indirectly, through action, dialogue, or descriptions of char-acter or setting, themes are, in most cases, implicit. Sometimes they are stated explicitly, but even when they are, the rest of the work carries them out in some way that must be established. Because themes are implicit and abstract, inexperi-enced readers may at first have difficulty articulating them. It is therefore usually a good idea to ask questions about theme only after discussing other formal ele-ments from which themes can be inferred. It is much easier for these readers to generalize about a work's central ideas once the details and incidents that reflect or dramatize them have been explored. Discussions of theme should help enrich readers' understanding and reduce their tendency to oversimplify and moralize them. You can help readers identify themes by asking them to locate patterns in the actions, among characters, in the setting, or in the language (by patterns, we mean repetitions, oppositions, processes, and causalities). For instance, "What do the conflicts you have identified have in common?" or "You have identified many images of darkness in this story. What idea or ideas does the author seem to be exploring by using them?" might be asked.

Asking impressionistic and evaluative questions

These questions are especially useful in helping readers formulate topics for essays, but they can, as well, be used to stimulate discussion of a work and may lead to considerations of formal elements. One type of inquiry is to ask readers what questions, puzzles, or ambiguities remain unresolved. For instance, having discussed a poem with a reader, a tutor might comment, "You said that the speaker seems to be criticizing his mistress even as he praises her. How can you resolve that seeming contradiction?" or, more generally, the tutor might say, "Does anything puzzle you about the speaker?" or, still more generally, "Do you have any questions about this poem?" Sometimes literature creates but does not solve these puzzles, as in some contemporary fiction that ends inconclusively. In such cases, you could ask the reader what further actions or outcomes she could imagine and which seem the most likely. If, on the other hand, the reader has not resolved some issue about which the work is clear, you can lead the reader back to the text to find the conclusive evidence. Another way of encouraging readers to react impressionistically to works is by asking what similarities and differences can be observed between two characters, incidents, settings, or themes in a work or in two works. This is often a useful approach when the reader is taking a literature course that includes works treating similar ideas or works by the same author. An additional means of stimulating readers' impressionistic responses to literature is to ask them to list a few words that come to them as they think about a work, then to write down their opposites and to form a sentence from the combined lists. This approach is particularly helpful when readers are trying to form essay topics. We know of one such reader who, having completed *One Flew Over the Cuckoo's Nest,* wrote down "madness" and "cruelty" when asked to follow this procedure. He then added their opposites, "sanity" and "kindness." From these oppositions, he generated this sentence: "In this book, those whom society considers mad are kind while those whom society deems sane are cruel," and he eventually developed a paper on the ironic mislabelings in the novel. (This approach is described at greater length in Chapter 4.)

Asking readers what they like or dislike about a work can also help them generate ideas about the literature, but such questions are useful only when followed by queries about on what basis the reader has formed a judgment. You can ask what the strong or distinguishing characteristics of the work are or whether some failings can be identified (for instance, is anything missing, implausible, inartistic, illogical?). Later in the chapter, we will consider how you can respond to unsupported interpretations or evaluations, but for now let us offer the general advice that you try to help readers trace the sources of their reactions by talking about how the text works.

Typical Problems in Writing about Literature and Some Strategies for Resolving Them

So far, this chapter has treated commonly experienced reading problems. As we have pointed out before, reading and writing are related activities, and a person who has trouble with one is apt to have trouble with the other. Someone who has not comprehended or interpreted a work will be unlikely to offer more than a written, often faulty, reconstruction of it, or, if attempting interpretation, will draw erroneous, unsupported conclusions. Someone who does not approach a text with questions will have to struggle to form an essay topic. Problems in writing about reading are predictable, then. Most result, directly or indirectly, from problems in reading. To alert you to the kinds of problems you will probably find in inexperienced writers' essays about literature, we describe the following typical trouble spots: formulating topics, paraphrasing and listing without interpreting, and interpreting faultily.

Trouble in forming a topic

Often, writers experience difficulty in forming topics about literature because they have not asked themselves the kinds of analytical questions that we have mentioned, and their readings are therefore superficial. Your first task, in such an instance, is to stimulate a reader's thinking about the work. Once the reader has analyzed the formal elements or has explained the bases for his impressionistic or evaluative responses, you can help him formulate a topic from the ideas he has generated. To give you an example of this procedure, we have included Tillie Olsen's short story, "I Stand Here Ironing," with a dialogue about it between Naomi, a tutor, and Vito, a student in an introductory literature course. He has asked Naomi for help because he must write "an analysis of some aspect of the story." After you have read it and the dialogue, write a critique of Naomi's strategy. Include in your comments answers to the following questions:

- Which of the kinds of questions listed above does Naomi employ, and to what advantage or disadvantage?
- What is Naomi's main objective and to what extent does she accomplish it?
- What might you have done differently?

I STAND HERE IRONING

I stand here ironing, and what you asked me moves tormented back and forth with the iron.

"I wish you would manage the time to come in and talk with me about your daughter. I'm sure you can help me understand her. She's a youngster who needs help and whom I'm deeply interested in helping."

"Who needs help." . . . Even if I came, what good would it do? You think because I am her mother I have a key, or that in some way you could use me as a key? She has lived for nineteen years. There is all that life that has happened outside of me, beyond me.

And when is there time to remember, to sift, to weigh, to estimate, to total? I will start and there will be an interruption and I will have to gather it all together again. Or I will become engulfed with all I did or did not do, with what should have been and what cannot be helped.

She was a beautiful baby. The first and only one of our five that was beautiful at birth. You do not guess how new and uneasy her tenancy in her now-loveliness. You did not know her all those years she was thought homely, or see her poring over her baby pictures, making me tell her over and over how beautiful she had been—and would be, I would tell her—and was now, to the seeing eye. But the seeing eyes were few or nonexistent. Including mine.

I nursed her. They feel that's important nowadays. I nursed all the children, but with her, with all the fierce rigidity of first motherhood, I did like the books then said. Though her cries battered me to trembling and my breasts ached with swollenness, I waited till the clock decreed.

Why do I put that first? I do not even know if it matters, or if it explains anything.

She was a beautiful baby. She blew shining bubbles of sound. She loved motion, loved light, loved color and music and textures. She would lie on the floor in her blue overalls patting the surface so hard in ecstasy her hands and feet would blur. She was a miracle to me, but when she was eight months old I had to leave her daytimes with the woman downstairs to whom she was no miracle at all, for I worked or looked for work and for Emily's father, who "could no longer endure" (he wrote in his good-bye note) "sharing want with us."

I was nineteen. It was the pre-relief, pre-WPA world of the depression. I would start running as soon as I got off the streetcar, running up the stairs, the place smelling sour, and awake or asleep to startle awake, when she saw me she would break into a clogged weeping that could not be comforted, a weeping I can hear yet.

After a while I found a job hashing at night so I could be with her days, and it was better. But it came to where I had to bring her to his family and leave her.

It took a long time to raise the money for her fare back. Then she got chicken pox and I had to wait longer. When she finally came, I hardly knew her, walking quick and nervous like her father, looking like her father, thin, and dressed in a shoddy red that yellowed her skin and glared at the pockmarks. All the baby loveliness gone.

She was two. Old enough for nursery school they said, and I did not know then what I know now—the fatigue of the long day, and the lacerations of group life in the kinds of nurseries that are only parking places for children.

Except that it would have made no difference if I had known. It was the only place there was. It was the only way we could be together, the only way I could hold a job.

And even without knowing, I knew. I knew the teacher that was evil because all these years it has curdled into my memory, the little boy hunched in the corner, her rasp, "why aren't you outside, because Alvin hits you? that's no reason, go out, scaredy." I knew Emily hated it even if she did not clutch and implore "don't go Mommy" like the other children, mornings.

She always had a reason why we should stay home. Momma, you look sick. Momma, I feel sick. Momma, the teachers aren't there today, they're sick. Momma, we can't go, there was a fire there last night. Momma, it's a holiday today, no school, they told me.

But never a direct protest, never rebellion. I think of our others in their three-, four-year-oldness—the explosions, the tempers, the denunciations, the demands—and I feel suddenly ill. I put the iron down. What in me demanded that goodness in her? And what was the cost, the cost to her of such goodness?

The old man living in the back once said in his gentle way: "You should smile at Emily more when you look at her." What *was* in my face when I looked at her? I loved her. There were all the acts of love.

It was only with the others I remembered what he said, and it was the face of joy, and not of care or tightness or worry I turned to them—too late for Emily. She does not smile easily, let alone almost always as her brothers and sisters do. Her face is closed and sombre, but when she wants, how fluid. You must have seen it in her pantomimes, you spoke of her rare gift for comedy on the stage that rouses a laughter out of the audience so dear they applaud and applaud and do not want to let her go.

Where does it come from, that comedy? There was none of it in her when she came back to me that second time, after I had had to send her away again. She had a new daddy now to learn to love, and I think perhaps it was a better time.

Except when we left her alone nights, telling ourselves she was old enough.

"Can't you go some other time, Mommy, like tomorrow?" she would ask. "Will it be just a little while you'll be gone? Do you promise?"

The time we came back, the front door open, the clock on the floor in the hall. She rigid awake. "It wasn't just a little while. I didn't cry. Three times I called you, just three times, and then I ran downstairs to open the door so you could come faster. The clock talked loud. I threw it away, it scared me what it talked."

She said the clock talked loud again that night I went to the hospital to have Susan. She was delirious with the fever that comes before red measles, but she was fully conscious all the week I was gone and the week after we were home when she could not come near the new baby or me.

She did not get well. She stayed skeleton thin, not wanting to eat, and night after night she had nightmares. She would call for me, and I would rouse from exhaustion to sleepily call back: "You're all right, darling, go to sleep, it's just a dream," and if she still called, in a sterner voice, "now go to sleep, Emily, there's nothing to hurt you." Twice, only twice, when I had to get up for Susan anyhow, I went in to sit with her.

Now when it is too late (as if she would let me hold and comfort her like I do the others) I get up and go to her at once at her moan or restless stirring. "Are you awake, Emily? Can I get you something?" And the answer is always the same: "No, I'm all right, go back to sleep, Mother."

They persuaded me at the clinic to send her away to a convalescent home in the country where "she can have the kind of food and care you can't manage for her, and you'll be free to concentrate on the new baby." They still send children to that place. I see pictures on the society page of sleek young women planning affairs to raise money for it, or dancing at the affairs, or decorating Easter eggs or filling Christmas stockings for the children.

They never have a picture of the children so I do not know if the girls still wear those gigantic red bows and the ravaged looks on the every other Sunday when parents can come to visit "unless otherwise notified"—as we were notified the first six weeks.

Oh it is a handsome place, green lawns and tall trees and fluted flower beds. High up on the balconies of each cottage the children stand, the girls in their red bows and white dresses, the boys in white suits and giant red ties. The parents stand below shrieking up to be heard and the children shriek down to be heard, and between them the invisible wall "Not To Be Contaminated by Parental Germs or Physical Affection."

There was a tiny girl who always stood hand in hand with Emily. Her parents never came. One visit she was gone. "They moved her to Rose Cottage" Emily shouted in explanation. "They don't like you to love anybody here."

She wrote once a week, the labored writing of a seven-year-old. "I am fine. How is the baby. If I write my leter nicly I will have a star. Love." There never was a star. We wrote every other day, letters she could never hold or keep but only hear read—once. "We simply do not have room for children to keep any personal possessions," they patiently explained when we pieced one Sunday's shrieking together to plead how much it would mean to Emily, who loved so to keep things, to be allowed to keep her letters and cards.

Each visit she looked frailer. "She isn't eating," they told us.

(They had runny eggs for breakfast or mush with lumps, Emily said later, I'd hold it in my mouth and not swallow. Nothing ever tasted good, just when they had chicken.)

It took us eight months to get her released home, and only the fact that she gained back so little of her seven lost pounds convinced the social worker.

I used to try to hold and love her after she came back, but her body would stay stiff, and after a while she'd push away. She ate little. Food sickened her, and I think much of life too. Oh she had physical lightness and brightness, twinkling by on skates, bouncing like a ball up and down up and down over the jump rope, skimming over the hill; but these were momentary.

She fretted about her appearance, thin and dark and foreign-looking at a time when every little girl was supposed to look or thought she should look a chubby blonde replica of Shirley Temple. The doorbell sometimes rang for her, but no one seemed to come and play in the house or be a best friend. Maybe because we moved so much.

There was a boy she loved painfully through two school semesters. Months later she told me how she had taken pennies from my purse to buy him candy. "Licorice was his favorite and I brought him some every day, but he still liked Jennifer better'n me. Why, Mommy?" The kind of question for which there is no answer.

School was a worry to her. She was not glib or quick in a world where glibness and quickness were easily confused with ability to learn. To her overworked and exasperated teachers she was an overconscientious "slow learner" who kept trying to catch up and was absent entirely too often.

I let her be absent, though sometimes the illness was imaginary. How different from my now-strictness about attendance with the others. I wasn't working. We had a new baby, I was home anyhow. Sometimes, after Susan grew old enough, I would keep her home from school, too, to have them all together.

Mostly Emily had asthma, and her breathing, harsh and labored, would fill the house with a curiously tranquil sound. I would bring the two old dresser mirrors and her boxes of collections to her bed. She would select beads and single earrings, bottle tops and shells, dried flowers and pebbles, old postcards and scraps, all sorts of oddments; then she and Susan would play Kingdom, setting up landscapes and furniture, peopling them with action.

Those were the only times of peaceful companionship between her and Susan. I have edged away from it, that poisonous feeling between them, that terrible balancing of hurts and needs I had to do between the two, and did so badly, those earlier years.

Oh there are conflicts between the others too, each one human, needing, demanding, hurting, taking—but only between Emily and Susan, no, Emily toward Susan that corroding resentment. It seems so obvious on the surface, yet it is not obvious. Susan, the second child, Susan, golden- and curly-haired and chubby, quick and articulate and assured, everything in appearance and manner Emily was not; Susan, not able to resist Emily's precious things, losing or sometimes clumsily breaking them; Susan telling jokes and riddles to company for applause while Emily sat silent (to say to me later: that was *my* riddle, Mother, I told it to Susan); Susan, who for all the five years' difference in age was just a year behind Emily in developing physically.

I am glad for that slow physical development that widened the difference between her and her contemporaries, though she suffered over it. She was too vulnerable for that terrible world of youthful competition, of preening and parading, of constant measuring of yourself against every other, of envy, "If I had that copper hair," "If I had that skin. . . ." She tormented herself enough about not looking like the others, there was enough of the unsureness, the having to be conscious of words before you speak, the constant caring—what are they thinking of me? without having it all magnified by the merciless physical drives.

Ronnie is calling. He is wet and I change him. It is rare there is such a cry now. That time of motherhood is almost behind me when the ear is not one's own but must always be racked and listening for the child cry, the child call. We sit for a while and I hold him, looking out over the city spread in charcoal with its soft aisles of light. *"Shoogily,"* he breathes and curls closer. I carry him back to bed, asleep. *Shoogily.* A funny word, a family word, inherited from Emily, invented by her to say: *comfort.*

In this and other ways she leaves her seal, I say aloud. And startle at my saying it. What do I mean? What did I start to gather together, to try and make coherent? I was at the terrible, growing years. War years. I do not remember them well. I was working, there were four smaller ones now, there was not time for her. She had to help be a mother, and housekeeper, and shopper. She had to set her seal. Mornings of crisis and near hysteria trying to get lunches packed, hair combed, coats and shoes found, everyone to school or Child Care on time, the baby ready for transportation. And always the paper scribbled on by a smaller one, the book looked at by Susan then mislaid, the homework not done. Running out to that huge school where she was one, she was lost, she was a drop; suffering over the unpreparedness, stammering and unsure in her classes.

There was so little time left at night after the kids were bedded down. She would struggle over books, always eating (it was in those years she developed her enormous appetite that is legendary in our family) and I would be ironing, or preparing food for the next day, or writing V-mail to Bill, or tending the baby. Sometimes, to make me laugh, or out of her despair, she would imitate happenings or types at school.

I think I said once: "Why don't you do something like this in the school amateur show?" One morning she phoned me at work, hardly understandable through the weeping: "Mother, I did it. I won, I won; they gave me first prize; they clapped and clapped and wouldn't let me go."

Now suddenly she was Somebody, and as imprisoned in her difference as she had been in anonymity.

She began to be asked to perform at other high schools, even in colleges, then at city and statewide affairs. The first one we went to, I only recognized her that first moment when thin, shy, she almost drowned herself into the curtains. Then: Was this Emily? The control, the command, the convulsing and deadly clowning, the spell, then the roaring, stamping audience, unwilling to let this rare and precious laughter out of their lives.

Afterwards: You ought to do something about her with a gift like that—but without money or knowing how, what does one do? We have left it all to her, and the gift has as often eddied inside, clogged and clotted, as been used and growing.

She is coming. She runs up the stairs two at a time with her light graceful step, and I know she is happy tonight. Whatever it was that occasioned your call did not happen today.

"Aren't you ever going to finish the ironing, Mother? Whistler painted his mother in a rocker. I'd have to paint mine standing over an ironing board." This is one of her communicative nights and she tells me everything and nothing as she fixes herself a plate of food out of the icebox.

She is so lovely. Why did you want me to come in at all? Why were you concerned? She will find her way.

She starts up the stairs to bed. "Don't get me up with the rest in the morning." "But I thought you were having midterms." "Oh, those," she comes back in, kisses me, and says quite lightly, "in a couple of years when we'll all be atom-dead they won't matter a bit."

She has said it before. She *believes* it. But because I have been dredging the past, and all that compounds a human being is so heavy and meaningful in me, I cannot endure it tonight.

I will never total it all. I will never come in to say: She was a child seldom smiled at. Her father left me before she was a year old. I had to work her first six years when there was work, or I sent her home and to his relatives. There were years she had care she hated. She was dark and thin and foreign-looking in a world where the prestige went to blondeness and curly hair and dimples, she was slow where glibness was prized. She was a child of anxious, not proud, love. We were poor and could not afford for her the soil of easy growth. I was a young mother, I was a distracted mother. There were the other children pushing up, demanding. Her younger sister seemed all that she was not. There were years she did not want me to touch her. She kept too much in herself, her life was such she had to keep too much in herself. My wisdom came too late. She has much to her and probably little will come of it. She is a child of her age, of depression, of war, of fear.

Let her be. So all that is in her will not bloom—but in how many does it? There is still enough left to live by. Only help her to know—help make it so there is cause for her to know—that she is more than this dress on the ironing board, helpless before the iron.

1953–1954

VITO: I don't understand this story, and I have to write a paper about it, so I guess I need some help.

NAOMI: Let's talk about the story, and maybe you'll get some ideas. What's the story about?

5   VITO: It's about a woman who's raising her daughter during the Depression and trying to support her. The husband goes to war and the woman has to work. Then the kid gets sick . . . *[Naomi interrupts.]*

NAOMI: You're just summarizing the plot. I was asking what the story is about. What are the ideas?

10 VITO: The ideas? I don't get what you mean.

NAOMI: I mean that it's a story about a mother–daughter relationship, about the way the mother raised the child and how that affected them both.

VITO: Uh-huh.

. . .

Naomi's questions are so general that they mislead Vito, frustrate him, and trap her into supplying ideas for him. Although it is possible that Naomi was trying to ask open-ended questions to allow Vito to think freely about the story, she phrases her queries too broadly. After all, her first question, "What is the story about?"

could reasonably be interpreted as a request for a plot summary, since "story" is often equated with plot, yet Naomi probably thought she was asking for something else, and unfortunately becomes impatient with Vito for not understanding her. Instead of rephrasing the question more precisely, she poses one that is equally general ("What are the ideas?"). Vito is now lost, Naomi sees no alternative but to say what she meant, and the dialogue breaks down.

If Naomi had asked specific questions using the language of literary analysis (which need not be highly technical, as you can see from the foregoing list), Vito might have begun to think analytically about the text. If she had asked, "What are the mother's conflicts and what are the daughter's?" or even "How about listing the characters' problems, so we can begin to see what the story is about?" Vito might have gotten a clearer sense of what she was asking. The dialogue might then proceed as follows:

NAOMI: How about listing the characters' problems so we can see what the story
15   is about?

VITO: Well, the mother has to support the kids, so she can't spend much time with the daughter, Emily.

NAOMI: Good. Is there anything else that keeps the mother from seeing Emily?

VITO: Um, she sends her away. But that's because she has to work. Let's see.

20 NAOMI: What happens when the mother remarries?

VITO: Oh yeah. She and the husband leave the kids alone at night. That's right. I remember about the talking clock.

NAOMI: OK, so how is all this a conflict for the mother?

VITO: The conflict is, um, between wanting to spend time with her husband and
25   wanting to care for her daughter.

NAOMI: Good, that's a second one. Want to jot that down? *[He does.]* How about phrasing the first conflict like that, too?

VITO: OK. *[writes]* "Wanting to support the family but wanting to be with the daughter."

30 NAOMI: Good. Anything else?

VITO: Well, she seems to feel guilty about the way the kid got messed up.

NAOMI: That's interesting. Why do you think that's a conflict?

VITO: Oh, well, gee. . . .

NAOMI: Do you hold her totally responsible for Emily's problems?

35 VITO: No. I mean, it wasn't her fault that her first husband left. And you can't blame the Depression or the war on her.

NAOMI: Sure. So does the mother seem aware that external circumstances contributed to her daughter's problems?

VITO: I'm not sure.

40 NAOMI: How about checking back through the text?

VITO: OK. Well, here on the first page, she talks about what couldn't be helped. So maybe she is aware.

NAOMI: It's great that you found that. It's good evidence. But now let's look at that entire sentence, "Or I will become engulfed with all I did or did not

45   do, with what should have been and cannot be helped." What does the "all I did or did not do" suggest that she's thinking about?

VITO: Oh yeah. Maybe that's her conflict. How responsible is she? Maybe she's figuring that out. Or trying to. Here she says, "if it explains anything."

NAOMI: Fine.

This time, Naomi's questions are more specific. She begins by calling for limited interpretations ("list the characters' problems") and directs Vito to search the text whenever he gets stumped. These strategies accomplish her original objective of getting Vito to decide "what the story is about." Let's suppose the discussion continues to the point at which Vito has listed the following conflicts or problems:

50   MOTHER'S PROBLEMS:

      1. Needing to work but wanting to be a mother

      2. Wanting to spend time with husband number 2 but wanting to mother

      3. Not knowing how responsible she is for Emily's problems

      4. Wanting child to be well (sent her to a convalescent home) but wanting child
55   with her

      5. Worrying about what will happen to Emily: should she resign herself or should she hope?

The dialogue could then continue:

NAOMI: OK, so how about listing Emily's problems now?

VITO: Oh, Lord, she has so many. That'd take forever. Can I just stick with the
60   mother and write about her?

NAOMI: That would be OK.

VITO: Except I can't just say this lady has a lot of problems and then just list them.

NAOMI: That's true. Let's see if we can do something with this list to shape it.
65   How can the items on the list be connected?

VITO: Well, the big problem seems to be how responsible she is for the kid's problems.

NAOMI: Uh-huh. *[pauses]*

VITO: Because the other things like needing to work and wanting to be home are
70   about that, right?

NAOMI: Sure.

VITO: I mean, every time, something seems to get in the way of this woman trying to be a good mother.

NAOMI: OK, like what?

75 VITO: The Depression and the war and both husbands leaving and, um, no money or good child care *[pauses]*, that school with the awful teacher and that convalescent home.

NAOMI: Great. So how about listing all those external circumstances that cause problems?

80 VITO: You mean how responsible she is for the kid's being screwed up?

NAOMI: Yes.

VITO: Well, looking at it this way, she doesn't look responsible at all.

NAOMI: OK, but you said that she seems to feel guilty. *[pauses]*

VITO: Well, let's see. *[pauses]* I guess yes and no. I mean, she talks about things
85   that couldn't be helped. She says that people feel guilty about things they
should have done or shouldn't have done, but she couldn't help it, so maybe
she is just telling this counselor person that she isn't responsible. But then
why does she feel she has to explain unless she feels responsible?

NAOMI: That's a good question.

90 VITO: Could I write about that? How responsible she feels and how responsible
she is, or maybe that she's trying to tell herself that she couldn't help it?

NAOMI: Fine. Sounds as though you want to write a paper that explores the theme
of "responsibility" in the story, and it certainly seems an important idea.
Let's see if we can use what you just said, along with the lists you wrote,
95   to develop this topic.

By asking Vito to name conflicts, Naomi has provided him with a way of identifying issues raised by the story. He has identified one of its complexities and has
begun to form a conception of "what the story is about." Although the discussion
of conflicts could have been more extensive, Naomi recognizes that Vito is not
eager for further exploration. She lets Emily's conflicts go unconsidered because
Vito has generated enough material to form a topic.

    Naomi might have chosen a different strategy for helping Vito analyze the story
➤ with equally good results. Before reading further, jot down some ideas about
alternative ways in which she might have proceeded.

            .   .   .

    Aside from asking Vito to identify conflicts, Naomi might have begun by ask-
ing him, "What causes problems for Emily and her mother?" and "Do these
causes form any pattern?" (see our suggested questions on theme). Alternatively,
she might have asked, "What sort of person is the mother?" and "What creates
that impression?" (see our questions on character and on narration). She might
even have asked Vito, "What is your reaction to the mother?" "Did you find her
sympathetic or believable?" (see questions on character). Any of these questions
would have made fruitful beginnings because they require a respondent to draw
conclusions (interpret) and to use the plot's details as supportive evidence (reconstruct), rather than as the focal point of discussion.

    Probably because Vito initially says he did not understand the story, Naomi
begins by asking reading questions instead of immediately helping him decide on
a topic. In this way, she gauges his grasp of the material, allows him to do some
thinking about the story, and lets the idea for a topic emerge gradually. If, however, Vito had said that he was having trouble deciding on a topic and Naomi
knew that his basic comprehension tended to be good, she might have begun the
session by helping him generate ideas for an essay. If, instead of focusing on
characters' conflicts, she had asked Vito to construct an oppositional list, for instance, the dialogue might have proceeded as follows:

NAOMI: You say you don't know what to write about. Well, when you think about
the story, what words come to your mind?

VITO: Hmmm. Poverty. Separation. Helplessness.

NAOMI: OK. Good. Write those down. What are their opposites?

5 VITO: Comfort, uh, togetherness, . . . control.

NAOMI: Good. Now see if you can make a sentence out of any of those terms.

VITO: Gee, I don't know. *[pauses]*

NAOMI: How about just starting with one of the words and see if you can connect it to any of the others.

10 VITO: OK, I'll say, "If you are poor, you don't have control. Because of the poverty, the mother and daughter have to be separated instead of being together. The mother is helpless to prevent the separations because she has to work to survive. And if they were not poor, she'd have more control over her life, and they'd have greater comfort."

15 NAOMI: Good. Now you're really getting somewhere. Now see if you can make a topic out of this, say, in a sentence.

VITO: Hmm. Well maybe something about what poverty does to a family?

NAOMI: Go on, try summing it up. Remember How-does-who-do-what? What does poverty do to the family?

20 VITO: It separates them, and that makes the mother feel helpless and turns Emily into a wreck. Let's see . . . *[writes]* "In 'I Stand Here Ironing,' poverty causes family separations that make the mother feel helpless and the daughter feel alienated."

NAOMI: Great. Now let's support that proposition with some of the ideas you've 25 mentioned.

Once Vito has reacted associatively to the story, he has some terms to work with. As he forms the oppositions, he generates further ideas that he then shifts about and pieces together. This dialogical process stimulates further thinking; he adds a new idea (alienation) and forms a predicated sentence (see Chapter 5 for more on predication).

Paraphrasing

In the previous chapter, we have already pointed out the tendency of inexperienced writers to reconstruct rather than to analyze literature. The questions that we have provided on pages 230–33 should move the writer beyond mere paraphrase or summary. To gain some experience in working with such writers, read the poem below and the student essay based on it. Then, using some of our questions, decide on a tutoring strategy or write a dialogue in which you try to assist the writer. Although starting with questions about the speaker is generally advisable, there is no single "right way" to plan a sequence of questions, so you might want to construct alternate approaches.

Sonnet 18

Shall I compare thee to a summer's day?
Thou art more lovely and more temperate;
Rough winds do shake the darling buds of May,
And summer's lease hath all too short a date;

Sometimes too hot the eye of heaven shines,
And often is his gold complexion dimmed,
And every fair from fair sometimes declines,
By chance or nature's changing course untrimmed;
But thy eternal summer shall not fade,
Nor lose possession of that fair thou ow'st,
Nor shall death brag thou wander'st in his shade,
When in eternal lines to time thou grow'st;
So long as men can breathe or eyes can see,
So long lives this and this gives life to thee.

William Shakespeare

"Shall I Compare Thee"
by Robert Egan
English 130

In this poem, the speaker compares his love to a beautiful day in May. He says that his loved one is more beautiful and even tempered than a day, which can become rough or too hot. Unlike a summer day, his lady will not change or grow less beautiful. She will not die or end like a day because in his poem she lives forever. Thus this poem is in praise of the speaker's loved one.

. . .

Robert's essay is a very literal paraphrase of much of the poem. He has not explored the implications of its language, the connotations of the words, or their rhetorical effect. He lists comparisons, but since he does not suggest how they work, the paper's sole interpretation and thesis, that the poem is written in order to praise, is not fully developed. Clearly, if Robert is to advance from reconstructing to interpreting literature, his tutor will need to consider what strategies will best lead Robert to listen to and think about the words more analytically.

Starting with questions about the central idea or the overall effect of the poem might not be wise because initially these issues are often too complex and abstract for inexperienced readers to handle, as we pointed out earlier. Instead, Robert's tutor could help him form a basis for a general interpretation by asking questions about the speaker or about the comparisons he draws between his loved one and nature. In either case, it would probably be a good idea to make use of a statement in the writer's essay. Robert's tutor might summarize a comment and then ask a question about it, such as, "You say that the speaker compares his lover to a summer's day. What sort of person would do that?" or "You say that in comparing his loved one to a summer's day, the speaker says she is more beautiful and even-tempered? What word in the poem corresponds to 'even-tempered'?" Both approaches would probably include questions about the speaker and about the comparisons he makes; the difference lies in the emphasis given to each idea and the sequence in which it will be discussed.

Listing but not interpreting poetic devices

Essays on poems are often sterile exercises because inexperienced writers tend merely to identify poetic devices without discussing their contribution to the meaning of the poem. This problem is understandable, for novice readers of poetry are usually students in introductory literature courses and are just beginning to master the technical vocabulary used to analyze poems. When they recognize a metaphor or a metrical pattern, they feel a sense of achievement. Since they have accomplished something new, they think they have accomplished all. They do not yet realize that labeling a poem's features is a means, not an end, that a more complete exploration would discuss the way a metaphor works, the contribution of rhythm to a poem's sense, and so on. Here is a typical example of this sort of writing. The student's essay is based on the first sonnet in Sir Philip Sidney's sequence, *Astrophel and Stella*. Mara, a student in an introductory literature course, was asked to write an analysis of the poem.

> Loving in truth, and fain my love to show,
> That she, dear she, might take some pleasure of my pain,
> Pleasure might cause her read, reading might make her know,
> Knowledge might pity win, and pity grace obtain,
> I sought fit words to paint the blackest face of woe,
> Studying inventions fine, her wits to entertain;
> Oft turning others' leaves, to see if thence would flow
> Some fresh and fruitful showers upon my sunburnt brain.
> But words came halting forth, wanting Invention's stay;
> And others' feet still seemed but strangers in my way.
> Thus, great with child to speak and helpless in my throes,
> Biting my truant pen, beating myself for spite,
> "Fool," said my Muse to me, "Look in thy heart and write."

Astrophel and Stella, Sonnet I
Mara Fitzer
English 130

   In this sonnet the speaker is trying to write a poem to his loved one, who does not seem to return his love. Unfortunately, he is unable to get the words out. The poet uses a metaphor to tell us what the speaker is feeling. When he describes telling his lover how sorrowful he is, he compares it to painting a "blackest face of woe." Then he reads other people's poetry to see if he can get some ideas, but he gets nowhere and becomes frustrated. This is expressed in a metaphor that compares his wish for inspiration to hoping for rain: "to see if thence would flow/Some fresh and fruitful showers upon my sunburnt brain." He feels dried up.

   In the next part of the poem, the speaker uses personification to describe his difficulty. "Invention," or his creativity, is compared to a child, "Nature's child." "Study," or what he learns from reading other poets, is pictured as an old woman who chases away the speaker's creativity. Continuing with the metaphor of the child, the speaker now sees himself as pregnant and helpless. The child, his poem, cannot be born. His pen is also compared to a child, a "truant" that runs away, won't work. Finally, the speaker gets the advice he needs from his Muse, who tells him to quit trying to imitate others and to "look in thy heart and write."

➤ Before reading further, identify the strengths and weaknesses of this essay. Then write down some questions that might help Mara improve her paper.

· · ·

Mara's essay reflects her understanding of the speaker's basic situation, but because she does not consider the connotations of and connections among the figures of speech, her interpretations are extremely limited and mechanical, though certainly more numerous that Robert's. If her tutor, Sue, were to ask her to compare and cluster some of the figures that she included in her essay, she might begin to experience the poem more fully.

SUE: You've identified some important metaphors here, but I want to know what they add to the poem. Let's look, for a minute, at the first one you pointed out, painting a face of woe. What kind of an activity is that? I mean, how is it different from or similar to giving birth to a child, which he mentions later?

5

MARA: Well, let's see. Painting is artistic, creative. I suppose you could say that giving birth is creative in another way.

SUE: OK. What's different about it?

MARA: Well, it's natural.

10 SUE: That's a useful word! If you can think of its opposite, maybe you'll have a way of thinking about painting a face of woe.

MARA: Well, in painting, he's putting something on outside; that's different from giving birth, where the baby comes from inside.

SUE: Great. Keep going. The baby comes from inside. . . .

15 MARA: Inside, outside. The baby comes from inside, so maybe that's why it seems natural. Painting a face of woe seems, um, more put on, artificial.

SUE: Wonderful. Write those terms down, natural/inside, artificial/outside. Now see if they fit any of the other images you picked out. You can list them underneath each category.

20 MARA: Well, there's all that stuff about children I mentioned, the truant and stuff. The would go with "natural."

SUE: OK. Anything else?

MARA: Natural . . . I'm stuck.

SUE: How about the fruitful showers on his brain?

25 MARA: Well, that's natural too, but they don't come from inside. But they do work on his brain.

SUE: True. Now let's see what the natural images describe and what the artificial ones describe.

MARA: The natural ones are about, let's see, being inspired, trying to write what you feel.

30

SUE: OK. Why can't he write what he feels?

MARA: He's stuck.

SUE: Why? What has he been doing?

MARA: He's been trying to write.

35 SUE: By doing what?

MARA: By studying what other poets did.

SUE: How does that compare with looking into your heart and writing?

MARA: I see, it's outside again, more artificial. So he's been trying to be fancy and instead of just letting his heart speak, sort of showing off for her.

40 SUE: Great. What language in the sonnet makes you think he's trying to show off for her?

MARA: Well, he explains in the first lines how he wants the poem to affect her, um . . . , he doesn't talk much about what he feels. He even uses the word "show"!

45 SUE: OK, good. Now what's the purpose of these artificial or external images? And the natural ones, too?

MARA: The purpose?

SUE: What's the effect of using them?

MARA: Well, the contrast lets you see how strongly he feels about her. The natural
50 images tell you how deep inside his feelings are and how strong they are. I mean, going through childbirth is really strong stuff. So maybe through the contrast he's telling her that his feelings aren't just superficial. He's not just being clever.

SUE: That's a good point. In fact, everything you've been saying helps me under-
55 stand how the metaphors are working. Let's see if we can get all these ideas into your paper.

➤ Before reading further, write a critique of Mara's approach. What did her objective seem to be? To what extent did she achieve it? What worked well? What would you have done differently?

. . .

The discussion of metaphorical language in this dialogue is very productive because Sue gets Mara thinking about how the figurative language works, how it means. On the other hand, the discussion of metaphor could have been more extensive. In particular, Sue could have asked Mara to distinguish the various references to children (especially since Mara referred to them in her essay). She might also have asked Mara to consider the different uses of the word, "invention" ("studying invention" and "Invention's child"). In other words, she might have helped Mara think about the ways in which a word takes on different meanings depending on its context and about how such differences illuminate a speaker's emotional or intellectual progress. This dialogue, however, is intended only as a brief illustration of ways in which tutors can encourage writers to begin to explore poetic diction, how metaphors mean, and how they reverberate when linked to similar and contrasting images.

In additional tutoring sessions, Sue and Mara might discuss other aspects of the poem. They might trace the sequence of images and their relation to the sonnet divisions. Sue might then ask questions about the way in which the rhythm and rhyme reflect the speaker's change in emotion and activity. If she were also to ask what the central idea of the poem seems to be, Mara might then consider the extent to which this is a persuasion poem or a self-mocking portrait of an artist. But in the preliminary conversation about the poem's figurative language, Mara has already made significant progress. She is no longer a mere hunter of metaphors.

➤ Sue chose to begin the dialogue with a discussion of metaphor. How else might she have begun? Answer this question by writing a dialogue between Sue and Mara, one in which Sue asks a different sequence of questions.

Problematic interpretations

When tutors and teachers raise doubts about the plausibility of writers' interpretations of literature, they often hear comments like, "How can you tell me I'm wrong? Brutus kills Caesar because Brutus wants to rule Rome himself. That's what I feel when I read the play. That's how I read his character, and my opinion is as good as anybody else's." It is particularly difficult to respond to such comments because reading literature *is* a subjective activity, more subjective than reading other kinds of texts since the reader is supposed to participate imaginatively in the work. Readers' reactions will therefore inevitably vary to some degree. No one knows, for example, precisely what Hamlet looks like, but each reader creates a mental picture of the character, and no one portrait is exactly like another. This sort of interpretive variation is to be expected and even to be desired. But to what extent are multiple interpretations of a text's meaning valid? While past critical theories assert the possibility of definitive interpretations, more recent schools of thought, particularly reader-response and deconstructionist criticism, argue that one reading can be as legitimate as another. While this position sounds like the one taken by the writer who misjudges Brutus's motives, it should not be confused with it. The idea that one person's interpretation is as good as another's may be tenable when readers disagree over subtle issues of connotation or syntactic connection, but it is not applicable when an interpretation is not textually substantiable: when a reader has not comprehended generally accepted meanings of words, has overlooked words, or has made inferences and judgments that are controverted by the text. It is well to keep these distinctions in mind when deciding whether or not to try to encourage a writer to revise an interpretation. Whenever you are in doubt about the validity of an interpretation, it is a good idea to ask the readers for substantiation and to judge the strength of the evidence before proceeding further. If the reader has erred, questions that draw attention to contradictory evidence are then in order (for example, "What motives does Antony impute to Brutus?").

At the same time that you should ensure that readers have basically comprehended a work and that their interpretations are supportable, you also need to guard against imposing your own, individualistic, subjective interpretations on others. Suppose Lloyd, a tutor, and Scott, a writer, were discussing the speaker in T. S. Eliot's "The Love Song of J. Alfred Prufrock," and they looked at the opening lines:

> Let us go then, you and I,
> While the evening is spread out against the sky,
> Like a patient etherized upon a table.
> Let us go, through certain half-deserted
> Streets, the muttering retreats
> Of restless nights in one-night cheap hotels,
> And sawdust restaurants with oyster shells:

If their dialogue went like this, how productive would you consider it?

LLOYD: What sort of person does the speaker seem to be, judging by these lines?
SCOTT: He sounds sort of depressed and lonely.

LLOYD: OK. What makes you think so?

SCOTT: The way he describes everything: the streets are deserted, and he thinks
5   about lonely nights in cheap hotels.

LLOYD: What makes you think the nights in the hotels are lonely?

SCOTT: Well, let's see. He describes them as restless, as if some poor guy is
      tossing.

LLOYD: What else could the person be doing?

10 SCOTT: Pacing the floor in a room by himself.

LLOYD: What else?

SCOTT: Having insomnia, being depressed.

LLOYD: What else?

SCOTT: God, isn't that enough? All those things are lonely!

15 LLOYD: But if they're cheap one-night hotels and restless nights, the speaker could
      be imagining the sort of place where you spend the night with a prostitute.
      Like a one-night stand.

SCOTT: I didn't think of that.

LLOYD: Well, it's worth considering as another aspect of the speaker's character.
20   It makes the whole scene sound seamy, like the word "cheap," which is
      different from your "lonely" idea.

➤ Before reading further, write a critique of Lloyd's approach: if he intended to help
Scott characterize the speaker, to what extent has he succeeded? What would you
have done differently? Why?

. . .

Lloyd does an admirable job of getting Scott to explain why he thinks the
speaker is lonely. Unfortunately, he never gives Scott credit for his useful responses, nor does he ask him to connect "restless nights" to other "lonely"-
sounding language. Lloyd seems more interested in getting Scott to read "restless
nights in one-night cheap hotels" as sexual encounter than he is in capitalizing on
what Scott does offer to support his contention that the speaker is lonely. While
the line may suggest some sort of assignation, why need it be with a prostitute,
and could not the line be read as Scott has interpreted it? Lloyd does not seem to
consider this, nor does he, having supplied his own interpretation, ask Scott if
such a sexual encounter could be linked to the idea of loneliness. While the tutor
seems a bit too insistent on having the reader interpret the line his own way, his
repeated question, "What else?" is useful up to a point, because it encourages
Scott to explore the richness of the language, to consider several connotations,
not merely one. However, the tutor would have done better to acknowledge the
validity of each of the reader's plausible interpretations and to help the reader use
➤ them to support his own inferences. With these suggestions in mind, write a revised dialogue between Lloyd and Scott.

Summary

As Chapter 11 points out, inexperienced writers are also apt to be inexperienced
readers. As with other reading, they do not know how to approach literature ac-

tively, so they neither glean information from it nor experience it fully for pleasure. While readers who have not previously analyzed literature may resist doing so at first, your patient questioning should gradually heighten their critical abilities and their enjoyment.

You can help readers look for behavioral, cultural, and historical ideas when they read for informational purposes, as in psychology, history, or sociology courses. You can help them find specific illustrations of general patterns of behavior, discover how a historical moment affects individual lives and the extent to which past social organizations and manners resemble or differ from our own.

By asking formal, impressionistic, and evaluative questions, you deepen readers' experience of literature and thereby increase their enjoyment. Formal questions concern literary elements such as plot, narration, setting. Impressionistic and evaluative questions call for readers' subjective responses to works: what puzzles, pleases, or annoys them; what similarities and differences they find between elements in one work or two.

These questions can help a writer form a topic for an essay that interprets rather than merely summarizes texts or lists poetic devices. If you doubt the validity of a reader's interpretation, you can tactfully ask for substantiation, and you should try to guard against imposing your own interpretations on a reader. Instead, you can foster independent thinking by helping a reader test tentative interpretations.

SUGGESTIONS FOR JOURNAL ENTRIES

1. What were your reactions to analyzing literature when you were first asked to do so? Were you resistant? Did you become a symbol seeker, a cataloguer of metaphors? Did you enjoy literature more? Experience it differently?

2. Compare and contrast your reactions (in exercise 1 above) to those of the writers with whom you are working. If the reactions are similar, in what way? If different, how do you account for the differences?

3. To what extent has writing about literature been different for you from writing about other kinds of reading? What accounts for the differences, if any?

SUGGESTIONS FOR FURTHER WRITING

1. Write a sequence of questions that you might address to an inexperienced reader who must write an essay about a short story of your choice. Or, write a dialogue between yourself and such a reader in which you discuss the story and help the reader form a topic.

2. Write a sequence of questions for an inexperienced reader who must write an essay about a poem of your choice. Or, write a dialogue between yourself and such a reader in which you discuss the poem and help the reader form a topic.

3. In the following dialogue, Carol, a tutor, discusses with Simon, a writer, his essay based on William Wordsworth's "There Was a Boy." Please write a critique of the dialogue, paying particular attention to the way the tutor handles the writer's interpretive problems. To what extent are the tutor's interventions justified? How tactful and constructive are his questions?

There Was a Boy

There was a Boy; ye knew him well, ye cliffs
And islands of Winander!—many a time,
At evening, when the earliest stars began
To move along the edges of the hills,
5   Rising or setting, would he stand alone,
Beneath the trees, or by the glimmering lake;
And there, with fingers interwoven, both hands
Pressed closely palm to palm and to his mouth
Uplifted, he, as through an instrument,
10   Blew mimic hootings to the silent owls,
That they might answer him.—And they would shout
Across the watery vale, and shout again,
Responsive to his call,—with quivering peals,
And long halloos, and screams, and echoes loud
15   Redoubled and redoubled; concourse wild
Of jocund din! And, when there came a pause
Of silence such as baffled his best skill:
Then sometimes, in that silence, while he hung
Listening, a gentle shock of mild surprise
20   Has carried far into his heart the voice
Of mountain-torrents; or the visible scene
Would enter unawares into his mind
With all its solemn imagery, its rocks,
Its woods, and that uncertain heaven received
25   Into the bosom of the steady lake.

    This boy was taken from his mates, and died
In childhood, ere he was full twelve years old.
Pre-eminent in beauty is the vale
Where he was born and bred: the churchyard hangs
30   Upon a slope above the village-school;
And through that churchyard when my way has led
On summer-evenings, I believe that there
A long half-hour together I have stood
Mute—looking at the grave in which he lies!

William Wordsworth

"There Was a Boy"
by Simon Gorda
English 130

    In this poem the speaker is grieving over the death of his son, in a country village in England. The boy died young and the father is remembering the liveliness of the boy, how playful he was, how close to nature. The father recalls the way the boy imitated birds and was touched by the beauties of summer rains, boulders, and woods. These recollections of
5   the boy's love of life sharpen your sense of loss, as does the way the poem is arranged. First you read about everything he did and he seems very alive. Only at the end do you learn that he died young. That comes as a shock and makes you feel terrible.

Carl: I really like what you said about how the way the lines are arranged sharpens a reader's sense of loss. That's a very thoughtful comment. I do have some questions, though, about some of the other things you said. Where did you get the idea that the boy liked summer rain?

5   *Simon:* From "mountain torrents," you know, torrents of rain.
     Carl: But if it comes from a mountain it's got to be like a river.
     Simon: Oh. OK.
     Carl: I would also like to ask you what makes you think that the speaker is the boy's father?
     Simon: Who else would visit the grave? Well, I suppose it could be anybody who loved the
10   boy and missed him. But he knew the boy well.
     Carl: What do you mean?
     Simon: He tells us a lot about him.
     Carl: What kinds of information?
     Simon: About all the things he did in the hills, hooting at owls and stuff.
15   *Carl:* Could anybody besides his father know about that?
     Simon: I guess so. Friends or anybody who was up there, but it just seemed like a father
     missing his son.
     Carl: What else might a father remember about his son?
     Simon: I don't know. Maybe things he did when he was a baby or things he said.
20   *Carl:* Sure. But that kind of information isn't in the poem. Also, does the speaker describe the
     boy as being with anybody or being alone?
     Simon: What do you mean?
     Carl: Does the boy play or talk with anybody?
     Simon: The birds, I guess. But no people. So how would the father know about all this if he
25   hadn't been up there?
     Carl: That's a good question. You might also ask yourself how anybody would know what
     went on inside the boy's mind. The speaker says "a shock of mild surprise/Has carried far
     into his heart the voice of mountain torrents." Who would know that?
     Simon: Nobody but the boy, really, but if anybody would guess, his father would.
30   *Carl:* Listen! You're simply going to have to get off this father kick! We already said that the
     speaker doesn't tell us a lot of intimate details about the boy, just what he did in nature.
     Then you said nobody would really know what effect nature had on his heart. This isn't a
     father talking. This is somebody who's like the omniscient narrator in that story you read
     last week, somebody who knows all, who can see into people's minds.
35   *Simon:* Oh. I didn't get that. But I still don't see why it can't be the father.
     Carl: I thought we went over that. The kind of detail that the speaker includes isn't intimate,
     doesn't really get personal. And also, think about the kinds of words the speaker uses, like
     "solemn imagery" and "uncertain heaven." That's not the language of a simple, country
     person. That's someone like Wordsworth, somebody who's thinking about big issues like
40   how children have a special rapport with nature.
     Simon: I guess you're right.

4. Write a dialogue between yourself and Simon (above) in which you improve upon Carl's approach.

SUGGESTIONS FOR CLASS ACTIVITIES

1. Compare your responses to the exercises in "Suggestions for Further Writing" with those of your classmates.

2. Bring to class copies of essays by writers with whom you are working and discuss your plans for helping the writers. Get suggestions from other class members.

3. If you have encountered any difficulties in helping people read or write essays about literature, discuss the problems and get suggestions from classmates.

4. Share with your classmates your successes in helping people read or write essays about literature. Try to generalize your approach so that others may use it.

SUGGESTIONS FOR FURTHER READING

Bleich, David. *Reading and Feelings: An Introduction to Subjective Criticism.* Urbana, IL: NCTE, 1975.

Booth, Wayne. *The Rhetoric of Fiction.* Chicago: University of Chicago Press, 1961.

Burke, Kenneth. *The Philosophy of Literary Form: Studies in Symbolic Action.* 3rd ed. Berkeley: University of California Press, 1973.

Ciardi, John, and Miller Williams. *How Does a Poem Mean?* 2nd ed. Boston: Houghton, Mifflin, 1975.

Faulkner, William. *Light in August.* New York: Vintage, 1972.

Fish, Stanley. *Is There a Text in This Class?* Cambridge, MA: Harvard University Press, 1980.

Hirsch, E. D. *Validity in Interpretation.* New Haven, CT: Yale University Press, 1967.

Holman, C. Hugh. *A Handbook to Literature.* 4th ed. Indianapolis: Bobbs-Merrill, 1980.

Kintgen, Eugene R., and Norman Holland. "Carlos Reads a Poem." *College English* 46 (1984): 478–491.

Le Bon, Gustave. *The Crowd.* New York: Penguin, 1977.

McCormick, Kathleen. "Theory in the Reader: Bleich, Holland, and Beyond." *College English* 47 (1985): 836–850.

Minot, Stephen. *Reading Fiction.* Englewood Cliffs, NJ: Prentice-Hall, 1985.

Newkirk, Thomas, Ed. *Only Connect: Relating Reading and Writing at the College Level.* Upper Montclair, NJ: Boynton/Cook, 1986.

Perrine, Laurence. *Sound and Sense: An Introduction to Poetry.* 2nd ed. New York: Harcourt Brace,, 1963.

Petersen, Bruce, Ed. *Convergences: Transactions in Reading and Writing.* Urbana, IL: NCTE, 1986.

Roberts, Edgar. *Writing Themes about Literature.* Brief ed. Englewood Cliffs, NJ: Prentice-Hall, 1982.

Rockas, Leo. *Ways In: Analyzing and Responding to Literature.* Upper Montclair, NJ: Boynton/Cook, 1984.

Scholes, Robert. *Semiotics and Interpretation.* New Haven, CT: Yale University Press, 1982.

———, and Robert Kellogg. *The Nature of Narrative.* New York: Oxford University Press, 1966.

Suleiman, Susan R., and Inge Crosman, Eds. *The Reader in the Text: Essays on Audience and Interpretation.* Princeton, NJ: Princeton University Press, 1980.

Tompkins, Jane P., Ed. *Reader-Response Criticism: From Formalism to Post-Structuralism.* Baltimore: The John Hopkins University Press, 1980.

13

Tutoring Spelling
and Vocabulary

The last two chapters pointed out that many people do not read *well* because they do not read *much*. Someone who reads infrequently may not recognize some written words because they are not part of his oral vocabulary. He may have trouble comprehending and therefore writing about a passage in which unfamiliar words appear. Just as vocabulary problems signal lack of exposure to the written word, so do many spelling errors. A writer who has rarely, if ever, seen a word in writing will probably not retain a visual memory of it, a memory that is crucial to good spelling. Although spelling and vocabulary problems may appear to be quite different, since one reflects orthographic, the other, semantic difficulties, both kinds of errors originate from the same fundamental sources:

> from the student's rootedness in spoken rather than written language, and his habitual preference for forms of English that diverge in a variety of ways from formal English; from a general lack of visual acuity and memory in relation to written letter and word patterns; from the student's efforts to stimulate a register or code he is not sure of. (Shaughnessy, 161)

This chapter, therefore, describes writers' difficulites in understanding, selecting, and transcribing vocabulary and suggests various strategies for helping writers to become more conscious of the look, the sounds, and the meanings of words.

Some Causes of Spelling Error

Shaughnessy describes the general underlying sources of difficulty, but you will also need to understand the specific causes of spelling problems in order to assess and address them effectively. Below we have listed some examples of typical errors. In some cases, their causes are obvious from the misspelling; in others reasons must be inferred. Please speculate as to why the writer of each example might have erred. Then continue with the chapter.

1. The room was extreamly cold.
2. More over, the company did not warn consumers that the product could have side effects.
3. At the trail, the judge ruled for my friend.
4. She tole the policeman everthin that happen and next day she was to sick to go to work.
5. They were always haveing company over.

Unpredictability of English spelling

A writer who misspells a relatively simple word like "extreamly" might appear unintelligent to someone who does not realize that many errors reflect a writer's assumptions about language (as Chapter 10 explains). Actually, the misspelling, "extreamly," makes sense: even though it is incorrect, it is phonetically accurate. The writer knew how the word should sound but did not how it should look, so she probably made an educated guess. Words like "dream," "cream," and "stream" use "ea," so why not "extreamly"? The danger with this approach is that one sound can be represented in several different ways. Thus, "extremely" could plausibly be spelled

extreamly	ecstreamly
extreemly	eccstremely
ekstremely	

and so on. A poor speller may be aware of only one of these letter combinations (graphemic alternatives) and so may assume that he has only one choice. Even if he is familiar with all of the alternatives, he may not have seen the word in question often enough to form the letter combinations automatically. Since there are no simple rules by which to indicate when to adopt one combination as opposed to another, phonetically identical one, the very unpredictability of spelling is a frequent source of error and discouragement. You can encourage poor spellers by letting them know that English spelling is not consistent, that some of their errors are understandable, even sensible. You can make the unpredictability comprehensible by explaining a bit about the rich, derivative history of the English language, and you can soothe writers by offering illustrations of the variety of graphemic choices that complicate a speller's lot. Our favorite illustration is George Bernard Shaw's famous example of "ghoti" for "fish," in which the sounds are "gh" as in "enough," "o" as in "women," and "ti" as in "station." Consolation alone, however, can deter progress by confirming writers' suspicions that English spelling is too inconsistent to be mastered. Actually, more *can* be learned about spelling. Many spelling rules have few or memorable exceptions. That in itself can encourage writers who believe otherwise and are frustrated and confused by the inconsistencies they encounter. Learning the rules also gives writers greater control over the system. Once they find that they can, indeed, rely on some principles, they are more apt to be attentive to spelling.

Problems in remembering, seeing, and transcribing words

Many but not all writers who read a good deal do not make errors like "extreamly" because they can rely on their visual memories. They do not have to use hunches as much as do writers who read little. Some, like the author of the second example, who represented "moreover" as "more over," may select the appropriate letters without knowing how they should look on the page. These writers therefore often make two words where there should be but one or join two words as one, as in "alot." Such errors might be slips of the pen in other people's writing but reflect inexperienced writers' poor visual memory or misunderstanding of word form.

Even when reasonably good spellers read a printed word and attempt to transcribe it, they may omit or reverse letters, as in sentence 3, where "trail" represents "trial." Anybody could make that kind of error, but not everybody would correct it in proofreading, for many writers have "trouble remembering what [they have] seen and seeing what [they have] written" (Shaughnessy, 173). If they proofread at all, inexperienced writers reread to make sure that they have said what they intended. Unlike more experienced writers, novices, when they are asked to look closely at words, often do not notice letter reversals or omissions. It is important, therefore, for you to watch writers edit and to listen to them read and spell out loud; by observing the degree to which the writers can distinguish individual letters, syllables, and other word parts, you can determine what the problem really is. The person who does not recognize an error obviously requires more extensive assistance than someone who does.

Problems caused by pronunciation

Someone who writes "tole" for "told," and "happen" for "happened" (sentence 4) is spelling by ear. As we pointed out in Chapter 10, in almost all English-speaking groups, some letters found in written forms of words are not sounded or are sounded differently from the pronunciation indicated by their standard spelling, for instance, the unsounded final "d" in "happened." Alternatively, he may hear different sounds and stresses from those indicated by the written words, "intire" for "entire," for example. The blurred or variant pronunciations that he hears mislead him when he spells because he has little or no awareness of the distinctions between his oral dialect and the standard grapholect. Writers who depend almost exclusively on their aural sense also do not distinguish homophones like "to," "too," and "two," or "there," "their," and "they're." Someone with problems such as these clearly needs to develop visual acuity and memory.

Unfamiliarity with word structure

Inexperienced writers also misspell words because they do not know how to change the form of a word in order to alter its tense, number, degree ("big" to "biggest"), or entire meaning ("pity" to "pitiless"). A writer might not know that a singular noun ending in "y" is pluralized by changing "y" to "i" and adding "es." Instead of transforming "fly" into "flies," a writer might write "flys" for the plural form, since the addition of "s" is the normal way to pluralize a noun.

Similarly, the author of sentence 5 does not know that a "silent 'e' " is dropped from most base words when a vowel suffix is added. Typically, inexperienced writers misconsolidate roots and affixes ("begining" for "beginning"), add superfluous syllables ("availiable" for "available"), or omit necessary ones ("econical" for "economical"). Unschooled in the system of affixation and unaccustomed to sounding words out syllable by syllable as they spell, they have little to guide them as they try to transform words.

Strategies for Helping Writers Improve Spelling

Raising consciousness and identifying patterns of error

The most basic guideline for working with writers on spelling is to help them concentrate on the issue. You can encourage them to think about how a word sounds as they try to write it, to look at words they have formed, and to observe them in other people's writing. A fundamental strategy for raising writers' spelling consciousness and overcoming their discouragement is to ask them to locate patterns of error in their compositions (the benefits of similar error analysis are described in Chapters 7 and 10). A major advantage of this approach is to make spelling problems seem manageable to writers who are frustrated by the number of errors marked on their papers. They wonder how they will ever learn to spell all the words they have misspelled. Further, they often assume that the rules are too numerous to be memorized and that learning them is not worthwhile anyway because they have so many exceptions. If you help writers detect the pattern of their errors and if you introduce only those rules or conventions relevant to it, the writers may feel less daunted by and more interested in spelling. Below is the kind of chart that you could ask writers to construct:

CORRECTED WORD	MISSPELLING	LETTERS INVOLVED
1. resistance	resistence	ance/ence
2. prettier	prettyer	i/y
3. silliest	sillyest	i/y
4. having	haveing	i/ei
5. extremely	extreamly	e/ea
6. independence	independance	ence/ance
7. carefully	carefuly	ly/lly
8. teachable	teachible	able/ible
9. their	there	eir/ere
10. relieve	releave	ie/ea
11. hopefully	hopefuly	ly/lly
12. reasonable	reasonible	able/ible
13. saving	saveing	i/ei
14. defiance	defience	ance/ence

The writer of this list could analyze it and identify his patterns of error. He could then group his errors in the following way:

TYPE OF ERROR	LETTERS INVOLVED	WORDS
Suffix problems	-ance/-ence	resistance
		independence
		defiance
	-able/-ible	teachable
		reasonable
	-i/-y	prettier
		silliest
	-ly/-lly	carefully
		hopefully
	-i/-ei	having
		saving
Long "e" problems	-e/-ea	extremely
	-ie/-ea	relieve
Homophone problems	-eir/-ere	their

Once he saw that he really had made three errors instead of fourteen, this writer would probably feel relieved. He would probably realize that when forming or proofreading words, he should pay extra attention to word endings, for that is where he most frequently errs. Not the least benefit of error analysis is that it helps writers anticipate problems.

It can also help writers to infer spelling principles. This writer's tutor, for instance, might ask him what the base words of "prettier" and "silliest" have in common (both "pretty" and "silly" end in "y") and how the addition of vowel suffixes changes them ("i" is substituted for "y"). The writer might then be able to formulate the following reminder: "Does the base word end in 'y'? Does the suffix begin with a vowel? If yes to both, change 'y' to 'i' and add the suffix." He could write this in an additional column on his second chart, or he might keep a separate checklist for future reference. This inductive process will be described at greater length later in this chapter, but since you may need to introduce a few basic spelling concepts before you can initiate it, we will describe them first.

Introducing phonic and syllabic principles

If writers are to correct their patterns of error, they must be familiar with a few basic principles of phonics and syllabication that underlie spelling rules. You cannot help a writer turn "dinning" into the intended "dining" by asking whether the "i" in dining is long or short if the writer knows neither what is meant by "long" and "short" nor to what specific sounds these terms refer. When writers are not familiar with the idea that letters can be pronounced in various ways or that different sets of letter combinations can produce identical sounds, you can introduce brief lists of simple words that illustrate phonic concepts. Some experts say that initially it is better to restrict such lists to simple oppositions in order to avoid confusing writers with subtler distinctions such as those among the "a" sounds of "par," "pare," and "pay." Below is the sort of list that could, instead, be used:

hat	hate
pet	peat/Pete
kit	kite
got	goat
cut	cute

You could ask a writer to read each pair of words out loud. Then, having made certain that she hears the differences in sounds, you could ask her to add other words containing the same sounds; next, you could introduce the terms "short vowels" and "long vowels" by writing them over the appropriate column and helping the writer discover that each long sound says the name of its letter (long a = the letter "a"). Finally, you could ask under what conditions, judging by the list, a vowel sound is short, and when long. The writer could infer that in a single syllable, the vowel (V) is short when single and surrounded by consonants (C): C V C = short sound, as in "cut." A long vowel is indicated either by C V V C, the second unsounded (diacritical) vowel functioning to make the first long as in "beat," or by C V silent "e" (diacritical "e"), in which the silent "e" makes the first vowel long, as in "cue." Admittedly, the list above does not cover all the possible letter combinations that produce the sounds, but it establishes the fundamental principle and provides some common combinations. The same kind of procedure could be used with consonants.

If writers tend to omit syllables when spelling but not when pronouncing words, you might suggest that they sound words out syllable by syllable as they spell. Listening to writers pronounce what they have written is a good way for you to distinguish spelling from vocabulary errors, as well as to determine whether mispronunciation causes the error. However, suggesting that words be sounded out is useful only if writers are familiar with syllabication principles. If the writer is not, some brief explanation will be necessary.

Two of the most common rules for breaking words into syllables are designated as C/VC, in which the break comes before the vowel, and VC/CV, in which the break comes between the consonants. If writers draw a line at each syllabic break and then sound out each syllable, they become more attentive to the number of sounds in a word. They also focus on the letter groups of each syllable. Such scrutiny promotes development of the visual memory required for accurate spelling. Additionally, learning how to syllabicate helps writers understand certain spelling conventions, as you will see in the dialogue below, in which Tina, a college freshman, discovers when to double a consonant. As she was composing, she tried to turn "red" into a verb by adding the suffix "en," but she spelled the word "reden" instead of "redden." She and her tutor, Ari, have already discussed rules of syllabication, and in this dialogue, he helps her use them to correct her error:

ARI: How about breaking "reden" into syllables? Maybe that will help you to see what the problem is.

TINA: OK, [*writes*] "re/den."

ARI: How would you pronounce that?

5   TINA: *(pronounces it correctly)* rĕ′ den.

ARI: Well, but take some other words like "defer" and "refuse." Break them into syllables.

TINA: [*writes, then pronounces*] "de/fer" "re/fuse." I pronounce *them* with a long "e" in the first syllable.

10   ARI: So what does that suggest about how you would pronounce r-e-d-e-n?

TINA: I see. The "e" in "re" would be long. So how do I get it to stay short since it isn't pronounced long?

ARI: Well, can you think of any words with a short vowel sound that change when you add a suffix?

15   TINA: Hmmm. Oh. "Sit" into "sitting."

ARI: Great. How do you spell that?

TINA: [*spells*] s-i-t-t-i-n-g.

ARI: OK. Now how has "sit" changed?

TINA: The extra "t" is added.

20   ARI: What happens if you take it away?

TINA: [*writes*] "siting." Oh. It's a different word. The "i" becomes long. How come?

ARI: Break each version into syllables and you'll see.

TINA: [*writes*] si/ting   sit/ting

25   So the extra "t" must keep the "i" short or something.

ARI: That's exactly right. Now go back to "red."

TINA: Well, it got to be r-e-d-d-e-n if you use the same logic. Is that right?

ARI: It certainly is. Let's look at some of the other words on your error chart and see if we can apply this idea to some of your other misspellings.

In this dialogue, Ari has helped Tina discover what must be added as well as why the addition is necessary. His first strategy, introducing "defer" and "refer" is a good one. Even if a few words like "preference" violate the principle, it obtains in most cases. By pronouncing "defer" and "refer," Tina sees how "re-den" would probably be pronounced. Then she must figure out a way to keep the "e" sound short. To help her do this, Ari suggests that she remember other words with a short vowel sound. Since Tina is able to think of and spell a word that uses a double consonant, Ari asks her to apply the VC/CV, V/CV rules to infer the reason for the additional consonant. If she had not thought of "sitting," Ari could have made a few suggestions as he did with "defer" and "refer." In the remaining minutes of the session, Ari and Tina could examine and correct other similar misspellings listed on her chart. Only then could Ari ask her to state the double-consonant rule because she would need to see several examples before she could form a general rule. In the dialogue above, Ari's strategies have worked well, but their success depended on Tina's acquaintance with a few phonic and syllabic principles.

Helping writers discover common spelling rules

You can help writers infer general spelling rules more easily if you are acquainted with a few that are commonly violated. You need not introduce them all to each writer, only those that a writer unwittingly breaks. Some writers find the rules illuminating because they give spelling a kind of logic. What once seemed mysterious and arbitrary begins to make sense, becomes systematic and therefore predictable once writers understand why words are spelled as they are. Some studies suggest that writers' spelling improves more when they discover the rules inductively than when they are merely asked to apply given ones. That is why we used Ari's work with Tina as an example and why we suggest that you help writers infer general principles by observing examples. We offer Shaughnessy's list of frequently violated rules (178), then, as information but not as the kind of list that should be handed to writers. Chapter 5 of *Errors and Expectations* contains additional rules and an excellent, detailed description of typical spelling errors. A spelling workbook such as Brown and Pearsall's *Better Spelling* or an English handbook could also be consulted.

1. "i" before "e"
   except after "c"
   or when sounded like "a"
   as in "neighbor" and "weigh"

   This rule works only where the student's confusion is between "ie" and "ei." For other spellings of the "e" sound, the rule is not useful ("reach," "extreme," etc.). Also, the rule does not apply to nouns that form their plurals by changing the "y" to "i" and adding "-es" ("democracies").

2. Is there an unpronounced "e" at the end of the word?
   Does the suffix begin with a vowel?
   If YES to both questions, drop the "e."

   Another rule can be attached to this that covers the main exceptions, namely, that when the "silent" "e" is preceded by "c" or "g" and the suffix begins with "a," "or," or "u," the "e" remains. However, the student can usually discover the phonemic principle that underlies the rule simply by seeing lists of words that retain the diacritic "e"—"manageable, "peaceable," etc.

3. Does the word end in a consonant + "y"?
   Change the "y" to "i" and add the suffix.

   Exception: Keep the "y" when suffix is "-ing," possessive " 's," or a proper name.

4. Rule for doubling the final consonant: Does the word end in one vowel plus one consonant?
   Is the accent on the final syllable?
   Does the suffix begin with a vowel?
   If YES to all three, double the consonant.

A word of caution about rules such as those listed above: they tend, as Shaughnessy points out, "to distort the student's sense of the larger pattern in English spelling unless they are applied during practice to a broad range of words . . . the unmistakable pattern of the language is not toward doubling or dropping but simply adding" (176). In other words, it is wise to help writers identify major spelling patterns as they formulate rules for minor ones. Shaughnessy also recommends that writers try to phrase rules as a series of questions, a sort of checklist that they can apply as they spell, for example, as in rule 4 above and our example of the "y" rule.

Helping with errors resulting from pronunciation

Since many spelling errors result from writers' pronunciation of words, you can make writers aware of differences between their pronunciation and the pronunciation indicated by the standard spelling. When writers drop word endings, blur or omit syllables, or mistake one sound for another, you can pronounce and sometimes spell the words (the latter if hearing them does not prompt a correction), so that writers can both hear and see the distinctions. Urging writers to alter their pronunciation is unwise because doing so is impractical and suggests that the writers' is inferior. Instead, you can help writers identify the patterns in their pronunciation that lead to misspellings so that writers can anticipate and avoid error. In the following example, Bill, a tutor from the Northeast, helps Lester, a student who grew up in the Deep South, correct misspellings that result from
➤ Lester's tendency not to pronounce final "ed" in verbs. Analyze the dialogue, including in your response answers to the following questions:

- What principles of verb formation, pronunciation, and spelling are raised and by whom?
- What strategies does Bill use? To what extent do they seem successful?

BILL: How about reading this sentence from your essay. [*points to a sentence*]

LESTER: [*reads*] He shine the shoes until they were spotless.

BILL: OK. Now let me say it and see if you hear any difference. "He shined [*emphasizing "d"*] the shoes until they were spotless." What did you hear?

5 LESTER: You said "d" on shined.

BILL: Right. Now let's see what that "d" sound is supposed to indicate. [*writes*]

I shine my boots weekly
I shined the boots yesterday

LESTER: So it means that it's happ'nin' in the past.

10 BILL: Right. Where you grew up, that ending wasn't pronounced, so you never heard it or said it and that's why you're not writing it.

LESTER: Doggone. Tha's the problem.

BILL: Let's make a list of your misspelled words and see if this principle can be applied to other verbs in your essay.

15   LESTER: Well, it's kinda hard to tell 'cause I don' know which ones work that way.

BILL: What do you mean?

LESTER: Well, like "eat" and "ate." I wrote "ate" in the essay for the past tense and I didn't hafta add an "ed" there.

20   BILL: No, you don't. That's a good point. Many commonly used verbs in English don't use "ed" to form the past tense, but it's a good principle to know because it's the main way to form past tenses. You can actually tell by sound whether the verb does use "ed" or not.

LESTER: Well, let's see if I kin tell here. The professor mark "plane" in "He 25   plane each board before he sanded it." Now *there*. "Sanded" has an "ed." But lessee here. What about "plane"? Should that be "planed"?

BILL: Great. How did you know?

LESTER: I did what ya'll said about tryin' out soun's. I tried "plone" and "pline" and they jes didn' soun' right. An' the word ended up jes like "sine" with 30   "n-e," so I figgered it hadda be.

BILL: Good. So if you use that kind of reasoning again, you'll probably avoid making an error the next time.

      .   .   .

In this productive session, Bill's first strategy is to get Lester to hear the difference between the two pronunciations. Then he writes sentences that permit Lester to see the correct spelling and to discover the function of the additional letter. Bill next explains the reason for Lester's pronunciation and misspelling in a way that does not degrade Lester's way of talking. When Bill suggests that Lester apply the principle (adding "ed" to form past tense), Lester notices that it does not apply to all verbs; this shows that he is becoming visually observant, a sign that augurs well for spelling improvement; however, his discovery momentarily halts him. Like many writers, he has found in the spelling system an inconsistency that seems to discredit a rule. However, Bill's explanation and his suggestion that Lester experiment with sounds to see whether a word follows the pattern prevent his discouragement. Bill might have taken the discussion a bit further by listing other irregular verbs and asking Lester to form their past tenses. He might then have introduced the terms, "regular" and "irregular," but perhaps he felt pressed for time and preferred that Lester apply the "ed" principle to other words in his essay. Lester is likely to become more aurally and visually alert and to improve as a speller if he and Bill continue to have such discussions of Lester's spelling errors.

While pronunciation can cause error, it can also aid in spelling. As we have already demonstrated, sounding out syllables can cue correct spelling once writers are familiar with a few phonic and syllabic principles. This approach is not a thoroughly reliable method because of variant pronunciations and because of the number of graphemic options for representing a sound. Nevertheless, the method works often enough to make it useful, and writers can consult a dictionary for confirmation.

Helping writers use charts, dictionaries, mnemonic devices, and proofreading to improve spelling

One way of helping writers overcome their own errors is to suggest that they assemble lists of commonly used graphemic alternatives for producing the same sound, such as

$$\text{long ``e''} \begin{cases} \text{ei} \\ \text{ee} \\ \text{ea} \end{cases}$$
$$\text{e-consonant-e}$$

When the writers are trying to spell a word that contains such a sound, they can experiment to see which of the alternatives look "right." They can then consult a dictionary to confirm the hunch. If it is wrong, they can repeat the process with other letter combinations. This limited trial-and-error procedure winnows writers' choices and helps them use the dictionary, which some poor spellers seldom consult because they don't know where to locate the words: "The dictionary doesn't do me any good because I need to know how to spell the word in order to look it up." Such a paradox can be avoided once writers become acquainted with graphemic alternatives. Using error charts like the ones reproduced on pages 289–90 can also help decide writers when a spelling might be questionable and when the dictionary work is in order. Suggesting that writers consult their error charts contributes to the "cultivation of doubt" that leads to better spelling (Shaughnessy, 186). Suppose that a writer frequently misspells words that end in "ence" and "ance." If she has charted this form of error, her tutor could suggest that she look up any word she wants to use that ends one way or the other. When she finds the correct spelling, she can add each word to her original chart and keep it by her side for reference when she writes. This writer could also be encouraged to use mnemonic devices to avoid "ance"/"ence" confusion. Harvey Wiener (119) offers the following example of this aid to memory, which is also useful for recalling homophonic distinctions.

WORD	TROUBLE SPOT	A WAY TO REMEMBER
abundance	abun*dance*	Have *a bun;* then *dance*
dilemma	dil*emma*	*Emma* has a dil*emma*
parallel	para*lle*l	*All* lines are para*lle*l

Finally, by indicating when and how to proofread, you can help writers spell more accurately. Since inexperienced writers tend, when they try to proofread, to think only about an essay's substance, not its surface, you can encourage them to review their essays several times, first reading for meaning, then for spelling and/ or punctuation. If the writers keep focusing on their ideas rather than on spelling, you can suggest that they read backwards, starting with the last sentence on the last page, proceeding to the next to last sentence, and so on. This process makes it harder for readers to become distracted from their purpose.

Typical Vocabulary Problems

People who read little, who look neither often nor carefully at graphic forms of words, are just as likely to experience vocabulary problems as to make spelling errors. Since their exposure to language occurs primarily through their speech communities, these individuals are unfamiliar with the sort of formal or technical vocabulary typical of speakers and writers in colleges and in many workplaces. While they may have heard or seen such language from time to time, they have not had enough contact with a word like "delineate" or "underwriter" to know its exact denotation, or they may know only one meaning for a word that has several. They may, for example, understand what is meant by "socialize" in "The men tend to socialize apart from the women," but not in "Children of this tribe are socialized by extended family members." Not only do they fail to recognize such semantic distinctions; they also fail to see that these are created by syntactical and grammatical variations (in this case, active and passive verb forms).

The working vocabularies of such adults are neither as large nor as diverse in register (tone) as those of more experienced readers, for even if they recognize some formal or "advanced" vocabulary in reading, they may not yet know how and when to use these words in speaking and writing. When they read, particularly when they read scientific texts, professional journals, and high canon literature, inexperienced readers become frustrated and demoralized by the forbidding, seemingly impenetrable language. Unaware that there are ways to comprehend vocabulary without consulting a dictionary, they may take this step needlessly or avoid it altogether. While the former strategy can be wearing, the latter is self-defeating.

Limited experience in reading and little exposure to speakers outside their own speech communities also lead to composition problems. Conscious that writing tends to be more formal that speech (as Chapter 10 explains), novice writers try to adopt a different register, try to imitate an academic or otherwise authoritative tone in their essays. Several kinds of errors may result. Writers may misuse words like "infer" for 'imply." They may inconsistently and dissonantly intermingle formal and informal words, as in "Hobbes's pessimistic view of man really threw me." They may get lexical forms wrong, as in "The author says that the drugs used to control hyperactivate children are dangerous." Or they may substitute similar-sounding words or word segments for those they intend, as in "It's a doggy dog world," and "I liked the way you disgust the animals in your lecture." Sometimes a writer's inventions are more than amusing malapropisms: they can convey unexpected, original meanings, for example,"The flowers were reboundant" (abundant). Such meanings, however, are usually unintended, and it is unfair to praise their creators for ingenuity without introducing them to the forms they were trying to imitate. Additionally, when writers try to adopt formal vocabulary in their sentences, they do not know what prepositions accompany the new terms. Sentences such as "The doctor should inform the patient to their options" are not uncommon. This example also illustrates one form of another typical vocabulary problem: pronoun use.

Many writers, as one of our students wrote, "are unformular with pronouns" (he meant unfamiliar). They confuse singular and plural pronouns, often because the writers' oral conventions differ from written ones, but sometimes because they do not know what the antecedents mean. Many think, for instance, that "everyone" means "all people" rather than "each one" or that "none" means "all [are] not" rather than "not one." Therefore, they mistakenly use plural pronouns. Most frequently, inexperienced writers use pronouns vaguely. "This" and "which," for instance, often appear without clear antecedents.

Such vague or general diction may reflect a writer's diffidence, her fear of committing herself to an idea, or her wish to sound more authoritative than she feels. This sort of vocabulary problem is not restricted to those who misuse pronouns or write "concernable" for "considerably." Even fairly proficient writers may use overgeneral, imprecise vocabulary, as in, "Things are getting worse all the time. People don't care. They just look out for themselves." What, exactly, is getting worse, and what does the writer mean by "care"? That people are not concerned about the deterioration or that they are inconsiderate of others? Typically, inexperienced writers use a limited number of general verbs such as "care," and, like more advanced writers, they also use "things," which actually denotes concrete objects, to refer to abstract concepts. Similarly, writers insert phrases like "the fact that" or "due to the fact that" when they are offering opinions rather than verified information. In "Capital punishment should be abolished due to the fact that human life is sacred," the writer may have chosen "due to the fact that" instead of "because" in the mistaken belief that the phrase sounds more convincing.

College students and mature professionals alike produce "gobbledegook" by mixing such vague and imprecise phrasing with technical, educational, psychological, and political jargons that conceal meaning. "Pentagonese" and other forms of political "doublespeak" often obscure the true intent and moral implication of an intended action, as in "defoliation of the landscape will optimalize surveillance." These and other jargons have infiltrated public consciousness through the media. The language carries an air of professionalism and power that many inexperienced writers admire, but the models are dubious at best. One example is perhaps all that is necessary to illustrate why: "Once it is known how the local campaigns will impact the public, we will be in a superior position to prioritize our strategies for the national campaign." What is wrong with simply saying, "Once we analyze the effect of our local campaigns, we can plan our strategies for the national ones"? In the first version, which is needlessly long and convoluted, the nouns "impact" and "priority" have been transformed into verbs, but English jargons more characteristically turn verbs into nouns by adding suffixes that elongate the words and therefore make them seem higher toned. Thus "priority" becomes "prioritize" and eventually "prioritization"; the verb "use" becomes "utilize," which is turned into "utilization." This transformation is called "nominalization," itself a nominalization from linguistics. It produces the kinds of sentence problems already considered in Chapter 8, so we do not describe them at length here; but later we will offer strategies for eliminating them that you will recognize if you have been reading the chapters consecutively.

A final vocabulary problem that deserves mention is the use of sexist or racist language. By this we mean language that, unbeknownst to the writer, expresses a bias. We do not mean racial epithets or other language that a writer consciously uses to degrade others; we have already discussed ways of dealing with such problematic thinking in Chapter 2. We are concerned here, rather, with a subtler and slipperier problem, one that arises, for instance, when a boss, who otherwise treats a female secretary respectfully, refers to her as a "girl"; when someone who intends no disrespect refers to a group of black men as "boys"; or when a writer adopts "he" exclusively as the impersonal pronoun. (You have probably noticed that we have alternated "he" and "she" in this book.) Since writers adopt such usage without realizing that it is problematic, usually they need only be alerted tactfully and may be asked if they can think of more neutral choices. If they cannot, they can be referred to the guidelines set forth for the "Guidelines for Nonsexist Use of Language in NCTE Publications," which is available from NCTE (see Nilsen).

Helping writers improve their vocabularies, like helping them learn how to spell more accurately, is inevitably a very slow process, both because of the range and number of problems that any one person may experience and because one acquires new words only through repeated exposure to and practice in using them. Sporadic tutorials cannot substitute for the steady and concerted work needed for substantial vocabulary development, but they can reinforce or extend such practice. In general, tutors can promote expansion and refinement of writers' vocabularies by helping writers to understand how words work semantically, by providing them with methods for discovering meaning, and by creating opportunities for using new words in speaking and writing.

Methods for improving reading vocabulary and those for improving writing vocabulary are most successful when introduced together. One type of work complements and reinforces the other. Newly acquired reading vocabulary is not likely to become part of long-term memory, nor does it ever become part of a working vocabulary if writers do not use the words in speaking and writing contexts. Many widely available vocabulary books offer word lists for memorization without providing such contexts, so we do not recommend them. They attract the sort of writer who feels

> a pressure to acquire facility with academic language speedily. . . . Just as abstract grammar study seems to hold out the answer to all his difficulties with inflections and syntax, so vocabulary drill seems to lead the way to an academic style. (Shaughnessy, 188)

If the vocabulary lists can be related and applied to subjects about which someone is reading and writing, however, and if that person receives guidance while trying to vary the forms of the words, the lists can be useful. Our suggestions below for helping writers develop their vocabularies reflect our view that writers need to read, hear, and write the words in a variety of contexts. Even though we have divided the strategies into two sections, one on helping writers improve vocabulary as they read texts, the other on helping writers improve vocabulary as they write, you will notice that in both sections, reading and writing activities are often combined.

Helping Writers Improve Vocabulary as They Read Texts

Looking up words as a first step: special occasions

Many people have been told, "If you don't know a word, look it up," but most ignore this advice because it takes too much time and effort. While consulting a dictionary may not always be necessary, as we point out later in this chapter, there *are* situations that require this step. Sometimes, readers should look up words even before attempting to get through entire passages. When, for instance, a text's major purpose is to introduce terminology, as is often the case with introductory natural and social science textbooks, readers can be advised to look over the glossaries often provided at chapter endings, or to skim for definitions in the text (see Chapter 11 on skimming). If every third or fourth word is unfamiliar, as is the case when readers are dealing with elevated, highly technical, or historically remote works, dictionary work should also precede any attempt to read a passage fully. In such cases, you can suggest that readers borrow a method familiar to foreign language students: underline all unfamiliar words; then, using the dictionary, pencil in definitions; and finally attempt the whole passage. By asking readers about their experience with a text, by watching them as they read, and by listening to them read aloud, you can determine whether the above strategy is in order. The occasions on which preliminary vocabulary work is appropriate are likely to occur less frequently than those in which readers encounter only a few unfamiliar words on each page.

Using contexts to discover meaning

When readers occasionally encounter unfamiliar vocabulary, you can help them learn to infer its meaning from the context in which it appears: from its lexical, grammatical, and syntactical features. In their discussion of the word "kickback" in *Catch 22* (see Chapter 11), Phillipa, the tutor, might use the context to help Joanna, the writer, form at least a rough definition. For instance, since raising his "kickback fees" was one of several moves the doctor made for financial gain, Phillipa might ask Joanna what the doctor's various activities seem to have in common. Joanna would probably respond that his other activities, handling too many patients and performing illegal abortions, are unethical ways to make money. Phillipa might then ask whether there is anything in the clause, "I upped my kickback fees" that could be connected to this idea, and Joanna would undoubtedly see that "fees" refer to money. She might also notice that "kickback" describes "fees," so from this contextual framework she might reasonably assume that a "kickback" was some sort of charge, probably an unethical or illegal one.

Analyzing syntax and word structure

Joanna would be able to guess that "kickback" describes "fees" from the placement of the two words. In English sentences, single adjectives normally precede nouns. Thus, "kickback" 's meaning derives from the *syntactic* as well as from the semantic context in which the word appears. By observing the position of a word in a sentence, readers can determine its function, which helps define its meaning. Suffixes can similarly indicate how a word functions. If Doc Daneeka had said, "I improved my financial situation," Joanna could infer that "financial" describes "situation" not only because of its position but also because of its "ial" ending.

Analysis of word structure, then, can also make dictionary work unnecessary. If you ask a reader if she recognizes some part of a word, be it a root, prefix, or suffix, the reader might be able to infer a definition. Of course, she would need to be familiar with common roots and affixes for this strategy to succeed. You can help readers learn to recognize them by suggesting that they list words that use them. For instance, a reader who does not understand what "monomaniacal" means could be asked if any parts of the word look familiar. If he said "maniac," you could then ask him to list words that use the prefix "mono." He might recall "monotony" or "monogamy," and you might help him define the prefix from these. Next, the reader could try to define "monomaniacal," and then you two could begin to look at the suffixes, how they differ, what they mean, where words using them are positioned, and so on. Many writing centers distribute lists of commonly used prefixes, suffixes, and roots, which can be useful when you and the reader do not have time to make extensive lists together. But supplying a handout is productive only if the reader uses it in a variety of ways, such as finding and listing examples of affixes in assigned readings and in his own essays, writing affixed words in sentences, and substituting affixes to form new words.

Using dictionaries selectively

If Joanna were to analyze word structure and contexts regularly, she would reduce her reading time. However, because the sort of reading in which she was engaged, literary analysis, requires attentiveness to connotation, Joanna should probably have underlined "kickback" and should have continued reading until she came to a convenient stopping place. Only then should she have looked up the word. Delaying dictionary work temporarily would afford her greater opportunity to glean meaning from a larger context. On the other hand, if Joanna had been reading for information and had been assigned hundreds of pages of a text, she would probably have needed to look up only those words whose meaning she could not understand at all from the context or repeated words that seemed to be key concepts. How closely you question readers about the vocabulary of a text and what advice you offer, then, depends on the readers' purposes as well as on the difficulty of the language.

Suggesting vocabulary notebooks

When a reader comes across new words, he can record them in a vocabulary notebook, a practice particularly valuable to readers who are eager to expand their vocabularies. If someone reads a word often enough to want to define and use it precisely himself, he could look it up, record both its dictionary definition and the sentence in which he saw it, write a context definition, and finally, make up an original sentence using the word. This strategy illustrates the interconnectedness of reading and writing activities. Looking up words can improve reading comprehension, but further exercises can expand speaking and writing vocabulary.

Helping Writers Improve Vocabulary as They Write

Approaching vocabulary problems tactfully

Working on vocabulary problems that appear in writers' essays is a delicate undertaking because wording is so much a matter of individual discretion. Thanks to the size of the English lexicon and to the availability of various syntactical patterns, one idea can be phrased in many different ways. Since writers' word choices express their individuality, they can be understandably touchy when their selections are questioned. After all, who is to say that one term is preferable to another, as long as the word suits the writer's purpose? This question contains a crucial qualification that can help you decide when to intervene: is the word suitable for the writer's purpose? A word can be considered "unsuitable" if its use results in semantic error, imprecision, repetition, or dissonance in register. It is not "unsuitable" if it differs from the word you would have used but nevertheless serves its function. In addition to your own assessment of "suitability," professors' marginal comments may indicate the need for vocabulary work (see Chapter 7 on using these to good advantage), but in either event, your approach must be tactful, particularly because choices that appear dubious may actually be defensible.

When someone uses a word questionably, incorrectly, or imprecisely, neutral comments like the following can be helpful: "Could you tell me what you mean here? I wasn't quite sure" or "I'm not certain what you mean by 'The private was prompted to the ranks of sergeant.' Could you explain, please?" (In the last example, the writer's response would disclose not only his intention but also whether he has made a spelling or a vocabulary error, or both.) In contrast, asking "What does 'prompted' mean?" is inadvisable. Because writers generally assume that they know fewer words than tutors, such a question would seem disingenuous. Substituting a word, as in, "Oh, you mean 'salutation' here, not 'salute,' don't you?" is not a good strategy either, for reasons that we hope are apparent to anyone who has read the first two chapters of this book. Offering words to writers is tempting when their vocabularies are limited or their usage rife with error, but there are a number of preferable strategies that help writers help *themselves* expand and refine their writing vocabularies. Substitution exercises, in which a writer supplies alternative words and phrases, activate someone with a limited or imprecise vocabulary. Questions like "In what way does this word sound different from the other words in this sentence?" can alert writers to problems of register, just as "Who does what?" can help them eliminate jargon or vagueness. These and a few other suggestions will be described in the following pages.

Using substitution exercises

In the most common version of this exercise, a writer is asked to prepare a list of synonyms by generating words or by gleaning a thesaurus. He is then asked to explore the connotative differences among the listed alternatives in order to become more conscious of their semantic distinctions. Because an inexperienced writer uses a limited number of basic verbs or vague terms, he can profit enormously from such a practice even without resorting to the thesaurus. He may think that his vocabulary is lacking; he may even be right, but he probably knows more words than he actually employs in his essays. A substitution exercise might convince him of this, sensitize him to linguistic choices, and provide him with a heuristic for future use.

The following example illustrates the strategy in use. Heather, a student in a freshman composition course, has brought to her tutorial a draft of a composition on a "frightening experience." In the draft, Heather recounts her childhood flight from some teenagers who had threatened her with a knife. The only verbs she uses to describe her escape are "run," "went," and "got out of there." Aware that Heather's assigned purpose is to convey her fright, her tutor, Dodi, tries to help her think of more precise, emotionally charged verbs:

DODI: When you were running, what kind of a run was it?

HEATHER: What kind of run? Like fast or slow? I mean I really moved.

DODI: OK. So it was fast? How did you feel when you were running?

HEATHER: Desperate. Dead scared. I was only eight and they were big and they
5   had a knife. I had to get out of there as fast as I could.

DODI: OK. Let's see if you can get that feeling into the essay by thinking of some
     other words for running.

HEATHER: "Run" is no good?

DODI: It's not that it's no good; it's that there are a lot of ways to run and you can
10   find a word to fit this specific situation.

HEATHER: But what is there besides run? Um. Gee, I can't think of anything.

DODI: That's not surprising since I put you on the spot. But there's a way out that
     you can use any time you get stuck like this. Try imagining how different
     people run or how animals run or even how inanimate objects move in ways
15   that are like running. Change the actor or change the situation and see what
     happens.

HEATHER: OK, let's see. Runners jog, but that's so relaxed. What about dash?

DODI: Ok, write both those down. How are they different?

HEATHER: Well the dash is real fast for a short distance. So that's great. That's
20   what it was. I'll use that.

DODI: It's a good one. But before you make up your mind, see if you can think
     up some other possibilities that may fit even better.

HEATHER: OK. Let's see. There's pressure when you dash. So what else has
     pressure? Oh, like water spurting. OK. Spurt I could use. *[writes]*

25 DODI: Good, keep going.

HEATHER: Um, pressure, force, OK, "streaming"; or how about "tearing"—oh, that makes me think of clothes. "Ripping." Can you rip down a street?

DODI: Sure.

HEATHER: OK *[writes "rip"]* Now, animals. Horses gallop.

30 DODI: What would that be like?

HEATHER: You know, noisy and thumping and bouncy but not scared. "Dash" and "tore" sound more scared to me.

DODI: I'm glad you are making these distinctions and that you are thinking about trying to get your fear across. Now, if you look at what you wrote, how
35 might you fit some of these words in? How about early in the essay when you first started running?

HEATHER: Yeah. Well, "tore" might be good there 'cause I'm breaking away from the kids.

DODI: Great. Why do you like it better than "run"?

40 HEATHER: It sounds more violent. I could use "streamed" when I ran for two blocks without stopping because that's like water flowing. You, know, steady.

DODI: That's great.

HEATHER: This is fun. Let's see. I could use "dash" at the end when I see my house.

45 DODI: Because. . . ?

HEATHER: Because there I had a short distance and could put on the speed.

DODI: OK. Now you've really made me see you run, I have a much clearer sense of what the speed and motion were like.

HEATHER: Yeah. I think it's better.

Using "change the actor and the situation" to stimulate substitution

Not everyone will respond as quickly and as discriminatingly as Heather, but we chose a ready pupil to illustrate the method. With another writer, a tutor might have to ask more questions about the connotative differences among the generated words. Even Heather, at first, finds it hard to think of synonyms, and Dodi's strategy at this point is worth noting: she suggests that Heather imagine different actors and different situations to bring new words to mind (lines 12–15). This very simple technique is often remarkably effective in unblocking writers. Often, it stimulates vivid, metaphorical usage.

Using antonyms to promote substitution

This variation works well when a writer cannot recall or has overused a word. If you ask, "What's the opposite of the word you are trying to think of?" when a writer temporarily cannot remember a word, she can often recall an antonym, add a prefix, or use the new word with "not." Naming an antonym also can often trigger memory of the original word being sought. As an example, let us say that Heather is now trying to generate a conclusion for her paper on a "frightening experience."

50 HEATHER: Well, I guess what bothers me is that nothing happened to those kids. They were never punished. I was the only one who suffered. It's another one of those cases where there's no . . . what's the word I am looking for? I know it but I can't think of it.

DODI: What's the idea you're trying for?

55 HEATHER: That it isn't fair.

DODI: OK. What's the opposite of "fair?"

HEATHER: Unfair.

DODI: OK. Can you think of another word for "unfair"?

HEATHER: Unjust. I got it. There's no justice. That's the word I was looking for.

60 It would have been easy enough for Dodi to supply the word for Heather, but Dodi is patient and wise enough to help Heather find the word herself.

Transforming word structures

Heather can recall "unjust" both because Dodi suggests that she think of an antonym and because she knows how to transform the adjective into the noun form. A writer who does not could benefit from another kind of substitution exercise, one in which he selects affixes and roots from a list and transforms words he has misconsolidated in his essays. The list could be a handout or a chart that the writer has made with your help (see page 301 of this chapter for a description of how this can be accomplished). If, for instance, a writer had written "conveniable" for "convenient," you could suggest that he try out different suffixes to see if they sound right. If his ear is unreliable, you can suggest trying another suffix or consulting a dictionary. He could also combine roots and affixes on the list to form new words when he is searching for a word that he cannot remember or wants to use one in a more formal register than a word in his original essay. These exercises work best when the charts group affixes with similar meanings and functions; for instance, suffixes commonly used to form abstract nouns might be clustered. The writer then has a basis for making selections.

Tutors can write sample sentences using the word to be transformed. Our "convenient" example can serve as illustration:

1. He finds using public transportation _____.
2. Public transportation is a great _____.
3. The bus was _____ located.

This sort of exercise helps writers transform words at the same time that it suggests various phrasing options. The exercise works best when it is followed by one in which writers create original sentences that vary a word's forms. In these, writers create the contexts themselves and make the transformations independently.

Using "Who does this sound like?" with register problems

We have said that writers who are trying to adopt the more formal language of written English have difficulty making the transition and often mix registers jarringly. Usually, the writer either does not detect the dissonance or else cannot think of a more formal term. The former is true in the following example, in which Casey, a student in a sociology of marriage class, writes, "Poor communication between marital partners can make their relationship go to pot." Notice how Nona, his tutor, alerts him to the change in tone:

NONA: How about reading that sentence aloud?

CASEY: OK. *[reads it]*

NONA: What differences do you hear between the first and the last parts of the sentence?

5 CASEY: I don't know. Gee.

NONA: Well, what's another way to say "poor communications between marital partners"? How would you say it if you were just talking to me?

CASEY: A husband and wife don't talk to each other.

NONA: Sure, now if that sounds like you talking, who does the other version sound
10   like?

CASEY: I guess more like the professor or the book.

NONA: Sure. Now who does "go to pot" sound like?

CASEY: Me.

NONA: You in what circumstances?

15 CASEY: Gee, I didn't think about it. I guess I'd use that with friends but maybe it should be fancier for school.

NONA: It doesn't have to be fancy, but maybe it should just sound more like the other words so you're not using two different voices. What other words say the idea of "go to pot"? What is happening to the relationship?

20 CASEY: It goes downhill. Well, that sounds like talking too.

NONA: Does it seem more or less formal than "go to pot"?

CASEY: More formal I guess.

NONA: It may not be as formal as you want, but write it down anyway and keep going. See if you can add some more.

25 CASEY: "Gets worse."

NONA: How can you make that into a single word, a verb I mean?

CASEY: Oh. You mean "worsens"?

NONA: Good. Any synonyms for "worsens"?

CASEY: Um, oh. "Deteriorates." That sounds good.

30 NONA: "Worsens" and "deteriorates" are both good. Is there any particular reason that made you like "deteriorates" better?

CASEY: Oh, I dunno. It's longer, I guess, so it sounds classier.

NONA: OK, but think about the differences in meaning, too, because length isn't always what tells you which one you want. When you think of "deteriorate,"
35   what do you picture? And what do you picture with "worsen"?

CASEY: I guess "worsen" is like a disease, but that's about all I can think of. And "deteriorates" is, like, well, slow and bit by bit, like what happens to buildings, you know? So maybe that's a reason to use it. The marriage doesn't just blow up, bang. It falls apart slowly.

Since Casey does not hear the register shift, Nona awakens him to it by having him rephrase the first part of the sentence colloquially. Her question, "Who does this sound like?" helps him see the need for consistency. Finally, Nona asks him to generate some more verbs and to think about their specific connotations so that he makes a considered choice. Nona's attempt to help Casey understand that different registers are appropriate for different occasions is good, although she might have pursued the issue by asking him why he wants to use a different register "for school." However, what she has implicitly and correctly acknowledged is that writers need to be able to express themselves with varying degrees of formality and that inexperienced writers require practice in using words more formal than those they habitually use in speaking (see also Chapter 10). Some unevenness of register may still result: sometimes writers will use language that is *too* high-toned or technical for the occasion or for the rest of the essay's register. While it might seem natural to ask, in such cases, "How would you say this if you were talking to a friend?" that question is more useful for helping writers to unscramble syntax (see Chapter 8) than for eliciting words in a lower but still formal register. Questions like "Say it in your own voice" or "How would you say this if talking to a friend?" call for the kind of colloquial vocabulary that is insufficiently formal for the writer's purpose. "What's another word for this?" or "What's another way of saying this?" are preferable because they encourage writers to use words from registers other than their informal speaking vocabularies. Once the writer has generated more words, their connotations and level of formality can be compared, as Casey considers "worsens" and "deteriorates" in the dialogue.

Using a thesaurus judiciously

If he had not been able to think of other verbs besides "worsens," Casey and Nona might have turned to a thesaurus, but the danger of suggesting this step to inexperienced writers is that they are likely to be unaware of the connotations and contexts for the formal words listed. A thesaurus can be helpful, however, if you explore the listed words with the writers and if together you write sentences that use each one in a context so that writers can begin to infer connotative and contextual distinctions.

Using "Who does what" for precision

Some inconsistencies in tone also reflect the problem of imprecision. In our earlier example, "Hobbes's pessimistic view of man really threw me," what does "threw me" mean? Is the writer surprised, puzzled, or disturbed? These and other vague word choices, including pronouns, can be amended if tutors ask versions of "who does what?" (first suggested in Chapter 8 as a way of correcting syntactical difficulties). Let us say a tutor, Gavin, asks Ada, the author of the sentence above, "What did you mean by 'threw me'? What did Hobbes' idea *do*? What effect did it have on you?" Ada might say, "It made me feel upset to think of man that way.'' Gavin could respond, ''OK, what did Hobbes' view *do,* then?'' Ada would probably say, ''It upset me.'' She could then adopt this verb, which is somewhat more precise and more in keeping with the register of the rest of the essay. Since the sentence does not reveal what, specifically, about Hobbes' view ''upset'' her, Gavin could then ask so that she would clarify further and expand her sentence.

''Who does what?'' is also useful when writers use words incorrectly. In the example below, a writer, Eric, has confused ''infer'' with ''imply'' in the sentence, ''In his essay about the morality of crowds, Le Bon infers that crowd members do not exercise independent judgment.'' Ilana, Eric's tutor, writes the following sample sentences to prepare a ''Who does what?'' exercise:

> In saying that intelligence is inherited, the writer implies that education has little to do with it.
>
> We can infer from the writer's statement on heritability of intelligence that education has little to do with it.

ILANA: In the first sentence, who is performing the action?

ERIC: The writer.

ILANA: And what is he doing?

ERIC: He is hinting at something he doesn't say directly.

5 ILANA: Good. How about the actor in the second sentence?

ERIC: It's the reader, and he's drawing a conclusion.

ILANA: Good. So that's a big difference. Now compare the actors: who hints and who draws conclusions?

ERIC: The writer ''hints'' and the reader draws conclusions, so ''imply'' is ''hint''
10 and that's what the writer does.

ILANA: How about writing that distinction down?

ERIC: *[writes]*:

> Imply: writer hints.
> Infer: reader draws conclusions.

15 ILANA: That's a good way to remember the difference. Now let's get back to your sentence. Who is Le Bon and what is he doing?

ERIC: He's the writer, so he's hinting. That means it should be ''imply.'' I got it now.

ILANA: Good. We have stated the distinction between ''infer'' and ''imply'' in
20 the writer-to-reader relationship. How about a speaker to a listener?

ERIC: I guess the speaker would be like the writer.

ILANA: Great. I think you understand it now.

Finally, ''Who does what?'' can help writers eliminate jargon. The question asks writers to name the actors and actions that are often missing from sentences containing nominalizations, as in this example, written by a student teacher who is reporting to her supervisor on one of her students: ''Education-wise, maximization of effort on arithmetic skills of computation are performance prerequisites for realizing potential.'' If the major action is ''maximize effort,'' that is, ''work hard on,'' who must do so, the student or the teacher? And what, exactly, must one or the other do? The answers to these and similar ''Who does what?'' questions would certainly clarify the writer's intended meaning.

Making Work on Spelling and Vocabulary a Steady, Integrated Activity

If writers are to improve spelling and vocabulary, they must follow the advice given by the Broadway magazine vendor to the Texas farm boy who had just arrived in Manhattan. ''How do ya get to Carnegie Hall?'' asked the Texan, looking about in confusion. Shaking his finger knowingly, the old man said, ''Practice, practice, practice.'' There is no other way. Like the Texan, however, most inexperienced writers do not dream of becoming virtuosos, so they need not spend four or five hours daily limbering their ''fingers.'' Some steady practice on spelling and vocabulary is necessary, nevertheless, for them to attain a moderate degree of accuracy and flexibility. A tutor who sees a writer regularly could devote a few minutes of each session to spelling and vocabulary; less frequent meetings still afford opportunities for recommending specific activities that writers can engage in independently. In either case, the vocabulary and spelling work should be connected to rather than separate from the reading or composition issue with which a particular writer is centrally concerned, be it the interpretation of a text or the revision of an essay.

Summary

Spelling and vocabulary problems arise chiefly from insufficient exposure to the written word. Writers misspell words because of the unpredictability of English spelling, because they have no visual memory of words, because they pronounce words differently from the sounds indicated by standard spelling, and because they are unfamiliar with word structure. You can encourage writers to concentrate on spelling by helping them locate patterns of error in their writing, a strategy that makes problems seem manageable. You can also introduce phonic and syllabic principles and help writers discover spelling rules inductively. Both of these strategies help writers understand the rationale of English orthography. If you alert them to differences between standard and their own pronunciations, they will be likely to anticipate and avoid error. Judicious dictionary use, mnemonic devices, and proofreading improve spelling as well.

People who read little are unfamiliar with the formal or technical vocabularies used in colleges and workplaces. When these readers approach texts, they are frustrated by the forbidding language and lack appropriate strategies for decoding it. As writers, infrequent readers attempting to sound authoritative may adopt inappropriate registers. They may also get lexical forms wrong and may misuse words. Novice writers use general verbs, inprecise phrases, jargons, and sexist language. Eradicating these problems is a slow process that you can abet with complementary work on reading and writing vocabulary.

As they read texts, writers should, in some instances, consult dictionaries or glossaries as a first step, but more often they should try to discover meaning from contexts and word structure before consulting a dictionary. To promote retention, you can suggest that writers keep vocabulary notebooks in which they write definitions and sentences that use the new words. To help writers use appropriate vocabulary, you can offer various kinds of substitution exercises. You can ask, "Who does this sound like?" to adjust register and "Who does what?" to promote precision and discourage jargon. You can explore with writers the connotations of words listed in thesauruses. A combination of these strategies should help writers expand and refine their reading and writing vocabularies.

SUGGESTIONS FOR JOURNAL ENTRIES

1. What steps do you take to monitor your own spelling? Has your spelling improved over the years? If you have observed any improvement, what accounts for it? Could any of the methods that you use to avoid spelling errors help writers whom you tutor?

2. How did your writing vocabulary develop? To what extent did you consciously try to expand it? What role did reading play in the development of your writing vocabulary? What other factors were influential?

3. What makes you remember the look and the meaning of words?

4. How conscious are you, as a writer, of using various registers for different writing purposes? Are you always comfortable in the registers you choose? Do you tend to mix registers on some occasions?

5. How do you react to jargon when you hear it? Does it impress you, offend you, amuse you? Do you ever use it? Why, if so?

6. Describe the spelling and vocabulary problems of writers with whom you are working. How are they similar to or different from those described in this chapter? From your own? What strategies seem most successful?

SUGGESTIONS FOR FURTHER WRITING

1. Identify the form and probable source of the errors present in the sentences below: Are they spelling or vocabulary errors, or could they be either kind of error? Why might each writer have erred?

    a. Reading this book enhanced me.

    b. Students with motivating difficulty do not see the good of education.

    c. Advancment in the business world is now possible for women.

    d. When I was twelve, this incident hapen to me.

    e. Conventionable weapons should be in place of A bombs.

    f. He did not know weather to tell his wife.

    g. He always asks about things before he tries it.

    h. Liveing conditions are poor here.

    i. The house was more quieter with the children gone.

    j. Religious background gives this sort of attitude.

    k. In this book, *The Right Stuff,* the author, Tom Wolfe extolls the guys who were the test pilots as the real heroes.

    l. When a person tells a lie to their friends, they feel guilty.

m. He went to the meeting regardless to the warning he got in the mail.

n. In the Faulkner story, he says that Joe Christmas knew he was a domed man but tried to ecscape anyway. This is what caused sympathy for him.

o. This author's lectioneering style gets in his way.

2. What strategies would you use to help each of the writers of the sentences above? Please explain your choices.

3. Here is an excerpt from an essay prepared for a "developmental" composition course in which the writer describes his job as an assistant in a center for brain-damaged children. Write a brief analysis of the excerpt's strengths and weaknesses. Speculate about the probable causes for the writer's spelling and vocabulary problems, making sure that you distinguish one from the other type. Then write a dialogue between yourself and the writer in which you try to help him. Finally, explain the rationale for your strategies and for the sequence in which you use them.

He over came his flustration as soon as he begun to see the children as indivual rather then rellating them to the norm. It did not matter much that they would not be normal on day. He seen a love in these children he hadnt seen befor in normal people. The children would always greet him with a warm hug. They showed aprecation for Chris' help with wide happy smiles. They did not refrane from showing afection or aprecation becuase some one was not goodlooking or charming. There love was unconditional, not limited to a person's exteror. They did not have to be friends with you befor they give you an afectionate hug.

4. Here is an excerpt written by another student in the same course as the writer in exercise 3. Please follow the directions provided in that exercise to complete this one.

In these three short stories, "Life Behind Bars" by Vladimir Bukovsky, "The Extraction" by Maya Angelou and "Letter to a Robber" all shared something in common and by Lois Gould the word I choose was defiance bold resistance to an opposing force or authority. Not a means of violence but in a nonviolent manner as Bukivsky did using his mind and a pen to upset the goverment and saying what he felt no matter what the outcome might have been. Lois Gould showed her defiance by writting a letter to the robber telling him of the fright he put in her and the children. hoping one day he might read the story. Maya Angelou showed her defiance when she went back into the dentist office to set him straight about his ugly words and discriminative actions in front of her grand daughter. She at time had saved him from going under and thats the thanks he gives her.

5. The following excerpt was written by a college junior in a natural science course. The essay, entitled "The Law of the Sea: Development of a Dilema" (sic), traces the history of the law and examines the Third World position on it. What follows is the first paragraph of the essay. Please analyze the spelling and vocabulary problems, speculate on their sources, and write a dialogue between yourself and the writer in which you address his problems. Then explain the rationale for your strategies and for the sequence in which you use them.

Richard Darman, Vice Chairman of the U.S. Delegation to the 1977 session of the Third United Nations Law of the Sea Conference, contends, in an atricle in *Foreign Affairs,* that the current impasse in those nogotiations is the result of "excessive artificial polerization between developed and developing countries." In his view, third world extreamists would welcome the opportunity to condemn economic imperialism that violates the common heritage of mankind. The U.S. position represents a moderant course. He concludes that if sympathetic third world opinion can be extracted from the obstructionist influence of the extreamist hy-jackers, progress will follow on the substantive issues before the commission. His assesment is constructive, but is it really veracious?

SUGGESTION FOR CLASS ACTIVITIES

1. Discuss with classmates your responses to the exercises in "Suggestions for Further Writing."

2. Bring to class copies of essays written by people with whom you are working, essays that contain spelling and/or vocabulary problems. Lead a discussion in which classmates analyze the patterns of error and consider strategies for working with the writers.

3. Having completed the discussion suggested in exercise 2, try out the strategies in a role-playing exercise. Since you are acquainted with the actual writer, you will probably be the best candidate to play the role of writer.

4. Discuss with classmates your own experiences in learning how to spell or to expand your vocabularies. Describe the kinds of activities that helped you and those that did not.

SUGGESTIONS FOR FURTHER READING

Bartholomae, David. "The Study of Error." *College Composition and Communication* 31 (1980): 253–269.

Blair, T. R. "Spelling and Word Attack Skills." *The Reading Teacher* 28 (1975): 604–607.

Brengelman, Frederick H. "Dialect and the Teaching of Spelling." *Research in the Teaching of English* 4 (1970): 129–138.

Brown, James I. *Efficient Reading.* Revised Form A. Lexington, MA: D. C. Heath, 1976.

———, and Thomas E. Pearsall. *Better Spelling.* 3rd ed. Lexington MA: D. C. Heath, 1985.

Buch, Jean L. "A New Look at Teaching Spelling." *College English* 38 (1977): 703–706.

Glazier, Teresa Ferster. *The Least You Should Know about Vocabulary Building.* New York: Holt, 1981.

Hanna, Paul R., et al. *Phoneme Grapheme Correspondences as Cues to Spelling Improvement.* Washington, DC: U.S. Dept. of Health, Education and Welfare, 1966.

———. *Spelling: Structure and Strategies.* Boston: Houghton, Mifflin, 1971.

Hartwell, Laurence, with Robert Bentley. *Open to Language.* New York: Oxford University Press, 1982.

Horn, Thomas D., Ed. *Research on Handwriting and Spelling.* Urbana, IL: NCTE, 1966.

Laurence, Patricia. "Error's Endless Train: Why Student's Don't Perceive Errors." *Journal of Basic Writing* 1 (1975): 23–43.

Mazurkiewicz, Albert J. *Teaching about Phonics.* New York: St. Martin's, 1976.

Nilsen, Alleen Pace. "Winning the Great *He/She* Battle." *College English* 46 (1984): 151–157.

Petty, Walter T., Curtis P. Herold, and Easline Stoll. *Vocabulary: The State of Knowledge about the Teaching of Vocabulary.* Urbana, IL: NCTE, 1968.

Shaughnessy, Mina P. *Errors and Expectations.* New York: Oxford University Press, 1977. Chapter 6.

Simons, Herbert D., and Kenneth R. Johnson. "Black English Syntax and Reading Interference." *Research in the Teaching of English* 8 (1974): 339–358.

Sklar, Elizabeth S. "Sexist Grammar Revisited." *College English* 45 (1983): 348–358.

Sloan, Gary. "The Subversive Effects of an Oral Culture on Student Writing." *College Composition and Communication* 30 (1979): 156–160.

Westfall, Alfred. "Can College Students Expand Their Recognition Vocabularies?" *School and Society* (January 1951): 25–28.

Wiener, Harvey S. *The Writing Room: A Resource Book for Teachers of English.* New York: Oxford University Press, 1981.

Williams, Joseph. *Style: Ten Lessons in Clarity and Grace.* Glenview, IL: Scott, Foresman, 1981.

Zuckerman, Marvin S. *Words Words Words: An English Vocabulary Builder and Anthology.* Beverly Hills, CA: Glencoe Press, 1974.

PART SIX

Tutors and Technology

14

Tutoring with Computers

While you have been reading this book, have computer assisted instruction (CAI) and word processing been putting writing teachers and tutors, bit by bit, out of business? Not as much as some software advertisements proclaim. In reality, tutors and CAI offer writers some of the same *kinds*—though not degree and quality—of help. Both afford individualized instruction and efficient use of writers' time, offering information, practice, or text analysis when a writer actually needs and can immediately use it. Both can encourage writers to generate ideas fluently without worrying prematurely about correctness. Both can provide pattern analysis of teachers' comments, of stylistic features, and of errors. Tutorial dialogue can render CAI and word-processing programs more useful to writers, and computers can further tutorial dialogue in virtually all aspects of composing: inventing and shaping ideas, encouraging correctness, and even analyzing reading materials. In contrast to CAI, word processing makes no claims to teach composition; however, it certainly enables most writers to apply composition instruction much more easily. Once you understand the theories and techniques presented in earlier chapters of this book, you are very well equipped both to use the powers and to compensate for the limitations of CAI and of word processing. This chapter has room to present only a few tutorial strategies for using computers. The rest depends on your understanding and ingenuity!

This chapter will not review CAI or word-processing software, although it will discuss a few programs as examples. If you have opportunities to help your writing centers evaluate software, you can consult the reviews that abound in general magazines (such as *Byte* and *Popular Computing*), in those devoted to specific hardware (such as *PC World* for the IBM Personal Computer), and in the *Journal of Educational Technology Systems*. Detailed descriptions of specific CAI programs are presented in *The Computer in Composition Instruction: A Writer's Tool*, edited by William Wresch. Readers interested in artificial intelligence (AI) and natural language processing (NLP) may consult *Artificial Intelligence*, the *Ameri-*

can *Journal of Computational Linguistics,* Roger Schank's *Scripts, Plans, Goals, and Understanding* and *Dynamic Memory: A Theory of Learning in Computers and People,* and Terry Winograd's *Language as a Cognitive Process.* After discussing some ways in which you can encourage writers to use computers, this chapter will present tutorial strategies for using five classes of programs: for invention, for organization, for grammar and mechanics drills, for text editing (including stylistic analysis), and for word processing.

Introducing Writers to Computers

Somewhere between the neo-Luddites, who fear that computers will dehumanize learning, and the Atari generation of computer enthusiasts stand the majority of people who increasingly rely on computers for word processing and, less frequently, for text editing. Many universities now include a personal computer in the tuition for every new student. Writing programs in all kinds of schools and colleges more and more commonly are using word processing. Publishers are producing texts such as *Interactive Writing: Composing with a Word Processor* by Helen J. Schwartz, Professor of English at Oakland University (Michigan). *English Microlab* by Arthur H. Bell and Sharon R. Anderson (Boston: Houghton, Mifflin, 1985) pairs a text with a disk. Understandably, many writers (and teachers) feel as the earliest amphibians must have felt: however much they want to scuttle back to comfortable waters, they know the future is on land—with computers. In several ways, you can help them feel comfortable with using computers.

Typing ability is often the key to who uses computers and how. Most CAI requires little typing skill. Since users control the pace with which they proceed from frame to frame, nontypists have time to hunt and peck. Word-processing programs, however, are largely if not completely wasted on nontypists, because they have to do too many different things at once: locating the keys and remembering a quasi-mnemonic vocabulary of commands distract them from thinking of what to say. Even skilled typists may feel computer-shy, worried that they might somehow damage the machine or lose their files. You can help these writers devise compromises with technology. For example, nontypists or writers who feel hesitant about composing directly on the computer may sneak up on word processing: they can write drafts longhand, then copy them into the computer and make whatever changes they want; they can then print a copy and write revisions on it longhand, then enter those changes into their files and print again (Bean). To initiates, such a process might seem like stirring one's coffee with a Cuisinart. But novices soon discover that the ease of making conceptual revisions and editorial changes without laborious recopying generously rewards their initial investment of time and energy in learning word processing. We hope, of course, that very soon most high-school students will elect typing courses as eagerly as they take driver's education; it is sad to see aspiring computer science or management majors laboriously entering their programs and papers by the Columbus method (find a key and land on it), holding up lines of fellow students anxious to use a terminal, and eventually changing to other majors because they simply cannot handle the keyboard efficiently enough. Meanwhile, tutors will find their ingenuity in encouraging writers to approach computers amply rewarded.

Although poor typing may interfere with people's willingness to use computers, most tutors find word processing especially helpful to writers with physical disabilities. For instance, programmed function keys or the keyboard "macros" can modify commands so that users need not hold down the control key while pressing the command key; they can then operate the keyboard with one hand, a straw, or a headstick. They may use keyboard guards that allow only one key to be struck at a time. (You will want to consult the vendors of your school's hardware periodically to find out what new aids are available.) Writers with hearing and/or speech impairments can "converse" via electronic networks. Voice recognition and speech synthesis systems now being developed (which will enable computers both to "hear" the writer's voice and to "read aloud" what she has composed) will soon enable writers with visual impairments to dictate, listen to, and revise their papers through computers. Similarly, those who read via tape recordings (or who have other people read aloud to them) will be able to dictate reading notes into the computer, which can then read them back aloud. Although few tutors will want to—or should—become typists for all of their tutees, under special circumstances you may enter text and execute whatever revisions the writers suggest. The relative speed with which these writers can then produce drafts, discuss them with you, and revise will significantly improve their writing.

Besides typing skill, other factors influence writers' willingness to use computers in their writing classes. Novelty may initially make computers more amusing to use than books, pencils, and legal pads, but the overly hearty tone that some CAI employs soon irks writers. For instance, if in response to an invention program's request, "Please type in your topic," John types in "The herring economy in medieval Denmark," then the computer may chuckle, "Well, John, the herring economy in medieval Denmark is a very interesting topic! You and I will have fun working on it!" John may smile. But if this is the tenth impossibly boring assignment the computer chuckles over as it asks, "Now please type in some information about the herring economy," John may type in, "I'll show you what's interesting. How would you like a herring in your disk drive?" When the computer answers, "I'm not sure I understand you. Please try again," John may resort to obscenities, evoking the computer's relentlessly polite "Please try again." As novelty fades, so may John's productive use of invention software. If tutors can select a similarly designed but less chummy program, the problem can be avoided. If not, they can point out to annoyed writers that at least the program designer was *trying* to make CAI humane, "user-friendly." Sitting together at the computer screen, a tutor and a writer may even collaborate in composing insults for the program; once they both let off steam, the tutor can make sure that the writer responds to the program's question. With practice, most writers can learn to ignore tone and provide the responses requested. The lesson that tone can affect a reader's response in ways a writer does not intend is, of course, useful for the writer's own papers. For most writers, CAI eventually turns out not to be a barrel of laughs—but neither are the workbook, the legal pad, and the old Olivetti.

Some writers may resent CAI and word processing because they seem impersonal. In many colleges and workplaces, no one else knows a writer as well as the writing teacher and tutor do. So, if they suggest that the writers use computers, the writers may feel even more isolated, as if their only friends have exiled them; referrals to the computer lab must be made with extra sensitivity and diplomacy (see Chapter 1). In the lab, you can sit at a distance, without hovering over writers at the terminals, for relative and temporary isolation can afford benefits to writers. For instance, the impersonality of CAI drill and editing programs may be good, in that writers need not fear making mistakes or looking "dumb" to an even dumber terminal. Likewise, the anonymity and ephemerality of word processing, which accepts any wild or intimate idea the writer wants to try out and allows for instantaneous erasure, can encourage risk taking, imaginative flights of speculation, and experimentation with absurd-seeming lines of analysis or argument. Thus, it can promote "thinking out loud" electronically. Composing at the computer is like whispering into a psychotherapist's ear what one fears to say aloud (Schwartz, "Teaching Writing with Computer Aids," 245). As rewarding as this means of prolonging and enriching the generative stages of composition may be, eventually real communication demands a live partner. An obvious antidote for impersonality is the tutorial conference.

Helping Writers Use Invention Programs

Invention programs, which are intended to help writers generate ideas, raise the most perplexing technological, philosophical, and pedagogical questions in CAI today, questions you should know something about before you encounter particular programs. At the present time, invention programs are understandably the most limited of all CAI used in writing instruction. The things that computers do best—make binary decisions, seek and match patterns (or "strings"), and whiz through the most complex algorithms in microseconds—are seldom involved in invention. Invention and analysis are not algorithmic; they depend on branching as intricate as the human mind. As the dialogues in this book illustrate, you must be ready to choose from an enormous array of alternative questions a "next question" that responds to an equally enormous range of statements writers may make within any given writing assignment and context. The permutations and combinations of questions in a tutorial dialogue are virtually endless. Although computers are capable of making thousands of branching decisions per second, the nature of each decision depends on the several ways in which the program designer imagines the writer may respond. Most designers of invention programs concede their limitations, and we can sympathize when we consider the immense difficulty of predicting writers' questions and responses. Current research in artificial intelligence, especially in computers' ability to "learn" by remembering patterns of user responses instead of relying entirely on what a programmer "tells" them, is making astonishing advances. For instance, once a computer is told the rules and strategies of chess, it can figure out the zillion possible sequences of moves; its "learning" ability enables it to recall all the moves made by a particular chess player, to figure out which are her favorite strategies, to predict which move she will probably make next, and—by sorting through its zillion alternative defenses in a microsecond—thwart her! Yet, chess, with its paltry sixty-four squares, thirty-two pieces of six kinds, each kind having its own set of moves, and two colors, is algorithmic, hence predictable. Chess is *easy,* compared to the variety of moves and strategies with which writers and tutors can approach most writing assignments.

Recognizing that because many situations are at least stereotypical, if not algorithmic, the kinds of questions one could ask about them are highly predictable, Yale University's Roger Schank and his colleagues in artificial intelligence research are working on programs that use "scripts." These are sets of content-specific questions that could be applied to particular domains of knowledge, domains about which a computer could be highly informed. Of course, scripts are much easier to program for CAI in, say, electronic wiring diagrams, where the vocabulary and information are very limited and the user's responses are of the "yes/no" variety, than for a writing assignment like "describe your neighborhood," much less "waste-water pollution in the San Joaquin Valley." Nevertheless, some composition researchers are exploring the use of scripts to promote invention; they hope to design CAI programs that ask topic-specific and assignment-specific sequences of questions following the "methods of proof" used in various disciplines (Bridwell and Ross, 116).

These absorbing technological questions should not distract those committed to liberal education from an equally challenging philosophical question: even if advancements in artificial intelligence and the use of scripts *could* enable invention programs to ask writers questions, *should* they? If the goal of liberal education is to cultivate a community capable of analytical thinking and critical synthesis of ideas, to what extent are scripts that ask all the questions desirable? When might technology begin to undermine the independent, critical abilities on which humane society depends? In the twentieth century, experience is often seen as a game. Philosophers analyze logic, mathematics, and language as games, with applications in marketing, collective bargaining, and war. People "play politics" and the "dating game," refer to their occupations as games ("the ad game"), and sigh in disappointment, "It's all in the game." To the extent that their domains are limited and their information is given by the program designer, scripts treat experience as a game: rules supplant "truth," validity supplants "meaning," shrewdness supplants "morality," and players' ability to "be cool" conceals their inner thoughts or feelings, as MIT philosopher Justin Leiber has argued. Developers of invention "scripts" proclaim that writers will gradually internalize the questioning processes of the various disciplines, and we hope they are right. However, we know physics students who say, "I can do the calculations, but I can't do word problems." Of course, *all* problems are word problems, that is, all problem solving entails figuring out conceptual relationships and relative values: How Does Who Do What and Why? Merely calculating one's way through a formula—or script—someone else has figured out is not analytical problem solving, but only number crunching, or idea crunching. However you might yearn, at four o'clock on winter afternoons after hours of helping writers generate ideas on "Describe your neighborhood," for scripts to lessen the costs in time and personal energy that such tutorial dialogues demand, you might do well to remember that the social, intellectual, and spiritual costs of scripts could be much greater.

Invention programs now available are much more rudimentary than the "scripts" being researched and developed. Some early programs developed by Major Hugh Burns at the Human Resources Laboratory of Lowry Air Force Base ask some of the same questions we have presented in Chapters 3 and 4: TOPOI uses Aristotle's classic questions of invention; BURKE uses Kenneth Burke's five-part grammar of invention [name, agent, agency (means), scene (background), purpose]; and TAGI uses Young, Becker, and Pike's tagmemic particle / wave / field matrix. A typical program might begin by asking writers to answer questions like "Why did you select this topic?" or "What is the audience of your paper?" Some programs ask further questions such as, "What ideas does your audience share with you about your topic?" or "What do you know about your topic that your audience does not know?" to help writers to elaborate their initial responses somewhat. Very soon, however, most programs' questions become extremely general: "Tell me more about . . ." or "That's the idea! Any more info?"

Tutors helping writers to use invention programs like these face an immediate problem: the unpredictability of writers' responses forces the programs' questions to become more and more general, whereas tutorial dialogue responds more and more specifically to the writer's statements (not to mention gestures and tones of voice). As the programs' questions become less focused, so will most writers' responses. You can suggest that writers bring printed copies of their answers to tutorial conferences, where together you can treat the copies as pieces of freewriting, glossing them longhand, adding further elaborations, asking further questions, and so on. You can also sit beside writers at the computer and ask questions that will help them elaborate their answers. Once writers see that they do in fact have some ideas about the topic, tutorial dialogue can proceed in ways we have discussed in other chapters.

SEEN, developed more recently by Helen J. Schwartz, asks questions that are more content-specific and assignment-specific than Major Burns' programs. For instance, SEEN asks the writer to state a hypothesis (such as "Don Quixote is an eccentric") and then to type in answers to general questions that, Schwartz claims, test the hypothesis (such as "What does Don Quixote say that proves he is an eccentric," "What does Don Quixote do that proves . . . ," "What do other characters say about Don Quixote that proves . . . ," and so forth). Sitting alone at the computer screen and answering the questions in private, without risking other people's judgments or interruptions, can have a very liberating effect. Nearly every designer of invention programs voices the same disclaimer that Schwartz makes about SEEN: the program

> does not and cannot judge the student's answers to these individualized form questions. However, it prompts the student to explore his own ideas and manages the questioning for him. With repeated use the student almost effortlessly internalizes the questions and can then leave this computer aid behind.
>
> ("Teaching Writing with Computer Aids," 240)

If you use programs like SEEN, you can help writers generate quite a lot of preliminary material for use in subsequent writing and tutorial dialogue. One danger, though, is that writers may merely print their responses to the invention questions and assume mistakenly that their papers are "finished." In other words, they may stop short of shaping what they have invented, and consequently they may not form concepts (see Chapter 6). You need to help SEEN's users deepen their understanding of "hypothesis" and of predication, since SEEN's hypotheses (for instance, that "Picasso's *Guernica* is an example of modernism" or that "Dreiser's settings are dreary") are in fact so obvious that no reasonable, well-informed person would disagree with them, and therefore no paper need be written. Once writers have generated plenty of information, you can ask, "How does who do what and why?" or can use some of the sentence-paradigms represented in Chapter 6 to help them establish predication. Tutors can also draw writers' attention to the *nature* of the questions asked, helping them to realize that questions like, "What does a character *say* that shows . . . ?" "What does a character *do* that shows . . . ?" and "What do *other characters say* about this character that shows . . . ?" are standard questions of literary analysis. By showing them some standard critical questions, you can help writers internalize the analytical process (see Chapters 11 and 12).

Foreseeing that writers working alone with SEEN might unknowingly enter incorrect information, might neglect subsequent analysis of information, and might not establish predication, Helen Schwartz uses an electronic network to enable writers to "converse" about their responses to the questions SEEN asks. Thus, her system helps writers not only to invent but also to shape their ideas. Electronic networks are, of course, available on any mainframe computer and increasingly for microcomputers; they need not be used with any particular invention program, because writers can "read" each other's drafts, questions, and comments written into the computer via word-processing programs. It is not SEEN's invention questions, but the conversation about them, be it in class or over the network or in tutorial conference, that actually accomplishes both the formulation and testing of real hypotheses. PAPERCHASE, a similar program for use by teachers, is now being developed by Dolores M. Burton at Boston University; it will help teachers to record and detect patterns in the comments they write on their students' successive drafts and papers and to plan conferences accordingly. If you use electronic networks, you can conduct a "conference" shared by a writer, his teacher, and perhaps his classmates, and can write messages asking the teacher for advice about assignments or comments. Networks also minimize the logistical problems of making tutorial appointments and finding meeting places. You can respond via networks to more writers at more stages of their drafts. In your person-to-person tutorial conferences, you can assess the extent to which writers are learning to ask themselves the analytical questions and form predications, so that eventually they can generate ideas without the aid of computer programs. We hope that reading Chapters 1 and 2 will help your balance computerized efficiency with personal attention and direct communication.

Helping Writers Use Computers to Shape Their Papers

Conversing via electronic networks can go a long way toward helping writers shape and revise their drafts. In addition, you can use an outline-making program with word-processing capabilities, like THINKTANK or MAXTHINK as well as certain functions of WRITER'S WORKBENCH and APPLEWRITER II, for these purposes. With computer graphic programs, writers can draw maps, diagrams, and matrices on the screen, but they can draw them more easily with paper and pencil. Although word-processing programs accept text in any form, they perform the visual manipulations of outlining quite inefficiently. That's why THINK-TANK, the first of its kind, was invented.

THINKTANK neither asks questions (as invention programs do) nor teaches writers how to outline; it is basically an electronic "storyboard." (As Chapter 4 explains, the "storyboard" is a movable outline; writers jot ideas on slips of paper and then move the slips around in various orders and patterns of subordination.) THINKTANK offers writers three main ways to manipulate text visually: indenting, hiding, and displaying. Its five levels of indentation (*not* laboriously numbered "I.A.1.a.(1)") allow writers either to indent while listing or to list first and indent later. With a few keystrokes, a writer can demote a single line from an important level to a subordinate level under a different heading, and vice versa. Groups of lines can be moved too, and ideas can be inserted or deleted at any time. The shape of a THINKTANK outline remains nearly as protean as the writer's thought processes.

THINKTANK's hide/display functions enable writers to see on the screen all the levels of an outline or to zero in on selected levels or sections. To view the main points, a writer can ask THINKTANK to display only the top (left side) one or two levels of indentation; to see what subordinate levels need further development, he can display only the fourth or fifth level of one small section. Under any heading, he can open a textfile and compose one or more paragraphs of development; then he can tell THINKTANK to hide (but save) these while he works on another section of the outline, later displaying or printing whatever parts of the outline and textfiles he chooses. The capacity of outline-making programs (sixteen pages for THINKTANK) is adequate for most college writing assignments, enabling writers to move recursively among several composing activities in one file: manipulating an outline, note-taking and freewriting in a textfile under particular headings, rearranging the outline and respective textfiles, later adding new headings, altering subordination, and so on. Of course, larger assignments can easily be divided among several THINKTANK files, which can later be merged or concatenated (strung together).

If you help writers to use THINKTANK, you will find the pencil-and-paper strategies of Chapters 3 and 4 useful. Very inexperienced writers might find THINKTANK's potential five-level intricacy intimidating; they might think, "I don't even have five things to say! How can I ever fill up the TANK?" If so, you could begin by talking over an assignment with them, pointing out that it probably does not call for five levels of analysis (and perhaps saying, "Just because a program *can* help you do something doesn't mean you *have* to do it."). You can help them do some preliminary listing, glossing, and mapping on paper. By the time visual clutter—the circles, arrows, cross-outs, and insertions that accumulate during the mapping process—begins to distract them, they will have enough ideas to make THINKTANK useful and approachable. As writers transfer ideas from the paper map to the computer screen, you can show them how glosses can become main headings and how items listed within each group can become subordinate points. Together you can experiment with alternative ways of restructuring the multidirectional map into linear order. If you are helping more experienced writers, you can suggest they temporarily place the key words in an assignment or some important problem-solving questions in main headings; these they can elaborate in subheadings, restructure, logically connect, and eventually rephrase as main propositions for the emerging paper. You can urge writers to open textfiles under any heading to accept stints of freewriting; these can be printed and then glossed by hand, or glosses can be written on the screen. After this second, analytical phase of freewriting, parts of files can be moved to other headings or other levels of subordination. Writers can print all or part of an outline at any time, work on it at home, jot longhand notes or add new paragraphs, and bring it all back to another tutorial conference.

A few words of caution: Some software that may be available in a computer lab may teach skills that are not appropriate to your or a teacher's pedagogy; for instance, if a teacher treats outlining as a sophisticated conceptual operation comparable to drafting, problems can arise for you and writers in her class if they use simplified outlining software. Another kind of oversimplification results from the limits of the twenty-line screen, which can accommodate much less manipulation of an outline than can a storyboard made of cards and laid out on a table. Split screens and "windows," while they compensate in part, have their own limitations. If an outline (or other task) calls for more than one page on the screen, we recommend that writers and you print out your results periodically, instead of trying to do everything on the screen.

Other programs enable writers, in effect, to "x-ray" their drafts, to see the structure underlying the details. Such programs operate on a draft that a writer has already typed into the computer via word processing and saved. She can ask WRITER'S WORKBENCH to display on the screen (or print) only the first and last sentences of every paragraph; the display amounts to an abstract. Less dependent on location, programs like APPLEWRITER II can automatically search a draft either for whatever word she selects (a search that is infallibly thorough!) or for whatever sentence she marks with special symbols as she reads the draft herself on the screen. The program then displays only the marked sentences or those containing the key word. Like THINKTANK's ability to hide details and display only selected headings, these programs can help writers avoid losing sight of logical structure among details.

You can use such programs to help writers check periodically on the organization of their drafts in progress. For instance, writers who have been taught to begin every paragraph with a topic sentence can use the WRITER'S WORK-BENCH displays (or printouts) to discern and check their lines of reasoning; if they have learned to end a paragraph with a sentence linking it either to the following paragraph or to the essay's main idea, the display can help them check for either kind of linkage. You and the writers can then discuss ways of clarifying logical connections, inserting, deleting, or rearranging paragraphs in a more useful way, and improving linkages; they can make changes on the screen or write them on printed copy. Similarly, a writer could ask APPLEWRITER II to display all sentences containing the word "feminist" or all sentences she has marked because they express her opinions of affirmative action (whether or not the sentences actually use the words "affirmative action"). With you, she could examine the displays for functional and nonfunctional repetitions of words and concepts, could discuss which to delete, and could gather scattered but similar sentences, condense them, and find them a useful location. Although these operations of THINK-TANK, WRITER'S WORKBENCH, and APPLEWRITER II do not differ in *kind* from what tutors and writers can do with pencil, marking pens, and paper, their efficient performance of visual manipulations can save you and writers a lot of tedious paper shuffling during tutorial sessions.

Helping Writers Use Computerized Drills

A lot of early CAI for drill on particular grammar, spelling, and punctuation skills amounted to little more than successive screens of questions scarcely distinguishable from the pages of an ordinary textbook. Tests of one such program, PLATO, indicated that it "had no consistent impact on either attrition or achievement" (Wresch, "Computers in English Class," 485). PLATO (like many workbook exercises) wasted writers' time and energy because its exercises were not connected to writers' actual practices and processes (as Chapters 8–10 advocate). More recent drill programs are somewhat more effective to the extent that they are more interactive and individualized. Designed by experienced basic writing teachers, these programs include instructional modules (very specific, sequentially arranged explanations with accompanying exercises) to explain and offer practice in correcting the more commonly made mistakes. Like a sequence of questions a tutor devises for a dialogue, a good program on subject–verb agreement would include modules to give writers practice in doing the following: identifying the verb, identifying the subject, distinguishing singular from plural verb and noun forms, and completing several exercises in choosing a verb that agrees in number with the subject. One such exercise might look like this:

PLEASE TYPE IN THE SUBJECT AND CORRECT VERB FORM:

ALL THE FISHING POLES IN THE SPORTING GOODS STORE IS/ARE ON SALE.

If the writer types in "FISHING POLES ARE" or "POLES ARE," a good interactive drill program would give her one or two more similar sentences and then offer her the choice to stop practicing what she obviously understands. A good drill program also offers alternative modules in response to various wrong answers writers might give. For example, if the writer types in "STORE IS," an alternative module might ask what you would ask: "What is on sale?" and might then explain in grammatical terms the nature of the writer's error. If the writer types in "POLES IS" or "GOODS IS," a third module would ask "What is on sale?" and might offer the writer further practice in identifying singular and plural forms. This kind of branching is binary, a "yes/no," "right/wrong" response to syntax, rather than the more complex mixture of semantic and pragmatic responses tutors make in the dialogues throughout this book. To be sure, even such simple branching avoids compelling writers to practice what they already understand. To the extent that it individualizes the pace and focus of drill instruction, such CAI software is useful. Programmers who consult with experienced writing teachers and tutors can design programs that are quite responsive to the variety of erroneous hyotheses inexperienced writers are most likely to form and test. The better we understand writers' errors as "interlanguage" (see Chapter 10), the more responsive we will be able to make CAI drill programs. However, such sophistication— dependent as it is on the computer's ability to resolve syntactical, semantic, and pragmatic ambiguities, as well as to interpret figurative language—lies on the research frontier of AI and natural language processing.

What can you do now? Using strategies suggested in earlier chapters of this book, you can sit beside writers who have been told to use CAI drill programs and can also augment the programs' explanations. When a writer types in a "wrong" answer that the program designer has not foreseen, hence has not provided instructional modules for, you can identify, discuss, and modify the incorrect hypothesis underlying the writer's "error." You can reduce writers' frustration when programs reject perfectly satisfactory answers that the program designers have failed to foresee. (In a program, the designer lists all the "right" answers she thinks of; if the user's answer does not match one of these, the program rejects it as "wrong.") For instance, one grammar drill asking the user to correct the sentence, "The child forgot their books," accepts only one answer: "The child forgot his books." Even though the same program contains a section on sexist language, it accepts neither "her" nor "The children forgot their books." A spelling program now on the market teaches writers to "change final -y to -i and add -es," but then it accepts "flys" as a correct answer. These flaws in program design are very easy to correct (even an amateur programmer can modify the program's list of "right" answers). Until corrections are made, the inexperienced writers who are most often assigned to use drill programs will need your reassurance when their alternative answers are, indeed, correct. Without such reassurance, writers may begin to suspect that computers "cry wolf" and may consequently distrust the computers' correct information. The resulting skepticism and confusion may seriously impair whatever effectiveness drill programs do have. Most important, you can help writers find in their own writing sentences that resemble those in the drills; then together you can apply what was learned in drill as they write and revise their own sentences.

Because drill programs *seem* relatively easy to write, many programmers, unaided by experienced writing teachers, are flooding the market with seriously flawed CAI software, with documentation full of typographical errors, with programs that set poor examples for inexperienced writers by beginning sentences with lowercase letters and using jargon like "your first journal write." Since in some colleges and workplaces the administrators and committees who buy CAI are not necessarily those who will use it, most tutors can expect sooner or later to find themselves compensating for CAI's conceptual errors and simple misinformation.

If you know your programs, you can minimize the damage and maximize the value. Eventually, you may participate in choosing—and we hope even in designing—better programs.

Helping Writers Use Text-Editing Programs

Text-editing programs perform their particular functions with far greater sophistication than other kinds of CAI do theirs. Bell Laboratories developed the original version of WRITER'S WORKBENCH to promote the use of uniform stylistic standards in technical documents, such as the Naval Air Systems Command's burgeoning technical manuals for aircraft: "In 1950, the manuals for one aircraft contained fewer than 2,000 pages; today, the manuals for one aircraft contain nearly 300,000 pages," far beyond merely human editorial capacities (Lawrence T. Frase. "The UNIX TM Writer's Workbench Software: Philosophy." *Bell System Technical Journal* 62 (1983): 1184). More recently, several states have enacted "plain language" legislation, requiring that public documents (such as tax regulations or social services documents) and business documents (such as insurance policies) be written simply and clearly. The designers of text-editing programs, not surprisingly, define "good writing" in stylistic and editorial terms:

> There is surprising consensus about how to write well. Aside from the obvious rules such as: 1) write grammatically, 2) use correct spelling, and 3) avoid wordy diction, there is consensus on less objective standards as well. [Experts including Strunk and White] agree on many aspects of writing: 1) avoid the passive voice, 2) use short concrete words, and 3) use verbs rather than nominalizations. (Nina H. Macdonald. "The Writer's Workbench: Computer Aids for Text Analysis." *IEEE Transactions on Communications* 30 (1982), 105)

To promote this kind of "good writing," WRITER'S WORKBENCH includes thirty programs on such aspects of style and editing. If you have access to mainframe computers, you may use the original version of WRITER'S WORKBENCH or the even more powerful EPISTLE being developed by IBM. But more often you are likely to encounter smaller programs (requiring less memory) such as THE WORD PLUS, HOMER, WANDAH, and GRAMMATIK, and a few may use programs dedicated to particular functions, such as the University of Michigan's JOURNALISM, which both proofreads and checks the context of articles for whose subjects information has been provided to the computer. The challenge for you is to figure out effective ways of using sophisticated text analyses to help inexperienced writers in workplace and academic settings.

All these programs are used to help writers—be they technical writers, journalists, graduate students at the Harvard Business School, or the considerably less experienced writers with whom most tutors work—to make their writing readable, comprehensible, and unambiguous. These programs work by matching patterns at both word and sentence levels. At the word level, they match a writer's text with lists in the program's dictionaries and suggest substitutions for wordy expressions (such as "conclude" in place of "bring to a conclusion"), for sexist words, jargon, and "officialese" (such as "use" in place of "utilize"), for vague or abstract words (finding endings like -ment, -ance, -ence, and -ion that signal nominalizations). They can find most spelling errors but cannot yet cope with homonyms, wrong words created through typographical errors, or proper names (unless these have been especially added to the program's dictionary). At the sentence level, they find syntactical patterns (such as split infinitives, misuses of a and an, and forms of the verb to be) and some punctuation patterns (such as paired parentheses or quotation marks, periods followed by capital letters, commas and periods inside quotation marks, semicolons and colons outside, and so on). Unlike other text-editing programs, EPISTLE's natural language processor can parse sentences. Therefore, it can identify examples of the problems that most often perplex inexperienced writers: subject–verb agreement, wrong pronoun case, noun–modifier disagreement (such as, "these kind of berries"), nonstandard verb forms (such as, "He has too many wrinkle shirts."), and nonparallel structures (see G. E. Heidorn, et al. "The EPISTLE Text-Critiquing Systems." *IBM Systems Journal* 21 (1982): 305–326). We know of no text-editing system that can handle apostrophes, accidental repetitions ("the the"), faulty comparisons (which fail to name the thing being compared), position of certain modifiers (such as "only"), or questions of judgment (such as whether to use a colon or semicolon)—*yet*.

What happens when a text-editing program "reads" a paper? After the writer saves a draft in the computer's memory, the draft disappears from the screen. In microseconds the program "reads" the draft all the way through *without* stopping, and the screen immediately displays a statistical report. How many and which features are reported depends on the capacity of the program being used. WANDAH allows a writer to select up to five features from the menu of features it can analyze, whereas other programs simply report everything they can find out. Sophisticated programs like WRITER'S WORKBENCH report many features: the percentages of simple, complex, compound, and compound-complex sentences; of imperative, declarative, and interrogative sentences; of content and function words; of prepositions, adjectives, adverbs, nouns, pronouns, of verb types ("to be" verbs, auxiliaries, and infinitives) as percentages of total verbs, of coordinating and subordinating conjunctions, and of expletives. The display reports the number of whichever kinds of grammar, spelling, and punctuation errors it can find. Finally, it reports "abnormal" percentages (such as "too many passive verbs" or "too many simple sentences"), the desirable or "normal" percentages having been previously established for the program by analysis of high-quality documents in a particular field, be they aircraft manuals, legal briefs, or—in theory, at least—academic papers such as "A" chemistry reports and "A" essays on Chaucer.

At this point, if you are scanning the displayed or printed report, you can help writers decide how to use the report's statistical information most productively. In contrast to textbooks' general lessons, the statistical report is custom-tailored to the individual style of the writer whose draft the program has just "read." Nevertheless, as readers of our Chapter 7 already know, writers can become confused and discouraged when confronted with too many different problems at once. Using the strategies of that chapter, you can help writers decide which problems to work on immediately, which to postpone, and perhaps (when a report is extremely detailed) which to ignore. Some percentages (for instance, the ratio of verbs to adjectives) are more useful than others (say, the number of prepositions). You can also adjust your interpretations of statistics according to the individual writer's needs, as Chapter 2 suggests. For example, you might congratulate very inexperienced writers for writing a high percentage of simple sentences (an indication that fragments are under control) and might encourage them to start writing more compound sentences. On the other hand, you might help more experienced writers cultivate variety and rhythm by interspersing compound-complex sentences with quite short, simple sentences for occasional emphasis. By comparing statistical reports on several papers by one writer, you and writers can identify which grammatical and stylistic problems are gradually being eliminated and which are persisting and need attention in tutorial conferences. Statistical confirmation of your own and writers' observations can indicate how your collaborative efforts are progressing.

Once priorities have been established, text-editing programs can help writers use their reports, usually in one of two ways: by offering electronic flashcards (in computer parlance, "on-line stylistic analysis and reference information") and by highlighting certain features in the text that has been recalled to the screen. Suppose that one report says that the percentage of passive-voice verbs is higher than normal. The writer will recall his text to the screen in order to make the corrections. If he asks for an explanation of "passive voice," the screen (or its top portion, for programs using split screens, or "windows") displays a message resembling a page from a conventional grammar handbook. The message explains what "passive voice" means and why writers should avoid it; it also gives examples of changing passive to active voice and perhaps a few exercises. As is often the case, a writer may understand the exercises but still have trouble identifying the problem in his own sentences. If so, he can close the flashcard "window" and ask the program to highlight the passive-voice verbs in his draft.

At this stage, if you are sitting beside the writer, you can help by relating the flashcards' perforce general lessons to the more particular contexts in which writers are composing, and especially by discussing when to heed or ignore the program's suggested changes. (In compensating for errors in drill programs, you can repair program designers' factual errors and incomplete predictions of all the possible correct answers users might give; however, in helping writers make stylistic choices, you will more often be compensating for the fact that most text-editing programs now available are "normalized" for only a few rhetorical situations.) For instance, a political speech or a chemistry report might, for quite different reasons, necessitate using passive voice. Language that the program deems "sexist" might be unavoidable in certain gender-specific contexts, such as a paper about a players' strike in major league baseball. Moreover, normalized percentages for various kinds of writing *could* in theory encourage everyone to write in the same style, a result much more desirable in aircraft manuals than in less technical contexts. The normal percentages for "A" papers on Chaucer are, thank goodness, yet to be calculated.

Also at this stage, you can help writers resist becoming too dependent on the highlighting. In early stages of work on a particular problem, highlighting can reveal recurrent problems. (We know of no programs that can print the highlighting as it appears on the screen, although somewhere at this very moment a program designer is probably working on such printing. Meanwhile, you and writers can easily print the text and use colored marking pens to copy the highlighting from the screen to paper.) Instead of tracking down examples, you and writers can spend your tutorial conferences discussing and refining writers' hypotheses about grammar, spelling, punctuation, and style (please see Chapter 10 on patterns of error, error analysis, and "interlanguage"). But you may need to urge some writers gradually to wean themselves from highlighting, to raise consciousness of persistent problems, and to identify and correct them independently of the text-editing program. After one session of flashcards and highlighting for passive voice, you could then help a basic writer to check subsequent papers "by hand," thus taking a first step toward independent mastery. In contrast, more advanced writers who already know the rules can use text-editing programs to provide prompts for proofreading.

For both you and writers, the most problematic statistic reported by some text-editing programs is the "readability score." Scores are calculated by formulae whose variables usually include the number of letters or syllables per word, of words per line or sentence, and of sentences per paragraph (Lorinda Cherry. "Writing Tools." *IEEE Transactions on Communications* 30 (1982): 100–105). Some programs automatically report the score: READABILITY = fourteenth grade. For many reasons, E. D. Hirsch and other composition theorists have repudiated the use of readability scores in composition instruction. The scores per se tell writers very little, and higher scores are not necessarily desirable. A writer whose paper is scored at fourth-grade level—or at fourteenth-grade level—might be pleased or chagrined, depending on her writing experience and expectations and on the purposes and audiences of the paper. Because inexperienced writers might be particularly vulnerable to discouragement by low readability scores, you might wisely avoid programs that automatically report them. If the text-editing program you are using automatically "tells all" instead of allowing users to choose what information is reported, we suggest that you dim the monitor, print the statistical report, and cross out with a heavy marking pen the readability scores, as well as other statistics that the writer you are helping might might not be ready to use productively.

Richard Lanham, whose deservedly popular textbook *Revising Prose* is automated in HOMER, gives good advice to teachers and tutors: "A machine can *help* teach style, but only a teacher can decide when and how to use the machine" (Lanham, in Wresch, *The Computer in Composition Instruction,* 90). Use your knowledge and ingenuity!

Helping Writers Compose and Revise with Word Processing

Word processing is becoming nearly ubiquitous in composition instruction. Children in elementary school use easy-to-learn but very limited programs like BANK STREET WRITER to compose directly into the computer. High school and college students learn more powerful programs like APPLEWRITER, WORDSTAR, and FINAL WORD, along with a variety of spelling checkers and thesaurus programs. These programs enable writers to enter new text and erase it instantaneously, to insert, delete, and move words, sentences, paragraphs, or whole sections within already established textfiles, to copy a draft and then revise the copied version without changing the original. Of course, anything that you and writers can do with pencil and paper—such as the listing, mapping, diagramming, glossing, and other techniques described in Chapters 3–6—you can do either on the screen of a computer or on whatever copies you may decide to print from time to time during your tutorial conferences.

The newest word-processing programs provide "windows," two or more portions of the computer screen that display several parts of one file or separate files and facilitate the transfer of text from one to another. Through "windows," writers can peek at lists of synonyms contained in a thesaurus file. They can view simultaneously two versions of one paragraph, or a draft's introductory and concluding paragraphs, or a list of points and some sentences that develop them, or a graph of data from page 3 and an interpretive paragraph from page 5, or some reading notes and a paragraph quoting or paraphrasing them, or a bibliography entry and a footnote entry based on it—the configurations are as various as writers' needs. Since writers can make changes without laborious recopying, word processing can remove much, if not all, of the anxiety and the physical drudgery from writing (see Diaute, "The Computer as Stylus and Audience"). With mainframe computers, word processors may additionally draw upon elaborate networks with access to various data bases, electronic message boards, and huge memories. Whatever its scale, word processing can help writers become much more willing and able composers and revisers.

It can—but it doesn't necessarily. How effectively writers use word processing for composition depends on how well they understand their own composing processes. Lacking such understanding, users of word processing may be overwhelmed by its editing powers and may neglect its capacities for generating ideas and forming concepts. By drawing on current theory and research in composition, you can make a tremendous difference in how writers use word processing.

Perhaps the most important thing you can do is to help writers resist using *too early* one of the things word processors do best: editing. Word-processing programs that include dictionary and thesaurus capabilities may prove particularly seductive; writers may be constantly tempted to open the thesaurus "window" on the screen and to substitute a fancier word than their original. Analyses of the commands given by writers using word processing indicate that because word substitutions and syntactical rearrangements can be done so easily, novice users— and some not so novice users—may spend too much time tinkering with the wording of passages which may later be discarded (see Chapter 4 on the differences between editing and critical analysis). One study reveals that inexperienced writers used word processing primarily to make word substitutions—many more than they made when writing longhand—but seldom revised in larger domains (Collier), a finding that is not surprising in view of Nancy Sommers' "Revision Strategies of Student Writers and Experienced Adult Writers" (see Chapter 7). You can remind writers that it is better to "satisfice," to use whatever word comes to mind or even to leave a blank, than to interrupt the flow of thinking in order to find the perfect word. You can help writers recall that generating, shaping, and revising generally should precede the editing of diction, syntax, spelling, and punctuation. Sitting beside writers as they enter text into computers, you can use the strategies presented in Parts Two and Three of this book to help writers resist the seductions of electronic editing.

A more effective tutoring technique is simply to ask writers to turn down the brightness on the screen and to compose invisibly for a while, essentially freewriting their ideas into the computer's memory without regard for order or correctness, all the while knowing that they can gloss, cut, rearrange, and correct hard copies of their texts later on. Invisible writing can preserve the writer's authentic rhythms, phrases, and tone of voice, which Peter Elbow says invigorate the first stage of freewriting. Sheridan Blau, who has experimented with invisible writing using carbon paper and dried-up ball point pens, suggests that the technique can draw on the intense concentration that builds up at the beginning of a writing task but may be depleted prematurely as the writer pauses to address editorial matters (305–306). Many people recognize computers as even more appropriate instruments—particularly since one can "shuttle" back to earlier sentences merely by turning a knob and, perhaps, using the "Find" command to locate a word. You can urge skilled typists, who can feel their fingers making typographical errors, to resist the urge to stop composing, turn up the brightness, and make corrections in midstream.

You can also help writers to avoid mistaking neatness for good writing. True, word processing can clear away the rubbish—the cross-outs, insertions, and arrows—that accumulates in writing drafts longhand, thus minimizing visual distractions to revision. However, a neatly printed text may make nonsense and vapidity *look* respectable. Therefore you need to help writers become willing to mess up neatly printed drafts as readily as they would coffee-ringed longhand drafts. You can urge writers to print drafts in several intermediate stages, glossing the margins, drawing arrows, and writing in changes as they would on longhand drafts. As writers become more proficient in word processing, they may learn to gloss by inserting key words or phrases on the computer screen, using these to gather similarly glossed passages into blocks that can then be moved to appropriate locations. If blocks get too large or if they are not going to be used for a while, you can suggest that writers write them out to separate files that can be called back if and when they are needed. (See Chapters 4 and 5 for ways to help writers "shuttle," gloss, analyze their drafts, and form concepts.)

The Future of Computers in Tutoring Writing

You can often influence the selection and even the design of the programs used in workplaces and academic environments. You can identify a good program by asking, "To what extent does it do what a good tutor would do?" Does it respect the personal rights of individual writers by treating them politely, considering their time constraints, and helping them focus on issues they really need help with, rather than on general-purpose exercises and unindividualized writing tasks? Does it anticipate writers' questions and problems, phrasing questions so as to avoid embarrassing, frustrating, or punishing writers for giving "wrong" answers to poorly phrased questions? Does the program, whenever possible, elicit writers' ideas? Does it, like a realistic tutor, frankly admit its limitations? (Programs that claim to help people write so-called poetry by plugging words from the user's or programmer's list into semantically marked sentences are, to put it kindly, overly optimistic.) Can reasonably skilled local programmers readily customize it according to users' suggestions on procedures and responses? Does it isolate writers from the social contexts in which genuine learning and communication are negotiated, or does it promote interchange? If you work in potentially isolating environments such as *drop-in* writing centers, and even more in all-purpose computer labs, you should particularly try to identify CAI (such as electronic networks) and hardware (such as large-screen monitors) that can be used in conferences and small-group workshops.

Just as tutors who have studied foreign languages can be especially helpful to ESL and nonstandard writers, so tutors who know some programming can be especially helpful to writers using computers. Tutors who know BASIC, PASCAL and LISP can consult with program designers about improvements in CAI software. The adventuresome can actually write modifications themselves. For instance, they could change the questions and responses of an invention program, could correct or enlarge the list of answers a drill program accepts as correct, or could tell a text-editing program not to print statistical information writers might not know how to use. (Changes like these are so simple, even amateurs like us can write them! Word-processing programs, however, should be tackled only by experienced programmers.)

Tutor-programmers can also use their knowledge to enhance writers' confidence. Because many high-school students today receive more computer instruction than composition instruction, they may feel more confident in programming than in writing. Tutors can help them recognize that the two processes are quite similar. Programs, like papers, are seldom written linearly but rather recursively. Above all, programming teaches a modular approach: divide and conquer. Using analytical strategies resembling those we describe in Chapter 4, a programmer begins by analyzing the language of the problem, considering what is already known, what the relationships are, what must be discovered, and who needs to use the results in what ways. After drawing alternative flowcharts of various methods for solving the problem, she might start writing one subroutine she feels confident about, gradually assembling and connecting pieces, changing her original plan to accommodate new insights into the problem and more efficient means of deriving the desired information or text manipulation, until her whole program looks ready to run. She runs it, and it probably crashes. Then the addition, deletion, and rearrangement of lines and maybe subroutines (like revision of sentences and maybe paragraphs) and the "debugging" (or editing) begins. Anyone who has constructed successful programs can apply these processes to writing, which then seems less mysterious and less dependent on "talent." You can help people see writing, like programming, as learnable.

Programming can help you and writers become more detached, clear-thinking readers and revisers of drafts, because good programs resemble good papers in many ways. Both require precision in vocabulary, syntax, and punctuation: like "You know?" in writing, the as-yet-uninvented but profoundly wished for DWIM (Do What I *Mean*) command accomplishes nothing. Papers have theses, introductions, paragraphs (to demonstrate particular points), and conclusions; programs have announced purposes, "top-down" introductory outlines, subroutines (to perform particular calculations or text management functions), and results. Papers are rhetorically styled for certain audiences; programs, too, try to be "user-friendly." Papers use logical transitions to demonstrate how paragraphs are connected to each other and to the main idea; in fact, writers often identify irrelevant paragraphs when no logical connector sounds "right." Similarly, programs articulate their functions through mathematical signs and computer commands (a BASIC program might say, "If $B > Q*(C+(A/2))$ then GO TO 2000 ELSE STOP" but never, "Oh, by the way, did you ever wonder about Q!"). Learning to check syntactical precision and logical structure in papers, as in programs, is one way of becoming a stronger writer. You can use programming language and concepts to help writers who are more experienced in programming than in composition.

Both research in AI and the development of improved CAI programs depend to a great extent on insights into "modes of inquiry" in various disciplines and into how individuals think. AI researchers agree that part of their "research" is an attempt to watch *themselves* think. Tutoring, too, entails such insights and observations. CAI cannot accomplish certain aspects of writing instruction—yet. But by the time this book is printed, many of the problems this chapter describes may already have been solved. We hope that some of our readers may use their knowledge of composition theory and their experience as tutors to help AI research solve the problems that remain—as well as to remind us all, without undue sentimentality, that certain aspects of communication, such as critical analysis and value judgments, are best left entirely to people.

Summary

Composition courses and writing labs increasingly use computer-assisted instruction (CAI) and word processing, but many writers need encouragement to use them. You and the writers with whom you work can rest assured of several facts: typing skill (while helpful) is not essential; computers are especially helpful to writers with physical impairments; computers are not fragile nor files easily lost; paper-and-pencil composing processes (and tutoring strategies) are compatible with computers.

Computers are most helpful for freewriting, rearranging, revising, and editing. You can use the rudimentary questions of invention programs to get a writer started with generating ideas; then, her preliminary responses can be discussed via an "electronic network" and further developed in tutorial conferences through strategies we describe in Chapters 3 and 4. To help her shape a draft, you can suggest she use an outlining program to try out alternative arrangements, a text-editing program to "x-ray" her already-written draft by displaying whichever kinds of sentences she designates, and/or a word-processing program to freewrite, print, gloss, and revise by using techniques we describe in Chapters 5 and 6. If she is required to use drill programs, you can augment the explanations they offer and, if she repeatedly errs, can help her identify the mistaken hypotheses that underlie her pattern of error. You can reassure her when the drill program rejects a perfectly correct response unforeseen by the program's designer, and you can help her relate computerized drills to sentences of her own. If she must use a text-editing program to analyze her essay's style, you can help her interpret, apply, or ignore the information it reports. If she uses word processing, you can help her to resist the temptation of premature editing and instead to employ its capacities for freewriting, reshaping, and revising drafts with ease. Beyond helping individual writers, you can choose to employ your growing expertise as a tutor by collaborating with researchers in composition and in artificial intelligence to develop more useful programs for new generations of writers.

SUGGESTIONS FOR JOURNAL ENTRIES

1. If you have overcome initial reluctance to use computers, write about how you did so.

2. If you have written on a word processor, write about how and to what extent the computer influenced your composing processes.

3. If you have used CAI, in composition or other courses, write about the ways in which it did and did not help you. What kinds of learning seem best accomplished through CAI?

SUGGESTIONS FOR FURTHER WRITING

1. If you have not already done so, go to your computer lab and try out a CAI or word-processing program. Write a critical review of its usefulness, including your judgments about how comprehensive its capabilities are and how readily one can learn to operate it.

2. On the basis of exercise 1, write a dialogue in which you help one of your tutees to feel more comfortable about using a CAI or word-processing program.

3. Construct a sequential list of modules for a CAI program you might use to help a nonstandard or ESL writer drill subject—verb agreement or another grammatical problem of your choice. (You may wish to refer to the dialogues in Chapter 10 for ideas.) Try to design your program to be as interactive as possible by providing opportunities for clarifying whatever mistaken hypotheses the writer may make.

4. If you know something about programming, construct a flowchart for the program you have described in exercise 3.

5. If you know a lot about programming, write the program in exercise 4 and ask your tutees to try it out.

6. If you have used or helped others use electronic networks for exchanging comments on assignments and on papers, write a short paper comparing such discussions with those that ordinarily take place in writing classrooms and in conferences. What are the advantages and disadvantages of electronic networks?

SUGGESTIONS FOR CLASS ACTIVITIES

1. Discuss your own experiences in using CAI and word processing.

2. Discuss your experiences in using CAI and word processing with the writers with whom you work. Which programs seem most helpful? In what ways?

3. What would you like to say to the designers of the CAI and word-processing programs you have used?

SUGGESTIONS FOR FURTHER READING

Bean, John C. "Computerized Word-Processing as an Aid to Revision." *College Composition and Communication* 34 (1983): 146–148.

Blau, Sheridan. "Invisible Writing: Investigating Cognitive Processes in Composition." *College Composition and Communication* 34 (1983): 297–312.

Bourque, Joseph H. "Understanding and Evaluating: The Humanist as Computer Specialist." *College English* 45 (1983): 67–73.

Bridwell, Lillian S., and Donald Ross. "Integrating Computers into a Writing Curriculum; or, Buying, Begging, and Building." In *The Computer in Composition Instruction.* Ed. William Wresch. Urbana, IL: NCTE, 1984. 107–119.

Burns, Hugh L., and George H. Culp. "Stimulating Invention in English Composition through Computer-Assisted Instruction." *Educational Technology* 20 (1980): 5–10.

Catano, James V. "Computer-Based Writing: Navigating the Fluid Text." *College Composition and Communication* 36 (1985): 317–322.

Cohen, Michael E., and Richard A. Lanham. "HOMER: Teaching Style with a Microcomputer." In *The Computer in Composition Instruction.* Ed. William Wresch. Urbana, IL: NCTE, 1984. 83–90.

Collier, Richard M. "The Word Processor and Revision Strategies." *College Composition and Communication* 34 (1983): 149–155.

Diaute, Colette. "Can the Computer Stimulate Writers' Inner Dialogues?" In *The Computer in Composition Instruction.* Ed. William Wresch. Urbana, IL: NCTE, 1984. 131–139.

———. "The Computer as Stylus and Audience." *College Composition and Communication* 34 (1983): 134–145.

Fluegelman, Andrew, and Jeremy Joan Hewes. *Writing in the Computer Age: Word Processing Skills for Every Writer.* New York: Anchor, 1983.

Harris, Jeanette. "Student Writers and Word Processing: A Preliminary Evaluation." *College Composition and Communication* 36 (1985): 323–330.

Hubbard, Francis A. "Writing and Word Processing." *College English* 46 (1984): 128–133.

Jaycox, Kathleen M. *Computer Applications in the Teaching of English.* Illinois Series on Educational Applications of Computers, 19e. Urbana: University of Illinois Press, 1979.

Kiefer, Kathleen E., and Charles R. Smith. "Textual Analysis with Computers: Tests of Bell Laboratories' Computer Software." *Research in the Teaching of English* 17 (1983): 201–214.

Lanham, Richard. *Revising Prose.* New York. Scribner's, 1979.

Lawlor, Joseph, Ed. *Computers in Composition Instruction*. Los Alamitos, CA: SWRL Educational Research and Development, 1982,

Leiber, Justin A. *Structuralism: Skepticism and Mind in the Psychological Sciences*. Boston: G. K. Hall, 1978. 121–138.

Oates, William. "An Evaluation of Computer-Assisted Instruction for English Grammar Review." *Studies in Language Learning* 3 (1982): 193–200.

O'Shea, Tim, and John Self. *Learning and Teaching with Computers: Artificial Intelligence in Education*. Englewood Cliffs, NJ: Prentice-Hall, 1983.

Rodrigues, Raymond J., and Dawn Wilson Rodrigues. "Computer-Based Invention: Its Place and Potential." *College Composition and Communication* 35 (1984): 78–87.

Schank, Roger. *Dynamic Memory: A Theory of Learning in Computers and People*. Cambridge: Cambridge University Press, 1982.

———. *Scripts, Plans, Goals, and Understanding*. Hillsdale, NJ: Lawrence Erlbaum, 1975.

Schwartz, Helen J. *Interactive Writing: Composing with a Word Processor*. New York: Holt, Rinehart and Winston, 1985.

———. "Monsters and Mentors: Computer Applications for Humanistic Education," *College English* 44 (1982): 141–152.

———. "Teaching Writing with Computer Aids." *College English* 46 (1984): 239–247.

———, and Lillian S. Bridwell. "A Selected Bibliography of Computers in Composition." *College Composition and Communication* 35 (1984): 71–78.

Selfe, Cynthia L. *Computer-Assisted Instruction in Composition: Create Your Own*. Urbana, IL: NCTE, 1986.

———, and Billie Wahlstrom. "The Benevolent Beast: Computer-Assisted Instruction for the Teaching of Writing." *The Writing Instructor* 2 (1983): 183–192.

Sudol, Ronald A. "Applied Word Processing: Notes on Authority, Responsibility, and Revision in a Workshop Model." *College Composition and Communication* 36 (1985): 331–339.

Winograd, Terry. *Language as a Cognitive Process*. Reading, MA: Addison-Wesley, 1983.

Wresch, William. "Computers and Composition Instruction: An Update." *College English* 45 (1983): 794–799.

———. "Computers in English Class: Finally beyond Grammar and Spelling Drills." *College English* 44 (1982): 483–490.

———, Ed. *The Computer in Composition Instruction: A Writer's Tool*. Urbana, IL: NCTE, 1984.

Zinsser, William. *Writing with a Word Processor*. New York: Harper and Row, 1983.

INDEX